The Catholic Biblical Quarterly
Monograph Series

51

The Temple Administration and the Levites in Chronicles

BY

Yeong Seon Kim, FMM

The Catholic Biblical Quarterly
Monograph Series
51

Produced in the United States of America

Library of Congress Cataloging-in-Publication Data

Kim, Yeong Seon, 1965-
The Temple administration and the Levites in Chronicles / by Yeong Seon Kim, FMM. — First edition.
pages cm. — (The Catholic Biblical quarterly monograph series ; 51)
Includes bibliographical references and indexes.
ISBN 0-915170-50-7 (alk. paper)
1. Bible. Chronicles—Criticism, interpretation, etc. 2. Priests, Jewish—Biblical teaching. 3. Levites. I. Title.
BS1345.52.K56 2013
222.6067—dc23

20130034902

Contents

List of Tables

Questions about the Temple Administration during the Achaemenid Era and the Book of Chronicles[1]

It is a truth almost universally acknowledged that the Jerusalem Temple in the province of Yehud functioned as a socio-economic, political, and religious center. The cumulative results of recent research suggest, moreover, that the Temple, during the Achaemenid era, was run by the high priest as a counterpart of the governor who was appointed by the Persian king.[2] Scholarly unanimity proceeds thus far. But when it comes to questions of the Temple's day-to-day administrative realities, what we do not know can seem daunting indeed. How was the administrative staff of the Temple organized? How many levels were in the administrative system? Was service hereditary? How long did individuals hold their positions? How were

[1] When I use the phrase "Temple administration" in relation to the book of Chronicles, it includes any information related to the Temple personnel, their functions in the Temple, or its organization/installation.

[2] The majority of scholars admit that the high priest had authority over cultic affairs during the Persian period, but not over civil affairs. See Rainer Albertz, "The Thwarted Restoration," in *Yahwism After the Exile* (ed. Rainer Albertz and Bob Becking; Assen: Royal Van Gorcum, 2003) 1-17, here 11-12; Jeremiah W. Cataldo, *A Theocratic Yehud? Issues of Government in a Persian Province* (LHBOT 498; New York: T & T Clark, 2009) 175-85; James C. VanderKam, *From Joshua to Caiaphas: High Priests after the Exile* (Minneapolis: Fortress, 2004) 43-111; Steven James Schweitzer, "The High Priest in Chronicles: An Anomaly in a Detailed Description of the Temple Cult," *Biblica* 84 (2003) 388-402; and many others. However, some scholars argue that the political authority of the Persian era Yehud was transferred to the high priest in the fourth century B.C.E., such as Joel Weinberg, *The Citizen-Temple Community* (trans. Daniel L. Smith-Christopher; JSOTSup 151; Sheffield: JSOT Press, 1992) 125-26; Jon L. Berquist, *Judaism in Persian's Shadow: A Social and Historical Approach* (Minneapolis: Fortress, 1995) 135-56; and Jonathan E. Dyck, *The Theocratic Ideology of the Chronicler* (Biblical Interpretation Series 33; Leiden: Brill, 1998).

they paid? And for that matter, how can we find answers to any of these questions?

Among historians who seek to understand how the Temple was administered in the Achaemenid era, the book of Chronicles is a central resource.[3] Chronicles provides more information about temple administration than any other biblical book. And since Chronicles was written sometime in the Persian period (from the sixth century B.C.E. to the fourth century B.C.E.),[4] the Chronicler's material illuminates the history of the province of Yehud during the Persian period.[5] Moreover, scholars have long posited

[3] André Lemaire, "Administration in Fourth-Century B.C.E. Judah in Light of Epigraphy and Numismatics," in *Judah and Judeans in the Fourth Century B.C.E.* (ed. Oded Lipschits et al; Winona Lake: Eisenbrauns, 2007) 58, 60-61; O. Lipschits, "Achaemenid Imperial Policy, Settlement Processes in Palestine, and the Status of Jerusalem in the Middle of the Fifth Century B.C.E.," in *Judah and Judeans in the Persian Period* (ed. O. Lipschits and Manfred Oeming; Winona Lake: Eisenbrauns, 2006) 39; Ephraim Stern, "The Religious Revolution in Persian-Period Judah," in *Judah and Judeans in the Persian Period*, 199-205, here 203-4; Hugh G. M. Williamson, "The Temple in the Books of Chronicles," in *Templum Amicitae: Essays on the Second Temple Presented to Ernst Bammel* (ed. W. Horbury; JSNTSup 48; Sheffield: JSOT Press, 1991) 15-31; Melody D. Knowles, *Centrality Practiced: Jerusalem in the Religious Practice of Yehud and the Diaspora in the Persian Period* (SBL Archaeology and Biblical Studies 16; Atlanta: Society of Biblical Literature, 2006).

[4] Several markers of time in Chronicles indicate that the author of Chronicles had precise knowledge of the Persian era, such as, the reference to Cyrus in 2 Chr 36:23, the reference to *darics*, Persian gold coins in 1 Chr 29:7, and the reference to Zerubbabel's descendants whose origin is clearly from the Persian period in 1 Chr 3:19-24. Based on such inner-textual evidence, the majority of scholars propose a fourth-century B.C.E. date for Chronicles. For instance, Gerhard von Rad, Wilhelm Rudolph, Otto Eissfelt, Sara Japhet, H. G. M. Williamson, Isaac Kalimi, Gary N. Knoppers, and the like. Detailed bibliographical information about these scholars' works is provided in the related section of Chapter One.

[5] In this work, the term "the Chronicler" designates the author of Chronicles. This could be one person or a group of people who shared similar ideas which are presented in the book of Chronicles. However, I do not consider that the Chronicler was also responsible for the composition of the book of Ezra-Nehemiah. Although there are significant similarities between the book of Chronicles and the book of Ezra-Nehemiah, the differences in language, style, literary method as well as in theological views outweigh the similarities. Thus I agree with scholars who argue that Chronicles and Ezra-Nehemiah were written by two different authors and at two different times. The proponents of separate authorship of Chronicles are as follows: S. Japhet, "The Supposed Common Authorship of Chronicles and Ezra-Nehemiah Investigated Anew," *VT* 18 (1968) 330-71; idem, "The Relationship between Chronicles and Ezra-Nehemiah," in *From the Rivers of Babylon to the Highlands of Judah* (Winona Lake: Eisenbrauns, 2006) 169-82; H. G. M. Williamson, *Israel in the Books of Chronicles* (Cambridge: Cambridge University Press, 1977) 1-70; Roddy Braun, "Chronicles, Ezra and Nehemiah: Theology and Literary History," in *Studies in the Historical Books of the Old Testament* (ed. J. A. Emerton; Leiden: Brill, 1979) 52-64; Simon J. de Vries, *1 and 2 Chronicles* (Grand Rapids: Eerdmans, 1989) 7-11; Steven L. McKenzie, "The Chronicler as

that the Chronicler retrojected his contemporary understanding of temple administration into the earlier history of the monarchy.[6] Thus, even parts of the book that ostensibly pertain to the Monarchic era may reveal socio-economic and political realities of Achaemenid Yehud.

Chronicles has therefore long been seen as a good starting point from which to reconstruct the administration of the Jerusalem Temple during the Achaemenid era. I will argue, however, that in some cases, the Chronicler's descriptions of issues pertaining to both the first and second Temples reflect not the *actual* practices of his own day, but an *idealized* representation of temple practices he wished to see enacted. Indeed, I shall argue that the Chronicler's description of the temple administration was intended to persuade his readers to accept his own ideas about who *should* run the Temple, and how the Temple *ought* to be administered. With these ideas in mind, much can be learned from the Chronicler's treatment of issues pertaining to temple administration and from the ways he formulates his argument to legitimize his particular view of the Jerusalem Temple and cult. Through his dialectic approaches to Pentateuchal traditions and to contemporary cultic situations, the Chronicler reveals a remarkable ability to enlist Pentateuchal regulations in the service of his particular ideologies.

The case for my argument must be made through careful consideration of three interrelated questions. First, what does the Chronicler say about the temple administration? Second, does his description of the temple administration cohere with information found in other biblical or extra-biblical resources? Finally, if the Chronicler's description does depart from other evidence, are these departures intentional, and if so, what was their purpose?

Redactor," in *The Chronicler as Author: Studies in Text and Texture* (ed. M. Patrick Graham and Steven L. McKenzie; JSOTSup 263; Sheffield: Sheffield Academic Press, 1999) 71-80; Gary N. Knoppers, *1 Chronicles 1–9: A New Translation with Introduction and Commentary* (AB 12; New York: Doubleday, 2004) 93-100; and Ralph W. Klein, *1 Chronicles* (Hermeneia; Minneapolis: Fortress Press, 2006) 6-10.

[6] See for example S. Japhet's (*I & II Chronicles: A Commentary* [OTL; Louisville: Westminster/John Knox, 1993] 843) comment on 2 Chr 24:5: "Reflecting the actual situation of the Chronicler's own time, they (*the regulations of Nehemiah's covenant*) were seen as anachronistically retrojected to the monarchical period." Italics are mine. For similar observations, see H. G. M. Williamson (*1 and 2 Chronicles* [NCBC; Grand Rapids: Eerdmans, 1982] 321) on 2 Chr 24:8; R. W. Klein (*1 Chronicles*, 481) on 1 Chr 25:1; S. L. McKenzie (*1–2 Chronicles* [AOTC; Nashville: Abingdon, 2004] 363) on 2 Chr 35:1-19 and G. N. Knoppers (*1 Chronicles 10-29* [AB 12A; New York: Doubleday, 2004] 620) on 1 Chr 15:16.

My approach to the Chronicler's descriptions of the temple administration proceeds in three steps. In the first step I choose certain passages from Chronicles that are related to the temple administration for further study, applying the following criteria: (1) A passage or section that is related to the temple administration should be found in the Chronicler's unique material, with no parallels elsewhere in the Bible. This criterion makes it very likely that a selected passage contains the Chronicler's own idea about the temple administration. (2) To ensure the consistency of the Chronicler's presentation of a given topic, the idea which a selected text portrays should be identified elsewhere in the book. (3) Among the select texts which meet the preceding two criteria, a specific passage is to be chosen when it is specifically related to economic activities in the Temple.

The first chapter of this work establishes which texts fulfill the above criteria. I will demonstrate that the Chronicler's distinctive views on the temple administration are found in three sets of texts pertaining to (1) gatekeepers (1 Chr 9:17-32; 26:1-19), (2) treasurers (1 Chr 9:26-28; 26:20-32), and (3) tax collectors (2 Chr 24:5-11; 34:9-13), all of whom are described by the Chronicler as Levites. Asserting the levitical identification of these officials, I shall argue, is a particular preoccupation of the Chronicler; as we shall see, it should be interpreted as a part of his plan to establish a legitimate temple administration, rather than as a demonstration of his tenacious pro-levitical partisanship.

Having selected the texts that will provide the basis for this study, in the balance of this chapter I will examine the inner textual evidence that suggests a fourth-century B.C.E. date for Chronicles to ask whether the Chronicler *intended* his work to be understood in the setting of Persian-era Yehud. Then I will consider alternative arguments that posit the book's complex redactional literary evolution. My interpretation of Chronicles depends, in large part, on the book's literary unity. I will therefore argue, in contrast to redactional theories, that passages I identify as "David's Installation Block" bespeak the unity of Chronicles and provide insight into the overall plan of the work.

In Chapter 2, my main task of the second step is to determine exactly what the Chronicler claims about the Temple's gatekeepers, treasurers and tax collectors. I present a literary analysis of these temple administration texts and challenge some common scholarly interpretations of them. My analysis shows that in some cases, the Chronicler retrojected a complex of *ideal* cultic practices in relation to the temple administration of the Persian period into the monarchic past. That is to say, it is unlikely, in several cases, that the policies or practices which he envisions as having been instituted in the distant past were actually in effect in his own day. This analysis helps identify ten different literary methods that the Chronicler used to encode elements of the temple administration that he envisioned for his own *ideal and unrealized* temple, in his narrative of the past.

In Chapter 3, in order to show that the Chronicler's description of temple administration is indeed unique, I examine three topics in Chronicles (as the third step of the present work) that relate to economic activities of the Temple and compare them to other Persian era biblical and extra-biblical depictions of the same issues.[7] I consider data from Chronicles and from other texts that deal with (1) *Loci* of economic activities in the Temple: gates, store-chambers and treasuries; (2) Temple revenue: tithes, priestly gifts, the temple tax, and imperial taxes; and (3) Temple staff. As we shall see, in contrast to other biblical traditions, the Chronicler incorporates all the non-priestly temple personnel into one category, that is, the Levites. Furthermore, he claims that such incorporation was a continuation of the tradition which had been established since the wilderness period. The Chronicler also expands the levitical involvement in certain cultic duties which had been assigned only to priests in Priestly traditions. One of the Chronicler's most innovative claims in cultic matters appears in his presentation of the cultic personnel's remuneration: the priests and Levites were to be paid with the priestly gifts and tithes that the people offered. Ultimately, the comparative analysis reveals that while some of the Chronicler's descriptions of the temple administration do reflect, to some degree, the practices of his own time, more frequently they reflect the Chronicler's ideal image of the temple administration as he would wish it to be. Thus, it becomes clear that the Chronicler is shaping his material to achieve a persuasive purpose, not merely to present an accurate reconstruction of contemporary practices.

[7] I limit the topics in the area of economic activities among various duties discharged by the staff of the Temple. This limitation is set by the availability of comparable data from material and textual sources originating in the Persian period. The current popularity of Second Temple studies has produced new data about material culture, and new insights concerning literary texts and socio-economic circumstances in Yehud and neighboring regions. These new data and insights provide us with a vantage point to explore the Persian-era Yehud. I take the best advantage of them to discern the Chronicler's plan in his work.

In the fourth and final chapter, I examine the Chronicler's distinctive presentation of the temple administration over and against other biblical descriptions of the Levites. I also examine the roles of the Levites in texts that post-date the composition of Chronicles, such as Deutero-canonical and pseudepigraphic works that originated in the Hellenistic and Hasmonean periods, including the Dead Sea Scrolls. Based on this comparative approach, I conclude this chapter with an argument that the Chronicler's description of the temple administration should be understood as his ideal views on who should run the Temple, and how the Temple is supposed to be administered, rather than as a presentation of "what really happened" in regard to the temple administration of his own time. The Chronicler's ideal views on the temple administration reveal his exegetical and creative approaches to known Pentateuchal traditions and to the contemporary debates among competing priestly circles concerning membership in the legitimate priesthood.

CHAPTER ONE

Groundwork

1.1. Selection of Texts from Chronicles

In the section that follows, I will establish the corpus of texts that lie at the center of my argument that the view of the economic administration of the Temple presented in Chronicles is to some degree an idealized portrait, rather than a historically accurate reconstruction. Three main themes, all of which are unique to Chronicles, emerge in this body of texts: first, the Levites occupy multiple administrative roles. Second, David is credited with having installed the Levites in their distinctive offices. Third, Chronicles uses kings' compliance with David's assignment of the Levites to these offices as the criterion of regnal evaluation.

Among all the Chronicler's descriptions of the temple administration, the tasks of the levitical gatekeepers, treasurers and tax collectors are particularly related to the economic activities in the Temple.[1] Thus, the following texts are directly relevant for the current project: those concerning (1) gatekeepers (1 Chr 9:17-32; 26:1-19),[2] (2) treasurers (1 Chr 9:26-28; 26:20-32),[3] and (3) tax collectors (2 Chr 24:5-11; 34:9-13). Before we turn to

[1] I exclude 1 Chr 15:1–16:43 from my analysis because it discusses Levites' service as temple musicians, rather than administrators.

[2] Gatekeepers are also mentioned elsewhere in Chronicles: 1 Chr 15:18, 23; 16:38; 23:5; 2 Chr 8:14; 23:4, 19; 34:13; 35:15. These references to the gatekeepers are to be considered when I discuss the gatekeepers in order to evaluate the consistency of the Chronicler's depiction. The references to the gatekeepers in Ezra 2:42, 70; 7:7; 10:24; Neh 7:1, 45, 73; 10:28, 39; 11:19; 12:25, 45, 47; 13:5 are to be compared with the Chronicler's depiction of the gatekeepers. See section 2.1 in the present work.

[3] The other references to the temple treasurers are found in 2 Chr 12:9; 16:2; 31:11-16; and 36:18. They are treated in section 2.2.3.

these texts however, it may be useful to consider the Chronicler's perspective on the Levites more generally.

1.1.1. 1 Chronicles 5:27-41 and 1 Chronicles 6

1 Chronicles 5:27-41 and 1 Chronicles 6 indicate that the Levites are a significant group for the Chronicler. The first passage (1 Chronicles 5:27-41) presents the genealogies of the high priests under the rubric of "the sons of Levi."[4] The second passage, 1 Chronicles 6, introduces the genealogies of the tribe of Levi and the list of the levitical cities.[5] The prominence of the levitical genealogy for the Chronicler is underscored by its central position among the genealogies of the twelve tribes of Israel presented in 1 Chronicles 1–9, and by its length and level of detail, which are second only to the genealogy of Judah.[6]

According to both passages, the tribe of Levi consists of three important groups: priests, Levites and levitical singers. Initially, the Chronicler's presentation of the priestly and levitical duties corresponds with that of the Priestly tradition, since the Chronicler asserts that both clerical services originated from the Mosaic installation (ככל אשר צוה משה עבד האלהים 6:34).[7] A novelty

[4] This list has been interpreted as the genealogy of the high priests at least since the time of Josephus, in the mid-first century C.E. However, the list does not include several well-known high priests, such as Amariah during the reign of Jehoshaphat (2 Chr 19:11), and Johoiada during the reigns of Athaliah and Joash (2 Chronicles 22-24// 2 Kings 11-12). Therefore, G. N. Knoppers ("Classical Historiography and the Chronicler's History: A Reexamination," *JBL* 122 [2004] 627-50) suggests that the genealogy of the priests (1 Chr 5:27-41) is not that of the high priests, but a genealogical list intended to legitimate a line of priests in Persian Yehud.

[5] The Chronicler's list of the levitical settlements seems to depend on that of Joshua 21, but with some redactional changes of it. Whereas the list of Joshua 21 is organized by the distribution and number of the levitical cities within the individual tribes of Israel, the Chronicler's is reorganized by the order of cities of the Aaronide priestly families (1 Chr 6:39-45) and the cities of non-priestly levitical families (1 Chr 6:46-66), which suggests the Chronicler's perspective on a definite distinction between the priests and the Levites, as S. Japhet (*I & II Chronicles*, 147) comments. The historicity of the list of the levitical cities has been a subject of scholarly discussions. Considering the fact that the great majority of the listed cities were out of the borders of the province of Yehud, the Chronicler's list of levitical cities seems to propose "the unequivocal right of the sacerdotal orders to settle in the land." See *I & II Chronicles*, 165 and also Knoppers, *1 Chronicles 1–9*, 442-50.

[6] McKenzie, *1–2 Chronicles*, 89.

[7] The Priestly duties are succinctly summarized in 1 Chr 6:34 and each of the functions is also mentioned in the Pentateuchal traditions: (1) to make offerings upon the altar of burnt offering (Exod 29:38-42; 30:1-10; Lev 8:1–9:24) and the altar of incense (Exod 30:1-8), (2) to

here resides in the Chronicler's claim that David appointed Levites as singers before the Ark (1 Chr 6:16-17).[8]

1.1.2. 1 Chronicles 9:17-32

1 Chronicles 9 provides the Chronicler with another general opportunity to highlight the roles of the Levites. The chapter begins with a list of people who returned from the exile and settled in Jerusalem.[9] They are categorized in four groups: Israelites, priests, Levites and temple servants (1 Chr 9:2).[10]

---

perform all the tasks of the most holy place (Exod 26:33-34; Num 18:1-5); and (3) to make atonement for Israel (Lev 4:20; 16:17; 23:28). See Knoppers, *1 Chronicles 10-29*, 424-25. On the other hand, the levitical duty, described in 1 Chr 6:33, is also mentioned in Exod 38:21; Num 1:50-51, 53 and 8:19-22.

[8] The installation of the levitical singers by King David is introduced in detail in 1 Chr 15:1-16:43 and I Chronicles 25. The Chronicler's description of David's installation of the musical liturgy does not have any parallel in the Priestly sources or in Deuteronomy. Due to this silence about singers and musicians in the ritual rites in the Pentateuch, Y. Kaufmann, N. Sarna, M. Haran, M. Greenberg, and I. Knohl have asserted that the priestly cult was a silent one. I. Knohl ("Between Voice and Silence: The Relationship between Prayer and Temple Cult," *JBL* 115 [1996] 17-30) argues:

> The school of the "Priestly Torah" developed a religious language that rejected nearly every aspect of personality or anthropomorphism in connection with God. ... By its very nature, the language of prayer and hymn is permeated with anthropomorphic language concerning God. The refusal to ascribe any kind of characteristics or actions to God makes any positive speech concerning God impossible. Hence, the sole alternative open to one standing before the holy is absolute silence.

I. Knohl also argues that the verbal cult only existed outside the priestly realm, and the arrangement for levitical song took shape during the Second Temple period. In this sense, the Chronicler's description of the choral rite draws our attention. The Chronicler's statement concerning Davidic arrangement of the levitical singers shows a more developed stage in terms of cultic history over against the distinction of Levites and singers in Ezr 2:41, Neh 7:44, as H. G. M. Williamson (*1 and 2 Chronicles*, 73) points out. For an extensive treatment about the Chronicler's description of the choral rite, see John W. Kleinig, *The Lord's Song: The Basis, Function and Significance of Choral Music in Chronicles* (JSOTSup 156; Sheffield: Sheffield Academic Press, 1993).

[9] Its parallel list is found in Neh 11:3-19. Concerning the relationship between 1 Chronicles 9 and Neh 11:3-19, refer to Ralph W. Klein's summary (*1 Chronicles*, 263-65). In brief, the list of Neh 11:3-19 is somewhat different from one of 1 Chronicles 9 in that the former intends to list "the chiefs of the province who lived in Jerusalem." Furthermore, in Nehemiah 11, the gatekeepers are not included among the Levites (Neh 11:21). Due to the differences in their overall intentions and contents, the Chronicler's dependence on Nehemiah 11 has been debated and has not won scholarly consensus.

[10] The term "Temple servants (נתינים)" appears only here in Chronicles. Temple servants are the lowest orders of the clergy in Ezra-Nehemiah (Ezr 2:43, 58; 8:17, 20; Neh 3:31; 7:46, 60; 10:29; 11:21), but not included in the cultic organization of Chronicles. Following

The Chronicler then turns his attention to specific temple personnel, listing the names of the priests in 1 Chr 9:10-13, and those of the Levites and levitical gatekeepers in 1 Chr 9:14-16 and 1 Chr 9:17, respectively. At this point, the first detailed explication of levitical administrative functions appears: 1 Chr 9:18-34 outlines various levitical functions, but focuses primarily on the duties of levitical gatekeepers.[11] The gatekeepers not only guard the four temple gates, they also take care of chambers, treasuries, inventory and upkeep of the furniture and the holy utensils, and guard the supplies for the regular temple service. The link among these varied responsibilities lies in their connection to the temple economy which revolves around maintaining the Temple and continuing cultic practices in the Temple. 1 Chr 9:17-32, because of its specific interest in the roles of the gatekeepers, will comprise one of the base texts in our corpus as we seek to discern the Chronicler's vision of the ideal temple. It is worth noting as well that in the course of the description of the gatekeepers' duties, the Chronicler repeatedly stresses (one might even say unnecessarily) the gatekeepers' affiliation to the Levites.[12]

1.1.3. 1 Chronicles 23–26

The Chronicler describes the temple administration quite extensively in 1 Chronicles 23–26.[13] This section clearly reveals the Chronicler's interest

S. Japhet (*I & II Chronicles*, 208), I consider that the reference to Temple servants in 1 Chr 9:2 reflects the inadvertent survival of a textual detail from Nehemiah 11.

[11] The functions of the Levites are presented in the following order: gatekeepers (vv. 18-29), priests (v. 30), Levites and singers (vv. 31-33). This shows that the Chronicler's cultic organization consisted of these four groups: gatekeepers, priests, non-priestly cultic assistants, and singers. All of these cultic personnel belong to the tribe of Levi. In other words, the Chronicler integrates the temple clergy into the Levites. This is the Chronicler's novel presentation which draws further attention.

[12] The Chronicler's emphasis on the gatekeepers' integration to the Levites led S. Japhet (*I & II Chronicles*, 204) to assume that the controversy against the gatekeepers' levitical affiliation was not yet silenced in the Chronicler's own time. The Chronicler's incorporation of gatekeepers to the rank of Levites will be treated in the continuing discussion of the present study.

[13] Several scholars in the past have considered 1 Chronicles 23–26 as a later addition to the Chronicler's work. Adam C. Welch (*The Work of the Chronicler, its Purpose and its Date* [London: Oxford University Press, 1939] 81-96) points out the lack of homogeneity of these chapters and concludes that 1 Chronicles 23–26 was revised by a writer with an intention to rearrange the material in order to divide the several classes of Temple officials into twenty-four courses each. M. Noth (*The Chronicler's History* [trans. H. G. M. Williamson;

in the Levites, and attributes every detail of the Jerusalem cultic institutions to David's initiative.[14] According to the Chronicler, the status of the Levites changed with David's transfer of the Ark to Jerusalem: since the Levites no longer needed to carry the Ark (1 Chr 23:26), David assigned them different duties (1 Chr 23:28-32). Freed from the burden of the Ark, the Levites became cultic assistants to the priests (הלוים), officers (שׂטרים) and judges (שׂפטים), gatekeepers (שׂערים) and musicians (משׂררים). Since this project is limited to exploring administrative activities specifically related to economic undertakings in Temple, I will include in our corpus of base texts only the passages directly related to the inflow and outflow of Temple revenue, namely 1 Chr 26:1-19 (the list of the gatekeepers and their organization) and 1 Chr 26:20-28 (a list of treasurers and their responsibilities).

It is worth noting, while 1 Chronicles 23–26 is before us, what minimal interest the Chronicler seems to have in the priests themselves! According to the Chronicler, the priests comprise only one branch of the tribe of Levi;

JSOTSup 50; Sheffield: JSOT Press, 1987] 31-33) also considers this section as "a massive insertion" since it interrupts the original connection of 1 Chr 23:1-2a to 1 Chr 28:1. Since Noth's analysis of Chronicles mainly depends on its literary coherence, it is not surprising that he considers this section as secondary. The following scholars concede M. Noth's argument: Wilhelm Rudolph (*Chronickbücher* [HAT 21; Tübingen: J. C. B. Mohr, 1955] 152-53) and Thomas Willi (*Die Chronik als Auslegung: Untersuchungen zur literarischen Gestaltung der historischen Überlieferung Israels* [FRLANT 106; Göttingen: Vandenhoeck & Ruprecht, 1972] 194-204). On the other hand, Williamson ("The Origins of the Twenty-four Priestly Courses: A Study of 1 Chronicles XXIII-XXVII," *Studies in the Historical Books of the Old Testament* [VTSup 30; Leiden: Brill, 1979] 251-68; and *1 and 2 Chronicles*, 157-58) argues that a part of 1 Chronicles 23–26 originated from the Chronicler, but a significant part of it is post-Chronistic additions by a pro-priestly reviser (1 Chr 23:13b-14, 25-32; 24; 25:7-31; 26:4-8, 12-8; 27). Against these scholars' arguments for the secondariness of 1 Chronicles 23–26, S. Japhet (*I & II Chronicles*, 406-10) defends the originality of the section because of its literary integrity with the other parts of Chronicles, and attributes the incongruence of the section to the Chronicler's use of varying sources. Favoring Japhet's view on the literary integrity, I treat 1 Chronicles 23–26 in this study. My stance on this point is to be defended in the section of David's Installation Block of this chapter where I deal with the question of redactional layers in 1 Chronicles 23–26.

[14] The Chronicler's apparent favoritism for the Levites has led scholars to speculate that the Chronicler came from levitical circles. For example, Simon J. de Vries ("Moses and David as Cult Founders in Chronicles," *JBL* 107 [1988] 619-39, here 636) states: "It would not be unreasonable to speculate that the Chronicler was himself a Levite, perhaps even a member of the order of singers." See also G. von Rad, *Das Geschichtsbild des chronistischen Werkes* (BWANT 4; Stuttgart: Kohlhammer, 1930) 81-119; P. R. Ackroyd, "The Theology of the Chronicler," *LTQ* 8 (1973) 101-16, here 111-12; Williamson, *1 and 2 Chronicles*, 16-17; and McKenzie, *1–2 Chronicles*, 28-29.

the Chronicler's treatment of the priests is limited to describing their organization into divisions and their assignment to cultic duties by casting lots (1 Chr 24:1-19).[15] In contrast, for all other levitical groups, the Chronicler provides a much more detailed description of their tasks (1 Chr 23:28-32; 25:1-6; 26:14-18, 20-32).[16]

Might the Chronicler's unbalanced treatment reflect a certain tension between the two groups? The Chronicler admits the priests' exclusive right to certain cultic activities, such as atonement and burning incense, and does not deny that the levitical personnel are subordinate to the priests.[17] Nevertheless, the extent of levitical engagement in cultic activities is greatly expanded in Chronicles, when compared with the Priestly tradition.[18] Indeed, 1 Chronicles 23–26 promotes the Levites as a "multi-functional group" in the Temple.[19]

1.1.4. 2 Chronicles 17–19; 29–31; and 34–35

Having established earlier that David appointed the Levites to their administrative duties, the Chronicler then uses successive kings' compliance with David's levitical policies as a criterion by which to evaluate their reigns.

[15] The system of the twenty-four divisions (מחלקות) of the priests is believed to begin in the early stage of the Restoration period. See Japhet, *I & II Chronicles*, 423-24.

[16] Japhet, *I & II Chronicles*, 424-25.

[17] S. S. Tuell, *First and Second Chronicles* (Louisville: John Knox, 2001) 100.

[18] In the Priestly tradition the Levites are described as hierodules for the priests. Their cultic role is distinguished from that of priests. In the books of Exodus and Numbers, the Levites are to carry the tabernacles and all its equipment (Num 1:50), to substitute for all the firstborn (Num 3:12) and to serve at the Tabernacle (Num 8:15). All these roles of the Levites should be done under the direction of the priests (Exod 38:21; Num 3:9, 32; 8:11). The Chronicler follows the Priestly tradition in terms of the genealogical distinction between the Aaronide priests and the Levites and the general distinction between their cultic roles. However, the Chronicler deviates from the Priestly tradition by expanding their roles as officers and judges, gatekeepers and temple musicians as well as minor clerics. Some of the Levites' cultic activities in Chronicles encroach on the priests' exclusive duties defined in the Pentateuchal tradition. For example, "the showbread" (Exod 25:30; 35:13; 39:36; Num 4:7; cf. 1 Chr 9:32; 23:29), "fine flour for the cereal offering" (Lev 2:1; 6:15, 20; *et al.*), "the griddle" (only in Lev 2:5; 6:21; 7:9; cf. Ezek 4:3), "the unleavened wafers" (Lev 2:4; 7:12; Num 6:15), and "flour mixed with oil" (Lev 2:5; 7:10; 9:4; 23:13; Num 7:13, 19, 25) can be handled only by the priests in the Priestly tradition, but in Chronicles, the Levites are in charge of them. According to 2 Chr 31:14, all categories of priestly gifts, which should be given to the priests in Pentateuchal legislation, are distributed to the priests and the Levites. I treat this issue in detail in section 3.2.2.

[19] A. Labahn, "Antitheocratic Tendencies in Chronicles," in *Yahwism after the Exile* (ed. Rainer Albertz and Bob Becking; Assen: Royal Van Gorcum, 2003) 115-35, here 128-29.

According to Chronicles, the levitical roles in the temple administration that David instituted in 1 Chronicles 23–26 were not unanimously respected throughout the history of Israel. Rather, recognition of the Levites' importance becomes emblematic of the piety and wisdom of, specifically, Solomon, Jehoshaphat, Hezekiah and Josiah.[20] The Temple's inauguration gets off to a good start, the Chronicler implies, when Solomon precisely implements David's levitical policies (2 Chronicles 5, 7, 8). Solomon's concern for his father's chief legacy will be followed by Jehoshaphat, Hezekiah and Josiah, who embark on additional cultic and judicial reforms involving the Levites (see Table 1, below).[21]

[20] The roles of the Levites are also highlighted in the times of Johoiada and Joash in Chronicles. However, these two kings are not included into Table 1 for the following reasons. First, 2 Chr 23:2-9 asserts that the Levites were deeply involved in Jehoiada's coup against Athaliah, whereas its parallel passage 2 Kings 11-12 completely neglects to recognize their participation in the same event. However, S. Japhet (*I & II Chronicles*, 822) argues that 2 Chr 23:2-9 should not be interpreted as glorification of the levitical role since the Chronicler's interest here is not in the Levites, but in his religious conviction that the entry to the Temple is absolutely limited to the priests and the Levites. See also Williamson, *1 and 2 Chronicles*, 316. Furthermore, McKenzie (*1–2 Chronicles*, 310-12) considers the Chronicler's presentation about this coup as "ideologically changed" and "unrealistic picture." Due to these commentators' varied interpretations of this passage, it is excluded from the list of Table 1. Nevertheless, it appears to me that the Chronicler tried to set up Jehoiada as another figure who restored the cult according to David's ordinances. For example, in MT 2 Chr 23:18, Jehoiada appointed the levitical priests to take charge of the house of the Lord, *according to the order of David* after the success of the coup against Athaliah. The emphasis is mine. Unfortunately, MT 2 Chr 23:18 does not give any detail about the measure that Johoiada took to reorganize the cult. This happened because of the textual corruption of MT 2 Chr 23:18 by scribal error (*homoioteleuton*). LXX 2 Chr 23:18 gives a more detailed information. It reads:

> Jehoiada assigned the care of Yahweh's Temple to the priests and the Levites, *and he assigned the divisions of the priests and the Levites* whom David had organized...

MT 2 Chr 23:18 does not have the text in italics, which must have been lost by a skip of the eye from the first occurrence of "the priests and the Levites" to the second one. If we follow the reading of the LXX, it (2 Chr 23:18-19) shows that Jehoiada's cultic restoration perfectly reflects the Chronicler's ideal for the cultic system. Second, King Joash's special treatment of the Levites (2 Chr 24:6-11) is also excluded from the list of Table 1 since the text will be dealt with later in relation to the tax collection in the Jerusalem Temple.

[21] Raymond B. Dillard, *2 Chronicles* (WBC 15; Waco: Word Books, 1987) 228-29. In the present study, the historicity of the Chronicler's treatment of these kings' reformative measures is not my concern. My focus is on what the Chronicler intended to transmit to his audience or readers through his descriptions of these reforms, especially concerning the Levites.

During the reign of Jehoshaphat, the Levites' tasks expand to include teaching the Book of Torah of YHWH (ספר תורת יהוה) (2 Chr 17:7-9),[22] participating in judicial activities in the royal court (2 Chr 19:8-11),[23] and praising God as musicians on the battle field (2 Chr 20:21-22).

[22] What the Chronicler refers to by "the Book of Torah" in 2 Chr 17:9 is debatable. Some scholars have speculated that it could have been a royal law code or edict. See Jacob M. Myers, *II Chronicles* (AB 13; Garden City, N.Y.: Doubleday, 1965), 99-100. However, 2 Chr 17:7-9 clearly shows that Jehoshaphat promulgated not his own royal code, but God's law, as Gary N. Knoppers ("Reform and Regression: The Chronicler's Presentation of Jehoshaphat," *Biblica* 72 [1991] 508-9) points out. S. Japhet (*The Ideology of the Book of Chronicles and Its Place in Biblical Thought* [BEATAJ 9; Frankfurt: Peter Lang, 1989] 234-44) and J. R. Shaver (*Torah and the Chronicler's History Work: An Inquiry into the Chronicler's References to Laws, Festivals and Cultic Institutions in Relation to Pentateuchal Legislation* [BJS 196; Atlanta: Scholars, 1989] 73-86) have suggested that it could be a version of the Pentateuch. See also Williamson, *1 and 2 Chronicles*, 282. Regardless of the identity of this book, the Chronicler's account is noteworthy since it describes that the Levites were chosen as instructors to teach the Torah. The Levites' instructional role as teachers of the Torah is mentioned once again in 2 Chr 35:3. The role of teachers is often considered one of the priestly prerogatives elsewhere in the Hebrew Bible (Lev 10:11; Deut 31:9-13; Jer 18:18; Ezek 7:26; Hag 2:11; Neh 8:1-8). Nevertheless, the Chronicler's description of the Levites' instructional role has "an astonishing parallel" in Ezra 7:25, as S. Japhet (*I & II Chronicles*, 749) comments. For this reason, S. Japhet asserts that the Chronicler's account is an anachronistic projection of a post-exilic reality to the monarchic period. See also R. North, "The Chronicler: 1–2 Chronicles, Ezra, Nehemiah," in *The New Jerome Biblical Commentary* (ed. R. E. Brown et al.; New Jersey: Englewood Cliffs, 1990) 362-98, here 377.

[23] As Gary N. Knoppers ("Jehoshaphat's Judiciary and 'The Scroll of YHWH's Torah'," *JBL* 113 [1994] 59-80, here 71-79) comments, the Chronicler's account of Jehoshaphat's judiciary can be compared with the account of Moses' delegation of his judicial duties to certain magistrates in Exod 18:13-27; Deut 1:9-18, or with the Deuteronomic division of judiciary powers between local courts (Deut 16:18-20; 17:2-7) and a royal court (Deut 17:8-13). The Chronicler's description of Jehoshaphat's juridical reform has been interpreted in various ways, either as the Chronicler's justification of the contemporary judicial system (such as, Julius Wellhausen, *Prolegomena to the History of Ancient Israel* [Atlanta: Scholars, 1994) 191; repr. of *Prolegomena to the History of Israel* [trans. J. Sutherland Black and Allan Enzies, with preface by W. Robertson Smith; Edinburgh: Adam & Charles Black, 1885]; trans. of *Prolegomena zur Geschichte Israels* [2nd ed.; Berlin: G. Reimer, 1883]; McKenzie, *1–2 Chronicles*, 293; Robert R. Wilson, "Israel's Judicial System in the Pre-exilic Period," *JQRNS* 74 [1983] 229-48), as the Chronicler's ideological blueprint for the future (see Knoppers, "Jehoshaphat's Judiciary," 59-80), or as a reflection of historical reality in the ninth century B.C.E., based on his own sources which are no longer extant (see W. F. Albright, "The Judicial Reform of Jehoshaphat," in *Alexander Marx Jubilee Volume* [New York: The Jewish Theological Seminary of America, 1950] 61-82; Williamson, *1 and 2 Chronicles*, 289; Japhet, *The Ideology of the Book of Chronicles*, 436; Bernard S. Jackson, "Law in the Ninth Century: Jehoshaphat's 'Judicial Reform'," in *Understanding the History of Ancient Israel* [ed. H. G. M. Williamson; New York: Oxford University Press, 2007] 369-97; and Hanoch Reviv, "The Traditions Concerning the

In the Chronicler's account of Hezekiah's reform, the Levites' involvement is prominent (2 Chronicles 29–31). Here, the Levites participate in purifying the Temple (2 Chr 29:4-19), perform the paschal offering with the priests (2 Chr 30:15-18), and appear to be *more punctilious than the priests* in purifying themselves (2 Chr 29:34).[24] Hezekiah also installs the work rotations of the priests and the Levites according to their divisions and makes provision for the maintenance of the clergy (2 Chr 31:2-19). It should be noted, incidentally, that while the levitical involvement in the ritual activity is justified as part of the written Law of Moses in 2 Chr 35:6, 12, specific laws for it are *not* found in Pentateuchal legislations.[25] In Hezekiah's reform, then, we find two instances of the Chronicler's apparent cultic elevation of the Levites.

Josiah reinstitutes Hezekiah's reforms.[26] The Chronicler's narrative of Josiah's repair work on the Temple (2 Chr 34:8-13) also demonstrates that king's favorable treatment of the Levites. By making several changes to his source (2 Kgs 22:3-7), the Chronicler emphasizes that the Levites were involved in collecting people's contributions for repairing the Temple. The idea that the Levites collected and oversaw funds for temple restoration also occurs in the Chronicler's version of Joash's restoration of the Temple (2 Chr 24:5-11//2 Kgs 12:5-11). This overlap has led some commentators to argue that the Chronicler retrojected contemporary practices of tem-

Inception of the Legal System in Israel: Significance and Dating," *ZAW* 94 [1982] 566-75). However, these scholarly discussions have not emphasized the question of why the Chronicler included the large number of Levites in Jehoshaphat's juridical system, or of how the levitical involvement in juridical system would be significant to the Chronicler.

[24] S. Japhet (*I & II Chronicles*, 930) argues that this verse (2 Chr 29:34) has been misinterpreted as "the ultimate proof of the Chronicler's negative view of the priesthood, and his clear favoritism of the Levites." She proposes that this verse should be interpreted within its immediate context, which underlines the unexpected situation of widely spread priestly impurity.

[25] Michael Fishbane, *Biblical Interpretation in Ancient Israel* (Oxford: Clarendon, 1988) 138.

[26] The Levites' participation in slaughtering animals for sacrifice is mentioned in the Chronicler's both accounts of Hezekiah's and Josiah's reforms. Hezekiah allowed the Levites to kill the Passover lambs and to assist the priests when they dashed the blood (2 Chronicles 30). But it was a temporary measure due to the lack of the number of purified priests (2 Chr 30:17). This levitical service was perpetuated during the reign of Josiah (2 Chr 35:6, 11). In Chronicles, the Levites' involvement in the cult has been gradually expanded since Solomon's reign and reached its fruition in Josiah's Passover celebration. See Louis C. Jonker, *Reflections of King Josiah in Chronicles: Late Stages of the Josiah Reception in 2 Chr 34f.* (TSHB 2; Gütersloh: Gütersloher Verlagshaus, 2003) 60.

ple tax collection into these two narratives.[27] If so, this bolsters the idea that for the Chronicler, the Levites must be indispensably related to the management of the temple economy. The narratives of Josiah and Joash's (2 Chr 24:5-11 and 34:9-13) are therefore prime candidates for our corpus of texts that depict the Levites' economic duties, and I shall consider them in greater depth in Chapter 2.

Table 1. The Levites' Involvement in the Three Kings' Reforms

King	2 Chronicles	2 Kings
Jehoshaphat	▪ In the third year of his reign, he sent 5 officials, 9 Levites and 2 priests to teach the Torah in all the cities of Judah (17:7-9). ▪ Jehoshaphat appointed judges in every city of Judah, and then in Jerusalem he appointed some Levites, priests and ancestral chiefs of Israel for judgment for YHWH and for disputes (19:4-8). ▪ While Jehoshaphat prepared himself to do battle with the Moabites and Ammonites, he worshipped God, and the Levites praised the God of Israel on the battle field (20:1-27).	
Hezekiah	▪ Hezekiah invited the Levites to purify the Temple (29:4-5, 12-16). ▪ He made the Levitical musicians and singers attend the sacrifice in the Temple according to the commandment of David and prophets (29:25-27). ▪ The Levites were allowed to help the priests when they flayed the burnt offerings (29:34). ▪ When Hezekiah and the people celebrated the Passover, the Levites helped the priests who were sprinkling the blood (30:16). Moreover, the Levites were in charge of slaughtering the Passover lambs (30:17).	

[27] See Edward L. Curtis and Albert A. Madsen, *A Critical and Exegetical Commentary on the Books of Chronicles* (ICC 11; New York: Scribner's, 1910) 435; Rudolph, *Chronikbücher*, 274; Japhet, *I & II Chronicles*, 842-3; Dillard, *2 Chronicles*, 189-91; and Williamson, *1 and 2 Chronicles*, 321.

Hezekiah	▪ In Hezekiah's reform, the Levites were given outstanding roles in many ways and the fact is emphasized in the text (30:22, 25, and 27). In 30:27, the Levites blessed the people together with the priests. ▪ After finishing his purification of the Temple, Hezekiah set up the work-rotations of the priests and the Levites by their divisions (31:2). Then he also ordered people to give the portion due to the priests and the Levites (31:4-7). The Levites were appointed for the storerooms of contributions, tithes, and consecrated things (31:12-15).	
Josiah	▪ After purifying the Temple, Josiah wanted to repair the Temple. Thus the money collected by the Levites, guardians of the threshold, was given to Hilkiah, the high priest (34:9). ▪ The Levites oversaw the workers who repaired the Temple (34:12-13). ▪ The scribe Shaphan brought the king the book of Torah that Hilkiah found in the Temple (34:15-18). When celebrating the Passover, Josiah appointed the Levites, who taught all Israel, to a new mission as David had done. According to their division, the Levites will stand in the sanctuary (35:1-10). The priests dashed the blood with the help of the Levites, and the Levites did the flaying (35:11).	The money was collected by the guardians of the threshold (22:4). The scribe Shaphan brought the king the book of Torah that Hilkiah found in the Temple (22:8-10).

1.1.5. Summary

We have now gained significant ground in the quest to discern the Chronicler's distinctive portrayal of the Levites' roles in the Temple. For the Chronicler, the temple personnel are composed of priests and Levites, an arrangement that he claims originates with David. While both groups belong to the tribe of Levi, priests are specifically designated as "the descendants of Aaron" and play a largely superior role in cultic affairs, as 1 Chr 23:28 specifies. Yet, as is apparent in his versions of Josiah's and Joash's reforms, there can be no doubt that the Chronicler raises the Levites' status in areas related to the Temple's economic administration. Thus we find that the Levites, either as members of the temple treasury committee (1 Chr 28:12;

2 Chr 31:12-16) or as the head of that committee (1 Chr 26:24, 29), are deeply engaged in the in-and-out-flow of the temple revenue. And as we shall see in Chapter Two, the Levites (at least in the Chronicler's depiction of them) also possess significant authority over the Temple's purse-strings in their roles as the temple gatekeepers.

In subsequent chapters, I examine the texts that relate to the Levites' administrative roles to see what the Chronicler actually tells us about the functions of gatekeepers, treasurers and tax collectors and to consider the implications of the Chronicler's divisions of labor. Before I undertake this task however, it is necessary to lay additional methodological groundwork regarding the origins of Chronicles and its literary unity.

To justify my way of reading Chronicles, I need to establish (1) How one may read the Chronicler's description of the temple administration in the temporal and geographical setting of Persian-era Yehud even though the Chronicler's narrative describes situations of the First Temple and (2) How one might argue that the selected texts from Chronicles represent the Chronicler's particular views on the temple administration? In other words, what is the basis on which to read Chronicles as the work an author with a particular program? I will treat these matters in order. First, I will point to temporal indicators that situate the book's origins in the Persian period. Then, I will treat the question of literary unity by identifying passages I designate as "David's Installation Block" which argue for Chronicles' literary unity.

1.2. Temporal Setting for Chronicles

Despite its focus on the history of pre-exilic Israel, a near consensus holds that the Chronicler's work is likely to have originated in the Persian period, most likely in the late fifth or fourth century B.C.E.[28] Below I summarize some of the arguments—some highly speculative, some with a reasonably firm basis in probability—that scholars are currently advancing with regard to the date of Chronicles.

[28] In fact, for a date of Chronicles, a wide range of over three hundred and fifty years (from late sixth century to the mid-second century B.C.E.) has been suggested. Each of the proposed dates, whether early or late, has its strengths and weaknesses. The fourth-century B.C.E. dating of Chronicles now represents the mainstream of scholarly opinion.

(1) Depending on the way in which one reconstructs the text of 1 Chr 3:21, the genealogy of Jehoiachin (1 Chr 3:17-24) may indicate a fourth-century B.C.E. date for Chronicles. Unfortunately, the line of descent in this genealogy is ambiguous and may permit a range of between five to fourteen generations.[29] Nevertheless, calculating twenty years per generation, the possible date of birth for Anani, the last name on the list, can be placed in a range of 486 B.C.E.–300 B.C.E.[30] Clearly the genealogy of Jehoiachin in 1 Chr 3:17-24 cannot be a determining factor in establishing a *terminus ad quem* of the Chronicler's composition since it depends on a speculative reconstruction of 1 Chr 3:21. Nevertheless, the genealogy confirms a date for this passage sometime in the fifth or fourth century B.C.E., i.e. the Persian period in Yehud.[31]

[29] The genealogy of Jehoiachin contains text-critical, grammatical and syntactical problems which hinder an exact accounting of the number of generations. Gary N. Knoppers (*1 Chronicles 1–9*, 328-30) and R. W. Klein (*1 Chronicles*, 14-15, 119-23) count eight generations from MT 1 Chr 3:17-24, but twelve generations from LXX 1 Chr 3:17-24 (as well as the Syriac and Vulgate versions). The preceding passage (MT 1 Chr 3:10-17) relates eighteen generations of the descendants of Solomon approximately from 950 B.C.E. to 586 B.C.E. This reveals that the Chronicler calculated one generation with the twenty-year figure (18 generation × 20 years per generation = 360 years. Then, 950–360 = 590 B.C.E.). If we apply this figure to the genealogy of Jehoiachin (1 Chr 3:17-24), we arrive at the approximate date of 426 B.C.E. (from the MT) or 346 B.C.E. (from the LXX). S. Japhet (*I & II Chronicles*, 94) and H. G. M. Williamson (*Israel in the Books of Chronicles*, 83-84) also agree upon this calculation.

[30] Knoppers, *1 Chronicles 1–9*, 115.

[31] Japhet, *I & II Chronicles*, 94; and Williamson, *Israel in the Books of Chronicles*, 83-84. Most recently, Israel Finkelstein ("The Historical Reality behind the Genealogical Lists in 1 Chronicles," *JBL* 131 [2012] 65-83) suggests a second-century B.C.E. dating of Chronicles based on his archaeological survey on places mentioned on the genealogical lists in 1 Chronicles 2-9. He ("The Historical Reality," 71) asserts that the Persian period is not an option for the date of Chronicles since eleven sites out of thirty-nine surveyed places were not inhabited and eight sites were sparsely inhabited in the Persian period. However, Finkelstein presupposes that the places of the genealogical lists in 1 Chronicles 2-9 were intended to reflect historical realities, whether of the late Iron II period or of the Persian period. Because of this presupposition, many other places from the genealogical lists, specifically places taken from the Chronicler's earlier sources (the books of Joshua and Judges), are excluded from his survey. Without considering the Chronicler's intention to include such towns in the list, I. Finkelstein ("The Historical Reality," 82) asserts that the genealogical lists were intended to legitimize Jewish rule over the area where the Hasmonean state occupied. What if the Chronicler did not intend to reminisce about the past glory of the late Iron II period nor to spill to sketch the realities in his own time? What if the Chronicler intended to suggest an idealistic picture of Israel based on his earlier sources, memories of the past, and possibilities for the future? Finkelstein's argument for a second-century B.C.E. dating for Chronicles is not strong enough to deny a Persian-era dating of Chronicles.

(2) 1 Chronicles 9 (cf. Nehemiah 11) strongly indicates that the backdrop of the book of Chronicles is the post-exilic period, in that it addresses the identity, pedigree, and destination of exilic returnees.[32] Although the literary dependence of 1 Chronicles 9 on Nehemiah 11 cannot be ascertained, the Chronicler's description of the levitical gatekeepers reflects more a systematized institutional development than appears in the parallel material in Nehemiah.[33] Although 1 Chr 9:2-17 is almost identical with Neh 11:3-9, its middle section (1 Chr 9:18-33) provides new material about the duties of the gatekeepers, which are described in a single verse in Nehemiah 11 (v. 19). Moreover, the gatekeepers are included among the Levites only in Chronicles, whereas they are treated as an independent order among the temple personnel in Ezra-Nehemiah (Ezra 2:42, 70; 7:7; Neh 7:1, 3, 45, 73; 10:28,39; 12:47; 13:5). Thus, Chronicles' expansiveness with regard to the gatekeepers makes it reasonable to speculate

[32] The relationship between 1 Chronicles 9 and Nehemiah 11 has long been a subject of debate. Moreover, the distinctiveness of the list of gatekeepers in 1 Chr 9:17-34 has complicated scholarly debates on this matter. What follows is a summary of various scholarly opinions on the literary dependence of 1 Chronicles 9 on Nehemiah 11. For this summary, I referred to R. W. Klein's concise summary (*1 Chronicles*, 263-64), but inserted some additions and changes.

(1) The literary dependence of Nehemiah 11 on 1 Chronicles 9 is no more argued in recent decades.

(2) The literary dependence of 1 Chronicles 9 on Nehemiah 11 is argued by W. Rudolph (*Chronikbücher*, 85, 94); S. Japhet (*I & II Chronicles*, 202-19); R. Braun (*1 Chronicles*, 132-36); R. W. Klein (*1 Chronicles*, 263-64); I. Kalimi ("The View of Jerusalem in the Ethnographical Introduction of Chronicles (1 Chr 1–9)," *Biblica* 83 [2002] 556-62); and W. Johnstone (*1 Chronicles 1–2 Chronicles 9: Israel's Place among the Nations* [Vol. 1 of *and 2 Chronicles*; JSOTSup 253; Sheffield: Sheffield Academic Press, 1997] 120-21).

(3) A hypothesis of the common earlier source which the Chronicler and the author of Nehemiah 11 reworked independently is argued by E. L. Curtis and A. A. Madsen (*The Books of Chronicles*, 168); J. M. Myers (*1 Chronicles*, 66-73); H. G. M. Williamson (*1 and 2 Chronicles*, 87-88); and Gary N. Knoppers ("Sources, Revisions, and Editions: The Lists of Jerusalem's Residents in MT and LXX Nehemiah and 1 Chronicles 9," *Textus* 20 [2000] 141-68). Gary N. Knoppers (*1 Chronicles 1–9*, 510-11) states that the Chronicler's indebtedness to Nehemiah is only one possible explanation of the data. He argues that the Chronicler's source for the list in1 Chronicles 9 is not the same one that the author or editor of Nehemiah used for the list in Nehemiah 11since the differences between the two lists are significant: a great number of non-parallel sections in each of the two lists; different numerical totals; and the significant differences between the MT and LXX versions of 1 Chronicles 9 and Nehemiah 11. Thus, Knoppers concludes that each of them reworked and expanded his own source in very distinctive ways. Oded Lipschits ("Literary and Ideological Aspects of Nehemiah 11," *JBL* 121 [2002] 428-29) concedes Knoppers' conclusion without providing additional evidence in his studies of the list in Nehemiah 11.

[33] Klein, *1 Chronicles*, 263-65.

that 1 Chronicles 9 derives from a time later than the time that implied by Nehemiah 11.

On a related note, the Chronicler portrays the Levites, priests, singers and gatekeepers as organized into twenty-four units (see 1 Chr 23:6-24; 24:1-19; 25:1-31; and 26:1-19). The twenty-four priestly divisions, which 1 Chronicles 24 first introduces in the Hebrew Bible, continue to appear in texts of the post-biblical period.[34] The system of the twenty-four divisions of each clerical group is not mentioned in Ezra-Nehemiah. Considering the continuance of the twenty-four priestly divisions, the Chronicler's picture of cultic institutions is likely to reflect a later practice than that of Ezra-Nehemiah.[35] If this speculation is correct, Chronicles is likely to have been written later than the late-fifth century B.C.E.[36]

[34] S. Japhet, "The Supposed Common Authorship of Chronicles and Ezra-Nehemiah Investigated Anew," *VT* 18 (1968) 345-46. According to Japhet, the priestly twenty-four divisions are attested to in *m. Taᶜan.* 4:2; *t. Taᶜan.* 2; *y. Taᶜan.* 4:2; and *b. Taᶜan.* 27a, b. This fact underlines that the system of the twenty-four priestly divisions remain unchanged into the post-biblical period. Gary N. Knoppers (*1 Chronicles 10-29*, 841-42) also lists texts written later than Chronicles which attest to the priestly divisions as follows with a conclusion that these texts significantly evince the existence of the priestly divisions in the Second Temple period although the texts do not agree with one another about the number of priestly courses: (1) Twelve fragmentary manuscripts from Qumran cave 4 (4Q320-330, 337) which explain calendars of priestly courses. As for further discussions about these calendars, see Florentino García Matínez and Eibert J. C. Tigchelaar, eds., *The Dead Sea Scrolls Study Edition* (2 vols.; Leiden; Boston; Köln: Brill, 1997–1998) 678-705, 707; Shemaryahu Talmon and Israel Knohl, "A Calendrical Scroll From A Qumran Cave: Mišmarot B[a], 4Q321," in *Pomegranates and Golden Bells*, 267-301; and S. Talmon with the assistance of J. Ben-Dov, "Calendrical Documents and Mishmarot," *Qumran Cave 4. XVI: Calendrical Texts* (ed. S. Talmon, J. Ben-Dov, and U. Glessmer; DJD 21; Oxford: Clarendon, 2001) 2, 8-28. (2) The works of Josephus: *Ant.* 7:366 (which describes that the priestly courses were distributed by lot); *Life* 1:2 (which mentions about twenty-four priestly courses); and *Against Apion* 2:108 (where four courses of the priests are mentioned). (3) Luke 1:5 which attests to the existence of priestly divisions; (4) *m. Sukkah* 5:8 and *m. Tamid* 5:1-5:6 and 6:1-6:3 which explain that various priestly roles were allotted to different priestly families by lottery.

[35] S. J. de Vries (*1 and 2 Chronicles,* 10, 16-17) suggests that Chronicles was composed later and canonized later than Ezra-Nehemiah. S. Japhet (*I & II Chronicles*, 27) also states:

> In the absence of comparative material it is difficult to draw precise chronological conclusions from this general portrayal of the cult organization, but since a prolonged and complex process is involved, a later provenance, certainly later than the one assumed by Ezra-Nehemiah, must be presupposed.

[36] Since a large section of Ezra-Nehemiah (from Ezra 7 to Nehemiah 13) recounts the events of 458–433 B.C.E., the book of Ezra-Nehemiah must have been written later than 433 B.C.E. To determine the *terminus ad quem* of Ezra-Nehemiah is another conundrum since it depends on how one understands the process of the composition of Ezra-Nehemiah, as well as how to interpret the mandate of Ezra (458 B.C.E. or 398 B.C.E.?). Johanna W. H. van Wijk-

(3) The Chronicler relates that King David collected ten thousand *darics* for the construction of the temple in Jerusalem (1 Chr 29:7). Since *darics* are Persian gold coins, this expression is obviously anachronistic.[37] The *daric* became the chief gold currency in the world of trade over the course of several centuries. Obviously, the appearance of the word *daric* in Chronicles indicates that Chronicles was written after *darics* were circulated throughout extensive regions of the Achaemenid Empire in the fifth century B.C.E. at the earliest. Unfortunately, several ancient Greek authors give different data for the date of the first minting and circulation of *darics* (Harpocration: before Darius I [earlier than 522 B.C.E.]; Xenophon: Cyrus II [559–530 B.C.E.]; and Herodotus: Darius I [522–486 B.C.E.]).[38] Archaeological findings thus far lend support to Herodotus' report: no *darics* have been discovered in the archaeological excavations of the foundation of the *apadana* in Persepolis, which was built between 517 and 514 B.C.E. (and otherwise yielded four silver Greek coins as well as gold and silver plates with the inscriptions of Darius I).[39] Based on this fact, M. A. Dandamaev and V. G. Lukonin argue that the minting of *darics* should be dated to a time after 517 B.C.E., when the *apadana* was being built.[40] In contrast, a horde of *darics* were found in a buried treasure on the Athos canal, which

Bos (*Ezra, Nehemiah, and Esther* [Westminster Bible Companion; Louisville: Westminster John Knox, 1998] 14) suggests that the writing and editing process of Ezra-Nehemiah may have taken place in the early part of the fourth century B.C.E. Concerning the dating issue of Ezra-Nehemiah, several scholars reserve their judgment on it with a very cautious comment, such as: "It is important to recognize that we have no real supporting evidence from other sources which enables us to date either Ezra or Nehemiah" (R. J. Coggins, *The Books of Ezra and Nehemiah* [CBC; New York: Cambridge University Press, 1976] 6-7). See also D. J. A. Clines, *Ezra, Nehemiah, Esther* (NCBC; Grand Rapids: Eerdmans, 1984) 12-14.

[37] This fact was first pointed out by William M. L. de Wette. See De Wette, Vol. II of *A Critical and Historical Introduction to the Canonical Scriptures of the Old Testament* (trans. Theodore Parker; 2 vols.; 3rd ed.; Boston: Rufus Leighton, 1859) 264-65. Some scholars, though citing the late date of this verse, do not consider that it could be a conclusive indicator of the fourth century B.C.E. dating of Chronicles since they consider 1 Chronicles 29 was added by a later redactor. For example, R. Mosis, *Untersuchungen zur Theologie des chronistischen Geschichteswerkes* (FTS 92; Freiburg: Herder, 1973) 105-6; and M. Throntveit, *When Kings Speak: Royal Speech and Royal Prayer in Chronicles* (SBLDS 93; Atlanta: Scholars Press, 1987) 89-96.

[38] Concerning these Greek authors' and their comments on *darics*, refer to M. A. Dandamaev and V. G. Lukonin, *The Culture and Social Institutions of Ancient Iran* (New York: Cambridge University Press, 1989) 195-97.

[39] Dandamaev and Lukonin, *The Culture and Social Institutions of Ancient Iran*, 196.

[40] Dandamaev and Lukonin, *The Culture and Social Institutions of Ancient Iran*, 196.

was built by Xerxes in 480 B.C.E.[41] Thus, Dandamev and Lukonin assert that 480 B.C.E. could serve as the *terminus ante quem* for the minting of *darics*.

(4) The Chronicler had access to all of the major textual traditions of ancient Israel. He cites or alludes to texts from Genesis, Exodus, Numbers, Leviticus, Deuteronomy, Isaiah, Jeremiah, Ezekiel, Zechariah, and the Psalms.[42] Second, the Priestly tradition and the Deuteronomic tradition are occasionally harmonized in Chronicles.[43] As an example, we may examine 2 Chr 7:8-10, where the Chronicler describes the eight-day celebration of the feast after the Temple was built.[44] The Chronicler's description harmonizes the narrative of 1 Kgs 8:65-66 and the requirement of the priestly law.

[41] Dandamaev and Lukonin, *The Culture and Social Institutions of Ancient Iran*, 196.

[42] Louis Jonker ("The Chronicler and the Prophets: Who were his Authoritative Sources?" *SJOT* 22 [2008] 275-95) argues that 2 Chr 36:15-21 has a strong literary connection with the book of Jeremiah, such as an allusion to Jer 29:10. It has been suggested that in 2 Chr 16:9, the seer Hanani's speech probably would be a quotation from Zech 4:10. See R. W. Klein, *1 Chronicles*, 15; and Kai Peltonen, "A Jigsaw without a Model? The Date of Chronicles," in *Did Moses Speak Attic? Jewish Historiography and Scripture in the Hellenistic Period* (ed. Lester L. Grabbe; JSOTSup 317; Sheffield: Sheffield Academic Press, 2001) 225-71, here 230. There seems to be more connections between the two books, such as Zech 1:2-4 and 2 Chr 30:6-7 and Zech 8:10 and 2 Chr 15:5-6. S. Japhet (*The Ideology of the Book of Chronicles*, 183) comments on this fact as such: "The many verses of classical prophecy quoted by the Chronicler particularly in his speeches prove his familiarity with this corpus." See also P. Beentjes, "Prophets in the Book of Chronicles," in *The Elusive Prophet: The Prophet as a Historical Person, Literary Character and Anonymous Artist* (ed. J. C. de Moor; OtSt 45; Leiden: Brill, 2001) 45-53; idem, "Tradition and Transformation: Aspects of Inner Biblical Interpretation in 2 Chronicles 20," *Bib* 74 (1993) 258-68.

According to P. Beentjes ("Psalms and Prayers in the Book of Chronicles," in *Psalms and Prayers* [ed. Bob Becking and Eric Peels; OTS 55; Leiden; Boston: Brill, 2007] 9-44, here 11, 43-44), the Chronicler cites a psalm or part of it seven times in Chronicles. Psalms 96; 105; 106 are incorporated in 1 Chr 16:8-36, and Ps. 132:8-10 in 2 Chr 6:40-42. 1 Chr 16:41; 2 Chr 5:13; 7:3, 6; 20:21 refer to the phrase "Give thanks to YHWH for He is good, for his loyalty endures forever." This phrase frequently appears in the following psalms: Pss. 106:1; 107:1; 118:1, 29; 136:1. Beentjes points out that these quotations from the Psalter are always found in highly liturgical contexts. This fact indicates that the Chronicler was familiar with such liturgical contexts.

[43] In 1930 Gerhard von Rad (*From Genesis to Chronicles: Exploration in Old Testament Theology* [Minneapolis: Fortress, 2005] 232-42; repr. of *From Genesis to Chronicles: Exploration in Old Testament Theology* [trans. E.W. Trueman Dicken; Edinburgh; London: Oliver & Boyd, 1966]; trans. of *Gesammelte Studien zum Alten Testament* [Theologische Bücherei 8; Munich: Kaiser, 1958]) already demonstrated that the Chronicler's work stands on both the P and D traditions.

[44] This feast seems to be the feast of Tabernacles since 2 Kgs 8:2 reports that the installation of the Ark took place in *Ethanim* (the Seventh month).

According to 1 Kgs 8:65-66, Solomon and all of Israel observed "the festival" for seven days; on the eighth day, the celebrants went home. In other words, they had a seven-day celebration of the feast of Tabernacles. This complies with the Deuteronomic tradition (Deut 16:13-15), which defines this feast as a seven-day fall harvest festival. However, the Priestly law has different regulations for this feast. The Priestly law requires an eight-day celebration of the feast by adding a regulation for the holy assembly on the eighth day (Lev 23:33-36; Num 29:35-36). Thus, the Chronicler harmonizes the narrative in Kings in accordance with the requirements of the Priestly law in 2 Chr 7:8-10.[45]

Similarly, in 2 Chr 35:13, the Chronicler describes the cooking of the Passover lamb: "they boiled the Passover lamb with fire" (באש יבשלו הפסח כמשפט). Here, the Chronicler harmonizes the two contradictory Pentateuchal requirements for the preparation of the sacrificial meat for the Passover: "to roast over the fire" (צלי־אש) in Exod 12:9 and "to boil" (בשל) in Deut 16:7.[46]

The Chronicler's interest in harmonizing Pentateuchal legislation serves as a reliable indication that the book of Chronicles was written in the post-exilic period, when both the Priestly tradition and the Deuteronomic tradition were brought together to create the present form of the Pentateuch.[47]

(4) Scholarly consensus places the *terminus ad quem* for the composition of Chronicles in the mid-third century B.C.E. for two reasons. First, Chronicles was translated into Greek (*Paraleipomena*) in the mid-third century B.C.E., and reused in 1 Esdras in the second century B.C.E.[48] Second,

[45] I. Kalimi, *The Reshaping of Ancient Israelite History in Chronicles* (Winona Lake: Eisenbrauns, 2005) 147-48; and Fishbane, *Biblical Interpretation*, 151-53.

[46] Ehud Ben Zvi, "Revisiting 'Boiling in Fire' in 2 Chronicles 35:13 and Related Passover Questions: Text, Exegetical Needs and Concerns, and General Implications," in *Biblical Interpretation in Judaism and Christianity* (ed. Isaac Kalimi and Peter J. Haas; LHBOT 439; New York/ London: T & T Clark, 2006) 238-50; and Fishbane, *Biblical Interpretation*, 134-38.

[47] In general scholars agree that the Pentateuch must have been come into existence in the post-exilic period. Since the Greek translation of the Pentateuch was made in the middle of the third century B.C.E, it is likely the Pentateuch was completed at the beginning of the Hellenistic period. See Frank Crüsemann, *The Torah: Theology and Social History of Old Testament Law* (trans. Allan W. Mahnke; Minneapolis: Fortress, 1996) 332-34.

[48] Additional evidence for the determination of the *terminus ante quem* is provided by G. N. Knoppers (*1 Chronicles 1–9*, 106-11): Eupolemus' citation of *Paraleipomena* in the second century B.C.E.; an allusion of Dan 1:1-2 to 2 Chr 36:6b-7; an allusion of Sir 47:9-10 to 1 Chr 24:1-19; and the testimony to Chronicles in the Temple Scroll and the War Scroll.

the absence of Hellenistic influence in Chronicles suggests that the *terminus ad quem* is the end of the Persian period.[49]

(5) Some scholars date Chronicles to the Persian period based on their linguistic observations. For instance, the Chronicler frequently uses the verb יחש relating to genealogical registration in Chronicles.[50] Of the twenty occurrences of this verb in the Hebrew Bible (always in the *hithpa'el*), fifteen occur in Chronicles (ten in the genealogies of 1 Chronicles 1–9). The other five occurrences are all in Ezra and Nehemiah.[51] The verb is always used in the context where the issue of identity matters in the community. In Chronicles, the majority of the occurrences of this verb are found in the first nine chapters, the so-called "genealogical hall."[52]

P. C. Beentjes' study on the significance of the verb יחש in Chronicles gives some insight into socio-historical situations which may have produced such a predilection for verb יחש.[53] Beentjes concludes that the verb יחש is

---

Thus, he concludes: "The collective evidence points to a mid-third-century date as the latest reasonable time for composition."

[49] Some scholars suggest that the Hellenistic influence in the Levant began even before the conquest of Alexander the Great. Nevertheless, the lack of any vestige of such influence in Chronicles indicates that the influence was not pervasive in the Chronicler's time. See Einat Ambar-Armon and Amos Kloner, "Archaeological Evidence of Links between the Aegean World and the Land of Israel in the Persian Period," in *A Time of Change: Judah and Its Neighbors in the Persian and Early Hellenistic Periods* (ed. Yigal Levin; Library of Second Temple Studies 65; New York: T & T Clark, 2007) 1-22. P. Welten (*Geschichte und Geschichtsdarstellungin den Chronikbüchern* [Neukirchen-Vluyn: Neukirchener Verlag, 1973] 98-114), interpreting the word חשבון in 2 Chr 26:15 as a Greek catapult used in the third century B.C.E., has suggested the existence of the Hellenistic influence in Chronicles. But this interpretation has been refuted by several scholars, such as Williamson (*1 and 2 Chronicles*, 337-38) and G. H. Jones (*1 & 2 Chronicles* [OTG; Sheffield: JSOT Press, 1993] 92-93). A military device for shooting arrows and great stones had been used even before the Persian period as the Assyrian reliefs of the siege of Lachish portray. Thus, the word חשבון in 2 Chr 26:15 cannot be used as evidence for dating Chronicles in the Hellenistic period.

[50] The word פקד is used most frequently in the Hebrew Bible to express "register, or enroll," such as Exod 30:12, 13, 14; 38:25, 26; Num 1; 2; 3; 4; 26 (total 69 times); 1 Sam 11:8; 13:15; 24:2, 4; and 1 Chr 23:24. The word כתב is also used to render the same idea in Num 11:26; Isa 10:19; Ps 69:28; Ezra 13:9; 1 Chr 24:6. See BDB 507, 823. The Chronicler does not use these two words to designate tribal enrollments in his genealogical section (1 Chronicles 1–9). There, his preference to יחש is obvious.

[51] Knoppers, *1 Chronicles 1–9*, 367.

[52] This term is coined by M. Oeming in his book, *Das wahre Israel: Die 'genealogische Vorhalle' 1 Chronik 1–9* (BWANT 7; Stuttgart: W. Kohlhammer, 1990).

[53] Beentjes, *Tradition and Transformation in the Book of Chronicles*, 187-91.

used in Chronicles as "literary and theological glue" to bind the forgotten tribes to the rest of the tribes in order to express his ideal of all Israel.[54]

S. Japhet is cautious about taking this evidence to confirm any specific date for Chronicles since the absence of the verb יחש in other books does not necessarily mean that the verb was introduced into Hebrew only at a later phase. It could just reflect a certain author's stylistic preferences.[55] Thus the Chronicler's Late Biblical Hebrew and his preference for certain vocabulary are of limited usefulness in determining a specific date for the composition of Chronicles.[56]

On the other hand, Persian loan words appear in Chronicles, although with less frequency than in Ezra-Nehemiah. Only four cases are found: נדן (1 Chr 21:27); פרבר (1 Chr 26:18); גנזך (1 Chr 28:11); and אדרכנים (1 Chr 29:7).[57] The term "province" (מדינה), a basic administrative unit in the Achaemenid Empire, never occurs in Chronicles. S. Japhet considers this scarcity of Persian loan words in Chronicles as the Chronicler's deliberate elimination of any explicit indication of the Persian influence.[58] At any rate, the occurrence of Persian loan words in Chronicles definitely indicates that the Chronicler's work originated in the Persian period.

All in all, all these markers of date of Chronicles point to a specific temporal context through which the entire book of Chronicles should be read, namely, Persian-era Yehud. Furthermore, the Chronicler places two important markers of time, the genealogy of Jehoiachin (1 Chr 3:17-24) and 1 Chronicles 9, in the prologue of Chronicles, whereas he puts another marker of time, the edict of Cyrus (2 Chr 36:23), at the end of the book. By bracketing the beginning and the end of his work with indicators of time, the Chronicler seems to design it to be read against the backdrop of the post-exilic period.

1.3. David's Installation Block

Since the present study examines the Chronicler's descriptions of the temple administration by analyzing three sets of texts concerning gatekeep-

[54] Beentjes, *Tradition and Transformation in the Book of Chronicles*, 191. See also Peter B. Dirksen, *1 Chronicles* (HCOT; Dudley, MA: Peeters, 2005) 25.

[55] Japhet, *I & II Chronicles*,168.

[56] It is argued that the language of Chronicles, which is Late Biblical Hebrew (henceforth: LBH), sets the upper limit of the composition of the book no earlier than the post-exilic period. See Japhet, *I & II Chronicles*, 25.

[57] See I. Kalimi, *An Ancient Israelite Historian: Studies in the Chronicler, His Time, Place and Writing* (Assen: Royal Van Gorcum, 2005) 41.

[58] Japhet, *I & II Chronicles*, 207.

ers (1 Chr 9:17-32; 26:1-19), treasurers (1 Chr 9:26-28; 26:20-32), and tax collectors (2 Chr 24:5-11; 34:9-13), it is necessary to establish the basis on which I argue that these texts derive from the same pen (perhaps, a single editorial circle), not from diachronically distinct redactional levels.

Chronicles, to put it mildly, is not an easy or an aesthetically pleasing read. Many scholars have accounted for the lack of literary smoothness by positing that multiple redactional literary strands were added over time to create the book in its present form. M. Noth offered a highly influential theory in this vein when he argued that 1 Chronicles 23-27 was a secondary addition that interrupted the original narrative connection between 1 Chr 23:1-2a and 1 Chr 28:1 and the following verses.[59] He then classified any passage as secondary which traces the origins of the late post-exilic divisions of the various cultic servants back to King David, as 1 Chronicles 23-27 does. [60] Thus, Noth considered the following passages—which include all of the "base texts" essential to the current project— as secondary: 1 Chr 9:1-34; 12:1-23; 12:24-41; 15:4-10, 16-24; 16:5-38, 41-42; 22:17-19; 23:3-27:34.[61]

Yet the approach that Noth and his followers have applied to Chronicles does not explain sufficiently the literary function of the presumed secondary passages in the overall narrative structure of Chronicles. Furthermore, the basis on which Noth identified 1 Chronicles 23-27 as secondary is untenable. Noth considered the resumptive repetition between 1 Chr 23:1-2 and 1 Chr 28:1 as evidence for attributing the intervening material to a redactor. But there are several cases of resumptive repetition in Chronicles, such as 2 Chr 12:2, 9 (cf. 1Kgs 14:25) and 2 Chr 16:7, 10 (cf. 1Kgs 15:22ff) where that literary technique indicates the Chronicler's reworking of his original sources, rather than insertion of secondary material. I. Kalimi provides many examples of resumptive repetition which the Chronicler used not only in narrative passages but also in lists.[62] Concerning the Chronicler's usage of this technique, Kalimi comments:

> The examples adduced below clearly demonstrate the considerable use that the Chronicler made of this literary technique in giving a renewed literary appearance to the passages that he took from the

[59] M. Noth, *The Chronicler's History* (trans. H.G.M. Williamson; JSOTSup 50; Sheffield: JSOT Press, 1987) 31-33.

[60] Noth, *The Chronicler's History*, 31-32.

[61] Noth, *The Chronicler's History*, 31-42.

[62] Kalimi, *The Reshaping of Ancient Israelite History*, 295-324.

books of Samuel-Kings. It turns out to have been one of the most prominent writing devices of the Chronicler.[63]

Moreover, three thematic threads run through 1 Chronicles 23–26 and attest to its unity: first, each corps of levitical personnel established by David in these chapters is divided into 24 divisions (1 Chr 23:6-24 [the divisions of the Levites]; 1 Chr 24:1-19 [the divisions of the priests]; 1 Chr 25:1-31 [the divisions of the musicians]; and 1 Chr 26:1-19 [the divisions of the gatekeepers]). Second, the literary coherence of 1 Chronicles 23–26 is established by the repeated references to an action of casting lots which would decide the order of shifts for the duties of the Levites (see 1 Chr 24:5, 31; 25:8; and 26:13).[64] Lastly, reiteration of the word מחלקות and of a similar phrase which emphasizes an equal footing also exhibits the literary coherence of 1 Chronicles 23–26.[65]

Despite its manifold weaknesses, Noth's basic stance was followed by many scholars, most notably W. Rudolph and more recently Roddy Braun, who argue for many such additions.[66] Similarly, recent scholars, such as T. Willi, R. Mosis, M. Throntveit, and P. Welten, view some of the so-called levitical portions of Chronicles as the product of later redactions.[67]

However, the approach that Noth and his followers applied to Chronicles does not explain sufficiently the literary function of the presumed

[63] Kalimi, *The Reshaping of Ancient Israelite History*, 296.

[64] Concerning the significance of lot casting in the Hebrew Bible, see Anne Marie Kitz's article, "The Hebrew Terminology of Lot Casting and Its Ancient Near Eastern Context," *CBQ* 62 (2000) 207-14.

[65] Phrases used to indicate equal footing include: "all alike" (אלה עם־אלה) in 1 Chr 24:5; "the chief as well as the youngest brother" (הראשׁ לעמת אחיו הקטן) in 1 Chr 24:31; "small and great, teacher and pupil alike" (לעמת כקטן כגדול מבין עם־תלמיד) in 1 Chr 25:8; and "small and great alike" (כקטן כגדול) in 1 Chr 26:13. S. Japhet (*I & II Chronicles*, 409) points out, regarding the unity of 1 Chr 23-27, "An unprejudiced consideration of chs. 23-27 will reveal that they exhibit a transparent structure, integrate nicely with the literary methods of the book, voice the same views as and have close affinities with the other parts of Chronicles."

[66] Rudolph, *Die Chronikbücher*, 152-85. Rudolph further suggested more than one redactional layer in the section of 1 Chronicles 23-27 since he found there the lack of unity of form or incoherence of the content. Roddy Braun (*1 Chronicles* [WBC 14; Waco: Word Books, 1986] xix) argues that major additions and revisions have been introduced to the Chronicler's work, principally in the genealogies of 1 Chronicles 1–9 and 1 Chronicles 23-27, although he considers the greater part of 1 and 2 Chronicles as the work of the Chronicler.

[67] See T. Willi, *Die Chronik als Auslegung* (FRLANT 106; Göttingen: Vandenhoeck & Ruprecht, 1972) 194-204; R. Mosis, *Untersuchungen zur Theologie des chronistischen Geschichteswerkes*, 44; M. Throntveit, *When Kings Speak*, 1–9, 115-25; and P. Welten, *Geschichte und Geschichtsdarstellung in den Chronikbüchern*, esp., 180-85, 201-6.

secondary passages in the overall narrative structure of Chronicles. Scholarly skepticism toward Noth's approach has led some scholars to re-examine what Noth thought were secondary materials. H. G. M. Williamson made the first move in this direction.[68] Through a careful literary analysis of 1 Chronicles 23-27, Williamson discerns two main literary layers in 1 Chronicles 23-27: the earlier, much shorter layer of the Chronicler's original composition and the secondary layer added about a generation later by a pro-priestly reviser under the influence of the institution of the system of twenty-four priestly courses.[69] Thus, Williamson ascribes the following passages to a pro-priestly redactor, not to the Chronicler himself: 1 Chr 15:4, 11, 14: 16:6; 23:13b-14, 25-32; 24:1-19, 20-32; 25:7-31; 26:4-8, 12-18; 27:1-34, and a few isolated other passages. Williamson's layer model is followed by several scholars, such as Simon J. de Vries, Peter B. Dirksen, and Ralph W. Klein although the way in which they identify the literary layers varies.[70]

[68] H. G. M. Williamson (*1 and 2 Chronicles*, 14) argues that Chronicles constitutes a substantial unity, yet with minor later additions. He includes 1 Chronicles 1–9 as an integral part of Chronicles.

[69] See H. G. M. Williamson, "The Origins of the Twenty-Four Priestly Courses: A Study of 1 Chronicles 23-27," in *Studies in Persian Period History and Historiography* (FAT 38; Tübingen: Mohr Siebeck, 2004) 127-40; and idem, *1 and 2 Chronicles*, 14-15. Primarily based on his literary critical approach to the text, Williamson (*1 and 2 Chronicles*, 15) surmises that the pro-priestly reviser intended to correct the Chronicler's neglect of the importance of the priests in their relationship to the Levites, and to present Davidic legitimation for the recently emerged priestly and Levitical orders. Similarly, A. C. Welch (*The Work of the Chronicler*, 5-6) argues that Chronicles was written by a pro-Levitical author to substantiate Levitical claims over against the priests about 515 B.C.E., and later annotated by pro-priestly redactors to defend their case. S. L. McKenzie ("The Chronicler as Redactor," 78-80), however, disapproves Williamson's argument by pointing out that inner-connection among the texts in Williamson's pro-Priestly layer is not strong enough to hold them together as one layer. My own critique of Williamson's conclusion is to be given in the sections of literary analysis of each selected text in Chapter Two.

[70] Simon J. de Vries (*1 and 2 Chronicles* [FOTL 11; Grand Rapids: Eerdmans, 1989] 12-14) suggests the following passages as secondary expansions: 1 Chr 2:34-41, 42-50ab, 52-55; 6:35-38 (50-53); 15:23-24; 23:24b-32; 24:1-19, 20-31; 25:7-31; 26:4-8, 12-18; 27:1-34; 2 Chr 24:5b-6; 29:25; 34:6-9,11-16. He argues that these additional passages do not fit comfortably in their context, but rather tend to create disharmony. After analyzing the secondary material, he concludes that it reflects a constant struggle of the clerical orders to gain higher dignity. Yet, he admits that linguistic evidence is not strong enough to reach a conclusion whether one or a few or many were responsible for all these expansions. Peter B. Dirksen (*1 Chronicles* [HCOT; Dudley, MA: Peeters, 2005] 4-5, 274-77) suggests the following passages are secondary: 1 Chr 1:32-33; 5:27-41; 6:33-34; 9:26b, 28-33; 12:28-29; 15:4-10, 17-18; 16:35-38; 1 Chronicles 23-27; 1 Chr 28:12b-18a; 29:6, 8, 21, 22. Ralph W. Klein (*1 Chronicles*, 11, 487) thinks 1 Chr 26:4-8, 12-18 is secondary.

A lack of literary uniformity in Chronicles has pushed some scholars further to suggest multiple redactional layers. Most recently, E. M. Dörfuss, by applying a hyper-critical literary analysis to Chronicles, has suggested a late (Maccabean) "Moses redaction" of Chronicles which aimed to challenge the idealization of the Davidic kingdom and the Jerusalem Temple in favor of Moses' authority and the Sinaitic institutions, while also giving hope for theocratic leadership in the future.[71] G. Steins goes even further. He suggests three levels of redaction, each level composed of multiple layers: (1) the first level: a cultic personnel layer, two musician layers and a "musician-gatekeeper" layer; (2) the second level: the community level; and (3) the third level: a cult layer and a northern layer.[72]

Redaction critics' literary analyses of Chronicles are intended to give a better explanation for the considerable unevenness in the text of Chronicles, but they have resulted instead in the production of over-complicated hypotheses for the reconstruction of its redaction. A hypothesis of multiple redactional layers demands speculation about the socio-historical and ideological backdrop of each layer, and in turn such speculations make the whole hypothesis tenuous. Indeed, theories that posit multiple layers of redaction eventually make it difficult to recognize the significant themes which run throughout the whole book of Chronicles. S. Japhet's critique rings true:[73]

> Even the most severe forms of literary criticism did not achieve meticulous harmony of the details, and the problems they raised were sometimes greater than those they solved. More problematic was the recognition of how arbitrary some of the arguments actually were. While the possibility of secondary elaboration during the course of transmission was not ruled out—in particular in the lists, which are most susceptible to change—it seemed that a better explanation of the book's variety and composition is the view that it is one work, composed essentially by a single author, with a very distinct and peculiar literary method.

[71] E. M. Dörrfuss, *Mose in den Chronikbüchern: Garant theokratischer Zukunftserwartung* (BZAW 219; Berlin: W. de Gruyter, 1994).

[72] G. Steins, *Die Chronik als kanonisches Abschulussphänomen: Studien zur Entstehung und Theologie von 1/2 Chronik* (BBB 93; Weinheim: Beltz Athenäum, 1995).

[73] Japhet, *I & II Chronicles*, 7.

In fact, in my view, we can identify the "distinct and peculiar literary method" of the Chronicler, and can ascertain, within reason, the literary unity of Chronicles by turning our attention to a set of four passages (1 Chr 6:31-38; 1 Chr 9:17-32; 1 Chr 16:4-43 and 1 Chronicles 23–26) that I designate as "David Installation Blocks" (henceforth, "DIB"). All of the passages that I identify as DIB share specific characteristics that point to the literary unity of Chronicles. First, they indicate that for the Chronicler, King David was the founder and guardian of the Jerusalem temple as an institution. Second, they share a uniform conception of the levitical involvement in the temple administration. Table 2 (p. 32) illustrates the prominence of these dual traits in 1 Chronicles 23–26.

The DIB passages unite the genealogical preface of Chronicles with the body of the book: two DIB passages (in 1 Chr 6:31-38 and 1 Chr 9:17-32) appear in the preface of Chronicles (1 Chronicles 1–9), whereas the other two blocks (1 Chr 16:4-43 and 1 Chronicles 23–26) are in the main body of Chronicles. The first two blocks provide complementary information about the roles of levitical singers and gatekeepers, which are presented again at length later in the other two blocks (1 Chr 16:4-43 and 1 Chronicles 23–26). Thus these DIBs link the preface of Chronicles to the rest of the book by means of specific shared content and vocabulary.

Furthermore, a relatively large section of 1 Chronicles 23–26 seems to function programmatically in Chronicles, in that, as I noted above, it establishes the criteria for Chronicles' evaluation of kings, which are reflected in the subsequent treatments of Solomon, Hezekiah, and Josiah.[74] Similarly, in the Chronicler's description of the Passovers during the reigns of Hezekiah and Josiah (1 Chr 30:15-16; 35:5-6, 10-12), the priests and the Levites work closely together in the sacrifice, displaying coordination which reflects the

[74] R. K. Duke ("A Rhetorical Approach to Appreciating the Books of Chronicles," in *The Chronicler as Author*, 120-22) also points out that in the Chronicler's portrayal of David, the king is explicitly the model to which the succeeding kings are compared. According to the Chronicler, Solomon established the priestly and levitical divisions "*according to the ordinance his father David*" (כמשפט דויד אביו) (2 Chr 8:14). Jehoiada assigned the priests and Levites to care for the Temple *as David had organized* (2 Chr 23:18). Hezekiah's reformative measure for the levitical musicians was done "*according to the commandment of David*" (2 Chr 29:25). Josiah's preparation for the Passover celebration was also done "*following the written directions of King David of Israel and the written directions of his son Solomon*" (2 Chr 35:4). In this celebration of Passover, the levitical singers participated in the rite "*according to the command of David*" (2 Chr 35:15). All these italicized phrases (the emphasis is mine) underscore the literary function of the David Installation Block in the Chronicler's narration of the history of monarchic Israel.

Table 2 The Reference to David in 1 Chronicles 23–26

Verse	The Reference to David	Notes
1 Chr 23:2	"David assembled all the leaders of Israel and the priests and the Levites."	The initiation of the census of the Levites.
1 Chr 23:6	"And David organized them in divisions corresponding to the sons of Levi: Gershon, Kohath, and Merari."	The organization of the Levites according to their ancestral houses.
1 Chr 23:27	"For according to the last words of David these were the number of the Levites from twenty years old and upward."	The redefinition of the age of the Levites at their initiation into service.
1 Chr 24:3	"Along with Zadok of the sons of Eleazar, and Ahimelech of the sons of Ithamar, David organized them according to the appointed duties in their service."	The organization of 24 divisions of the priests.
1 Chr 25:1	"David and the officers of the army also set apart for the service the sons of Asaph, and of Heman, and of Jeduthun, who should prophesy with lyres, harps, and cymbals."	David's installation of the temple musicians and their 24 divisions.
1 Chr 26:32	"King David appointed him and his brothers, two thousand seven hundred men of ability, heads of families, to have the oversight of the Reubenites, the Gadites, and the half-tribe of the Manassites for everything pertaining to God and for the affairs of the king."	This verse governs only the preceding verse.

Chronicler's careful definition of the relation between the priests and the Levites, presented in 1 Chr 23:28-32.[75]

[75] William M. Schniedewind, *The Word of God in Transition: From Prophet to Exegete in the Second Temple Period* (JSOTSup 197; Sheffield: Sheffield Academic Press, 1995) 165-69.

All of these observations indicate that DIB passages, particularly 1 Chronicles 23–26, are indispensable for the interpretation of Chronicles. Indeed, the emphasis on upholding the levitical prerogatives established in the DIB passages underscores the underlying unity of passages in Chronicles that might otherwise seem disparate.

My "David's Installation Block" model is part of a recent scholarly reevaluation of Chronicles which defends the essential unity of Chronicles. Leading the charge is S. Japhet, who defends the literary unity of Chronicles, while attributing inconsistencies found in Chronicles to the variety of sources that the Chronicler used.[76] Similarly, Isaac Kalimi, based on his extensive study on the Chronicler's historiographical methods and literary techniques, concludes that Chronicles is the product of a single writer.[77] He also argues that inconsistency and lack of systematization do not always stem from late additions and redactions in a biblical work which deals with a wide span of histories of Israel, such as Chronicles.[78] Gary N. Knoppers is also skeptical of the claims that Chronicles underwent one or more major Priestly, levitical, or Deuteronomistic redactions.[79] Without ignoring the literary heterogeneity within Chronicles, Knoppers pays more attention to the Chronicler's concern to mediate different perspectives within the context of the author's contemporary world.[80] Similarly, Raymond B. Dillard focuses on the traces of a unitary purpose in the narratives of Chronicles.[81] I hope to contribute to the evidence in favor of Chronicles' literary unity by demonstrating that the David's Installation Block passages play programmatic literary functions across the entire work.

[76] See Japhet, *I & II Chronicles*, esp. 5-7, 34-41.

[77] Kalimi, *The Reshaping of Ancient Israelite History*, 407.

[78] Kalimi, *The Reshaping of Ancient Israelite History*, 410-11.

[79] Knoppers, *1 Chronicles 1–9*, 90-93.

[80] Concerning the Chronicler's harmonistic tendency, M. Fishbane (*Biblical Interpretation*, 134-38, 151-58) pays due attention to it and points out the Chronicler's exegetical technique in harmonizing different traditions in the passages of 1 Chr 7:8-10; 2 Chronicles 30; and 2 Chr 35:12-13.

[81] Raymond B. Dillard's following comment (*2 Chronicles*, 7) underscores the literary unity of Chronicles:

> Whatever speculation scholars may indulge in regarding the history of redaction of the individual literary units and sources the Chronicler had at his disposal, in several extended periscopes there remain the traces of a unitary purpose and of a contrivance in structure that most naturally comport with a single author of considerable skill and genius.

Having reviewed much of the essential scholarship on questions related to Chronicles' unique interest in the expanded roles of Levites, diachronic origin, and literary unity, and having established the corpus of texts which will occupy the rest of this study, we can now proceed to the central question of the project, namely, how the Chronicler's claims about the Levites reveal his ideological interests and idealized visions for the Temple.

CHAPTER TWO

Analyses of Gatekeeper, Treasurer, and Tax-Collector Texts

In this chapter we will turn our attention to the Chronicler's specific claims regarding the historic and contemporary roles of levitical personnel as temple gatekeepers, treasurers and tax-collectors. The passages that concern these administrators are dense with detail and therefore require patient unraveling. But this painstaking analysis allows us to discern the ways that the Chronicler insistently though unobtrusively argues for the Levites' legitimate access to temple administrative offices by demonstrating that such access was normative in the periods of the First Temple and Tent of Meeting.

The Chronicler takes a comprehensive approach to his task: he employs intricate genealogies, coins innovative terminology, and even presses the character of Samuel, judge, prophet and seer, into the service of his cause. Indeed, the Chronicler used no fewer than ten different literary methods to encode elements of the temple administration of his own day in his narrative of the past. Yet the fact that the Chronicler finds it necessary to employ such a wide variety of devices to make the legitimacy of the Levites' administrative roles seem both obvious and irrefutable is quite telling: it reveals that the Chronicler is working to counter a perception that the roles occupied by Levites in his own era are innovative and potentially suspect.

2.1. Gatekeepers in Chronicles and Elsewhere in the Hebrew Bible

The presence of cultic gatekeepers is attested throughout the Hebrew Bible, but their identification as Levites varies across sources. While sources generally dated to a relatively early period tend not to identify temple gatekeepers as Levites, later sources trend in the direction of such identification. Thus we find that Ezek 44:10-11 depicts the gatekeepers of the future temple as Levites. Similarly, according to Neh 13:22, it is Nehemiah himself who, in his second term, appoints Levites to guard the gates to preserve the sanctity of the Sabbath.[1] Elsewhere, however, some gatekeepers are certainly priests: 2 Kgs 12:10 clearly establishes that "the keepers of the threshold" (שמרי הסף) are priests. The same phrase appears in 2 Kgs 12:10; 22:4; 23:4//2 Chr 34:9; 2 Kgs 25:18//Jer 52:24; Jer 35:4, and R. W. Klein argues on this basis that priests were probably the keepers of the threshold in pre-exilic times.[2]

However, this interpretation goes beyond the available evidence. Indeed, 2 Chr 34:9, which is parallel to 2 Kgs 23:4, explicitly designates the keepers of the threshold as Levites, while the other occurrences of the phrase contain no indication of the keepers' familial or tribal identity. Thus it is not possible to determine whether or not the keepers of the threshold were exclusively priests in pre-exilic times. It is however possible to infer that the gatekeepers' levitical status became controversial in the exilic and post-exilic periods but was ultimately upheld by the writers of Ezekiel, Ezra-Nehemiah, and of course, the Chronicler, for whom the matter is settled: as we shall see below, in Chronicles, the gatekeepers are all Levites.[3] At present, it may be useful to explore the Chronicler's specific descriptions of the gatekeepers in 1 Chr 9:17-32 and 1 Chr 26:1-19. The first gatekeeper section (1 Chr 9:17-32) is part of a list of those who settled in the province of Yehud in the post-exilic period (1 Chronicles 9). The second gatekeeper section (1 Chr 26:1-19) is found in the narrative where the Chronicler describes David's installation of cultic personnel in the temple that Solomon, his successor, will build (1 Chronicles 23-27).

[1] Klein, *1 Chronicles*, 489. S. Japhet (*I and II Chronicles*, 213-14) notes that the gatekeepers are usually registered between the singers and the temple-servants (Ezr 2:70; 7:7; cf. Neh 7:72; 10:29, in which the gatekeepers are listed before the singers). Interestingly, in Ezra-Nehemiah, the gatekeepers initially constitute an independent order among the temple personnel and are not identified as Levites (Ezra 2:42//Neh 7:45; 10:24; Neh 7:1, 45; 11:19; 12:25; 13:5).

[2] Klein, *1 Chronicles*, 276. See also Braun, *1 Chronicles*, 137; and D. Olson, "What Got the Gatekeepers into Trouble?" *JSOT* 30 (2005) 223-42, here 224.

[3] Exceptionally in 2 Chr 23:4-5, the priests and Levites were hired as gatekeepers in order to guard the young king who hid himself in the Temple during Johoiada's coup against Athaliah, since the temple precinct was restricted to the clergy.

2.1.1. The First Gatekeeper Section (1 Chr 9:17-32)

The first gatekeeper section (1 Chr 9:17-32) introduces the levitical status of the gatekeepers and their tasks in the temple.[4] This section belongs to the long genealogical prologue which covers the first nine chapters of Chronicles.[5] In chapter 9, we find our first example of the Chronicler's interest in the theme of historical continuity. In chapters 1–8 of the prologue, the Chronicler rehearses the past events and major figures of Israel's history by way of genealogies. In chapter 9, he presents the list of those who settled in the province of Yehud after the Babylonian exile (1 Chr 9:1-34).[6] A great many links bind chapter 9 to the preceding chapters. For

[4] In the Hebrew Bible, the office of gatekeepers is referred to in several ways. The most common expression is שׁוֹעֵר, or שֹׁעֵר and its plural form שׁערים. The term שֹׁעֵר is found thirty-five times in the Hebrew Bible and all but three of these occurrences (2 Sam 18:26; 2 Kgs 7:10, 11) are in Chronicles and in Ezra-Nehemiah. See John R. Spenser, *The Levitical Cities: A Study of the Role and Function of the Levites in the History of Israel* (Dissert. of The University of Chicago, 1980) 110. Spenser mentions 37 occurrences of שֹׁעֵר or שׁערים, but the two cases are excluded from my counting because they are merely designating "doors." The term is found 19 times in Chronicles, 4 times in Ezra, and 9 times in Nehemiah. Another term for the office of guard is שֹׁמֵר, or שֹׁמְרִים. It occurs in Judg 1:24; Isa 21:11, 12; 62:6; Jer 35:4; 51:12; Song 3:3; 5:7; Ps 130:6; 1 Kgs 14:17//2 Chr 12:10; Neh 3:29; 11:19; 12:25; Neh 13:22. Ran Zadok ("Remarks on Ezra and Nehemiah," *ZAW* 94 [1982] 296-98) points out that the phrase שמר שער (Neh 13:22) does not occur before Nehemiah's time. The combined expression of שמר שער indeed appears only in Nehemiah (Neh 3:29; 11:19; and 13:22), but the term שֹׁמֵר as a designation of the office of guard is found widely in the Hebrew Bible as the given examples prove. פקדה is also used to designate the office of guard in combination with other words which clarify the object of guard, such as פקדת משמרת (Num 3:36); פקדת כל־המשכן (Num 4:16); פקדות על־בית יהוה (2 Kgs 11:18//2 Chr 23:18; Mic 7:4); and פקדת ישׂראל (1 Chr 26:30). The Chronicler clearly prefers to use שער, or שערים. However, the duty of the gatekeepers is expressed with four main verbs: שמר in 1 Chr 9:23; 26:12, 16; 2 Chr 8:14; Neh 3:29; 12:45; שרת in Ezek 44:11; 1 Chr 26:12; 2 Chr 8:14; עבד in Num 8:26; and צבא in Num 4:23; 8:24; Deut 18:16. In Chr 9:17-32, the Chronicler chiefly uses the verb שמר to express the duty of the gatekeepers, and sometimes chooses another verb, שרת. Concerning the usage of the three verbs (שמר, שרת, and צבא) in relation to gatekeepers, see J. R. Spencer, *The Levitical Cities*, 67-86; and idem, "The Tasks of the Levites: šmr and ṣbʾ," *ZAW* 96 (1984) 267-71.

[5] Scholars have discussed whether the genealogical prologue (1 Chronicles 1–9) is an original component of the entire work of the Chronicler (S. Japhet, G. N. Knoppers) or a late redactional addition (M. Noth). Since the parallels to the Chronicler's genealogical prologue are found in Greek historiography, scholarly contention that 1 Chronicles 1–9 is an intentional part of the Chronicler's historiography has become mainstream. See Japhet, *I & II Chronicles*, 8-10; Knoppers, *1 Chronicles 1–9*, 253-60; Noth, *The Chronicler's History*, 36-42; and Kenneth G. Hoglund, "The Chronicler as Historian: A Comparativist Perspective," in *The Chronicler as Historian* (ed. M. Patrick Graham et al; JSOTSup 238; Sheffield: Sheffield Academic Press, 1997) 21-23.

[6] This chapter breaks up the connection between 1 Chr 8:29-40 (the genealogy of the

example, 1 Chronicles 2-8 demonstrates the Chronicler's particular interest in the tribes of Judah, Levi and Benjamin, a feature which finds its match in 1 Chr 9:1-34 which names Judah first among other tribes (1 Chr 9:3) and provides long lists of the descendants of Levi and of Benjamin.[7] Similarly, just as 1 Chronicles 2-8 highlights five tribes, Judah, Benjamin, Manasseh, Ephraim and Levi, so 1 Chronicles 9 focuses on these tribes in the restored community.[8] By highlighting these commonalities, the Chronicler underscores the continuity of the post-exilic community with monarchic era Israel.

2.1.1.1. The Immediate Context of 1 Chr 9:17-32, the First Gatekeepers Section

On an initial reading, 1 Chr 9:17-32, the first gatekeepers section, may seem somewhat jarring in its immediate context. But this passage also binds the

Saulides) and 1 Chr 10:1-14 (the account of Saul). Moreover, the last section of 1 Chronicles 9 (1 Chr 9:35-44) introduces the second lineage of the Saulides which is a clear case of resumptive repetition of 1 Chr 8:29-40. However, I argue that the seemingly intrusive character of 1 Chronicles 9 does not prove that it is secondary to Chronicles. First, each lineage of the Saulides has a different literary function in the Chronicler's prologue. The first lineage of the Saulides, presented in 1 Chr 8:29-40, concludes a long catalogue of the pedigree of the twelve tribes of Israel, whereas the second genealogy of Saul (1 Chr 9:35-44) introduces an account of Saul (1 Chr 10:1-14). The second genealogy (1 Chr 9:35-44) makes a good transition between the genealogies and the historical narrative. The second genealogy of the Saulides (1 Chr 9:35-44) does not include the lineage of Ulam which appears in the first genealogy (1 Chr 8:39-40). S. Japhet (*I & II Chronicles*, 205) considers that abridgment intentional since it helps one's focus move to Saul which is introduced in the following narrative. See also Aaron Demsky, "The Genealogy of Gibeon (1 Chronicles 9:35-44): Biblical and Epigraphic Considerations," *BASOR* 202 (1971) 16-23, here 17.

[7] The Chronicler's favorable treatment of these three tribes is shown quantitatively. His intention behind this strategic structural plan, however, is not self-evident. Scholars have generally hypothesized that it may be related to the author's contemporary situation in which these three tribes were the main components of the restored community in Yehud. See Knoppers, *1 Chronicles 1–9*, 263.

[8] Marshall D. Johnson (*The Purpose of the Biblical Genealogies: With Special Reference to the Setting of the Genealogies of Jesus* [2nd ed.; SNTSMS 8; Cambridge: Cambridge University Press, 1988] 69) comments that the reference to the tribes of Manasseh and Ephraim underlines the inclusion of the northern tribes. He also argues that this reference indicates that the Chronicler considered them as the core of the northern kingdom. On the other hand, Yigal Levin ("Who Was the Chronicler's Audience? A Hint from His Genealogies," *JBL* 122 [2003] 229-45) argues that the Chronicler's genealogies of the central tribes of Judah, Benjamin, Ephraim, Manasseh, and (southern) Asher plausibly reflect the reality of the Chronicler's own day. The genealogies of these five tribes are largely expanded in 1 Chronicles 2-8, whereas those of the other tribes are telescoped into a simple summary of genealogical information found in the Pentateuch.

Chronicler's contemporary time to Israel's storied history, by emphasizing the continuity of the office of gatekeepers during the wilderness and monarchic periods, as well as in the post-exilic period. In its function, therefore, the section on gatekeepers is exactly that of the more conventional tribal genealogies that precede it.

2.1.1.2. Analysis of 1 Chr 9:17-32

I divide the first gatekeepers' section (1 Chr 9:17-32) into two units: 1 Chr 9:17-23 and 1 Chr 9:24-32.[9] The first unit confirms the levitical status of the gatekeepers and explains the origins of their office in the history of Israel. The second unit details the specific functions of the gatekeepers in the temple precinct.

2.1.1.2.1. The First Unit (1 Chr 9:17-23): The Gatekeepers' Levitical Ancestry

In the first unit of the first gatekeepers' section (1 Chr 9:17-23), the Chronicler confirms the levitical lineage of gatekeepers (v. 17) and emphasizes the continuity of the offices held by gatekeepers since the time of David and even earlier (v. 22-23). The major devices that establish this continuity are the Chronicler's identification of the gatekeeper named Shallum with his levitical ancestors, and his use of two novel phrases that establish a link between the gatekeepers of the Tent of Meeting and those of the Second Temple.

The Chronicler presents Shallum as a major figure in 1 Chr 9:17-23 and mentions him twice in verses 17-18. He is said to have been the chief among the gatekeepers of the Persian period (v. 17) and to have been stationed at "the King's gate on the east" (v. 18).[10] More importantly, perhaps, for

[9] R. Braun (*1 Chronicles*, 141-42) divides this section in the same way: 1 Chr 9:17-23 and 1 Chr 9:24-32, but other scholars propose alternatives, such as 1 Chr 9:17-22 and 1 Chr 9:23-32. There is no obvious literary marker to divide this passage into two units except for its content. However, I found a strong reason to divide it after verse 23 in the following observations. The word אהל appears in verses 19, 21, and 23. This word serves to establish the continuity of the office of the gatekeepers throughout the history of Israel. I consider this word as a "rhetorical unit marker" which L. Allen named. According to L. Allen ("Kerygmatic Units in 1 and 2 Chronicles," *JSOT* 41 [1988] 21-36), the Chronicler repeated specific terms as "rhetorical unit markers" to divide the text into "assimilable portions." Moreover, verse 23 begins with *waw* conjunctive, which means that it is connected to the preceding verse, while verse 24 clearly indicates a new beginning. For these reasons, I include verse 23 in the first unit (1 Chr 9:17-23).

[10] Regarding the primacy of the east gate, refer to Japhet, *I & II Chronicles*, 213-14;

the Chronicler's purposes, he is a descendant of the Korahites, a levitical family which guarded the threshold of the Tent in the wilderness period (v. 19).[11] The Chronicler's focus on the Korahites is remarkable in light of the fact that in Priestly traditions, the Korahites are mainly known for the involvement of one of their number, Korah the son of Kohath, in the doomed rebellion of Abiram and Dathan against the exclusive authority of the Aaronide priesthood in the wilderness period, for which he was punished by God (Num 16:1-32). Despite Korah's untimely end, Num 26:11 takes care to note that Korah's descendants survived, a detail which provides the Chronicler with an interpretive opportunity. It is not clear in the Priestly traditions whether the Korahites could have continued serving in the Tent of Meeting after Korah's rebellion, as the Levites were commissioned to do in Num 3:5-9. For the Chronicler, though, no such ambiguity exists. Rather, the Chronicler draws a genealogical link between Shallum and Zechariah son of Meshelemiah, himself a Korahite, who was gatekeeper during the reign of David (vv. 22-23; cf. 1 Chr 26:1, 14).[12] Shallum is thus presented as a living levitical link between Israel's cultic past and its present.

Williamson, *1 and 2 Chronicles*, 90; McKenzie, *1–2 Chronicles*, 112; Braun, *1 Chronicles*, 141; and also, D. Olson, "What Got the Gatekeepers into Trouble?" 236. Both Williamson and Braun suppose the most prestigious status of the king's gate based on Ezek 46:1-8, according to which the king's gate would be opened on the occasions of Sabbath and the new moon, and only the king would enter the gate to offer sacrifices.

[11] Verse 19 confirms that the gatekeepers were the Levites by providing detailed genealogical information about Shallum: "And Shallum is the son of Kore, son of Ebiasaph, son of Korah" (ושלום בן־קורא בן־אביסף בן־קרח). The identification of the Korahites as guardians of the Tent is the Chronicler's innovation. Priestly tradition introduces a general function of the Levites as guardians at the Tent as follows: "They shall keep all the furnishings of the Tent of Meeting and attend to the duty of the Israelites by doing the service of the Tabernacle." (Num 3:8). However, it never connects that function specifically to the Korahites.

[12] The identity of Zechariah reveals clearly the Chronicler's intention for verse 21. Here, Zechariah son of Meshelemiah is introduced without any temporal marker. Two other verses from Chronicles (1 Chr 26:2 and 14) referring to Zechariah reveal his identity: Meshelemiah, a Korahite, who was the gatekeeper of the eastern gate during the reign of David. Zechariah was his first son, who was in charge of the northern gate (1 Chr 26:14). Thus, Zechariah is another Korahite who took the office of gatekeeper during the reign of David. The Korahites' involvement in the office of gatekeepers is again confirmed in 1 Chr 26:1 and 19. 2 Chr 31:14 also introduces another Korahite, Kore who was the son of Imnah the Levite. He was the keeper of the East Gate during the reign of King Hezekiah. The name Kore appears only in Chronicles: 1 Chr 9:19; 26:1; and 2 Chr 31:14. The first two Kores are the Korahites. Thus the Kore in 2 Chr 31:14 is likely to be a Korahite.

Having established the ancestral link that binds a present day gatekeeper to his predecessors, the Chronicler now embarks on a terminological campaign intended to persuade readers that the Second Temple is itself the legitimate heir of its institutional predecessors. First, in verse 18, the Chronicler again makes it clear that the gatekeepers are indeed Levites: "they were the gatekeepers belonging to the Levite camp" (המה השערים למחנות בני לוי).[13] The term "the Levite camp" (מחנות בני לוי) seems intended to recall the camp of Levi stationed near the Tent of Meeting (cf. Num 1:53; 2:17).[14] With this phrase, the levitical status of the gatekeepers is again traced back to the wilderness period.[15] Moreover, 1 Chr 9:19 states that the Korahites were the "guards of the threshold of the Tent" (שמרי הספים לאהל) and that their ancestors had been the "guards of the entrance of the camp of the Lord" (על־מחנה יהוה שמרי המבוא). These two phrases are neologisms, unique to the Chronicler, which intimate the continuity of the offices of gatekeepers throughout the history of Israel. The phrase "guards of the threshold of the Tent" (שמרי הספים לאהל) appears only in 1 Chr 9:19. However, "the guards of the threshold" (שמרי הסף) occurs in 2 Kgs 12:10; 22:4; 23:4; 25:18; 2 Chr 34:9; Jer 35:4; 52:24; Esth 2:21; and 6:2.[16] With the exception of the uses of this phrase in Esther, שמרי הסף refers to the guards of the threshold of the Temple, i.e. gatekeepers.[17] It is likely then that the phrase "guards of the threshold *of the Tent*" was coined

[13] S. Japhet (*I & II Chronicles*, 213-14) considers this phrase as the echo of an independent source that the Chronicler used since it represents a different view of the gatekeepers from the one introduced in Ezra-Nehemiah.

[14] Gary N. Knoppers (*1 Chronicles 1–9*, 505) points out the Chronicler's tendency of using the Priestly terms to describe cultic activities around the temple, such as in 2 Chr 31:2 ("at the entrance of the camp of Yahweh" בשערי מחנות יהוה). Verse 18 is another example of such a tendency. Here, the Chronicler adapts a Priestly term to legitimize his contemporary cultic activities. By using the Priestly terms, the Chronicler establishes their conformity to Pentateuchal traditions.

[15] Piet B. Dirksen, "1 Chronicles 9:26-33: Its Position in Chapter 9," *Bib* 79 (1998) 91-96, here 92. The Chronicler introduces another Korahite gatekeeper, Zechariah son of Meshelemiah in 1 Chr 29:21.

[16] 2 Chr 34:9 is a parallel to 2 Kgs 22:4. This verse mentions the keepers of the threshold during the reign of Josiah. 2 Kgs 22:4 does not specify that these keepers are priests or the Levites. However, its parallel text 2 Chr 34:9 states that they are the Levites. According to Jer 35:4, during the reign of Johoiakim, a certain Maaseiah son of Shallum was the guardian of the threshold. Jer 52:24 is a parallel to 2 Kgs 25:18, in which three unnamed keepers are mentioned among the officials executed by Nebuchadrezzar after Jerusalem fell into the Babylonians.

[17] Knoppers, *1 Chronicles 1–9*, 505.

by the Chronicler to strengthen the appearance of continuity between the Tent of Meeting in the wilderness period and the Jerusalem Temple. The unique term "guards of the threshold of the Tent," ties both institutions together very neatly. Indeed, according to 2 Chr 5:5, the Tent of Meeting was absorbed into the First Temple at its completion, making the continuity of the two sacred spaces not only a conceptual but a concrete reality.[18]

The connection between the two institutions is supported by the other terminological innovation found in 1 Chronicles 19:9b, "guards of the entrance of the camp of the Lord" (על־מחנה יהוה שׁמרי המבוא). This phrase explains specifically what kind of cultic function the ancestors of the Korahites carried out: they were the guards of the Tent of Meeting in the wilderness period (cf. Num 1:53), a fact that is again emphasized by the reference to Phinehas in the following verse, 1 Chr 9:20, which introduces Phinehas as the ruler of the guards in the wilderness period: "and Phinehas son of Eleazar was chief officer over them" (ופינחס בן־אלעזר נגיד היה עליהם). This appears to be the Chronicler's innovation: Num 3:32 presents Eleazar as the leader of the "guards of the Tabernacle" (שׁמרי משמרת הקדשׁ).[19] What can account for the Chronicler's revision of this detail?

I suspect that the substitution of Phinehas for Eleazar is intended to associate the Phinehas incident in Num 25:2-8 with the task of gatekeepers.[20] Phinehas, readers will recall, achieves renown in Num 25:6-8 by killing

[18] Before Solomon built the temple in Jerusalem, regular sacrificial services had been offered before the Ark and the Tent of Meeting (1 Chr 6:17; 23:32). When Solomon completed the construction of the temple, the Ark and the Tent of Meeting were brought into the temple and became constituent parts of the temple (2 Chr 5:5). Gary N. Knoppers (*1 Chronicles 1–9*, 506) points out that such an association between the Tabernacle and the Jerusalem Temple appears in the Apocrypha (Judith 9:8; Sir 24:10-11; cf. 2 Macc 2:4-5), but it is not emphasized as strongly as in Chronicles.

[19] Numbers 3 does not state explicitly that to guard the Tabernacle is a levitical duty. But there are several clues to conclude that it is a levitical duty. First, the levitical duties are expressed by the verb שׁמר in Num 3:7, 8, 25, 28, 32). Second, the levitical duties are summed up with the phrase "attending to the duties of the sanctuary" (שׁמרי משמרת הקדשׁ) in Num 3:28, 32. Lastly, Num 1:53 explicitly mention the Levites' guarding duty for the Tabernacle with the phrase "the guard duty of the tabernacle of testimony" (משמרת משכן העדות).

[20] Japhet, *I & II Chronicles*, 216; and Knoppers, *1 Chronicles 1–9*, 506. S. L. McKenzie (*1–2 Chronicles*, 113) suggests that for the Chronicler, Phinehas would be a better model for the combined cultic and martial duties of the gatekeepers. Interestingly, in the later Levi-Priestly Tradition (which I deal with in Chapter Four), Phinehas' zeal for God is connected with Levi's zeal to punish the Shechemites (Genesis 34), as well as the Levites' involvement in punishing the apostates at Mt. Sinai (Exod 32:25-29). The Levi-Priestly Tradition is found in *Aramaic Levi*, *Testament of Levi* and *Jubilees* 30:1-32:9, which are dated to around the

the Israelite man and Midianite woman who were having intercourse. 1 Chr 9:20 does not identify the place where the Phinehas incident happened. However, it is likely that the Chronicler anticipated his readers' knowledge of Num 25:6-7, in which Phinehas sees the idolatrous couple first at the entrance of the Tent of Meeting (פתח אהל מועד). Significantly, the Chronicler refers to the exact phrase פתח אהל מועד in the next verse (1 Chr 9:21) to indicate the office of Zechariah the gatekeeper during the reign of David: "Zechariah the son of Meshelemiah was gatekeeper at the entrance of the Tent of Meeting" (זכריה בן משלמיה שער פתח לאהל מועד). By describing his office with the term "שער פתח לאהל מועד", the Chronicler brings together the role of guards of the Tent of Meeting (Phinehas) with that of temple gatekeepers which was instituted by David (Zechariah).[21]

The Chronicler reinforces this association in the following verse (v. 22) where he legitimizes the offices of gatekeepers by stating that they were not only originally established by David but also divinely authorized by Samuel the seer: "David and Samuel the seer established them in their office of trust" (המה יסד דויד ושמואל הראה באמונתם).[22] 1 Chr 9:22 is thus a con-

second-century B.C.E. It is not known, however, to what extent the Chronicler's replacement of Eleazar by Phinehas is related to that later tradition.

[21] The term "the entrance of the Tent of Meeting" (פתח אהל מועד) frequently appears in Exodus (9 times), Leviticus (25 times) and Numbers (12 times). Outside of the Pentateuch, it appears only in 1 Chr 9:21; Josh 19:51 and 1 Sam 2:22; the last two are related to the Tent of Meeting in Shiloh. Thus this phrase also reflects the Chronicler's general tendency of emphasizing the continuity of the First Temple and the Tent of Meeting in the wilderness period.

[22] David's installation of temple gatekeepers is expressed by the phrase of ... יסד באמונה. The word באמונה appears thrice in 1 Chr 9:17-32 (vv. 22, 26 and 31). The exact meaning of it in 1 Chr 9:22 is still in debate. Scholars have translated it either "because of trustworthiness or faithfulness" (*e.g.*, M. Oeming, *Das wahre Israel*, 203: "because of their reliability" [*wegen ihrer Zuverlässigkeit*]), or "in permanent official duty" (e.g., R. W. Klein, *1 Chronicles*, 278). See also *HALOT*, 62-63. I argue that the present context requires reference to a certain position or duty rather than to an attribute of gatekeepers. Since a *piel* form of the verb יסד is used to express "to found something" or "to appoint someone in a certain position," the translation of the word באמונה should be "in their office of trust" or "on their permanent duty." See *HALOT*, 417.

The prophets' involvement in installing the cultic offices is also witnessed in 2 Chr 29:25. According to 2 Chr 29:25, the establishment of the singers is authorized by both David and the prophets (Gad and Nathan). Nevertheless, the reference to Samuel is peculiar. It seems that the Chronicler mentions Samuel here because of the functions that Samuel performed in the temple at Shiloh and because of his levitical lineage with which the Chronicler invested him (see 1 Chr 6:12-13). See also Braun, *1 Chronicles*, 137; Japhet, *I & II Chronicles*, 214-215; and Williamson, *1 and 2 Chronicles*, 72. I. Kalimi (*The Reshaping of Ancient Israelite History*, 152)

cise summary of 1 Chronicles 26, which contains the detailed account of David's installation of the office of gatekeepers. Indeed, this verse bridges the two gatekeepers' sections (1 Chr 9:17-32 and 1 Chr 26:1-19): both sections clearly indicate that the Chronicler locates the origin of the office of temple gatekeepers in David's reign, yet views the office as a continuation of an ancient institution from the wilderness period.[23]

The final verse of the first gatekeeper section makes explicit what the preceding verses have consistently implied. Here the Chronicler equates the house of the Lord (בית־יהוה) and the house of the Tent (בית־האהל) to underscore the continuity between the Tent of the Meeting and the Temple.[24] The term "the house of the Tent" (בית־האהל) appears only in 1 Chr 9:23.[25] It must have been coined by the Chronicler to link the two different institutions, as he previously did in verses 19 and 21.[26]

Why did the Chronicler make such an effort to legitimize the levitical gatekeepers by grounding their office in the history of Israel?[27] Was the presence of these gatekeepers in the post-exilic period innovative or unwel-

---

argues that the Chronicler made Samuel a Levite since his service in the sanctuary was diametrically opposed to Pentateuchal traditions which permit only Levites to minister in the sanctuary (Num 1:50-51; 3:5-9; 18:2-4, 22-23). I. Kalimi's argument is convincing when one considers the Chronicler's tendency to resolve contradictions found in earlier textual traditions. By providing Samuel with the levitical lineage, the Chronicler probably attempted to harmonize the narrative in Samuel with the above-quoted verses of the Pentateuch.

[23] Japhet, *I & II Chronicles*, 217.

[24] Japhet, *I & II Chronicles*, 216.

[25] Knoppers, *1 Chronicles 1–9*, 506; and Avi Hurvitz, "Terms and Epithets Relating to the Jerusalem Temple Compound in the Book of Chronicles: The Linguistic Aspect," in *Pomegranates and Golden Bells: Studies in Biblical, Jewish, and Near Eastern Ritual, Law, and Literature in Honor of Jacob Milgrom* (ed. David P. Wright et al.; Winona Lake: Eisenbrauns, 1995) 165-83, here 179-80. In this article, A. Hurvitz examines the following seven terms, which were employed in Chronicles to refer to the temple compound: בית (ה)מקדש; בית (ה)קדש; בית קדש קדשים; בית הכפרת; בית מנוחה; בית זבח; and בית האהל. A. Hurvitz suggests that all these expressions, coined by the Chronicler, seem to be intended to express the continuity between the Tabernacle in the wilderness and the Second Temple. The phrase, "the house of the Tent" (בית האהל) in 1 Chr 9:23 is one of these seven terms that the Chronicler coined.

[26] G. N. Knoppers (*1 Chronicles 1–9*, 506) points out that the Chronicler often used such a strategy to establish the antiquity of a relatively new system of worship. For example, when King Abijah spoke to Jeroboam and all northern people, he claimed that the cult of the Jerusalem Temple was the continuation of that of the Sinaitic era (2 Chr 13:4-12). See also Curtis & Madsen, *The Books of Chronicles*, 176.

[27] M. Oeming (*Das wahre Israel*, 203-4) poses the same question, but he does not develop his question further, and concludes: "the new classification and honorable furnishings of the gatekeepers indicate a cultic innovation of the post-exilic period."

come enough to require such a rationalization? I shall take up this question in Chapter Four, a conclusion of the present work.

2.1.1.2.2. The Second Unit (1 Chr 9:24-32):
The Gatekeepers' Duties and Prerogatives

Having established the continuous status of the Levites as gatekeepers, the Chronicler now presents us with his specific claims regarding the gatekeepers' duties and prerogatives. As we shall see, there is no single, easily identifiable ideological program at work here: on occasion, the Chronicler's account of the gatekeepers' duties departs from those presented in Priestly or other literary sources, but as frequently he emphasizes continuity and conformity with Priestly tradition.

Verse 24 begins by stating what might seem an obvious point, namely that the primary duty of gatekeepers is to guard the four sides of the Temple, likely temple gates: "the gatekeepers were on the four sides, east, west, north, and south" (לארבע רוחות יהיו השערים מזרח ימה צפונה ונגבה). This duty will be performed by the gatekeepers who reside in their own villages, along with the four chief levitical gatekeepers who were on permanent duty (כי באמונה המה ארבעת גברי השערים) and who therefore lived in the immediate environs of the Temple[28] These four chiefs had multiple duties connected with the chambers and the treasuries of the Temple: "They were in charge of the chamebrs and the treasures of the house of God" (היו על־הלשכות ועל האצרות בית האלהים).[29]

[28] Verse 26 begins with כי which introduces a clause indicating the cause of items specified in either the previous clause or the following one. In this case, verse 26 seems to be connected with the preceding sentence since the next clause is linked with another causal clause, which also begins with כי. Therefore verse 26 provides the reason why the gatekeepers who dwell in their own villages need to come up to Jerusalem to guard the temple gates.

[29] Throughout the history of Israel, supervision over the chambers and treasuries has been assigned to the Levites in general and not specifically to the gatekeepers (2 Chr 31:12; Neh 13:13). In 2 Chr 31:14, however, Kore, the keeper of the east gate, was in charge of the freewill offerings and was responsible to apportion them to the temple personnel during the reign of Hezekiah. See Klein, *1 Chronicles*, 278. John W. Wright ("Guarding the Gates: 1 Chronicles 26:1-19 and the Roles of Gatekeepers in Chronicles," *JSOT* 48 [1990] 69-81, here 77) also points out that the gatekeepers were responsible for collecting funds during the reign of Josiah (2 Chr 34:9). These two cases show that the gatekeepers were occasionally in charge of the chambers or treasuries in the Temple. But in 1 Chr 23:28-29 and 26:20-28, supervision over the chambers and the treasuries is not specifically the task of the four chief gatekeepers. To explain this contradiction, P. B. Dirksen ("1 Chronicles 9:26-33: Its Position in Chapter 9," 92-95) suggests an alternative reading of 1 Chr 9:26: to link v. 26a directly with v. 27, by omitting 1 Chr 9:26b-c as a later redactor's addition. Then he reads these two

Priestly traditions concur that guard duty (משמרת) is a levitical duty, so in this respect, the Chronicler is well within the conventions of the traditions he works with. In the wilderness period, the Levites were commissioned to defend the sanctuary against lay encroachment (Num 1:53; 3:7-8, 25-26, 36-37; 18:3-5, 22-23; 31:30, 47).[30] Similarly, Ezekiel assigns guard duty to the Levites in his blueprint for the future utopian cultic organization (Ezek 44:11).

However, the Chronicler's descriptions of the duties of gatekeepers deviate from Priestly traditions in verses 28-32. Verse 28 states that some of gatekeepers (presumably, the chief gatekeepers) were in charge of the utensils of service which needed to be counted when they were used: "Some of them had charge of the utencils of service, for they should carry them in by number, and carry them out by number" (ומהם על־כלי העבודה כי־במספר יביאום ובמספר יוציאום).[31] According to Numbers 4, assembling or disassembling the vessels of service (כלי השרת, Num 4:12) used in the sanctuary was the sole prerogative of Aaronide priests; the Kohathites' duty was merely to carry these items when the camp moved (Num 4:15). With regard to the

verses (v. 26a and v. 27) as an explanation of the four chief gatekeepers' permanent duty which is in contrast to the temporal duty of the gatekeepers who live outside Jerusalem (v. 25). If it was the case, one must explain why a later redactor inserted 1 Chr 9:26b-c in such an interrupting way although there is a possibility of adding it right before 1 Chr 9:28. Dirksen explains it as a redactor's habit of abrupt insertion, but I find this view unconvincing for two reasons. First, as I have argued in the previous footnote, 1 Chr 9:26b-c explains why the four chief gatekeepers needed assistance of village-gatekeepers. Second, the disagreement between two different sets of texts (1 Chr 9:29 and 1 Chr 23:28-29; 26:20-28) can be explained without assuming a different literary layer if one reads them according to the time frame which the Chronicler included. See section 2.2.3.

[30] Knoppers, *1 Chronicles 1–9*, 507.

[31] P. B. Dirksen (*1 Chronicles*, 153) argues that 1 Chr 9:28 was added by a later editor, for two reasons: first, charge over "the vessels for the service" (כלי העבודה) is not specifically assigned to the gatekeepers elsewhere in Chronicles; and second, the same term appears in 1 Chr 28:13, 14. Thus, he concludes that 1 Chr 9:28 must have been written by the same redactor as 1 Chr 28:13, 14. His argument is solely based on the occurrence of the same term כלי העבודה in two different places (1 Chr 9:28 and 1 Chr 28:13, 14). But it is not tenable because the term כלי העבודה is not peculiar enough to be assigned to a specific time or author. In the Hebrew Bible various terms are used to designate the vessels for the cultic service, such as כלי המשכן in Exod 27:19; כלי הקדש in Num 4:15; 18:3; 1 Kgs 8:4; 1 Chr 9:29; 2 Chr 5:5; כלי המקדש in Neh 10:40; כלי בית־האלהים in 2 Chr 28:24; 36:18; Neh 13:9; כלי בית־יהוה in Ezr 1:7; Jer 27:16; 28:3, 6; כלי העבודה in Exod 39:40; Num 4:26; 1 Chr 9:28; 28:13, 14; and כלי השרת in Num 4:12, 32; 2 Chr 24:14. These references to the vessels of the cultic service indicate that the Chronicler uses the diverse terms to designate them. Furthermore, the term כלי העבודה is neither coined nor preferred by the Chronicler.

vessels' accessibility in the cult, Num 18:3 specifically prohibits the Levites from approaching either the utensils of the sanctuary or the altar.[32]

The Chronicler further opposes Priestly traditions by saying that the chief gatekeepers were also in charge of the fine flour, the wine, the oil, the incense, and the spices, which are all necessary for daily sacrificial services (v. 29). The term הסלת (the fine flour or the choice flour) is used primarily in the Priestly texts, but never in relation to Levites' duties.[33] In the Priestly texts, הסלת is always connected with priestly sacrificial duties.[34] This picture becomes somewhat more complicated subsequently, when the Chronicler interrupts his description of the gatekeepers' charge over "flour, wine, incense and spices" (v. 29), to explain who actually prepared these items in verses 30-32: the spices were prepared by the priests (v. 30), but the flat cakes and the showbread by other Levites (vv. 31-32).[35]

The unexpected interpolation of a priestly duty in verse 30, in the middle of the description of the levitical duties, has given rise to much schol-

[32] A similar contradiction between Chronicles and the Priestly material is evident in verse 29, where the Chronicler asserts that some of the chief gatekeepers were appointed over "the furniture" (הכלים) and "all the holy utensils" (כלי הקדש). On the contrary, as noted above, the Priestly source expressly forbids the Levites from approaching these utensils (Num 18:3). The Priestly sources are unusual in presenting such a clear-cut distinction between priestly duties and levitical duties in handling the holy vessels. 1 Kgs 8:4 (//2 Chr 5:5) presents a much blurrier picture: it relates that the priests and Levites brought up the Ark, the Tent of Meeting, and all the holy vessels which were in the Tent, to the Temple at the command of Solomon, without indicating who carried what. Another passage, Neh 10:38-39, does not offer support for the levitical involvement in keeping the holy vessels secure, but it does say that the Levites could freely approach the storehouses in the Temple to bring the tithes there, where the equipment of the sanctuary was also kept.

[33] It appears 39 times among the total 54 occurrences in the Hebrew Bible: Gen 18:6; Exod 29:2, 40; Lev 2:1, 4, 5, 7; 5:11; 6:8, 13; 7:12; 14:10, 21; 23:13, 17; 24:5; Num 6:15; 7:13, 19, 25, 31, 37, 43, 49, 55, 61, 67, 73, 79; 8:8; 15:4, 6, 9; 28:5, 9, 12, 13, 20, 28; 29:3, 9, 14; Josh 19:12; 1 Kgs 5:2; 2 Kgs 7:1, 16, 18; 18:17; 1 Chr 9:29; 23:29; Prov 16:17; Isa 7:3; 36:2; Ezek 16:13, 19; 46:14.

[34] Gary N. Knoppers (*1 Chronicles 1–9*, 508) quotes Ezek 46:14 as a similar example with the Priestly tradition. However, Ezek 46:14 is ambiguous since it does not specify who is in charge of הסלת.

[35] This passage (1 Chr 23:28-32) is very interesting in that it defines the levitical duties by using the apparent priestly vocabulary, as a few examples show: "bread of the presence" (לחם הפנים in the Priestly texts, such as Exod 25:30; 35:13; 39:36; Num 4:7; cf. "showbread" לחם מערכת in 1 Chr 9:32; 23:29), "fine flour for the cereal offering" (סלת למנחה) (Lev 6:15, 20, *et als*; cf. 1 Chr 23:29), "the griddle" (מחבת) (only in Lev 2:5; 6:21; 7:9; Ezek 4:3; cf. 1 Chr 23:29), "the unleavened wafers" (רקיקי המצות) (Lev 2:4; 7:12; Num 6:15; cf. 1 Chr 23:29), and "what is well-mixed" (מרבכת) (Lev 6:14; 7:12; cf. 1 Chr 23:29). These are all technical terms of the Priestly texts which never associate them with the Levites. They solely belong to the priestly prerogatives. Thus the Chronicler's presentation obviously deviates from Priestly traditions.

arly speculation. Certainly verse 30 reflects the Priestly tradition in which the concoction of the anointing oil and the preparation of the incense are considered an absolute prerogative of the priests (Exod 30:23-33 and 34-38).[36] P. B. Dirksen claims that this verse was added by a later redactor who emphasized the prerogatives of the priests as opposed to the Levites.[37] E. L. Curtis considers this verse a gloss, which was intended to limit the work of the Levites in connection with the spices, but he does not specify who added this gloss.[38]

On the other hand, Steven S. Tuell attributes the awkwardness of this verse to the Chronicler's synthetic approach in combining various sources as exemplified in the genealogies and in the treatment of David's stories.[39] Tuell's approach to the verse is appropriate and convincing. If one does not assume that the so-called "original" Chronicler is always opposed to the Priestly tradition, this verse can be read to reflect the Chronicler's effort to harmonize earlier traditions with the temple practice of his own day. It is clear that the Chronicler admits the priests' exclusive right to conduct certain cultic activities, such as atonement (1 Chr 23:13), and does not deny the levitical role as cultic assistants (1 Chr 23:28).[40] Indeed, 1 Chr 23:28 seems to stress the Levites' subordination to the Aaronide priests.[41] These passages indicate that the Chronicler is committed to cultic propriety, and

[36] Knoppers, *1 Chronicles 1–9*, 508.

[37] Dirksen, *1 Chronicles*, 153.

[38] Curtis and Madsen, *The Books of Chronicles*, 177.

[39] Tuell, *First and second Chronicles*, 41.

[40] Steven J. Schweitzer ("The High Priest in Chronicles," 394) emphasizes the Chronicler's perspective on this issue as follows:

> Priestly duties and Levitical duties are clearly distinguished throughout the larger complex of 1 Chronicles 23–27 in terms consistent with the first occurrence of this language in 1 Chr 6:48-53, and subsequent details given in 1 Chr 9:17-34.

Paul D. Hanson also points out that the non-emphatic acknowledgment of the superior status of the priests characterizes the whole Chronicler's history. See Paul D. Hanson, "1 Chronicles 15-16 and the Chronicler's View on the Levites," *"Sha'arei Talmon" Studies in the Bible, Qumran, and the Ancient Near East Presented to Shemaryahu Talmon* (ed. Michael Fishbane et al.; Winona Lake: Eisenbrauns, 1992) 69-77, here 74.

[41] For this reason, these passages have been considered as secondary by the scholars who defend the Chronicler as pro-Levitical, such as De Wette, Van Rad, De Vries, Williamson, Welch, and others. See Gary N. Knoppers, "Hierodules, Priests, or Janitors? The Levites in Chroniclers and the History of the Israelite Priesthood," *JBL* 118 (1999) 49-72, here 51-52. Japhet (*I & II Chronicles*, 927-28) points to another example which also shows the Chronicler's respect for the Priestly tradition. In the Chronicler's treatment of the musicians in the Temple, the horn (שופר) and trumpet (חצצרה), the sacerdotal instruments, are always played by the priests and never sounded by Levites.

does not act solely as a partisan in a competition between the priests and Levites in regard to cultic practices.[42]

In the final two verses of the second unit (1 Chr 9:31-32), the Chronicler introduces those who were in charge of preparing "flat cakes" (חבתים) and "showbread" (לחם המערכת) for the regular cultic service. Mattithiah, the first son of Shallum, is in charge of the preparation of the flat cakes (v. 31).[43] The term "flat cakes" (חבתים) is a *hapax legomenon* which presumably means the "flat cake baked on the griddle,"[44] which was handled only by the priests in Priestly tradition.[45] Therefore, Mattithiah's involvement in preparing the "flat cakes" (חבתים) is likely an example of the expanded participation of the Levites in cultic practices of the Post-exilic period.[46] It is worth noting that the preparation of the griddle-cake (מחבת) is also assigned to the Levites in 1 Chr 23:29, which delineates cultic duties assigned to the Levites by David, so we find in this detail evidence for the Chronicler's consistency in his presentation of this matter.

[42] Dyck, *The Theocratic Ideology of the Chronicler*, 139, and 227-28. See also M. Oeming who understands verse 30 in a similar way: "The Chronicler partly continues the tradition, but puts his own time (or his own program?) next to and against to it." M. Oeming, *Das wahre Israel*, 202. He also claims that the concurrence of logically contradictory and not rigidly systematized arrangement of the tradition and its commentary, which is seen in Chronicles, became characteristics of later rabbinic Judaism. Simiarly, A. H. J. Gunneweg (*Leviten und Priester. Hauptlinien der Traditionsbildung und Geschichte des israelitisch-jüdischen Kultpersonals* [FRLANT 89; Göttingen: Vandenhoeck & Ruprecht, 1965], 210) comments on this verse as such: "This contradiction is identical to that between the theory and practice at the time of the Chronicler."

[43] I argue that the Shallum of verse 17 is the same individual as the Sallum of verse 19, but not as Meshelemiah, the father of Zechariah, (v. 21) who was a contemporary of King David. This removes a difficulty in harmonizing verse 21 (Meshelemiah the father of Zechariah) and verse 31 (Shallum the father of Mattithiah). If Meshelemiah of verse 21 were the same individual as Shallum of verse 31 and as Shallum of verses 17 and 19, one needs to explain why Meshelemiah of verse 21 and Shallum of verse 31 are introduced in a different way. Since R. Braun (*1 Chronicles*, 142) argues that Shallum in v. 19 is the same individual as Meshelemiah in v. 21, he tries to explain the obvious contradiction between verse 21 and verse 31, by suggesting that the text (1 Chr 9:17-32) was revised and updated through a period of at least three generations (Shallum, Zechariah, and Mattithiah), in which the role of gatekeepers was undergoing substantial review. Steven L. McKenzie (*1–2 Chronicles*, 113) proffers a similar opinion on this verse.

[44] The word's meaning can be inferred from the word מחבת, which appears in Lev 2:5; 6:14; 7:9; Ezek 4:3; and 1 Chr 23:29. The word מחבת means a metal plate, pan or griddle, but sometimes designates flat, round cake (esp. in 1 Chr 23:29). *HALOT*, 289 and 567.

[45] Klein, *1 Chronicles*, 279.

[46] Oeming, *Das wahre Israel*, 203.

Finally, in verse 32, the Chronicler states that the preparation of the showbread (לחם המערכת) for each Sabbath is the duty of Kohathites.[47] In contrast, in Priestly traditions, the "bread of the presence" (לחם [ה]פנים) and even the "table of the bread of the presence" (שׁלחן הפנים) were off-limits to the Levites (Num 4:4-7).[48] This conflict between the Chronicler's description and the Priestly tradition raises the question of whether the Chronicler's description is designed to sidestep the Priestly restriction. Or could it be a reflection of the Persian-era *cultus* in which the non-priestly class took a more prominent role than the Priestly tradition allows? These questions will be dealt with in Chapter Four of the present work.

2.1.1.3. Summary

The Chronicler's presentation about the gatekeepers in 1 Chr 9:17-32 can be summarized as follows: (1) The gatekeepers are included among the Levites; (2) The office of the gatekeepers originated in the wilderness period and continued throughout the history of Israel; and (3) The gatekeepers are involved not only in guard duty but also in the administration of the Temple, where some of their duties seem to encroach on traditional priestly roles. Thus, the Chronicler's presentation reflects his effort to establish the continuity between the temple administration in his day and the received traditions. At the same time, it is clear that the Chronicler does not simply mirror the traditions, but proposes new, innovative interpretations of them, either to support current practices, or perhaps to present his view of an ideal Temple; the Temple as it should be.

2.1.2. 1 Chronicles 26:1-19: The Second Gatekeeper Section

In the second section on gatekeepers, the Chronicler begins to make a case for the levitical gatekeepers' legitimate access to certain specific duties

[47] In Priestly traditions, the Kohathites was a levitical clan who carried the most holy objects when the Tent moved (Num 4:15, 19). The Kohathites's privileged status among the levitical clans in the wilderness period might have a relation to the Chronicler's singling out this levitical clan for the duty concerning showbread. However, there is no way to confirm it without further evidence.

[48] Knoppers, *1 Chronicler 1–9*, 509. The Priestly tradition makes clear that this bread belongs to Aaron and his sons: היתה לאהרן ולבניו(Lev 24:9). The Priestly tradition uses the term "the bread of the presence" (לחם [ה]פנים) to designate the bread displayed on the table before the Tabernacle (Exod 25:30; 35:13; 39:36; see also 1 Sam 21:7; 1 Kgs 7:48//2 Chr 4:19), whereas the Chronicler prefers another term "the rows of bread or showbread" (לחם מערכת) or its shorten form המערכת, which appears mainly in the Post-exilic texts (1 Chr 9:32; 23:29; 28:16; 2 Chr 2:3; 13:11; 29:18; and Neh 10:34; cf. Lev 24:6, 7 where המערכת occurs, but it denotes a layer or row rather than the bread itself).

related to the economic administration of the temple. Again, a fair amount of exegetical excavation is required: but once we clear away some of the textual and linguistic miscellanea, we find that the Chronicler presents two main points. First, the Chronicler is careful to show that the number of gatekeeper divisions, and the number of gatekeepers on duty on a daily basis, is always 24. Second, the Chronicler situates the origins of the appointments of various levitical families to specific posts in the time of David. The discussion below will begin to point to several of the questions that scholars have raised regarding the historical veracity of the Chronicler's claims; we will take up these issues more thoroughly in the following chapter.

2.1.2.1. 1 Chr 26:1-19: Gatekeepers' Divisions and Posts

1 Chr 26:1-19 is comprised of two distinct sections: (1) vv. 1-12 and (2) vv. 13-19.[49] The former section establishes that precisely 24 divisions of gatekeepers were appointed to guard Solomonic temple while the latter section describes how each family of gatekeepers was assigned certain posts by the casting of lots.

2.1.2.1.1. The First Unit (1 Chronicles 26:1-12): The Twenty-four Divisions of Gatekeepers

Once again, the larger context of the passage at hand proves informative as we attempt to discern the import of the Chronicler's particular interest

[49] This passage can be divided differently, such as vv. 1-11 and vv. 12-19, as R. Klein does (Klein, *1 Chronicles*, 487). Its division depends on how one understands the function of verse 12. I consider, with Japhet (*I & II Chronicles*, 450), verse 12 as a concluding sentence of the first section (vv. 1-12). On the other hand, the originality of this passage has been suspected by several scholars. While G. von Rad (*Das Geschichtsbild des chronistischen Werkes*, 116-18) argued vv. 4-8 as secondary, several other scholars have treated both vv. 4-8 and vv. 12-18 as secondary, such as, J. W. Rothstein and J. Hänel (*Das erste Buch der Chronik* [Leipzig: D. Werner Scholl, 1927] 469-73), Williamson (*1 and 2 Chronicles*, 169-71), and Braun (*1 Chronicles*, 250-51). Among those who argue both vv. 4-8 and vv. 12-18 as secondary, some consider that the later addition originated from a pro-priestly reviser under the impact of the institution of the system of twenty-four priestly courses, such as, Williamson ("The Origins of the Twenty-Four Priestly Courses: A Study of 1 Chronicles 23-27," in *The Historical Books of the Old Testament* [ed. J. A. Emerton; Leiden: Brill, 1979] 251-68), Klein (*1 Chronicles*, 487), and S. L. McKenzie (*1–2 Chronicles*, 199-201). Others argue that those verses were later added by the Chronicler himself. See Welch, *The Work of the Chronicler*, 91-93; and Dirksen, *1 Chronicles*, 308. On the other hand, G. Stein (*Die Chronik*, 327-31) considers vv. 4-8, 12-13 and 16b-18 as secondary, and categorizes them into a "Musician-Gatekeeper-Redaction" (Musiker-Torwächter-Bearbeitung), which was added later to an older text.

in the gatekeepers. In 1 Chronicles 23–26, a section I identified earlier as a "David's Installation Block," several groups of temple personnel (Levites, priests, musicians, treasurers) are introduced with a formula which attributes their organization to David (see 1 Chr 23:2, 6; 23:27; 24:3; 25:1 and 26:32). In each case, the groups are comprised of 24 familial divisions. The lists of the divisions of gatekeepers (1 Chr 26:1-19), however, are introduced without the formula that indicates Davidic appointment. For this reason, some scholars have considered this section as a secondary addition.[50] It should be noted, however, that other passages from Chronicles clearly indicate that the divisions of gatekeepers were installed by David (1 Chr 23:28-32, 2 Chr 8:14). Moreover, there is little doubt that 1 Chr 26:1-19 should be read in connection with the previous chapter since 1 Chronicles 25 does not end with a summarizing phrase which appears in the end of each sub-section in 1 Chronicles 23–26, such as 1 Chr 23:24, 31b-32; 24:19; 26:12, 19.[51]

The first unit of the second gatekeeper section (1 Chr 26:1-12) is framed by an *inclusio* "the divisions of the gatekeepers" (למחלקות לשערים in v. 1 and לאלה מחלקות השערים in v. 12). Within this structural framework, the genealogical information and the numbers of three different families of the gatekeepers are introduced.

The structure of the first unit is as follows:

1a: The introduction
1b: The Korahites
  2-3: The genealogy of Meshelemiah
  4-7: The genealogy of Obed-edom[52]

[50] W. Rudolph (*Chronikbücher*, 173) argues 1 Chr 26:1-19 as secondary since this passage deviates from Ezra-Nehemiah's categorization of gatekeepers. For Rudolph, the Chronicler is the author of both books of Chronicles and Ezra-Nehemiah. Thus, he suggests that 1 Chr 26:1-19 could not have been written by the same author. However, once freed from this basic assumption that the books of Chronicles and Ezra-Nehemiah were written by one author (the Chronicler), one can easily make the case that 1 Chr 26:1-19 integrates nicely with the whole section of 1 Chronicles 23–26. I argue that 1 Chr 26:1-19 is an integral part of 1 Chronicles 23–26 for three reasons. First, the section shares the structural patterns which characterize 1 Chronicles 23–26 as I argued before, such as twenty-four divisions, lot casting to decide the order of shifts, and the common phraseology. This proves that 1 Chr 26:1-19 is a part of structural patterns that the Chronicler designed for the whole section of 1 Chronicles 23–26.

[51] Steins, *Die Chronik*, 305-7.

[52] The Chronicler's treatment of Obed-edom is very peculiar in terms of his incorpora-

8: The number of gatekeepers of Obed-edom
9: The number of gatekeepers of Meshelemiah
10-11a: The genealogy of Hosah, the Merarite
11b: The number of gatekeepers of Hosah
12: The conclusion

This passage is neatly designed as one literary unit. The number of each family of gatekeepers is reported formulaically: a number + ל family name (לעבד אדם [v. 8b], ולמשלמיהו [v. 9], and לחסה [v. 11b]) + a phrase of בנים ואחים (vv. 8, 9 and 11b). Additionally, as S. Japhet notes, there is an inner chiastic structure between vv. 2-7 and vv. 8-9, by which the unity of this passage is expressed.[53]

The chiasm of this unit serves a specific function, namely, to establish the shared Korahite ancestry of the families of Meshelemiah and Obed-Edom, in distinction from the origins of the family of Husah. The first gatekeeper family of the Korahites is introduced by the phrase of משלמיהו בן־קרא מן־בני אסף in verse 1: Meshelemiah is said to be the son of Kore, of the sons of Asaph. Within the narrative framework of 1 Chronicles 23–26, Meshelemiah emerges as a contemporary of David, selected as a gatekeeper during

tion of Obed-edom into the Levites and of his unusally frequent references to Obed-edom (fourteen times: 1 Chr 13: 13, 14 [twice]; 15:18, 21, 24, 25; 16:5, 38 [twice]; 26:4, 8 [twice]; 2 Chr 25:24). See Nancy Tan, "The Chronicler's 'Obed-dom': A Foreigner and/or a Levite?" *JSOT* 32 (2007) 217-30, here 218. As S. Japhet (*I & II Chronicles*, 281-82) suggests, the Chronicler seems to combine all the available traditions about Obed-edom to to make Obed-edom a worthy man of keeping and carrying the Ark in order to rationalize David's action to move the Ark to Obed-edom's house. The Chronicler's work on Obed-edom can be viewed as a precursor of "overkill" phenomenon, which is found commonly in the later Rabbinic exegeses. J. Kugel ("Levi's Elevation to the Priesthood in Second Temple Writings," *HTR* 86 [1993] 1-64, here 7) says:

> The "overkill" phenomenon usually comes about when the author of a particular text is aware of two earlier versions of a story or two different explanations for the same phenomenon; unable or unwilling to decide between them, the author seeks to incorporate both into a single telling. In so doing, however, the author inevitably ends up "overkilling" something in the story, giving two reasons why a particular thing happened or two different ways in which it took place.

By using this "overkilling" technique, the Chronicler intended to give an impression that the Ark was never mistreated nor desecrated by any foreigner. This argument is supported by the facts that Obed-edom appears only one more time (2 Chr 25:24) after 1 Chr 26:1-19, and that none of his family members are included in the list of gatekeepers of the post-exilic period (1 Chr 9:19-32). The Chronicler's interest in Obed-edom is limited to establish his levitical status.

[53] Japhet, *I & II Chronicles*, 451.

the last years of King David.[54] Meshelemiah has seven sons (vv. 2-3), all of whom will head divisions of gatekeepers.

In 1 Chr 26:1-19, Obed-edom is also connected to the Korahites—but by means of syntax, rather than by an explicit genealogy. Verse 4, which introduces the eight sons of Obed-edom, begins with the *waw* conjunctive, which joins it syntactically to verse 1. In other words, the *waw* conjunctive establishes that the family of Obed-edom belongs to the Korahites as much as that of Meshelemiah does, even if the ancestry of Obed-edom is not provided. [55] Further genealogical information about Obed-edom is provided in 1 Chr 26:6-7: Shemaiah, Obed-edom's first son, branches out to form a separate household, which consists of six sons. Thus, the family of Obed-edom forms thirteen houses of gatekeepers, bringing the total number of divisions that descend from Korah to twenty.

While Meshelemiah and Obed-edom are affiliated with the Korahites, Hosah is affiliated with the Merarites. Hosah is first introduced in 1 Chr 16:38 as a gatekeeper before the Ark in Jerusalem, but his family of origin is mentioned only in 1 Chr 26:10. According to 1 Chr 26:10-11a, Hosah has four sons. Thus, the total number of the chief men (ראשי הגברים: v. 12) of the gatekeepers is twenty-four: seven of Meshelemiah, thirteen of Obed-edom and four of Hosah.[56] The twenty-four divisions of gatekeepers exactly parallel those of priests and musicians. As I mentioned earlier in section 1.2, the twenty-four priestly divisions were first introduced by the

[54] Since this Meshelemiah shares exactly the same ancestry as Shallum in 1 Chr 9:19, S. Japhet (*I & II Chronicles*, 452) argues that he is the same individual as Shallum. As I have argued in section 2.1.1.2, however, her proposal disregards the temporal setting of the text that the Chronicler constructed quite deliberately. This Meshelemiah is a contemporary of David, whereas Shallum in 1 Chr 9:19 is a gatekeeper in the post-exilic period. I may suggest that Meshelemiah, a figure in the time of David, is singled out or invented by the Chronicler to emphasize the Korahites' position as gatekeepers. The Chronicler traces back the Korahites' possession of the office of gatekeepers to the wilderness period (1 Chronicles 9), and now to David's time (1 Chronicles 26).

[55] Japhet, *I & II Chronicles*, 455-56; and Klein, *1 Chronicles*, 490. It is possible that the Chronicler intends his readers to identify this Obed-Edom with the Gittite of the same name, about whom 1 Chr 13:14//2 Sam 6:11 relates: "the LORD blessed Obed-edom and his entire household." Commentators often connect this blessing with phrase "for God has blessed him" (כי ברכו אלהים) in 1 Chr 26:5. Obed-edom's large family (total sixty-two in 1 Chr 26:8) is understood to reflect this divine blessing.

[56] G. Steins (*Die Chronik als kanonische Abschlußsphänomen*, 304) points out that the phrase of "chief men" (ראשי הגברים) appears only one more time in the entire Hebrew Bible: 1 Chr 24:4 which is non-gatekeeper section. This fact also supports the literary integrity of 1 Chr 26:1-19 to the David's Installation Block (1 Chronicles 23–26).

Chronicler in the Bible, but continued to be mentioned in the post-biblical period.[57] The Chronicler's attribution of the organization of gatekeepers to David seems to be his retrojection of his ideal for gatekeepers, based on the priestly organization.[58]

2.1.2.1.2. The Second Unit (1 Chr 26:13-19): Assignment of Gate Posts

In the second unit (1 Chr 26:13-19), each clan of gatekeepers receives its appointment to guard a certain gate or area of the temple. Verse 13 states that the process of appointment was strictly impartial, in that each clan of gatekeepers cast a lot for each guard post on an equal footing: "and they cast lots, small and great alike, according to the house of their fathers, for each gate" (ויפילו גורלות כקטן כגדול לבית אבותם לשער ושער). The attractiveness of lot-casting lies in its usefulness as a means of divination, or as a means of ensuring an equal chance to all the parties concerned, as the phrase "small and great alike" (כקטן כגדול) in 1 Chr 26:13 also implies.[59] Lot-casting to ensure equal access is mostly reported in post-exilic texts (1 Chr 24:31; 25:8; 26:13, 14; Neh 10:34; 11:1) and in post-biblical texts, such as *M. Tamid* 5:1-5:6 and 6:1-6:3; and Philo, *On the Special Law* 1:156.[60] This evidence suggests that the Chronicler's description of gatekeepers in 1 Chronicles 26 reflects his contemporary situation, even though he ascribes the organization of the temple personnel to David.[61]

Verses 14-16 introduce the guard posts assigned to the three main families of gatekeepers in the order of their introduction in the previous unit: "Shelemiah" goes first, followed by the family of Obed-edom, and then the

[57] See section 1.2, esp. n. 38.

[58] For a further discussion of this topic, see section 3.3.3.

[59] Anne Marie Kitz, "The Hebrew Terminology of Lot Casting," 207-14; and Johannes Lindblom, "Lot-casting in the Old Testament," *VT* 12 (1962) 164-78. See also A. M. Kitz, "Undivided Inheritance and Lot Casting in the Book of Joshua," *JBL* 119 (2000) 601-18. Kitz notes that when the land was allotted to the tribes in the time of Joshua, lots were cast by each tribe (Josh 18:6, 8, 10). Similarly, according to Neh 10:24, lots were cast by each ancestral house among the priests, the Levites, and the people to determine who would bring the wood-offerings to the temple

[60] See Frances Schmidt, "Gôrâl versus Payîs: Lots at Qumran and in the Rabbinic Tradition," in *Defining Identities: We, You, and the Other in the Dead Sea Scrolls: Proceedings of the Fifth Meeting of the IOQS in Groningen* (ed. Florentino García Martínez and Mladen Popović; Studies on the Texts of the Desert of Judah 70; Leiden; Boston: Brill, 2008) 175-85, esp. 181-83; and Everett Ferguson, *Backgrounds of Early Christianity* (3rd ed.; Grand Rapids: Eerdmans, 2003) 566; and Barbara Burrell, *Neokoroi: Greek Cities and Roman Emperors* (Leiden: Brill, 2004) 5.

[61] Japhet, *I & II Chronicles*, 458-59.

family of Hosah.[62] The most prestigious place—the east gate— is assigned to the family of Meshelemiah. The primary status of the east gate is well known: elsewhere in Chronicles it is called the "King's gate" (1 Chr 9:18).[63] Even in the wilderness camp, the east side of the Tent of Meeting was assigned to the most prestigious leaders, Moses and Aaron and his sons (Num 3:38).[64] Verse 14a could serve as an etiological explanation of why the family of Meshelemiah held the most prestigious place in the Chronicler's own time (see 1 Chr 9:17-32).

The guarding post of Zechariah, son of Shelemiah, is introduced in verse 14b.[65] Zechariah's lot came out to the north. Thus, the family of Meshelemiah is now assigned to the east gate and to the north gate.[66]

[62] Since "Shelemiah" appears here instead of the expected Meshelemiah in accordance with verses 1, 2, and 9, this verse has been often considered to come from a different (or later) hand. However, as S. Japhet suggests (*I & II Chronicles*, 452-53), the different orthography of Meshelemiah does not necessarily mean that it came from a different hand. See also Knoppers, *1 Chronicles 10-29*, 864. Shelemiah is likely an alternate form of Meshelemiah since they share the same genealogy. There is no doubt that Shelemiah is the same individual as Meshelemiah, since the first son of Meshelemiah is Zechariah (1 Chr 26:2), and Shelemiah's son is also Zechariah. In verse 14, only Zechariah is introduced as a son of Shelemiah. It implies that Zechariah is probably the first son of Shelemiah. This genealogical relation hints that the two figures are one and the same.

[63] McKenzie, *1–2 Chronicles*, 491.

[64] Ezekiel also confirms the primacy of the east gate by saying that Yahweh entered the Temple by the east gate (Ezek 44:2-3) and that the prince would come and go to the Temple through this gate (Ezek 46:12).

[65] W. Rudolph (*Chronikbücher*, 170) suggests reading the beginning of verse 14b (וזכריהו) as ולזכריהו by referring to the LXX and the Vulgate. In my reading of v. 14b, I follow Rudolph. On the other hand, LXX 1 Chr 26:14b renders זכריהו בנו יועץ בשׂכל ("and Zechariah his son, a prudent councilor") as Ζαχαρια υἱοὶ Σωάζ [Bc$_2$: cf. Ιωαζ: A] τῷ Μελχια. Here, יועץ (*Qal* participle of verb יעץ) is rendered by the LXX^A as Ιωιας, and by the LXX^B as Σωάζ. Both renderings imply that the translator(s) understood the word as a proper noun and transliterated it. Furthermore, another phrase τῷ Μελχεια or τῷ Μελχια in LXX^{AB} is totally unrelated to the MT's בשׂכל. E. L. Curtis (*The Books of Chronicles*, 286) suggests that it would be a transliteration of the Aramaic gloss מליך for יועץ. Unlike the LXX, the Vulgate, the Targum and the Peshitta follow the MT. The Lucianic recension (LXX^{be2}) also reflects the MT. The renderings of LXX seem to reflect a corrupted text. Neither Soaz/Joas nor Malchiah appears in the genealogy of Meshelemiah (1 Chr 26:2-3). Furthermore, two more names in verse 14 do not seem to fit in the structural pattern in which verses 14-16 are arranged. Each verse introduces only the head of the family and one name of its sub-branch and their guarding posts. Therefore I follow the MT reading of verse 14b.

[66] Zechariah, son of Meshelemiah, appears only in Chronicles: 1 Chr 9:21; 26:2, 14. A certain Zechariah appears with Meshullam in 2 Chr 34:12 which depicts the process of restoring the Temple during the reign of Josiah. According to 2 Chr 34:12, Zechariah and Meshullam are both the Kohathites. Along with Jahath and Obadiah, the Merarites, they supervised the process of the restoration of the Temple. In 2 Chr 34:12, the relationship

Obed-edom's guarding post is introduced in verse 15: לעבד אדם נגבה ולבניו בית האספים:. Since verse 15 is connected to the phrase הפילו גורלות in verse 14 by the prefixed preposition *lāmed* before Obed-edom, I translate this verse as follows: "[They cast lots and the lot] for Obed-edom [fell] to the south and for his sons to the store-house."[67] Thus, according to 1 Chr 26:15, the guarding duties for the south gate and the store-house are assigned to Obed-edom and his sons.

The presence of the south gate of the Temple in the pre-exilic period is subject to debate: the Solomonic Temple is believed to have been connected with the royal house on the south, which would seem to imply that there was no need to station any guards at the south gate.[68] E. L. Curtis claims that the reference to the south gate reflects the Chronicler's anachronistic

---

between Zechariah and Meshallum is not clarified. In Ezra 8:16, Zechariah also appears with Meshullam. They were among the nine leaders who were sent by Ezra to Iddo to bring some Levites to the Land. Here the relationship between Zechariah and Meshullam is not known to us, either. They appear together at the scene in which Ezra read the Torah (Neh 8:4). Both of them stood at the left side of podium where Ezra read the Torah. One more time Zechariah and Meshullam appear together in Neh 12:16. They are among the heads of the priestly clans: Zechariah is the head of the Iddo clan, but Meshullam, the head of the Ginnethon clan. In this manner, the pair Zechariah and Meshullam appears together several times in the post-exilic texts, but their relationship is often not clarified. Furthermore, neither of them is designated as gatekeepers. Thus, I can say that there is no strong ground to identify Zechariah and (Me)shelemiah in 1 Chronicles 26 with post-exilic figures, Zechariah and Meshullam.

[67] LXX 1 Chr 26:15 is deviant from the MT. The majority of LXX manuscripts (hereafter, LXX^{M}) have τῷ Αβδεδομ νότον κατέναντι οἴκου εσεφιν, which can be translated as "to Abed-edom the south, opposite the house of Esephim." The difference seems to be caused by a confusion between ב and פ due to graphic similarity of the two letters or by a phonetic error (both are labial), as L. C. Allen (*Textual Criticism*. Vol. 2 of *The Greek Chronicles: The Relation of the Septuagint of I and II Chronicles to the Massoretic Text* [VTSup 27; Leiden: Brill, 1974] 124) and D. Osen ("What Got the Gatekeepers into Trouble?" 227) suggest. The LXX^{M} probably reflects לפני instead of the MT's ולבניו. Furthermore, the Lucianic recension (LXX^{be2}: hereafter, LXX^{L}) of 1 Chr 26:15 clearly reflects the MT's rendering. Thus, the MT 1 Chr 26:15 is likely closer to the original reading than the LXX^{M}.

[68] See Curtis and Madsen, *The Books of Chronicles*, 285; and Williamson, *1 and 2 Chronicles*, 170-71. This argument is based on Ezek 43:8, in which Ezekiel claimed that the temple was adjoined to the palace by the same wall, and such proximity meant that the Temple was easily defiled by the abominations that the royal families committed. However, this text does not demonstrate the absence of a south gate in the First Temple. Ezek 43:8 seems to imply the opposite since it mentions thresholds ספים and doorposts מזוזות between the two buildings. Furthermore, Ezekiel's blueprint for a new Temple includes the south gate as well as several other gates for the Temple: the east gate (Ezek 44:1-3; 46:1, 12); the north gate (Ezek 44:4; 46:9 and 47:2); the gates of the inner court (Ezek 44:17); and the south gate (Ezek 46:9).

projection of a later situation onto the monarchic period.[69] In contrast, R. W. Klein contends, on the basis on 2 Kgs 11:11, (where Jehoiada the priest commands guards to stand from the south side of the Temple to the north side of the Temple during the coup against Athaliah), that there was indeed a south gate during the monarchic era.[70] I argue in section 3.1.2.1 of the present study that "the gate behind the guards" (שער אחר הרצים) and "the gate Sur" (שער סור) in 2 Kgs 11:6 was located in the southern wall separating the Temple and palace compounds. Thus, the Chronicler's reference to the south gate in 1 Chr 26:15 reflects the historical reality of the Temple architecture at least in the monarchic period.

The text does not provide much information about the store-house, the guarding post for the sons of Obed-edom. The word אסף or אספים originates from Akkadian *asuppu* (pl. *asuppāti*), which means "a type of building erected of less durable materials than a house, used in outbuildings and on top of the buildings."[71] It is not possible to determine from verse 15 whether each Temple gate had such a store-house or outbuilding, or whether only a specific gate had such an additional building. In any case, the store-house that the sons of Obed-edom were assigned to guard would probably have been at the south since the other gates were assigned to other families.[72]

The guarding post for Hosah, the third gatekeeper family, is introduced in verse 16 which is also connected with the phrase הפילו גורלות of verse 14: לשׁפים ולחסה למערב עם שער שלכת במסלה העולה משמר לעמת משמר. Regrettably, text-critical and exegetical problems hinder our ability to dis-

[69] Curtis and Madsen, *The Books of Chronicles*, 285. H. G. M. Williamson (*1 and 2 Chronicles*, 170-71) also considers the reference to the south gate as a proof of the post-exilic origin of this paragraph.

[70] Klein, *1 Chronicles*, 492.

[71] The word occurs only three times in the Hebrew Bible: 1 Chr 26:15, 17 and Neh 12:25. *HALOT*, 75; *CAD* A II, 349; and see also Japhet, *I & II Chronicles*, 459-60. The Greek translator(s) of the LXX only transliterated this word, which suggests that its meaning must have not been known to him (them). See L. C. Allen, *The Translator's Craft*. Vol. 1 of *The Greek Chronicles: The Relation of the Septuagint of I and II Chronicles to the Massoretic Text* (VTSup 25; Leiden: Brill, 1974) 62. The definition of the Akkadian word *asuppu* does not indicate how such a building might have been used in antiquity. That definition is more about the building structure. Although I admit that אסף is a cognate of *asuppu*, I translate אסף as a storehouse to designate its probable usage.

[72] D. Kimḥi (Yitzhak Berger, *The Commentary of Rabbi David Kimhi to Chronicles: A Translation with Introduction and Supercommentary* [Providence: Brown Judaic Studies, 2007] 170), without giving any concrete evidence, asserted that the store-house (בית האספים) was located outside of the Temple court to the south of it.

cern who cast lots and what posts were assigned to the family of Hosah: indeed, in the MT the verse fairly bristles with difficulties which alternative versions do little to resolve. Luckily, since the Chronicler consistently asserts that gatekeepers were assigned to the four directions around the Temple (in both gatekeeper sections: 1 Chr 9:24 and 26:14-16) and since only one direction remains to be allotted, we can reasonably place the family of Hosah at the western gate.[73]

The Chronicler notes in 1 Chr 26:16 that the western post was near to the Shellecheth gate (שַׁעַר שַׁלֶּכֶת), a highly puzzling toponym. The MT's שַׁלֶּכֶת is a *hapax legomenon*, possibly a case of metathesis of the first two consonants.[74] Ancient translations support this conclusion.[75] I favor the

[73] The first exegetical problem is that lots seem to have been cast for two people, Shuppim and Hosah. However, לשפים is text-critically problematic. W. Rudolph (*Chronikbücher*, 172) suggests deleting the phrase since it resulted from a scribal error (dittography of the preceding word [האספים] in the end of verse 15). Commentators generally follow this suggestion and delete it because Shuppim is not expected here and never appears together with Hosah elsewhere. Once לשפים is deleted, verse 16 states that the lot for Hosah fell to the west (למערב). The second exegetical problem in verse 16 is how to understand the relationship between למערב and שַׁעַר שַׁלֶּכֶת. The location of Hosah's guarding post is closely related to one's interpretation of the preposition עם which comes before שַׁעַר שַׁלֶּכֶת. P. B. Dirksen (*1 Chronicles*, 306) translates it as "with," so that Hosah's guarding posts are two: the west (gate) and the Shellecheth gate. W. Rudolph (*Chronikbücher*, 172), E. L. Curtis (*The Books of Chronicles*, 285), S. Japhet (*I & II Chronicles*, 860) and R. Braun (*1 Chronicles*, 248) render it as "at." According to this translation, Hosah is responsible for guarding the west at the gate of Shellecheth. This seems more reasonable for the following reasons. First, when the preposition עם is used of a locality, it generally means "close to," or "beside" (see BDB 768). Second, if the Shellecheth gate is another guarding post for which Hosah is responsible, שַׁעַר שַׁלֶּכֶת should be prefixed with the preposition *lāmed*, like למערב. But שַׁעַר שַׁלֶּכֶת is not prefixed with *lāmed*, and connected with the preposition עם. Thus, I may say that Hosah's guarding post is on the west side by the Shellecheth gate, which is not known to us. The third question is what למערב designates. It could simply mean somewhere on the west side of the Shellecheth gate. Thus Hosah is responsible for the west side of the Temple which is near to the Shellecheth gate. Some scholars doubt the existence of a west gate to the Temple. See Jacob Liver, *Chapters in the History of the Priests and Levites: Studies in the Lists of Chronicles and Ezra and Nehemiah* (Jerusalem: Magness, 1968) 115; and Japhet, *I & II Chronicles*, 460. I shall deal with the question of the existence of the western gate later in section 3.1.2.2.

[74] Japhet, *I & II Chronicles*, 460; and Knoppers, *1 Chronicles 10-29*, 864.

[75] Concerning שַׁעַר שַׁלֶּכֶת, only the Targum corresponds with the MT's witness. The Targum's תרעא דמתרמיא is a literal Aramaic translation of שַׁעַר שַׁלֶּכֶת, which means "the gate of casting forth." On the contrary, the majority of LXX texts reflect שַׁעַר לִשְׁכַּת, "the gate of chamber," and the Peshitta also witnesses to a similar rendering: לתרעא דמתקן, which means "to the gate of preparation" or "the gate of setting aside the priestly gifts." Even the Lucianic recension (LXX[be2]) does not reflect the MT's reading at all. Such a situation is quite rare since the Lucianic recension of Chronicles clearly shows a conservative tendency by

LXX's rendering לשכת which can be understood to mean that Hosah's post was "in the west side by the chamber gate."[76]

The location of the chamber gate is specified by the phrase במסלה העולה. Neither ancient nor modern translations of this phrase help us determine the location of this gate. The Lucianic recension (ἐν τῇ τρίβῳ τῆς ἀναβάσεως), Targum (תרעא דמתרמיא), Peshitta (ܒܫܒܝܠܐ ܕܣܘܠܩܐ), and the Vulgate (*ad viam ascensionis*) render it consistently: "on the ascending road or highway."[77] Since מסלה in the Hebrew Bible is often understood as "highway," all modern translations adopt this interpretation more or less.[78] Thus, the chamber gate is said to be located somewhere on the ascending road. However, the context requires מסלה העולה to be somewhere in or near to the Temple precinct.[79]

N. L. Tidwell argues that מסלה refers to the approach road, which ascends from the base of the mound or hill where cities were usually located, to the main gate of the city on the mound.[80] Usually this road is the paved street leading to the temple or palace within the city walls.[81] However, the three instances of מסלה in Chronicles (1 Chr 26:16, 18 and 2 Chr 9:11) do not fit into this category. In 2 Chr 9:11, מסלות designates a kind of "passageway" leading up to the Temple and to the palace, which Solomon made of algum wood. A passageway made of expensive wood cannot be a paved street running from the bottom to the top of a temple mound. Rather, מסלה seems more likely to have been part of the architectural complex connected with the Temple.[82] David A. Dorsey's study on *mušlālu*, an Akkadian cognate of מסלה that designates a gate or a gatehouse for a temple or palace, provides an interpretation that better suits the evidence of Chronicles.[83] Dorsey

---

reflecting important Hebrew readings without taking out anything out of the original Greek translation, as E. Tov (*Textual Criticism of the Hebrew Bible*, 148) comments.

76 Curtis, Klein and Knoppers also follow LXX's reading. Curtis and Madsen, *The Books of Chronicles*, 285-86; Klein, *1 Chronicles*, 485; and Knoppers, *1 Chronicles 10-29*, 860. The Shellecheth gate (שער שלכת) only appears here in Chronicles, but the chamber gate (שער לשכת) is found elsewhere in the Hebrew Bible (*e.g.*, Ezek 46:19, though it is rendered in a slightly different way: השער אל־הלשכות הקדשה).

77 Interestingly, the LXX^{M} does not render the word, and simply dismiss it.

78 BDB 700; and *HALOT*, 606.

79 David A. Dorsey, "Another Peculiar Term in the Book of Chronicles: מְסִלָּה, 'Highway'?" *JQR* 75 (1985) 388.

80 N. L. Tidwell, "No Highway! The Outline of a Semantic Description of *Mesillâ*," *VT* 45 (1995) 251-69.

81 Tidwell, "No Highway! The Outline of a Semantic Description of *Mesillâ*," 269.

82 Knoppers, *1 Chronicles 10-29*, 864.

83 Dorsey, "Another Peculiar Term in the Book of Chronicles," 385-91. Akkadian

suggests that מסלה could be associated with "an entranceway or gateway into a temple complex," where gatekeepers would probably be stationed.[84] If מסלה had such a technical meaning in the exilic/post-exilic period, the location of Hosah's guarding post becomes much clearer. It is "in the west side at the gate of a chamber, which is in the ascending gateway to the Temple."

With the final phrase of verse 16 (משמר לעמת משמר), the process of allotment is completed; verses 17-18 now move into even more particular territory by stipulating the number of gatekeepers assigned to each post. Verse 17 states that six gatekeepers are stationed at the east (למזרח הלוים ששה), four gatekeepers at the north (לצפונה ליום ארבעה), and another four gatekeepers at the south (לנגבה ליום ארבעה). However, it is not clear how many are stationed at the storehouses (ולאספים שנים שנים): two or four? It depends on how one interprets the phrase שנים שנים.[85] If two, then the second שנים must have been added by a scribal error (dittography).

On the other hand, the phrase שנים שנים appears in Genesis 7:9 and 7:15, where it means "two of each."[86] D. Kimḥi interprets שנים שנים of MT 1 Chr 26:17 in the same way.[87] He concludes that there were two storehouses with two guards posted at each, making a grand total of four storehouse guards.

I follow Kimḥi and translate verse 17, "At the east (there were) six daily, at the north four daily; at the south four daily; two at each storehouses" making the total number of gatekeepers thus far stationed at their respective positions eighteen.[88]

The number of gatekeepers stationed at Hosah's guarding post is presented in verse 18, which is difficult to translate: לפרבר למערב ארבעה למסלה

mušlālu appears in a number of Neo-Assyrian royal inscriptions, mostly combined with the temple or the palace, such as *mušlālum ekalli ša qereb Aššur*, *mušlālum ša ekalli*, or *bīt mušlālu ša qereb ekalli*. See *CAD* M II, 277.

[84] Dorsey, "Another Peculiar Term in the Book of Chronicles," 388. John M. Monson (*The Temple of Jerusalem: A Case Study in the Integration of Text and Artifact* [Ph.D. diss., Harvard University, 1998] 75) also suggests that מסלה denotes "a ramp into the gateway of the temple complex" in Chronicles.

[85] The MT's reading (שנים שנים) is followed by the LXX^A and the Lucianic recension as well as the Targum and the Vulgate, while the Peshitta (ܬܪܝܢ) agrees with the LXX^B (δύο). According to W. Rudolph (*Chronikbücher*, 172) a few Hebrew manuscripts also do not have the second שנים.

[86] *HALOT*, 1605-6. In Hebrew syntax, the repetition of the cardinal numbers expresses distributives. See also Gesenius §134q.

[87] Berger, *The Commentary of Rabbi David Kimhi to Chronicles*, 170.

[88] What I mean by "daily" here is "each day" (i.e. 24-hour period), not "daytime shift."

שׁנים לפרבר:. What פרבר designates is unclear, and the presence of the second פרבר suggests, to some scholars, that scribal error has corrupted the verse. The locations of the phrase לפרבר are indeed grammatically awkward, so W. Rudolph and others recommend deleting the first לפרבר, understanding it as a dittography of the second לפרבר.[89]

I want to suggest an alternative explanation, which requires that we examine the possible connotations of פרור/פרבר, a word which appears only three times in the Hebrew Bible: here in 1 Chr 26:18 (twice) and in 2 Kgs 23:11 (in its plural form: פרורים). In 2 Kgs 23:11, we find that פרורים, where the horses and chariots dedicated to the sun were kept, were located at the entrance of the Temple near by a chamber (לשׁכה). This passage suggests that פרורים could be a space connected with the entrance of the Temple and in proximity to a chamber of some sort.

Extra-biblical uses of the word confirm this interpretation. According to J. Maier, who examined all the instances of פרבר in the Temple Scroll, the probable meaning of the word is "a colonnaded porch," and a proper Greek translation of it would be *περίστυλον* or *στοά*.[90] Thus, פרבר in the Temple Scroll likely designates a colonnade in the west of the Temple.

[89] Rudolph, *Chronikbücher*, 172. The following scholars adopt his suggestion: Japhet, *I & II Chronicles*, 460; Knoppers, *1 Chronicles 10-29*, 865; Dirksen, *1 Chronicles*, 313; and Klein, *1 Chronicles*, 486. R. W. Klein suggests another possibility to understand the first לפרבר as a *casus pendens*: "As for the colonnade on the west." However, other commentators, such as R. Braun, H. G. M. Williamson, and S. L. McKenzie, have not commented on this text-critical problem with little attention to the meaning of the word פרבר.

[90] J. Maier, "The Architectural History of the Temple in Jerusalem in the Light of the Temple Scroll," in *Temple Scroll Studies: Papers Presented at the International Symposium on the Temple Scroll, Manchester, December 1987* (ed. George J. Brooke; JSPSS 7; Sheffield: Sheffield Academic Press, 1989) 23-62, here 26. פרבר appears in 11QT 5:13; 35:9-10; 37:6, 9; 42:8-9. According to 11QT 35:10, פרבר is a place in the west of the sanctuary and is to be built with many columns. For this reason, פרבר is translated as "a colonnade or a stoa." Florentino G. Martínez also translates פרבר either "a portico" or "a porch." See Florentino G. Martínez, *The Dead Sea Scrolls Translated: The Qumran Texts in English* (trans. Wilfred G. E. Watson; 2nd ed.; Leiden: Brill, 1996) 155, 163, 166. Donna Runnalls ("The Parwār: A Place of Ritual Separation?" *VT* 41 [1991] 324-31) expands Maier's studies and claims that פרבר originated from a biconsonantal verb *pr* in Hebrew, not from a Persian loan-word, *fra-bar* ("forecourt or vestibule") as has been argued previously. Runnalls argues, based on her reading of the Temple Scroll, that פרבר could originally have meant something like "the place of separation," where the purgation offerings of the priests could be kept separate from those of the laymen (11QT 35:10-15). The author of the Temple Scroll claims that this place should be built with many columns on the west side of the Temple (11QT 35:10). For this reason, Runnalls concludes that פרבר, which was originally a technical term for a place of ritual separation, could have been used to designate "a columned stoa." Concerning verb פרר II, refer to BDB 830.

Of course, one cannot apply a later technical meaning of פרבר from the Temple Scroll to an earlier text, 1 Chr 26:18, unless there is a common denominator between the usages of the word; as it happens, though, several links bind the biblical uses to the DSS uses. First, all sources indicate that the פרבר was located between the outer wall and the inner court of the Temple. Further, the Temple Scroll and MT 1 Chr 26:18 agree that פרבר was in the west side of the Temple, while both 2 Kgs 23:11 and MT 1 Chr 26:18 imply that פרבר is connected to the entrance of the Temple. Finally, 2 Kgs 23:11 and the Temple Scroll suggest that פרבר must have been a roofed area. Based on this evidence, I conjecture that פרבר would be something like "an open, but roofed space," which is connected to the ascending gateway to the Temple in the west.

This interpretation makes clear the purpose of the dual use of פרבר in 1 Chr 26:19 at the beginning and at end of the sentence: פרבר brackets the sentence, and thus conveys a graphic image:[91]

An open space (פרבר)	— an ascending gateway to the Temple —	an open space (פרבר)
(Two keepers)	(Two keepers)	(Two keepers)

Thus, at the west, six gatekeepers are stationed: one pair each at the two open spaces that bracket the ascending gateway, which is itself guarded by two other gatekeepers. Above, we concluded that the number of gatekeepers posted daily to the east, north, south and the storehouses was eighteen. If the six gatekeepers from verse 18 are added to this number, we find a total of twenty-four gatekeepers on duty.[92] The text seems to be geared to arrive at this number which reflects the Chronicler's ideal organization of gatekeepers, based on the twenty-four divisions of priestly families (see section 1.2).[93]

[91] A strategic positioning of the words can convey a vivid graphic image. A good example for it is Prov 8:22-31 where a strategic positioning of thematic words (the heaven, I [אני], and earth) gives a vivid graphic image that Wisdom has a place somewhere between YHWH and humankind and plays a role of mediator between the two. See Jean-Noël Aletti, "Proverbs 8:22-31: étude de structure," *Biblica* 57 (1976) 25-37; and Gale A. Yee, "An Analysis of Prov 8:22-31 According to Style and Structure," *ZAW* 94 (1982) 58-66.

[92] S. Japhet (*I & II Chronicles*, 460) counts the daily total of gatekeepers as twenty-two, but D. Kimḥi (Berger, *The Commentary of Rabbi David Kimhi to Chronicles*, 170-71), Gary N. Knoppers (*1 Chronicles 10-29*, 869), R. W. Klein (*1 Chronicles*, 494), and P. B. Dirksen (*1 Chronicles*, 309) count them as twenty-four although their interpretations of שנים שנים are not without dissent.

[93] D. Olsen's text-critical studies of LXX 1 Chr 26:17-18a are worth mentioning here

2.2. The Chronicler's Description of the Temple Treasurers

The Chronicler continues to emphasize the Levites' high administrative profile in his treatment of the temple treasurers. Two of the passages that I deem David's Installation Blocks present Levites as temple treasurers (1 Chr 9:26-29 and 1 Chr 26:20-28).[94] Insistence on the levitical identity of these officeholders is the only category in which the passages overlap: my analysis shows that these two texts are quite different in terms of the types of treasuries and offices presented. Should these differences be understood as discrepancies? Or can we understand the different presentations in light of the Chronicler's understanding of changes to the temple administration that occurred in response to Judah's changing historical circumstances?

2.2.1. 1 Chronicles 9:26-29

1 Chronicles 9:26-29 is embedded in the first gatekeeper section (1 Chr 9:17-32). As we saw in the analysis of that passage, 1 Chr 9:26-29 states that the four chief gatekeepers are in charge of the chambers (לשׁכות) and

---

since they are related to my conclusion in a certain way. Generally the first phrase of LXX 1 Chr 26:18a (εἰς διαδεχομένους) is believed to be a Greek translation of the first phrase לפרבר of MT 1 Chr 18a. However, D. Olsen ("What Got the Gatekeepers into Trouble?" 229-30) suggests that it is not a translation of לפרבר, but rather it would be a translation of משנים from the last phrase שׁני משנים, which is a result of his different division of MT's שׁנים שׁנים in 1 Chr 26:17. Olsen draws our attention to 2 Chr 31:12, where διαδεχομένους translates משנה (2 Chr 28:7; Esth 10:3 are also similar cases). According to 2 Chr 31:12, Conaniah the Levite is in charge of the store-chambers (לשׁכות) and Shimei his brother is second in rank (משנה). Based on this verse, Olsen concludes that LXX 1 Chr 26:17 would originally have ended with εἰς τὸ εσεφιν δύο εἰς διαδεχομένους as a translation of לאספים שׁני משנים, which he translates "in the gatehouses (there were) two relief guards." However, the exact retroversion of εἰς τὸ εσεφιν δύο εἰς διαδεχομένους would be לאספים שׁני למשנים. In Hebrew syntax, an adjectival form of cardinal number is directly attached to the word qualified without any prefixed preposition (see Gesenius § 97a and § 134). For this reason, שׁני למשנים cannot be the original reading. Olsen's speculation goes further in a different direction from mine, but it supports my conclusion that the original *Vorlage* of MT ends with שׁנים שׁנים, not with שׁנים. On the other hand, since LXX 1 Chr 26:18 is much longer than MT 1 Chr 26:18, it is doubtful whether or not they shared the same *Vorlage*. D. Alson ("What Got the Gatekeepers into Trouble?" 232) argues that LXX 1 Chr 26:18 describes the gatekeepers' day and night shift. However, my text critical analysis proves his argument untenable. LXX^{M} 1 Chr 26:18 is probably a repetition of the preceding verses 16-17 due to a scribal error, although a possibility that it reflects a different *Vorlage* from that of the MT cannot be entirely excluded.

[94] Beside these passages, 2 Chr 31:11-16, which describes Hezekiah's innovative measure for the upkeep of the Temple, is to be treated in this section.

the treasuries (אצרות) of the Temple (esp. v. 26). Their responsibility also covers the supervision of the utensils of service (v. 28), the furniture and all the holy utensils (v. 29) in the Temple, as well as the supply of the fine flour, wine, oil, incense, and spices, which are necessary for daily sacrificial services (v. 29).

If 1 Chr 9:26-29 generally reflects practices of the post-exilic period, the Chronicler's claim that the chief gatekeepers were involved in inventory control has significant implications for the temple administration in that period. The chambers and treasuries were vital to the running of the temple economy: the temple revenue was stored there and the major expenditures of the Temple were derived from there. In Chapter 3 of this study, I compare the Chronicler's claims with the known facts about temple treasuries in other sources. Before we grapple with questions that pertain to the historicity of the Chronicler's claims in 1 Chr 9:26-29, however, it will be necessary to take a detailed look at the other passage that pertains to temple treasurers and treasuries, 1 Chr 26:20-28. While the levitical identity of the officers of the treasury is upheld in 1 Chronicles 26, that passage contains no overlap between the duties of gatekeepers and treasurers, as in 1 Chronicles 9; rather, the treasurers appear to comprise a separate corps of personnel.

2.2.2. 1 Chronicles 26:20-28

The Chronicler's second passage about the temple treasurers (1 Chr 26:20-28) belongs to 1 Chronicles 23–26, a David's Installation Block, in which the Levites are assigned to four different offices. This particular section (1 Chr 26:20-28) introduces a list of treasurers and their responsibilities.[95] Specifically, the passage sets forth the administrative hierarchy that the Chronicler

[95] 1 Chr 26:10-28 does not follow the pattern of previous passages in 1 Chronicles 23–26. For the temple treasurers, the Chronicler mentions neither their twenty-four divisions nor their work shifts. Moreover, this passage is not homogeneous in its structure and literary style. Scholars have proffered various explanations of its heterogeneity in terms of its sources or its authorship. For instance, S. Japhet (*I & II Chronicles*, 454) argues that the Chronicler combined two different sources here with verse 23. P. B. Dirksen ("The Composition of 1 Chronicles 26:20-32," *JNSL* 24 [1988] 144-55) divides this passage into two sub-units: the Chronicler's source text (vv. 21b, 22-24) and his own composition (vv. 20, 21a, and 25-28). However, H. G. M. Williamson (*1 and 2 Chronicles*, 171) considers 1 Chr 26:20-28 to be a single literary unit derived from a source. I approach this text as a single literary unit and suggest an alternative way to explain its heterogeneity.

envisions as having been established at the time of David. Thus, we find that both the temple treasuries and the treasuries of the dedicated gifts are overseen by a chief administrator (נגיד, v. 24), Shebuel, whose immediate subordinates are Jehieli and his sons (v. 22) and Shelomoth and his brothers (v. 26) who have immediate charge over the day-to-day operations of the temple treasuries and the treasuries of the dedicated gifts respectively.

2.2.2.1. Analysis of 1 Chr 26:20-28: Two Types of Treasuries

The Chronicler claims in verse 20 that, during the reign of David, the Levites were assigned to be in charge of temple treasuries and the treasuries of the dedicated gifts: והלוים אחיה על־אוצרות בית האלהים ולאצרות הקדשים: (And the Levites, *their brethren*, were over the temple treasuries and over the treasuries of the dedicated gifts). The Chronicler's claims here are unique in two respects. First, the levitical affiliation of the treasurers is not presented as fact elsewhere in the Bible. Other authors present various professionals as temple treasurers, such as priests and scribes, as well as the Levites (e.g., Neh 13:13).

Second, the Chronicler's terminology in 1 Chr 26:20 is different from other references to the treasuries elsewhere in Chronicles: *e.g.*, 2 Chr 12:9 (//1 Kgs 14:26); 2 Chr 16:2 (//1 Kgs 15:18) and 2 Chr 36:18 (//2 Kgs 24:13). All of these verses distinguish the temple treasuries (אצרות בית־יהוה) from the royal treasuries (בית המלך אצרות).[96] However, in 1 Chr 26:20, instead of the royal treasuries, we find "the treasuries of the dedicated gifts" a classification which appears only appears here (1 Chr 26:20 and 26) and in 1 Chr 28:12.[97]

Verse 26 introduces Shebuel the Amramite, who, to judge from the wider context, acted as a chief administrator of the two treasuries: [98] ושבאל בן־

[96] The other references to the temple treasuries and the royal treasuries are 1 Kgs 15:18//2 Chr 16:2 (during the reign of King Asa); 2 Kgs 12:19 (during the reign of King Jehoash); 2 Kgs 14:14//2 Chr 25:24 (during the reign of King Amaziah);2 Kgs 16:8 (during the reign of King Ahaz); 2 Kgs 18:15 (during the reign of King Hezekiah); and 2 Kgs 24:13 (during the reign of Jehoachin). These references indicate that these two types of treasuries had existed throughout the monarchy once the Temple was built. See Gary N. Knoppers, "Treasures Won and Lost: Royal (Mis) Appropriations in Kings and Chronicles," in *The Chronicler as Author*, 181-208.

[97] Dirksen, *1 Chronicles*, 317. The peculiarity of the Chronicler's classification is to be dealt with further in my exegetical analysis of 1 Chr 26:23-28, which is related to the treasuries of the dedicated gifts.

[98] Rudolph, *Chronikbücher*, 177. S. Japhet (*I & II Chronicles*, 460-61) and H. G. M. Williamson (*1 and 2 Chronicles*, 172) also agree with W. Rudolph in this matter.

גרשׁוום בן־משׁה נגיד על־האצרות:.[99] This official prominence may account for the genealogical prominence which the Chronicler affords Shebuel, whom he presents (here and in 1 Chr 23:16) as the son of Gershom, the son of Moses.[100] In 1 Chr 23:16, in fact, Shebuel is designated as the chief among the sons of Gershom, the son of Moses. Elsewhere in the Hebrew Bible, however, Shebuel is not genealogically connected with Moses (cf. Exod 2:22; 18:3-4).

In light of Shebuel's high official status, why does the Chronicler wait until verse 24 to introduce him? If he is in charge of both treasuries, we would expect his name to appear at the beginning of the passage.[101] I suspect that the literary structure of 1 Chr 26:20-28 is intended to indicate Shebuel's leadership over the two treasuries. The passage begins (vv. 21-22) with the introduction of the clans of Ladan, the Gershonites, who were in charge of the temple treasuries. Verse 26 introduces Shelomoth and his brothers, the administrators (under the supervision of Shebuel) of the treasuries of the dedicated gifts: הוא שׁלמות ואחיו על כל־אצרות הקדשׁים. Verse 24, which introduces Shebuel as the chief officer of the treasuries, acts as a bridge connecting verses 22 and 26: Shebuel's responsibility is thus under-

[99] The texts of LXX^{AN} 1 Chr 26:24 correspond to the MT, but the manuscripts of LXX^{Bc2} do not have a corresponding word of נגיד. This loss can be explained by a scribal error (haplography). If the Greek word for נגיד in the original script that the copiest had was ἐπιστάτης, his eyes could have been easily skipped to the next word (ἐπὶ of ἐπὶ τῶν θησαυρῶν) since the next word begins with the same letters (*homoioarkton*). This is supported by the fact that LXX^{AN} 1 Chr 26:24 has another Greek word, ἡγούμενος for נגיד, instead of ἐπιστάτης. Thus, these minor textual variations do not affect our reading of the MT 1 Chr 26:24. See Knoppers, *1 Chronicles 10-26*, 875.

[100] The genealogy of Shebuel in 1 Chr 26:24 is a representative case of telescoped lineage, since Shebuel, a contemporary of David is directly connected with Gershom, the son of Moses. A purpose of telescoping in genealogy is to highlight the connection between the person concerned and the important ancestor(s). The same Shebuel is mentioned also in 1 Chr 24:20, where his name appears as Shubael. This verse is a part of 1 Chr 24:20-31, a passage which enumerates the names of the sons of Levi, who are not included in the divisions of priests (1 Chr 24:1-19). Shubael is named first in this list and is introduced as the Amramite, which implies first that Shubael was an influential Levite during the reign of David and second that he is the same individual as Shebuel the Amramite in 1 Chr 23:16 and 26:24.

[101] W. Rudolph (*Chronikbücher*, 177) attributes Shebuel's delayed appearance on the scene to his genealogical origin: the Amramite. Dissenting with Rudolph, P. B. Dirksen (*1 Chronicles*, 318-19) argues that 1 Chr 26:24-32 was taken from an independent source which does not share the same view of the temple treasuries as the David's Installation Block (1 Chronicles 23–26).

stood as pertaining to the oversight of both treasuries, a reading which Shebuel's title "chief officer" (נגיד) supports.[102]

The contents of the dedicated gifts treasuries are explained in verse 27. According to the Chronicler, these gifts were the booty of war (v. 27) dedicated for the maintenance of the house of the Lord: מן־המלחמות ומן־השלל הקדישו לחזק לבית יהוה׃.[103] The Chronicler enumerates the dedicators of the gifts in verses 26 and 28. They are David, the chiefs of the clans, the officers of thousands and hundreds, and the other army officers (v. 26), as well as Samuel, Saul, Abner and Joab (v. 28). This extensive list of dedicators for the Temple coincides with the Chronicler's overall concern about the maintenance of the Temple: the depiction of David's magnanimous support for the Temple underscores the importance of this theme in Chronicles.[104] See, for example, 1 Chr 18:10-11 which notes approvingly that David dedicated to the Temple "all sorts of articles of gold, silver, and of bronze," which King Tou of Hamath sent to him. In other places (1 Chr 22:4 and 29:2-5), the Chronicler underscores David's profuse contributions to the Temple and appeals to David's lay and military leaders to follow his example.[105] As a result, the chiefs of the clans and the military leaders are reported to have dedicated a huge amount of precious metals for the service of the Temple (1 Chr 29:6-7).[106]

[102] In Chronicles, נגיד designates a king (1 Chr 11:2; 17:7; 28:4; 29:22; 2 Chr 6:5; 11:22 [a crown prince]), a chief priest (1 Chr 9:11; 2 Chr 19:11; 31:13; 35:8), a tribal leader (1 Chr 5:2; 12:27; 27:4; 27:16), a military leader (1 Chr 13:1; 2 Chr 11:11; 32:21), or a chief officer (1 Chr 26:24; 2 Chr 31:12) and the like. See Japhet, *I & II Chronicles*, 495.

[103] I consider the phrase "from the booty of war" (מן־המלחמות ומן־השלל) as a hendiadys, following the interpretations of W. Rudolph (*Chronikbücher*, 174), Gary N. Knoppers (*1 Chronicles 10-29*, 876), and P. B. Dirksen (*1 Chronicles*, 319). And see also Bruce K. Waltke and M. O'Connor, *An Introduction to Biblical Hebrew Syntax* (Winona Lake: Eisenbrauns, 1990) 70. The LXX reads this phrase in an expansionary way: ἅ ἔλαβεν ἐκ τῶν πόλεων [LXX[Bbe2]: πόλεων; LXX[A]: πόλέμων] καὶ ἐκ τῶν λαφύρων (things which he took out of cities [wars] and from the spoils). Such a reading reflects that the translator did not consider the phrase מן־המלחמות ומן־השלל as a hendiadys, and tried to explain it in order to make a better sense of it. On the other hand, the Peshitta, the Targum and the Vulgate literally correspond to the MT. Thus, there is no need to emend the MT, based on the LXX.

[104] Klein, *1 Chronicles*, 495.

[105] According to 1 Kgs 7:51 (//2 Chr 5:1), when Solomon built the Temple, he brought "the things that his father David had dedicated, and stored the silver, the gold, and all the vessels" in the treasuries of the Temple. 2 Kgs 12:19 claims that other kings of Judah, especially, Jehoshaphat, Jehoram, and Ahaziah had also dedicated their votive offerings to the Temple.

[106] One could find a similar appeal in Josh 6:19, 24. It emphasizes that the precious

There is no explicit report elsewhere in the Hebrew Bible that Samuel, Saul, Abner and Joab also dedicated any booty of war to the sanctuary, but the Chronicler adds their names in the list of dedicators (v. 28). It seems that by adding the names of the earlier Israelite leaders, who led Israel militarily during the united monarchy, and thus collected war spoils, to the list of dedicators, the Chronicler intends to emphasize that the maintenance of the Temple is a duty of political and military leaders.[107] Verse 27b also expresses such an intention by clarifying that the purpose of these dedicated things is to maintain the house of the Lord (לחזק לבית יהוה).

2.2.3. The Consistency of the Chronicler's Descriptions of the Temple Treasurers

As I mentioned above, the Chronicler's treatments of the temple treasurers in 1 Chr 9:26-29 and 1 Chr 26:20-28 are quite different in terms of the types of treasuries and of the officeholders envisioned. However, the differences between the two texts should not be understood evidence for the inconsistency of the Chronicler's treatment of the temple treasurers. Rather, a comparison of the two texts *within the Chronicler's timeframe* helps us to make sense of the differences between them.

For this comparison, I want also to include an additional text, 2 Chr 31:11-16, which is directly related to the temple treasuries. There, Hezekiah orders that the store chambers be prepared in the Temple for the surplus of people's contributions for the clergy. He also appoints the temple staff to supervise the chambers, which would store the gifts (התרומה), the tithes (המעשׂר), and the sacred things (הקדשׁים), all of which were distributed to the priests and Levites.[108] The supervision of these store chambers would be the responsibility of Conaniah the Levite and his brother, assisted by ten more officials appointed by the king and high priest (v. 13). Furthermore, Kore, the keeper of the east gate, is placed in charge of the allocation of the freewill offerings (נדבה), gifts (תרומה), and the most sacred things (קדשׁי

metals taken as the booty of war should have been brought into the treasury of the Temple even way before the Temple was built.

[107] Klein, *1 Chronicles*, 495-96; Knoppers, *1 Chronicles 10-29*, 880; and also idem, "Treasures Won and Lost," 194-297.

[108] The definition and possible connotation of the gifts (התרומה), the tithes (המעשׂר), and the sacred things (הקדשׁים) in the different contexts are to be given in Chapter 3, where I deal with the temple revenue.

הקדשים) to the priests and Levites according to each group's share (v. 14). Kore was assisted by six more officials in the priestly towns (v. 15).

The Chronicler's claims about the temple treasurers in the three different passages (1 Chr 9:26-29, 1 Chr 26:20-28 and 2 Chr 31:11-16) are presented below according to the Chronicler's chronological framework.

Table 3. The Chronicler's Various Descriptions about Treasurers

Time	David's reign	Hezekiah's reign	The Post-exilic period
Text	1 Chr 26:20-28	2 Chr 31:10-11	1 Chr 9:26-29
Offices	האצרות בית יהוה and האצרות הקדשים.	הלשכות בבית יהוה, where people's contribution is kept.	The supervision of הלשכות and האצרות בית האלהים.
Officials	Shebuel was in charge of both categories of the treasuries; the Gershonites were in charge of האצרות בית יהוה and the Amramites were in charge of האצרות הקדשים.	For the process of storage, Conaniah and his brother were in charge and they were assisted by ten more officials, but for the process of distribution, Kore, the gatekeeper of the east gate, was in charge, and he was assisted by six more officials.	The four chief gatekeepers supervised the הלשכות and האצרות בית האלהים.

This table shows that "the treasuries of the dedicated gifts" (האצרות הקדשים) are not mentioned in the post-exilic context. But "the chambers" (הלשכות), said to have been built during the reign of Hezekiah, are mentioned in the post-exilic context.[109] These changes can be explained by the socio-historical changes in Israel and Judah. The treasuries of the dedicated gifts (האצרות הקדשים), which kept the war booty dedicated by the

[109] According to 1 Chr 28:11-12, David handed over his plan for the future Temple to Solomon. In this blueprint, the store chambers and treasuries of the Temple are already included. Thus the novelty of Hezekiah's measure to build the store chambers lies not in the chambers themselves, but in their purpose, that is to store the people's contribution.

king or military leaders, had no relevance in the post-exilic setting. In contrast, the significance of הלשכות, which kept the people's contribution for the support of the clergy, would have greatly increased in the post-exilic situation. The increased prominence of הלשכות is demonstrated by the fact that the references to הלשכות attached to the Temple mostly appear in exilic or post-exilic texts.[110]

The Chronicler consistently claims that the Levites were appointed to supervise and maintain the temple treasuries from the monarchic period through the post-exilic period, a claim that does not agree with other biblical authors' descriptions of the temple treasurers. The following section addresses the differences between the Chronicler's claim about the temple treasurers and other biblical authors' claims.

2.2.4. The Chronicler's Distinctive Claims about the Temple Treasurers

References to the temple treasurers are very rare in the Hebrew Bible. Only a few references are found outside of Chronicles, such as in Neh 12:44; 13:5, 12, 13.[111] According to Neh 12:44, Nehemiah appointed people over the chambers in the temple treasuries, but their identity is not included. The same book relates that, before Nehemiah's reform, a large chamber of the treasury was overseen by Tobiah (Neh 13:5). During his second term, however, Nehemiah appointed the temple treasurers, who included a priest, a scribe, a Levite and one officer (Neh 13:13).[112] Although each member's identity is not clear, it is evident that they were not all Levites,

[110] The word "a chamber" (לשכה) occurs 47 times in the Hebrew Bible: 8 times in Jeremiah; 23 times in Ezekiel 40-48; twice in Ezra; 7 times in Nehemiah; 5 times in Chronicles; once in 1 Sam 9:22 and in 2 Kgs 23:11. The references to the store chambers attached to the Temple can be roughly classified by their usages as follows: (1) treasury rooms in 1 Chr 28:12 and Ezr 8:29; (2) storerooms for offerings in Ezek 42:12-13; Neh 13:5; (3) storerooms for tithes of fruit, grain, wine and oil in Neh 10:38-40; Neh 12:44; 13:5; 2 Chr 31:11-12; (4) storerooms for frankincense in Neh 13:5; (5) storerooms for the sacred vessels in Neh 13:5; (6) the holy chambers for the priests for cooking of offerings in Ezek 46:19; (7) A washing room for offerings in Ezek 40:38; (8) a space for the sacrificial meal in Ezek 42:13 and the like. See A. Even-Shoshan, ed., *A New Concordance of the Bible: Thesaurus of the Language of the Bible Hebrew and Aramaic Roots, Words, Proper Names, Phrases and Synonyms* (Jerusalem: Kiryat-Sefer, 2000) 612; D. Kellerman, "לשכה," *TDOT* 3:33-38; and also Louis Jonker, "לשכה," *NIDOT* 1:822-23.

[111] Victor P. Hamilton, "אצר," *NIDOT* 1:487-89.

[112] J. Schaper ("The Temple Treasury committee in the Times of Nehemiah and Ezra," *VT* 47 [1997] 201-2) argues that the scribe in Neh 13:13 is the Zadokite since his name is Zadok, and another assistant Hanan is the Levite because of his genealogy. Thus, "the trea-

which coincides with other representations of cultic administration in Ezra-Nehemiah.[113]

In contrast, as we have consistently seen, the Chronicler claims that the Levites—and only the Levites—were temple treasurers throughout the history of Israel. Moreover, these were under the supervision of the four chief gatekeepers according to 1 Chr 9:26-29. Clearly, we need to ask what this insistence on levitical status can tell us about either the historical practices or the ideological interests of the Chronicler, questions I will take up in Chapter 3. Before moving to these topics, one set of texts pertaining to the Chronicler's presentation of levitical cultic administrators remains to be discussed: 2 Chr 24:5-11 and 2 Chr 34:9-13, the set of texts pertaining to levitical tax-collectors.

2.3. The Chronicler's Descriptions of Tax Collectors

2 Chr 24:5-11 and 34:8-13 are products of the Chronicler's redactional work on 2 Kgs 12:5-11 and 2 Kgs 22:3-7. Both texts describe repair work on the Temple during the reigns of Joash and Josiah respectively, and both articulate how, when, and by whom the funds for these renovations were procured. Unlike the texts which I dealt with previously, these two texts do not belong to a David's Installation Block. Nevertheless, both exhibit the characteristic features of the Chronicler's redaction, and contain the Chronicler's distinctive tendencies. These texts are important for the pres-

---

surers' committee," named by J. Schaper, is composed of two priests and two Levites, if his conjecture is correct.

[113] For instance, Ezra 8:33-34 mentions that the officials who weighed out the gold, the silver and the vessels which Ezra brought from Babylon, and recorded them were two priests and two Levites. Neh 10:39 also relates that the priests were with the Levites when the Levites received the tithes from the people. In the book of Ezra-Nehemiah the Levites are distinguished from the priests. Concerning the cultic activities, the Levites always accompany the priests to assist them (Neh 12:47). However, the Levites are a member of the assembly which is composed of priests, the Levites and the heads of the families (Ezra 1:5; 2:70; 3:12; *et als.*). The organization of the temple personnel seems to have already been fixed: the priests, the Levites, the singers, the gatekeepers, the temple servants, and the descendants of Solomon's servants (Ezra 2:40-55; Neh 7:43-60; 7:73; 10:28). The singers and gatekeepers are not included into the Levites, unlike in Chronicles. Nevertheless the multiple functions of the Levites are represented in the book of Ezra-Nehemiah. The Levites are depicted as teachers (Neh 8:7, 9), treasurers (Neh 13:13), tax collectors (Neh 10:37-39) and officers (Ezra 3:9) as well as cultic personnel.

ent study because they provide information concerning temple revenue, specifically the so-called "temple tax," and disclose the Chronicler's distinctive view on the matter of the temple tax.[114] I treat the two texts separately, and then consider them together in the end of this section (section 2.3.3).

2.3.1. Analysis of 2 Chr 24:5-11: Joash's Restoration of the Temple

2 Chr 24:4-14 concerns King Joash's restoration of the Temple. Since my concern is not with the restoration process itself, but with the levitical involvement in the temple economy, I focus on verses 5-11, where the Levites are involved in the collection of monies to fund the project. The Chronicler hews to the basic narrative of his source, 2 Kgs 12:5-11, where King Joash takes actions to secure the financing for repairing the Temple. However, the Chronicler deviates from his source in his descriptions of Joash's specific measures to secure the funds and of the agents who execute the king's policies.

The Chronicler's redactional fingerprints are easy to detect in this passage. Here, in concert with his interests elsewhere, the Chronicler includes the Levites in the process of restoring the Temple, even though they are not mentioned in 2 Kgs 12:5-11 (cf. 2 Chr 24:5, 6, and 11).[115] Additionally, the Chronicler leaves a trace of his editorial tendency to connect the Temple with the sanctuary in the wilderness period (2 Chr 24:6, 9), as I observed in the first gatekeeper section (1 Chr 9:17-32). Finally, the Chronicler highlights the people's reaction to Joash's new measures to secure funds for the restoration of the Temple as שׂמח; the people's joyful response here to the king's fundraising effort is characteristic of the Chronicler's crowd scenes (1 Chr12:40; 15:25; 29:9, 22; 2 Chr 7:10; 15:15; 20:27; 23:13, 21; 24:10; 29:36; 30:21, 23, 25, 26).[116]

[114] Here I use the term "temple tax" following other scholars who interpret the money collected in 2 Chr 24:5-11 and 2 Chr 34:8-13 as a tax. I also use the term "tax collectors" for those who were involved in money collection for the Temple, following the scholarly convention. But I argue in this section that the money collected for the temple was not a tax, but rather an offertory or contribution from people.

[115] See Dillard, *2 Chronicles*, 187.

[116] W. Johnstone (*2 Chronicles 10-36: Guilt and Atonement* [Vol. 2 of *1 and 2 Chronicles*; 2 vols.; JSOTSup 254; Sheffield: Sheffield Academic Press, 1997] 141) comments that "responding with joy" is the Chronicler's key term for the ideal, united response of the community.

Beyond these somewhat superficial indications of the Chronicler's activity, we can also discern several more weighty changes that he has made to his source material. Indeed, a close reading of 2 Chr 24:5-11,which parallels 2 Kgs 12:5-7, reveals that the Chronicler takes care to smooth out internal inconsistencies he finds in Kings, and provides legal justification for King Joash's apparently innovative policy of seeking funding for temple restoration from the populace of Judah and all Israel.

The Kings version begins with Joash commanding the priests to set aside monies which belonged to the following categories in order to repair the Temple: (1) כל כסף הקדשים אשר־יובא בית־יהוה (all the money offered as sacred donations); (2) כסף עובר איש כסף נפשות ערכו (the money for which each person is assessed-the money from the assessment of persons); and (3) כל־כסף אשר יעלה על לב־איש להביא בית יהוה (the money from the voluntary offerings brought into the Temple).[117] In the Kings' version, compli-

[117] The relationship between these three categories is not so obvious, but many commentators consider that the first כסף is articulated by the following three other כסף. See James A. Montgomery, *A Critical and Exegetical Commentary on the Books of Kings* (ICC; Edinburgh: T & T Clark, 1951) 428; Mordechai Cogan and Hayim Tadmor, *II Kings: A New Translation with Introduction and Commentary* (AB 11; New York: Doubleday, 1988) 135; Volkmar Fritz, *1 & 2 Kings: A Continental Commentary* (trans. Anselm Hagedorn; CCOT; Minneapolis: Fortress Press, 2003) 302; and Marvin A. Sweeney, *I & II Kings: A Commentary* (OTL; Louisville: Westminster John Knox Press, 2007) 347. I also interpret the first כסף encompassing all the subsequent כסף, following the majority of commentators. The first category, the money of the sacred donations (כל כסף הקדשים), originally belongs to the Temple treasuries. This could include a wide category of offerings, such as obligatory offerings, votive offerings, freewill offerings, contributions (תרומות) and the like. See Gray, *I & II Kings*, 585. Thus, it needs to be clarified which offerings should be deposited for financing the Temple's renovation. The following phrases (two and third categories of money) specify what the first category includes. The second category, כסף עובר איש כסף נפשות ערכו, is difficult to translate. כסף עובר of 2 Kgs 12:5 can be translated as "the current money" based on כסף עובר of Gen 23:16. Lev 27:2-8 provides an important clue to understand the rest of phrase, איש כסף נפשות ערכו, since it uses a similar phrase to explain how to offer votive offerings in accordance with an offerer's age and gender (Lev 27:2, בערכך נפשת). Thus, כסף עובר איש כסף נפשות ערכו of 2 Kgs 12:5 can be translated as "current money, the money that each one offers at one's valuation." Based on this reading, I may conclude that the second category means the votive offering, which is offered with respect to each one's age and gender. The third category, כל־כסף אשר יעלה על לב־איש להביא בית יהוה, is likely to be the voluntary offerings. On the other hand, 2 Kgs 12:17 confirms that guilt offerings and sin offerings were not deposited as the fund for the repair work of the Temple. Thus, these two offerings are excluded from the sacred donations (the first category), which were solicited for the Temple's renovation. In 2 Kgs 12:5, therefore, Joash directed the priests to separate the money for the votive offerings and for the voluntary offerings to finance the restoration of the Temple.

ance with the command is far from immediate: the priests do not obey the king's command until the twenty-third year of his reign.

Why this delay? The problem, perhaps, is that according to the Pentateuchal tradition (Lev 22:2-16; Num 18:8-10, 19), the sacred donations, both votive and voluntary, are for the support of the priests.[118] In brief, in the Kings version, Joash unlawfully commands the priests to reallocate a certain amount of money from their own share to restore the Temple.[119] In a broader context, this command is highly irregular: typically, the building or restoration of temples was initiated by the kings and funded from the royal treasury in the Iron II period of Ancient Near East.[120] It is no wonder that the priests did not comply with the king's command (2 Kgs 12:6-7).

The Chronicler's picture is somewhat different. First, whereas in 2 Kgs 12:5, the king summons only the priests (ויאמר יהואש אל־הכהנים), in 2 Chr 24:5, he commands the Levites as well as the priests (ויקבץ את־הכהנים והלוים ויאמר להם). Second, the Chronicler changes the king's command regarding the financing of the restoration. Instead of ordering the priests to tap into votive and voluntary offerings, as in 2 Kgs 12:5, the king commands the priests and the Levites to collect money annually from Judah and all Israel to repair the Temple (2 Chr 24:5).

It is evident that the Chronicler seems to have understood Joash's policy in Kings as unlawful since the king's command violated the priestly prerog-

[118] The Chronicler also considers sacred donations as belonging to the temple treasuries (1 Chr 26:20, 26-28; 28:12; 2 Chr 31:12, 14).

[119] Cogan and Tadmor, *II Kings*, 140; Fritz, *1 & 2 Kings*, 303.

[120] In the ancient Near East, one of the important royal duties was to make their patron god(s) satisfied and appeased to keep peace in the land, and to set order in the country. Either because of such religious sentiments or political motivation, kings built or rebuilt temples, provided new cult statues, or furnished cultic paraphernalia of all kinds as the royal annals of Mesopotamian kings state. In many instances, kings also regularly sent offerings to the temple, and granted land, and flocks to produce offerings in perpetuity. See A. Leo Oppenheim, "Babylonian and Assyrian Historical Texts," *ANET*, 265-317; J. F. Robertson, "The Social and Economic Organization of Ancient Mesopotamia Temples," in *Civilizations of the Ancient Near East* Vol. I (ed. Jack M. Sasson; New York: Simon & Schuster Macmillan, 1995) 445; and J. N. Postgate, "The Role of the Temple in the Mesopotamian Secular Community," in *Man, Settlement and Urbanism* (ed. Peter J Ucko et al.; Cambridge: Schenkman, 1972) 812. Concerning Joash's unusual command, scholars interpret it in various ways. On the one hand, R. Dillard (*2 Chronicles*, 188) explains the intentions of Joash as his attempt to reassert royal prerogatives over the cult. Thus the priests' response to this command is also interpreted as their resistance to royal power. On the other hand, E. L. Curtis (*The Books of Chronicles*, 434) suggests that Joash's attempt must have been caused by the impoverished condition of the royal treasuries.

ative. Thus, the Chronicler changes the king's command, making it both legal and reasonable; the requisite funds are to be obtained from a collection to be taken up for this specific purpose, not by diverting a percentage of the priests' own funds.

Scholars have conjectured that the Chronicler, through this change, retrojected contemporary practices into the monarchic period.[121] This conjecture is based on their reading 2 Chr 24:5 as connected with Neh 10:33: "We also lay on ourselves the obligation to charge ourselves yearly one-third of a shekel for the service of the house of our God." However, it is not clear that Joash's command is directly connected with the regulation of Neh 10:33. There is no linguistic connection between them except בשׁנה, a slender reed on which to build an argument for the connection of Joash's command in 2 Chr 24:5 and the regulation of Neh 10:33. Moreover, Joash's new measure does not explicitly stipulate the amount of money to be collected, unlike Neh 10:33. If Joash's command was meant to be a novel institution of a tax, the amount of money to be collected from each person should have been stipulated.

At any rate, the Chronicler reports that the Levites failed to go out to collect money (2 Chr 24:5b). The attribution of the failure to the Levites in 2 Chr 24:5b sounds unlike the Chronicler since he generally takes pains to praise the Levites at every opportunity. This is a major point in Williamson's argument that 2 Chr 12:5b-6 is a secondary gloss, which he claims belongs to "a pro-priestly reviser," who wanted to soften the criticism of the priesthood in 2 Kings 12.[122]

However, it is unlikely that 2 Chr 24:5b is intended to blame the Levites for the failure to implement the king's command. In 2 Chr 24:6, the king summons Jehoiada, the chief priest, and rebukes him for negligence. If 2 Chr 24:5b-6 was added by the pro-priestly reviser, as Williamson argues, why did the reviser not insert the Levites in verse 6 in order to make them responsible for the negligence?

[121] Japhet, *I & II Chronicles*, 843.

[122] H. G. M. Williamson (*1 and 2 Chronicles*, 320) develops Adam C. Welch's original argument that 2 Chr 24:5-6 was a later addition, by pointing out six reasons why these two verses came from the pro-priestly reviser (Welch, *The Work of the Chronicler*, 78-80). However, R. Dillard disputes Williamson's six points, one by one, and concludes that verses 5b-6 present some difficulties, but they may not be so great as to require positing a later author for the section (Dillard, *2 Chronicles*, 189-90). I found Dillard's argument to be more likely.

Without assuming a later reviser for this section, the Chronicler's comment on the Levites' failure (v. 5b) and Joash's reproach of Jehoiada's slackness (v. 6) can be explained by the Chronicler's systematic presentation of the relationship between the priests and Levites. As I have observed before, the Chronicler considers the ultimate responsibility for the cultic matters to rest with the priests. In 2 Chr 24:6, Joash, knowing his first command to have been neglected, summons Jehoiada (cf. 2 Kgs 12:8, in which Jehoiada and the priests were summoned) and reprimands him for not sending out the Levites to collect money.[123] 2 Chr 24:6 thus gives a hint as to why the Levites failed to collect money: they were not ordered by Jehoiada to do so. This statement coheres with my interpretation of 2 Chr 24:5b: the priests' resistance accounts for the Levites' noncompliance.

How are the Chronicler's readers intended to view the apparent impasse between priestly and royal powers? Is Joash overstepping the legitimate bounds of his authority? Is the priests' resistance ground for praise or blame? Perhaps what was lacking, in the priests' eyes, was legal justification for their participation in an innovative fund-raising scheme. It is this backing in Pentateuchal law that the Chronicler, speaking through Joash, now provides: in 2 Chr 24:6, the king implies that his fund-raising effort should be identified with an ancient tradition in the Pentateuch whose purpose was to provide funds for the then sanctuary ("the tax levied by Moses ... for the tent of the covenant"). By means of this legal fiction, Joash's initiative acquires a veneer of antiquity and legitimacy: the association of the command with Moses and the wilderness period, justifies the king's new measure to collect money from the people.[124]

What specific legal precedent does Joash invoke? The majority of commentators of Chronicles associate the Chronicler's version of Joash's command in 1 Chr 24:6 with Exod 30:12-16, the "census tax." However, the

[123] H. G. M. Williamson (*1 and 2 Chronicles*, 320) takes notice of an unusual form of the title of Jehoiada in the phrase "Jehoiada the chief" (יהוידע הראש) of verse 6 (הראש instead of כהן הראש, which is regularly used in Chronicles), and argues that this unusual title indicates the hand of a different author. See also De Vries, *1 and 2 Chronicles*, 345 and McKenzie, *1–2 Chronicles*, 316. However, W. Rudolph (*Chronikbücher*, 274), S. Japhet ("The Supposed Common Authorship," 343-44), and R. Dillard (*2 Chronicles*, 186) consider this title as an abbreviation of the Chronicler's ordinary designation "the chief priest" (כהן הראש) which occurs five times in Chronicles (1 Chr 27:5; 2 Chr 19:11; 24:11; 26:20; 31:10). I found the latter scholars' opinions more likely.

[124] See Rudolph, *Chronikbücher*, 275; Curtis and Madsen, *The Books of Chronicles*, 435; Japhet, *I & II Chronicles*, 844; and De Vries, *1 and 2 Chronicles*, 345.

linguistic connection between the Chronicler's description of the money to be collected from the people and the regulations of Exod 30:12-16 is not explicit. According to Exod 30:12-16, every male from twenty years old and upward (v. 14) shall pay "a ransom for himself" (כפר נפשו, vv. 12 and 15) of a half-shekel, as "an offering to Yahweh" (תרומה ליהוה, v. 13). This "atonement money" (כסף הכפרים, v. 16) will be assigned "for the service of the Tent of Meeting" (על־עבדת אהל מועד, v. 16). There is, then, a legal precedent that establishes that sanctuary maintenance may be funded by the extraction of funds from the populace. But the Chronicler does not actually use any of the terms which indicate the census tax in Exodus, such as כפר נפשו, כסף הכפרים, or even תרומה ליהוה.

Rather, the Chronicler uses משׂאת here and in verse 9 to indicate the people's contribution for the repair of the Temple.[125] It has been argued that the term designates a certain kind of taxation in the following three cases: 1 Chr 24:6, 9 and Amos 5:11. However, it is very unlikely that the usages in Chronicles refer to any kind of tax. If משׂאת did designate a tax, it should be stated how it would be levied and on who or what (a person, a product or an activity). 2 Chr 24:6 does not give any such details.

Furthermore, this term does not have any relation to the concept of expiation. By avoiding the terms denoting atonement, the Chronicler dissociates the money to be collected by Joash from the atonement money which was paid out only once in one's lifetime at the census. By means of this dissociation, משׂאת could be collected annually without violating the Mosaic regulation of Exod 30:12-16. Yet at the same time, by associating משׂאת with Moses as well as the congregation of Israel and by claiming that its purpose was for the service of "the Tent of Testimony" (לאהל העדות), the Chronicler provides Joash's command with antiquity and legitimacy.[126]

[125] משׂאת occurs 15 times in the Old Testament, and belongs to the semantic field of gifts or presents. *HALOT*, 640; and Gerald A. Klingbeil, "משׂאת," *NIDOT* 1:1113-15.

[126] In 2 Chr 24:6, the משׂאת is said to be decreed by Moses and the congregation of Israel. S. Japhet (*The Ideology of the Book of the Chronicles and its Place in Biblical Thought* [New York: Peter Lang, 1997] 417) considers the inclusion of "the congregation of Israel" (הקהל לישׂראל) here is an example of the "democratizing" trend in Chronicles, where the people are often considered as an active force in history, thereby limiting the monarch's exclusive authority. Concerning the phrase לאהל העדות, H. G. M. Williamson (*1 and 2 Chronicles*, 320) argues that it came from the pro-priestly reviser since that phrase occurs in Num 9:15; 17:22, 23; 18:2 and 2 Chr 26:6. However, considering the Chronicler's tendency of taking or creating a certain term from a relatively wide linguistic pool, I argue that a rare expression does not necessarily indicate a different redactor. R. Dillard (*2 Chronicles*, 190)

Through the Chronicler's reformulation of Joash's command, the king's exceptional measure to finance the repair work of the Temple with the people's contributions is firmly justified. This justification is strengthened by the next verse, where the king gives more explanation as to why the restoration funds are necessary. Simply, the sons of Athaliah had broken into the Temple and had used up all the dedicated things of the Temple for their gods: כי עתליהו המרשעת בניה פרצו את־בית האלהים וגם כל־קדשי בית־יהוה עשו לבעלים: (2 Chr 24:7).[127] As I observed in the previous sections concerning the temple treasuries, for the Chronicler, the purpose of the dedicated gifts of the Temple is to maintain the Temple (1 Chr 26:27b). Moreover, for the Chronicler it was specifically the king's responsibility to fill the treasuries of the dedicated things (1 Chr 26:26-28), so Joash's interest in "restoring" not only the bricks and mortar of the Temple but also, so to speak, its endowment, is laudable and legitimate.

In 2 Chr 24:8, Joash commands a chest to be made and put outside the gate of the Temple as an alternative method of collecting the funds for repairing the Temple: ויאמר המלך ויעשו ארון אחד ויתנהו בשער בית־יהוה חוצה:. Here the Chronicler changes two things from his source, 2 Kgs 12:10. The two texts suggest the same solution for collecting money, that is, to put a chest in the temple precinct, but the Chronicler comes up with a different idea concerning who took the lead in this matter, and where the chest was placed. In 2 Kgs 12:10, it is "Jehoiada" who made a chest and placed it "beside the altar on the right side" (אצל המזבח בימין). In 2 Chr 24:8, however, it is "the king" who made a chest put "outside the gate of the Temple" (בשער בית־יהוה חוצה). What do the Chronicler's two changes imply?

---

also disputes Williamson's opinion by arguing that the Chronicler's choice of העדות could have been influenced by his previous use of it in 2 Chr 23:11.

[127] The interpretation of the phrase בניה has been in debate among scholars since Athaliah had no sons when she became queen. Her husband, King Jehoram killed all his brothers when he became king (2 Chr 21:4), and the troops who came with the Arabs killed all the brothers of Ahaziah. He was the only son left to Athaliah (2 Chr 22:1). Some suggest interpreting בניה as "her adherents," rather than her biological sons, without changing its vocalization. See Curtis and Madsen, *The Books of Chronicles*, 435; and Williamson, *1 and 2 Chronicles*, 321. W. Rudolph (*Chronikbücher*, 274; see also McKenzie, *1–2 Chronicles*, 315) proposes changing its pointing slightly to בֹּנֶיהָ (her builders). Reading it as "her priests" (כבניה) has also been suggested. All these suggestions read too much into the text. בן has a wide range of semantic value in the Hebrew Bible, and it often designates "member or fellow of a group" (see *HALOT*, 137-38). Thus, בניה can be simply interpreted as "the follower or adherents" of Athaliah, without causing any contradiction to 2 Chr 21:4 and 2 Chr 22:1.

First, the king's initiative to make a chest perfectly conforms to the Chronicler's idea about the king's role responsibility for the upkeep of the Temple.[128] By this change, the Chronicler eliminates a problem contained in the Kings version (2 Kgs 12:7-9), which, after all, has Joash specifically excluding the priests from involvement in the fund-raising in verses 7-8, only to have Jehoiada instituting the collection box in verse 9!

Second, the change of the location of the chest seems to have been motivated by the inaccessibility of the chest placed beside the altar envisioned in Kings.[129] Since the laity could not enter the inner courts of the Temple, the priests who guarded the threshold took the money from the laity in order to put it in the chest beside the altar. The Chronicler's change of location simplifies the logistics: the laity could put their money directly into the chest. In fact, the Chronicler's change brings the situation into greater conformity to the king's command to restrict any priestly involvement in the collection of the money in 2 Kgs 12:8-9.[130]

[128] Joash's new measure, putting a chest at the entrance gate of the Temple, has often been compared with the practice in Babylonian temples. The Ebabbar temple archives reveal that the "royal basket" or "cash box" (*quppu*) was set at the entrance of the Ebabbar temple as well as the small sanctuaries in Sippar in order to collect the king's portion of temple income. In fact, this practice was introduced by Nabonidus (556–539 B.C.E.), and had been continued by the Achaemenid kings. For the supervision of this royal cash box, a special royal official (*ša muḫḫi quppi* or *rab quppi*) was dispatched by the king. The function of the royal cash boxes in the Neo-Babylonian temples is not identical with that of the chest that Joash installed. The former is for the benefit of the king, but the latter is for the upkeep of the Temple. Nevertheless, the presence of the cash box or chest at the entrance of the Temple would have been known throughout the ancient Near East. Concerning a royal cash box in the Neo-Babylonian temples, see A. C. V. M. Bongenaar, *The Neo-Babylonian Ebabbar Temple at Sippar: Its Administration and its Prospography* (Leiden: Nederlands Historisch-Archaelogisch Instituut te Istanbul, 1997); and Michael Jursa, *Neo-Babylonian Legal and Administrative Documents: Typology, Contents and Archives* (Münster: Ugarit-Verlag, 2005). For the references to *quppu*, see the two texts from Sippar: BM 64751 and BM 63917 from T. C. Pinches, *Cuneiform Texts from Babylonian Tablets in the British Museum*, Part 55-57 (London : The Trustees, 1982). See also Christopher Tuplin, "The Administration of the Achaemenid Empire," in *Coinage and Administration in the Athenian and Persian Empires: The Ninth Oxford Symposium on Coinage and Monetary History* (ed. Ian Carradice; Oxford: B.A.R., 1987) 151.

[129] Johnstone, *2 Chronicles 10-36*, 140.

[130] Many scholars have suggested that the Chronicler's phrase "outside of the temple gate" for the location of the chest reflects the practice of his own day since they consider that the access to the inner court had been restricted to the clergy from the Second Temple period. See Curtis and Madsen, *The Books of Chronicles*, 435; Williamson, *1 and 2 Chronicles*, 321; and Dillard, *2 Chronicles*, 191. However, it is not so obvious whether that practice originated from the Second Temple period. H. G. M. Williamson points out 2 Chr 6:13 and 2 Chr 23:13 as bases for his argument. R. Dillard proffers Amos 2:8 and 2 Chronicles 23 to support his

Since the chest was put outside the temple gate, it needed to be secured by the gatekeepers.[131] They were the ones who brought in the full chest daily according to 2 Chr 24:11. In this way, the Levites could still be involved in collecting the fund.

After convincing the clergy to collect money from the people, Joash issues a proclamation in Judah and Jerusalem to bring the same kind of contributions (משׂאת) [which had been imposed] on Israel in the wilderness by Moses.[132] By the Chronicler's new exegesis of Exod 30:12-16, Joash's measure is, as we have seen, justified by its connection to Moses (משׂאת משׁה) and to the wilderness period (במדבר). And this time, apparently, the legal justification persuades its audience: in 2 Chr 24:10, the king's proclamation is welcomed by the people with enthusiasm, a characteristic expression of the Chronicler: וישׂמחו כל־השׂרים וכל־העם ויביאו וישליכו לארון עד־לכלהה:. With this verse, the Chronicler underlines the fact that the money that the people put into the chest was their voluntary contribution, rather than their compulsory payment of taxes: all the leaders and people welcomed the proclamation with joy, and they thrust money into the chest until it was full.[133]

---

argument. Indeed, the passage of 2 Chr 23:5-6 seems to support their arguments, but this text does not specify in which court the lay people were standing. The division of the courts of the Temple into two was an already well-known architectural feature in the book of Kings ("the two courts": 2 Kgs 21:5; 23:12; the reference to "the inner court": 1 Kgs 6:36; 7:12; the reference to "the outer courts for king": 2 Kgs 16:18). In this matter, the Chronicler's treatment is not so different although it is not as systematic as in Ezekiel. The distinction between the court of the priests and the great court appears only one time in 2 Chr 4:9, but in Ezekiel 40-48, the inner court of the Temple is clearly distinguished from the outer court of the Temple. When the Chronicler refers to the laity in relation to their location in the temple courts, he does not specify where they stood either in the inner court or in the outer court. For example, the following texts refer to "the people who stood in the courts of the Temple," but without any clarification of which court it is: Jer 19:14; 26:2; 2 Chr 23:5; 24:21; 29:16; Neh 8:16; 13:7. If the prohibition of the laity's accessibility to the inner court was newly introduced in the Second Temple period, the Chronicler should have emphasized it, but he did not. It means that this practice had already been known to people before the Chronicler's own time, so that he did not need to do so. It is more likely that the modification of location of the chest reflects the Chronicler's intention to harmonize the king's command in 2 Kgs 12:8-9 and its implementation in 2 Kgs 12:10, as I argue.

[131] W. Johnstone (2 *Chronicles 10-36*, 141) proposes this gate to be the east gate, where other major transactions take place. For the basis of his suggestion, he points out 2 Chr 23:5, but this verse hardly supports his suggestion.

[132] The italicized words are not present in MT 2 Chr 24:9, but inserted to make a better sense of it.

[133] The translator of the Septuagint rendered the phrase ישׂמחו as ἔδωκαν, which reflects ישׂימו instead of ישׂמחו. W. Rudolph, *Chronikbücher*, 274, explains this change as a result

The final verse of the section (2 Chr 24:5-11) exhibits a certain degree of similarity to 2 Kgs 12:11, but some dissimilarities between the two are worth noting. The following table will help us to see the differences between them.

Table 4. A Comparison between
2 Chr 24:11 and 2 Kgs 12:11

	2 Chr 24:11	2 Kgs 12:11
(1) Who brought the chest in?	The Levites.	No mention of it.
(2) Who was responsible for emptying the chest?	The king's secretary and the officer of the chief priest.	The king's secretary and the high priest.
(3) What did they do with the chest?	They emptied it out and brought it back to its place.	They recast the silver and counted.
(4) How often did they do so?	Daily.	No mention of it.

As this table shows, the Chronicler provides a fuller description of the handling of the chest. In the Chronicler's picture, the priestly involvement is very limited. This conforms to the king's command, which cuts off the priests from the collection of money and from the repair work of the Temple (2 Kgs 12:7-8). But who, precisely, are the officials in charge of emptying the chest in Chronicles? The phrase פקדת המלך in 2 Chr 24:11 is traditionally translated as "the royal officers," whom many translators envision as middlemen, who take the chest from the Levites and deliver it to their superiors.[134] However, since פקדת is an abstract noun, it cannot be inter-

of the translator's puzzlement about the people's joy over the new imposition of the tax. Nevertheless, the Lucianic recension (LXX[be2]) reads it as εὐφράνθησαν, which reflects ישׂמחו; see Brooke et al. eds., *The Old Testament in Greek*, 523. The Peshitta, the Targum, and the Vulgate also agree with the MT's rendering. Thus, I consider ἔδωκαν of the LXX as a case of scribal changes. The enthusiastic response of the leaders and people echoes 1 Chr 29:6-9, where people offered willingly with their whole heart to build the Temple. See De Vries, *1 and 2 Chronicles*, 345.

[134] See Williamson, *1 and 2 Chronicles*, 322; and Dillard, *2 Chronicles*, 185. Several modern English versions, such as RSV, NRS, and JPS reflect such a traditional translation,

preted as a concrete plural noun "officers."[135] It would be more accurate to translate אל־פקדת המלך as "according to the king's appointment." Thus the Levites, who guarded the chest at the entrance gate of the Temple, were *appointed by the king* to bring the chest in.[136]

Subsequently, according to the Chronicler, the chest was emptied by the king's secretary and the delegate of the chief priest. In contrast, in the narrative of Kings, the king's secretary and the high priest Jehoiada empty the chest. The Chronicler's change from the high priest to his deputy can be explained as an attempt to distance the high priest from the process of the actual appropriation of the money according to the king's command (presented in 2 Kgs 12:7).[137]

Oddly, the Chronicler's description of what the king's secretary and the delegate of the chief priest do with the chest is much simpler than that in Kings. In 2 Chr 24:11, they simply empty the chest and bring it back to its place. But 2 Kgs 12:11 provides an additional detail: ויצרו וימנו את־הכסף. It is worth examining the two verbs which describe what the king's secretary and the high priest do with the money from the chest: צור and מנה. The verb צור has a wide range of meaning: "tie up or encircle," "attack or fight" and "form or cast."[138] If we understand צור in 2 Kgs 12:11 as "to form or to cast," what the king's secretary and the high priest did with the money was to recast silver before they counted (מנה) the money from the chest.[139] During the reign of Joash, donations that the people brought to

---

but NJB renders it as "for royal inspection," as E. L. Curtis (*The Books of Chronicles*, 435) and W. Johnstone (*2 Chronicles 10-36: Guilt and Atonement*, 141) translate.

[135] Japhet, *I & II Chronicles*, 845. See the following cases, where פקדת, as an abstract noun, designates "service," or "office": Num 4:16; 1 Chr 26:30; esp. 2 Chr 23:18.

[136] S. Japhet (*I & II Chronicles*, 845) suggests that the Levites here probably denote the clergy in general, but it seems not so. Her suggestion cannot explain why the Chronicler modified his source material.

[137] E. L. Curtis (*The Books of Chronicles*, 435-36) comments that the Chronicler's invention of the delegate of the chief priest is probably intended to place the high priest on the same level with the king. In other words, as the king sends his secretary, the high priest also sends a delegate. I. Kalimi (*The Reshaping of Ancient Israelite History*, 172, 183) also comments on this verse in a similar way. He states that the Chronicler creates the hierarchical balance here by making a reference to the delegate of the chief priest. However, Curtis's argument is not reconcilable with the Chronicler's overall tendency in this passage, where the role and responsibility of the king are greatly augmented, as S. Japhet (*I & II Chronicles*, 845) points out.

[138] *HALOT* 1015-16.

[139] Modern English versions, such as KJV, RSV, NRSV, NAS, and JPS render it as "tied it up in the bags," which reflect the rendering of the LXX. The Vulgate renders it as *effunde-*

the Temple were not in the form of coins. They were probably brought in the various forms and grades of silver or gold.[140] Thus, the verb צור in 2 Kgs 12:11 implies that there must have been foundries in the Jerusalem Temple as in Mesopotamian temples.[141]

On the contrary, the Chronicler does not mention the casting, and simply says that the box was emptied daily. Could it be that the Chronicler retrojected his contemporary situation, in which local coins circulated, into the past? That is to say, the Chronicler, writing in a later period, might have thought people donated their contributions in the form of coins. This could explain why he does not mention the casting: because one would have no need for it in a society with access to coinage.[142]

---

bant (poured it out), and the Peshita as ܐܣܩܘ (brought up). In all these translations, it seems that the process of the refinement of the precious metals, which were offered by the people to the Temple, was not taken into account.

[140] Ephraim Stern (*Aracheology of the Land of the Bible Volume II: The Assyrian, Babylonian, and Persian Period [732–332 B.C.E.]* [The Anchor Bible Reference Library; New York: Doublebay, 2001] 555-56) states that before the circulation of coins, which began only from the end of the fifth century B.C.E., metal ingots could have been used for mercantile transactions by weight as currency. Archaeological finds support Stern's statement. According to R. Kletter ("Iron Age Hoards of Precious Metals in Palestine-an 'Underground Economy'?" *Levant* 35 [2003] 139-52), more than 20 hoards of precious metals (silver/gold) have been found in Iron Age contexts in Palestine and these metals are in various shapes: damaged or cut pieces of jewelry and shapeless pieces of silver ("*Hacksilber*"). Scholarly interpretation of their function varies either as "a type of currency, that is, a medium of exchange" (see Seymour Gitin and Amir Golani, "A Silver-Based Monetary Economy in the Seventh Century BCE: a Response to Raz Kletter," *Levant* 36 (2004) 203-5, here 204) or as an indication of "a metal-weight economy (*Gewichtsgeldwirtschaft*)" existed already from the Middle Bronze II period (see "Coinage before Coins? A Response," *Levant* 36 [2004] 207–210, here 209). At any rate, such archaeological finds helps us understand the context of 2 Kgs 12:11 which implies that mixture of *hacksilber*, whole jewelry, beads, gold objects, and the like could have been offered by people to repair the Temple.

[141] Otto Eissfeldt, "Eine Einschmelzstelle am Tempel zu Jerusalem," *FuF* 13 (1937): 163-64; and Dillard, *2 Chronicles*, 190-91. A. C. V. M. Bongenaar (*The Neo-Babylonian Ebabbar Temple at Sippar*, 108) introduces practices of Babylonian temples in relation to the royal cash boxes. He states that the incoming silver collected in the cash boxes of the temple or of the king was transferred to the smiths for refining and casting. According to BM 74430, the incoming silver of the gate (*irbi ša bābi*) and that of the temples of *Annunītu* and *Gula* were handed over by the guardian of the cash box of the temple of *Gula*, to be smelted and cast. 2 Kgs 12:11 is one of the biblical texts (along with Zech 11:13) which indicate the existence of the foundry in the Jerusalem Temple.

[142] Nevertheless, the Chronicler seems not to be unaware of the process of casting or refinement of metal in the foundries of the Temple as 2 Chr 34:17 (see section 2.3.2 of the present study) demonstrates. As for the circulation of coinage in the post-exilic period, Yigal Ronen ("Twenty Unrecorded Samarian Coins," *Israel Numismatic Research* 2 [2007] 29-33) states that, in the late Persian period, during the fourth century B.C.E., there was extensive

Several scholars have theorized that the Chronicler's modifications of his source material (2 Kgs 12:5-11) reflect the actual situation in the Chronicler's own time, especially with regard to a yearly collection of tax (one-third of a shekel), and to the prohibition of the laity from access to the inner court of the Temple.[143] However, my analysis of 2 Chr 24:5-11 reveals that such a hypothesis is not very compelling. In 2 Chr 24:5-11, Joash's attempt to send the Levites to collect money from the whole country had failed. Thus, Joash had the chest set at the entrance of the Temple to collect משׂאת משה. As I argued, there is no basis for identifying this משׂאת משה with the annual temple tax known from Nehemiah 10:33. Rather, it is the people's voluntary contribution, which was collected especially for the repair work on the Temple. 2 Chr 24:14 implies that this collection was not meant to be a permanent measure: once the Temple was repaired, the rest of money from the chest was spent to make the sacred vessels.[144]

Moreover, the actual situation concerning the temple tax in the Chronicler's time is unknown. Neh 10:33 is the only evidence in the Hebrew Bible for the collection of revenue in kind for the Temple during the Persian period. In Neh 10:33 the people made a firm agreement (אמנה) upon the stipulation to give one-third of a shekel yearly for the service in the Temple.[145] However, it is not clear how extensively this stipulation was observed in the Chronicler's time. The existence of such a yearly collection should be confirmed before arguing that the Chronicler retrojected contemporary practices in 2 Chr 24:5-11.[146]

local minting of coins in the coastal cities of Gaza, Ashdod, Ascalon and Dor as well as at Samaria and Jerusalem (Yehud) in the hill country of the Land of Israel. If my conjecture is right, 2 Chr 24:11 can also be considered as an indicator of the Chronicler's time, although it cannot be specified as the fourth century B.C.E. or the early third century B.C.E., when the systematic use of coinage became commonplace.

[143] For example, S. Japhet's comment (*I & II Chronicles*, 842) on 2 Chr 24:5; W. Rudolph's comment (*Chronikbücher*, 274) on 2 Chr 24:6; E. L. Curtis' comment (*The Books of Chronicles*, 435) on 2 Chr 24:8; H. G. M. Williamson's comment (*1 and 2 Chronicles*, 321) on 2 Chr 24:8; and R. Dillard's comment (*2 Chronicles*, 191) on 2 Chr 24:8.

[144] McKenzie, *1–2 Chronicles*, 316.

[145] It needs to be emphasized that the poll tax in Neh 10:33 is not for the maintenance (חזק) of the temple, but rather for the regular services (לעבדה). On the contrary, משׂאת משה of 2 Chr 24:9 is collected to repair the Temple (לחזק את־בית יהוה, 2 Chr 24:12).

[146] The Chronicler does not demonstrate any knowledge about Nehemiah's stipulation in his version of Joash's measure to collect money from people. Evidently the Chronicler did not identify Joash's measure with Nehemiah's poll tax for the Temple, if he even knew about the latter. The second section (2 Chr 34:8-13), which is analyzed below, also shows no awareness of Nehemiah's poll tax.

2.3.2. Analysis of 2 Chr 34:8-13: Josiah's Restoration of the Temple

In 2 Chr 34:9-13 the Chronicler describes the process of the repair work to the Temple during the reign of Josiah. While the Chronicler's story is heavily dependent on that of 2 Kgs 22:3-7, he provides a very different picture of the process by restructuring his source material. The Chronicler's major alterations of 2 Kgs 22:3-7 are related to the role of the king and to the levitical involvement in the repair work on the Temple.

The story begins in the midst of Josiah's campaign of cultic reforms. The first verse of this section (2 Chr 34:8) says that after purging the land and the house of illicit practices and appurtenances of worship, Josiah took measures to repair the Temple in the eighteenth year of his reign. In other words, to the surprise of readers familiar with Kings, in Chronicles, Josiah's cultic reforms were executed *before* the discovery of the book of the law in the Temple.

In addition to this chronological shift, the Chronicler's description of the initiation of the Temple repairs differs from 2 Kgs 22:3-7 in two significant ways: first, in 2 Kings, Josiah sends only Shaphan as an emissary to the high priest Hilkiah to commission him to repair the Temple. In contrast, in 2 Chr 34:8-13, Josiah sends a three person delegation: Shaphan the secretary [הסופר, 2 Chr 34:15], Maaseiah the governor of the city [שׂר־העיר] and Joah the recorder [המזכיר]) whom he also orders to administer the whole project, effectively putting Hilkiah on the periphery of the project.[147] The implication of the Chronicler's account is that the repairs are under the jurisdiction of the king and duly appointed civil authorities, as the titles of the three figures indicate.[148]

[147] W. Rudolph (*Chronikbücher*, 321) argues that these three names had originally been included in the Chronicler's *Vorlage*, that is, 2 Kgs 22:3, but the latter two names were lost later due to their similarity of the final letter (ר). W. Rudolph does not provide any evidence for his argument. W. Rudolph's argument is followed by H. M. G. Williamson (*1 and 2 Chronicles*, 400) and S. L. McKenzie (*1–2 Chronicles*, 361). Both of them argue for the originality of these names in the Chronicler's *Vorlage* based on the commonality of the names and titles in the pre-exilic period. Although S. L. McKenzie provides the references to these names and titles (2 Kgs 18:18, 26, 37; 22:12, 14; 23:8), none of these references gives an exact parallel to the three men and their titles in 2 Chr 34:8. Thus, it is not conclusive that 2 Kgs 22:3 is a corrupted text, which lost the other two names from the original list.

[148] The titles of הסופר and שׂר־העיר are obviously related to the civil authority. See Nili Sacher Fox, *In the Service of the King: Officialdom in Ancient Israel and Judah* (Monographs of Hebrew Union College 23; Cincinnati: Hebrew Union College Press, 2000) 98, 102-3, 150-51. The third title המזכיר appears only 9 times in the Hebrew Bible, and only three people are entitled המזכיר: Jehoshaphat, son of Ahilud (2 Sam 8:16; 20:24; 1 Kgs 4:3//1 Chr 18:15); Joah, son of Asaph (2 Kgs 18:18, 37//Isa 36:3, 22); and Joah son of Joahaz (2 Chr 34:8). In these

The first step in both accounts is to finance the repair work. In the narrative of Kings (2 Kgs 22:4), Josiah directs Shaphan to let Hilkiah retrieve (תמם) the money kept in the temple treasury that had been collected from the people by the keepers of the threshold. In the Chronicler's version, the king's delegation approaches Hilkiah and they (Hilkiah and the three high officials) together "poured out" (יתכו) the money kept in the Temple.[149]

Thus, 2 Chr 34:9 describes that the king's delegation (three royal officials) went to Hilkiah and, with his consent, withdrew silver from the temple treasury in order to pay the laborers and to purchase supplies. The silver cast by Hilkiah and the king's delegation is then collected by "the keepers of the threshold" (שמרי הסף) in both Kings (2 Kgs 22:4) and Chronicles (2 Chr 34:9). The Chronicler now expands on his source: first, he specifies that the keepers of the threshold were Levites (הלוים שמרי הסף) in accordance with his general tendency (*e.g.*, 1 Chr 9:19-22; 2 Chr 23:4). These Levites, moreover, he credits with having accrued donations from the northern tribes (Manassites, Ephraimites and the remnant of Israel)

---

biblical references, המזכיר seems to be a king's spokesperson. The dearth of relevant information hinders one from defining specific activities of this office, but as the above evidence indicates, המזכיר was a high ranking government official during the monarchy. See Fox, *In the Service of the King*, 110-21. On the other hand, W. Johnstone (*1 Chronicles 1 – 2 Chronicles 9*, 213; and idem, *2 Chronicles 10-36*, 236) argues that Shaphan and Joah may well be Levites. Their genealogical information, such as "Shaphan son of Azaliah son of Meshullam" (2 Kgs 22:3) and "Joah son of Asaph" (2 Kgs 18:18), implies that they were Levites. However, what is more worth noting is that the Chronicler does not put any emphasis on the fact that they were Levites. It means that their levitical status, whether it is true or not, is not considered useful to build his own rhetoric here.

[149] Several scholars have argued to read the second verb of MT 2 Chr 34:9, נתן, as נתך based on 2 Chr 34:17. See Eissfeldt, "Eine Einschmelzstelle am Tempel," 163-64; Charles C. Torrey, "The Evolution of a Financier in the Ancient Near East," *JNES* 2 (1943) 295-301, here 301; Rudolph, *Chronikbücher*, 320; Williamson, *1 and 2 Chronicles*, 400; and McKenzie, *1–2 Chronicles*, 361. I adopt this reading for two reasons. First, the verb נתן requires an indirect object, that is, a recipient of the money in the case of 2 Chr 34:9; but no such object is indicated. The verb נתך does not require an indirect object and fits well in the context, as 2 Chr 34:17 indicates. This verse introduces Shaphan's report to the king about what the delegation accomplished (effectively summarizing 2 Chr 34:9-10). According to 2 Chr 34:17, they "poured out the money" (ויתיכו את־הכסף). Here a *Hiphil* form of the verb נתך is used, which means "to pour out" (in Job 10:10) "to melt down" or "to throw away money" (in 2 Kgs 22:9 and 2 Chr 34:17) or "to melt" (in Ezek 22:20). 2 Chr 24:11 also backs this reading: there, the chest was "emptied out" by the king's secretary and the delegate of the chief priest. Although a different verb (a *Piel* form of verb ערה) is used in 2 Chr 24:11, the basic idea is identical, that is, pouring out the money from the chest or the treasury for casting was done by or in the presence of the royal official(s) and the religious representative. It is likely that נתן found its way into 2 Chr 34:9 (ויתנו) by the influence of the following phrase ויתנו, which appears three times in verses 10-11 to refer to the actual delivery of money to those responsible for the repair work.

and the southern tribes, Judahites, Benjaminites, and the inhabitants of Jerusalem that are then put toward the renovation project.[150]

Does the Chronicler's expanded account imply that the Levites circulated throughout all Israel to collect taxes or other donations? S. Japhet comments that the Levites' itinerant collection of tax from all Israel functioned as "an established institution" at the time of Josiah, unlike the reign of Joash when the Levites failed to perform their task and another method was provided for the collection of the money (2 Chr 24:5-8).[151] Yet the Levites are here identified as the keepers of the threshold, not as itinerant tax collectors.[152] Moreover, the Chronicler does not endeavor to justify the practice of collecting money from the people at this time. Rather, he describes it as a *fait accompli*: the text does not provide us any information of how or where the money was collected, but it states unambiguously that the people's contribution for the upkeep for the Temple was collected during the reign of Josiah.

The next two verses (2 Chr 34:10-11) explain how the money was used. They are an almost verbatim repetition of 2 Kgs 22:5-6, but there are subtle differences between the two texts. First, the Chronicler's version has three ויתנו phrases that indicate how the funds were dispensed, whereas the version in Kings has two ויתנו phrases. The Chronicler's version makes it clearer than that of Kings that the money was distributed to three groups of people for payment of the laborers and for the purchase of supplies: the three groups are designated as (1) the overseers of the repair work; (2) workers; (3) the artisans and the builders.

[150] The Chronicler's expanded list of contributors can be explained by his general tendency to treat Israel as a comprehensive term which includes both north and south. See Williamson, *1 and 2 Chronicles*, 400. S. Japhet (*The Ideology of the Book of the Chronicles*, 269) comments on the Chronicler's broad definition of the people of Israel in this way: "The idea of 'all Israel,' that is, the people of Israel in its greatest and most inclusive sense, is indeed fundamental to the book of Chronicles. It appears not only in connection with David's reign or from the time of David on, but throughout the book." The "remnant of Israel" (שארית ישׂראל), as S. Japhet (*I & II Chronicles*, 1027) points out, appears in biblical prose only in Chronicles (1 Chr 12:39; 2 Chr 34:9). In these two occurrences, the term שׁארית ישׂראל seems to refer to "all the rest of people," without having a specific theological nuance as in the occurrences of prophetic texts (*e.g.*, Isa 46:3; Jer 6:9; 31:7; Ezek 9:8; 11:13; Mic 2:12; Zeph 3:13). In the final phrase of verse 9 (וישבי ירושלם), I read ישבי according to the *Ketib* (cf. *Qere*: וישבו). See De Vries, *1 and 2 Chronicles*, 407.

[151] Japhet, *I & II Chronicles*, 1026.

[152] W. Johnstone (*2 Chronicles 10-36*, 237) also comments that the Levites in 2 Chr 34:9 are not itinerant tax-gatherers.

The final two verses of the second section (2 Chr 34:12-13) introduce new information which is not found in 2 Kgs 22:7. First, the Chronicler identifies the supervisors who administered the repair work as Levites. Two of the Merarites, Jahath and Obadiah, and two of the Kohathites, Zechariah and Meshullam, are appointed to oversee the repair work (עליהם מפקדים ... לנצח v. 12). Secondly, the Chronicler notes that the levitical musicians are put in charge of the porters, supervising all the workers (vv. 12-13).[153]

Commentators have often pointed out the absence of the Gershonites in these two verses and the absurdity of the levitical musicians' role at a construction site. Various opinions concerning the former matter have been proffered. W. Rudolph points to 2 Chr 29:12, where the Gershonites are mentioned in the list of Levites who participated in the purification of the Temple during the reign of Hezekiah, and argues that the absence of the Gershonites in 2 Chr 34:12 must have been due to textual corruption.[154] W. Johnstone argues that the Gershonites are not in fact omitted in this list since Asaph's family, who is one of three important groups of the levitcal musicians, is the branch of the Gershonites (1 Chr 6:39-42).[155] These explanations miss the point that the Chronicler tries to make here: 2 Chr 34:12 is not intended to give a complete list of the Levites. As in 1 Chr 26:19, where the Chronicler mentions only two divisions of Levites (the Korahites and Merarites) when he summarizes the families of gatekeepers at the time of David, so here, the Chronicler is providing information about specific individuals' involvement in specific offices. Thus, it is not so strange that the Chronicler enumerates only four Levites, who belong to the Kohathites and the Merarites, i.e., the upper echelon of the temple administration.[156]

[153] At the end of 2 Chr 34:13, the Chronicler adds another list of the Levitical professions: scribes, officials and gatekeepers. The text itself does not clarify whether or how these individuals were involved in the repair of the Temple, but it is not too difficult to picture the presence of scribes, officials and gatekeepers at the construction site of the Temple. Considering the Chronicler's general tendency, the presence of the Levitical scribes, officials and gatekeepers would be essential in the repair work of the Temple since certain areas of the temple precinct were not accessible to lay people.

[154] Rudolph, *Chronikbücher*, 322-23. S. Japhet (*I & II Chronicles*, 1028-29) seems not to deny the possibility of the textual corruption, but she simply leaves this problem unanswered.

[155] Johnstone, *2 Chronicles 10-36*, 238.

[156] The number of the Levites in the upper echelon of the temple administration is worth noting. Here four Levites were appointed to oversee the repair work in the Temple (2 Chr 34:12). In 1 Chr 9:26-27, the four chief gatekeepers supervised the chambers and the

The presence of the levitical musicians at the construction site as the supervisors of the manual work (v. 12b) puzzles many readers. S. Japhet comments: "they are more probably a gloss, added to complete the series of "Levites, scribes, officers and gatekeepers" by the only class of Levites missing, the singers."[157] S. L. McKenzie also considers v. 12b as secondary and "out of place in the context of the report about building repair."[158] However, there is evidence that musicians played a significant role in directing or overseeing construction workers in antiquity.[159] One of Sennacherib's reliefs, entitled "Transport of a bull colossus" clearly shows four supervisors on top of the bull, and two of them are coordinating the traction and the lever with megaphones or trumpets.[160] Second, one of Assurbanipal's records also reveals that music was used in the oversight of brick workers at the construction site of the Temple *ridûti*. According to the Rassam Cylinder, Assurbanipal captured an Arab king and his people during battle and forced them to make bricks.[161] While molding bricks, they spent their days "to the accompaniment of music" (line 95).[162]

---

treasuries in the Temple as well as the guarding duties at the four gates. Interestingly, Nehemiah's temple treasurers' committee was also composed of four clergymen (Neh 13:13). Does this fact imply the presence of the four-member collegial body in the upper echelon of the Temple administration either in the monarchic period or in the post-exilic period? I deal with this question in Chapter 3 where I discuss the Temple staff.

[157] Japhet, *I & II Chronicles*, 1029.

[158] McKenzie, *1–2 Chronicles*, 361. S. J. de Vries (*1 and 2 Chronicles*, 407) also considers v. 12b as secondary.

[159] The following evidence was first pointed out in B. D. Eerdmans, *The Hebrew Book of Psalms: Translated from the Masoretic Text: Edited with Introduction and Commentary* (Leiden: E.J. Brill, 1947), 57-58, 63. W. Rudolph (*Chronikbücher*, 323) quotes this in order to argue the originality of verse 12b in his commentary. R. Dillard (*2 Chronicles*, 280) follows Rudolph's opinion without providing any textual evidence.

[160] For the relief, see Julian Reade, *British Museum Assyrian Sculpture* (Cambridge: Harvard University Press, 1999), 53, Picture 54 (Original Drawings I, 57, showing on WA 124820). For the explanation of the description, see John Malcolm Russell, *Sennacherib's Palace without Rival at Nineveh* (Chicago: The University of Chicago Press, 1991), 108.

[161] The Rassam Cylinder X: 89-95. The Rassam Cylinder was found in 1878 in the ruins of Kuyunjik and first published in H. C. Rawlinson's book, *The Cuneiform Inscriptions of Western Asia Vol V: A Selection from the Miscellaneous Inscriptions of Assyria and Babylonia* (London: Trustees of the British Museum, 1884), Plates 1-10. Its transliteration and translation was done by M. Streck in his book, *Assurbanipal und die letzten assyrischen Könige bis zum Untergang* II: Teil: Texte (Leipzig: Hinrichs, 1916), 2-91. For its English translation, I referred to Daniel D. Luckenbill, *Ancient Records of Assyria and Babylonia Vol. II: Historical Records of Assyria* (New York: Greenwood Press, 1968) 290-323.

[162] The transliteration of line 95 is: *ina elīli ningûti ubbalū ūmšun*. CAD gives its translation as "they spent their days in rejoicing and singing (*CAD* N:217-218).

These two examples of supervision of laborers by musicians are only a small fraction of numerous occasions in antiquity where manual labor was facilitated by musical rhythm. In addition, the usage of the Hebrew verb נִצַּח (*Piel* of נצח) in the Hebrew Bible also supports my interpretation of verses 12-13.[163] The Chronicler uses this verb to describe the levitical musicians' supervisory activity over laborers. The *Piel* form of נצח appears not only in Ezra 3:8, 9; 1 Chr 15:21; 23:4; 2 Chr 2:1, 17; 34:12, 13, but also as a part of the superscriptions for numerous psalms, where the *Piel* participle of נצח, that is, מנצח, designates a music director.[164] The verb also appears in several psalms, where the music director is asked to use נגינות (stringed instruments) to direct the choir (Ps 4:1; 6:1; 61:1; 67:1). Outside of Psalms, the other usages of the verb are mostly related to the construction work in the Temple and to the Levites.[165] It is the Levites who supervised (נצח) the construction work in the Temple. In Ezra 3:8-9, it is reported that the Levites were appointed to supervise the whole process of building the Second Temple. Thus, in the historical context of Ezra and the Chronicler, the levitical leadership in the construction or repair work of the Temple was taken for granted. The exercise of such leadership incorporated the Levites' musical performance, as well as their scribal or administrative skills. The Chronicler's reference to the levitical musicians' supervision of the repair work is not out of place in the present context and verse 12b should not be considered as secondary.[166]

2.4. Summary of Chapter 2

Having analyzed the passages in Chronicles that relate to the Levites' administrative roles in the Jerusalem Temple, what can we now say by way of summary? In synthesizing all of these sections, it is clear that the Chronicler's description of the temple administration shows a certain level

[163] Eerdmans, *The Hebrew Book of Psalms*, 57-58.

[164] *HALOT*, 716.

[165] Exceptionally, in 1 Chr 15:21, verb נצח is used to express the levitical musicians' role in leading the ritual procession.

[166] Josephus also gives a very interesting report concerning the building process of the Second Temple. According to *Antiquities* XV § 390, Herod made a thousand priests teach quarrying technique and carpentry to the workmen before they began to build the Temple. This is another example of clerical involvement in the construction work of the temples in antiquity. For this reason, 2 Chr 34:13b is neither unusual nor redundant. See also Curits and Madsen, *The Books of Chronicles*, 507.

of consistency on the following points: First, the Chronicler insists that the Levites were involved in the temple administration, particularly as gatekeepers and treasurers. Secondly, the Chronicler legitimizes the levitical involvement in the temple administration by tracing the origins of their duties not only to Pentateuchal traditions, but also to King David. That the Chronicler rehearses these themes multiple times should be abundantly clear. More interesting, perhaps, are the varied strategies and devices that the Chronicler uses to establish these points. Indeed, the benefit of examining the passages that deal with the Levites so closely is that we are now able to discern the precise, ingenious, and very subtle methods that the Chronicler uses to paint a portrait of levitical involvement in the temple economy.

2.5. The Chronicler's Methods

These methods can be summarized according to ten different categories.[167]

(1) To create or to highlight a particular genealogical connection:

Shallum is one of the gatekeepers in the Persian period (1 Chr 9:17).[168] By highlighting (inventing?) his genealogical connection to Korah (a Levite in the wilderness period: 1 Chr 9:19) and to Zechariah (a Korahite gatekeeper during the reign of David: 1 Chr 9:22-23 and 1 Chr 26:1, 14), the Chronicler establishes the continuity of the office of gatekeepers throughout the history of Israel, and also confirms that the gatekeepers are Levites. However, other biblical texts indicate that the levitical status of gatekeepers was not confirmed until late in the exilic or the post-exilic period, as I showed in section 2.1.1.3. Thus, Shallum's levitical lineage reflects the Chronicler's intention to bolster the levitical status of gatekeepers in his own time.

(2) To coin a new term:

The Chronicler coins a new term by combining well-known phrases taken from earlier biblical texts to convey a specific message. For example, the Chronicler uses a new term to connect the office of gatekeepers of his own day to that of the wilderness period, and to that of the First Temple,

[167] M. Fishbane (*Biblical Interpretation*, 380-440) and I. Kalimi (*The Reshaping of Ancient Israelite History*, 18-403) have extensively studied the Chronicler's exegetical techniques and literary methods. See also William M. Schniedewind, "The Chronicler as an Interpreter of Scripture," in *The Chronicler as Author*, 158-80. However, these scholars have not treated the texts at the core of the present study. Thus, the present study develops what they have already done.

[168] See section 2.1.1.2.

such as, "guards of the thresholds of the Tent" שמרי הספים לאהל (1 Chr 9:19) and "guards of the entrance of the camp of the Lord" על־מחנה יהוה שמרי המבוא (1 Chr 9:19). The first term is used to emphasize that the First Temple is the continuation of the Tent of Meeting,[169] and at the same time, the office of gatekeepers in the First Temple is a continuation of the one of the Tent of Meeting. The second term, על־מחנה יהוה שמרי המבוא, serves to highlight the Korahites' role as gatekeepers in the wilderness period. Since the Priestly tradition does not specify the Korahites' office of gatekeepers (it only mentions their general role of guarding the Tabernacle), the Chronicler traces the office of gatekeepers to the wilderness period by coining this term.

(3) To highlight levitical office holders:

To highlight the levitical status of gatekeepers, the Chronicler makes Levite gatekeepers frequent characters in his work; among the levitical gatekeepers we encounter are Zechariah, a Korahite gatekeeper at the time of David (1 Chr 9:21); the Korahite gatekeepers (1 Chr 26:1-19); and Kore, a Korahite gatekeeper during the reign of Hezekiah (2 Chr 31:14).

Similarly, the Chronicler hammers home the levitical identity of the temple treasurers. According to 1 Chr 9:20-26, the four chief gatekeepers, who supervised the chambers and treasuries of the Temple, were Levites. This fact is once again emphasized in 1 Chr 26:20-28, where David instituted the temple treasuries and appointed Levites to take charge of the treasuries of the Temple.

(4) To insert an explicit statement of the key point:

To confirm the gatekeepers' levitical lineage, the Chronicler explicitly adds a statement that the gatekeepers are Levites, such as השערים למחנ־

[169] The connection between the Temple and the Tent of Meeting is once again emphasized by the Chronicler's equation of "the house of the Lord" and "the house of the Tent" in 1 Chr 9:23 (see also 1 Chr 6:33, where the Tabernacle is combined with the Temple in a phrase משכן בית האלהים). James T. Sparks (*The Chronicler's Genealogies: Towards an Understanding of 1 Chronicles 1–9* [Atlanta: Society of Biblical Literature, 2008] 166) succinctly points out the Chronicler's attempt to establish continuity of the cult by creating such new phrases as follows:

> The Chronicler sought to combine all of the terminology he found in his sources into his text as synonyms for the temple of Yahweh in Jerusalem. In doing so he seeks to illustrate continuity in the worship of the people from the beginning of Israel's history until his own day. The Chronicler appears to have recognized the need for all of the cultic life of the postexilic community to be in conformity with the Torah.

נות בני לוי (1 Chr 9:18) and הם הלוים (1 Chr 9:26).[170] The Chronicler also adds three references to the Levites (1 Chr 24:5, 6, 11) not found in his source (2 Kgs 12:5-11), which instead refers to כהנים, to highlight the levitical involvement in the process of collecting funds to repair the Temple.[171] In 2 Chr 34:8-13, the Chronicler changes his source (2 Kgs 22:3-7) to highlight the levitical involvement in the repair work of the Temple, by specifying the guardians of the threshold as Levites and by adding the list of the Levites who participated in the repair of the Temple, either in the supervision of labor or in the administration of the process.[172]

(5) To legitimize a contemporary situation by harmonizing it with older traditions:

The Chronicler removes a contradiction between his contemporary practice in regard to the age of the Levites at their initiation into service and the Priestly regulation for it.[173] The difference between the initiation age of the Levites of his own day (twenty) and of the Priestly tradition (thirty) is attributed to David's organization of cultic matters. According to 1 Chr 23:24, 27, David changed the Levites' initiation age from thirty to twenty when he instituted new assignments for the Levites.

(6) To retroject his contemporary situation into the past:

According to 1 Chronicles 23–26, David organized the temple personnel in the pattern of twenty four divisions.[174] Since the evidence for the twenty-four priestly divisions is only found in the post-exilic period and afterward, this system evidently originated in or just before the Chronicler's own time. It appears that the Chronicler applied the contemporary system of twenty-four priestly divisions to the organization of the other cultic personnel, and retrojected his ideal for this cultic organization into the time of David.

[170] See section 2.1.1.2.

[171] See section 2.3.1.

[172] See section 2.3.2.

[173] The Priestly traditions show two different regulations for the initiation age of the Levites: (1) the age of thirty: Num 4:3, 23, 30, 35, 39; 43, 47; (2) the age of twenty-five: Num 8:24. The Chronicler seems not to have considered the regulation of Num 8:24 as a significant divergence from the first regulation (the age of thirty), since he did not mention the regulation of Num 8:24 (the age of twenty-five) in 1 Chr 23:3.

[174] See section 2.1.2.1.

(7) To exemplify figures for a didactic purpose:[175]

In 1 Chr 26:26-28, the Chronicler highlights David's magnanimous donations to the Temple, and the generous acts of Israelite leaders who followed David's example. The Chronicler specifically states that the chiefs of the clans, the officers of thousands and hundreds, and the other army officers (1 Chr 26:26) followed David's exemplary act. Furthermore, the Chronicler adds that Samuel, Saul, Abner and Joab (1 Chr 26:28) also dedicated some of the booty of war as David did so to maintain the sanctuary, even though there is no explicit report about their dedication of the booty in the Hebrew Bible.[176] By adding the names of Israelite leaders to the list of dedicators, the Chronicler seems to emphasize that the maintenance of the Temple is a duty of political and military leaders, and thereby instructs the contemporary generation to follow their great ancestors' examples.

(8) To resolve a contradiction between its source and Pentateuchal Traditions:

The Chronicler reworks Joash's command (2 Kgs 12:5) to be more in harmony with Pentateuchal traditions in 2 Chr 24:5, as I showed in Section 2.3.1. In 2 Kgs 12:5, Joash commands that a certain amount of money be set aside, which originally belonged to the temple treasuries, to secure the fund for the repairs of the Temple. But this command violates the priestly prerogative.[177] Thus the Chronicler changes the command into a neutral one: to go out and to collect money from people in the cities of Judah and Israel. Scholars have conjectured that the Chronicler, through this change, retrojected contemporary practices into the monarchic period. However, the Chronicler's change does not alter the original situation in his source where the king's first command was not carried out (2 Kgs 12:7). Likewise, the king's command, though it was changed into a neutral one, was not carried out in 2 Chr 24:5-6. It is likely that the Chronicler's alteration of the king's command was intended to correct its contradiction with the priestly

[175] I. Kalimi (*The Reshaping of Ancient Israelite History*, 166-74) deals with the same kind of methodology that the Chronicler applies here but he did not mention 1 Chronicles 26. See also Fishbane, *Biblical Interpretation*, 401.

[176] Knoppers, "Treasures Won and Lost," 196.

[177] See section 2.3.1. In 2 Kgs 12:5, Joash directs the priests to separate the money for the votive offerings and the voluntary offerings to finance the restoration of the Temple. However, according to Pentateuchal tradition (Lev 22:2-16; Num 18:8-10, 19), the money of the sacred donation is to be given to the priests.

tradition well known to the Chronicler, not to make it something relevant to his own time.[178]

(9) To provide a legal basis for a specific issue:

The Chronicler provides a legal basis for Joash's measure to collect the people's contribution especially for the purpose of repairing the Temple in 2 Chr 24:6, 9, by connecting it to the historical precedent of what Moses did in the wilderness period (Exod 30:12-16). At the same time, by eliminating the terms denoting atonement (כפר נפשו and כסף הכפרים), the Chronicler attempted to dissociate the money collected by Joash from the atonement money which was paid out only once in one's life time at the census. Due to this dissociation, משׂאת משה could be collected annually without violating the Mosaic regulation of Exod 30:12-16.[179] The Chronicler's effort to justify Joash's measure to collect money to repair the Temple must be related to his contemporary problem that the Jerusalem Temple was without any royal sponsorship after the monarchic period. The upkeep of the Temple had become the people's responsibility in the Persian period.

(10) To deviate from the Priestly traditions concerning a specific cultic practice:

In 1 Chr 9:28-32, the Chronicler describes certain duties of gatekeepers. Some of them, such as the responsibilities for the utensils of service (על־כלי העבודה) (1 Chr 9:28), the furniture (על הכלים) and all the holy utensils (על כל־כלי הקדש) (1 Chr 9:29), flour, wine, incense and spices (1 Chr 9:29), and the preparation of the flat cakes and the showbread, are assigned to the priests in Priestly traditions. However, the Chronicler describes them as part of the Levites' responsibilities (1 Chr 9:31-32; 1 Chr 23:28-32).

The Chronicler's emphasis on the Korahites' position as gatekeepers also deviates from Priestly tradition which dishonors Korah with the account of his rebellion against the Aaronide priesthood in the wilderness (Numbers 16). The Chronicler's effort to establish the continuity of the office of the Korahite gatekeepers from the wilderness period through the

[178] Thus, I argued that 2 Chr 24:5-6 does not support the existence of the itinerant tax collectors in the Chronicler's time.

[179] I challenged the traditional interpretation of 2 Chr 25:5-11 as a reflection of the actual situation in the Chronicler's own time, especially with regard to a yearly collection of tax (one-third of a shekel). I argued that משׂאת משה is not a compulsory tax but people's voluntary contributions, collected especially for the repair work on the Temple.

reign of David to his own time could have been intended to support the Korahites against the tradition depicted in Numbers 16.

These two cases show that the Chronicler's approach to Pentateuchal traditions is much more sophisticated than they may at first glance appear to be. On the one hand, the Pentateuchal traditions were considered authoritative to the Chronicler to the extent that he reinterpreted his sources by means of Pentateuchal cultic traditions. On the other hand, he did not hesitate to deviate from Priestly traditions when he needed to make his point in a certain cultic matter.[180]

In next chapter, I compare the Chronicler's description of the temple administration with other biblical and extra-biblical data which are related to the temple administration of Yehud in the Persian period. My comparison deals with (1) temple gates and treasuries as the major *loci* of economic activities of the Temple; (2) sources of temple revenue; and (3) temple staff. Specifically, I will examine several *loci* in the Temple where the major economic activities could have happened, based on the Chronicler's data: the temple gates, the store rooms and treasuries. I will ask how these places were portrayed in antiquity and whether one can hypothesize about possible economic activities that would have been conducted in those places.

[180] Rolf Rendtorff ("Chronicles and the Priestly Torah," in *Texts, Temples and Traditions: A Tribute to Menahem Haran* [ed. Fox, Michael V. et al; Winona Lake: Eisenbrauns, 1996] 266) also concludes his examination of the Chronicler's ideas about the sacrificial cult and his use of cultic language in 2 Chronicler 29–31 as such:

> The Chronicler has a good knowledge of the sacrificial service in the Temple, more or less in accordance with the Priestly texts of the Pentateuch. In at least one case, however, he mentions a detail not recorded in the Priestly texts, the receiving of the blood. On the other hand, he usually does not seem to quote directly from Pentateuchal texts or to be too eager to use exact cultic terminology. In one case he shows a totally non-Priestly use of a central Priestly word, namely *kippēr*. Thus the relations to the Priestly texts of the Pentateuch are not in terms of literary dependence but in terms of personal knowledge and experience with the cultic reality of his own time.

CHAPTER THREE

Temple Gates, Revenue, and Staff

As the previous chapter demonstrated, the Chronicler presents a relatively detailed description of the gatekeepers and the Temple treasurers. But his descriptions of cultic institutions do not necessarily provide an accurate reconstruction of cultic/administrative practices of Persian-era Yehud, nor do they necessarily cohere with the testimony of other sources. Why is the Chronicler's depiction of the Temple so often at variance with other both biblical and extra-biblical witnesses? This chapter will begin to grapple with this question by examining the Chronicler's depiction of the temple gates and treasuries in light of other reconstructions from archaeological, biblical and non-biblical sources. As we shall see, the Chronicler does not paint a consistent picture: at times "his" temple practices seem to reflect the practices of his own age, but more frequently, the Chronicler's description of the temple administration contains anachronistic details that seem to have been influenced by his literary knowledge of the First Temple and by his own ideological interests. To be clear, the present study does not aim to present a detailed reconstruction of the temple gates, revenue and administration staff in Persian era Yehud. Rather, it points out such evidence as a vantage point for understanding the Chronicler's concerns and interests.

3.1. *Loci* of Temple Economy: Gates, Store-chambers, and Treasuries

As I pointed out in the previous chapter, the Chronicler underscores that the levitical temple personnel were in charge of temple gates, store-chambers and treasuries. In this section, I approach the Chronicler's descriptions of these *loci* of the temple economy with two related questions: (1) What are the socio-economic implications of the practices described by the Chronicler? (2) Do his descriptions concur with other available information about the gate complexes of the Jerusalem temple?

To answer the first question, it is necessary to examine how the gate complexes would have been related to the temple economy in general. In antiquity, to control a temple's gates implies a significant influence over the temple economy. Thus, the Chronicler's emphasis on the levitical supervision of the temple gates should be understood as a loaded statement in need of examination.

For the second question, I compare the Chronicler's depictions of temple gates, store-chambers and treasuries with other available information about the gate complexes of the Jerusalem temple. On the one hand, the Chronicler's description of the store-chambers and treasuries reveals a growing interest in those institutions, which is also found in Nehemiah and other late authors. However, my comparison shows that the Chronicler's descriptions of the temple gates tend more to resemble the practices of the late monarchy. To be sure, we could wish for more evidence about the temples of both the monarchic and Persian eras! In particular, the lack of information about the store-chambers and treasuries of the Persian period still makes it difficult to determine whether the Chronicler's depictions of these institutions do or do not reflect the historical reality of his day.

3.1.1. The Significance of Temple Gates in Economic Activities

Studies of temple gates in particular have not attracted much scholarly focus up to now. However, the general structures and functions of city gates of the Late Bronze and Iron Ages in ancient Near East have been well known for over a century thanks to archaeological excavations. Happily, archaeologists suggest that temple gates, especially in their architecture and functions, were similar to city gates. Therefore I begin my exploration of temple gate complexes with a survey of city gates in antiquity.

In general, a fortified city had one or several city gates. Since the gate was by definition the weakest point in a city's defense, strengthening its security was critical.[1] For this purpose, a city gate was built with a pair of

[1] Gerald L. Mattingly, "Gateways and Doors," in *Dictionary of the Ancient Near East* (ed. Piotr Bienkowski and Alan Ralph Millard; Philadelphia: University of Pennsylvania Press, 2000) 125; B. Gregori, "Three-Entrance' City-Gates of the Middle Bronze Age in Syria and Palestine," *Levant* 18 (1986) 83-102; and Z. Herzog, "Settlement and Fortification Plan-

large gatehouses that had two or three pairs of piers that formed two or four chambers within the gate complex.[2] These chambers were designed to make room for the gates' opened doors in order not to hinder the flow of traffic through the gate itself. Typically, gates were manned by guards or other officials.[3] In the Iron Age, the gate chambers and their adjacent plazas were also used for social events, such as public meetings, religious functions or storage of goods. To strengthen their security, many gate complexes had towers that projected from the line of walls on the roofs of the gates. Sometimes the security of the gates was reinforced with a second gate, so that the gate complex would include an outer gate and inner gate, as at Tell en-Nasbeh, usually identified with the biblical city of Mizpah.[4]

In ancient Near East, city gates also functioned as "the legal boundary between the outside world and the world of the city."[5] They were "the dividing line for inclusion and exclusion of the communities."[6] Thus, it is not surprising that special significance attached to the gates and that those who had control over them exercised other forms of power and influence in the community.[7]

Biblical texts witness to these and other uses of city gate complexes. Among these, gate complexes functioned as places for various civic activi-

ning in the Iron Age," in *The Architecture of Ancient Israel: From the Prehistoric to the Persian Periods* (ed. A. Kempinski and Ronny Reich; Jerusalem: Israel Exploration Society, 1992) 271-74.

[2] Four-chamber gates have been found at Ur and Ashur in Mesopotamia, at Hattusha in Anatolia, and at numerous sites along the Levant from northern Syria to the Gulf of Aqaba. See G. R. H. Wright, "The Monumental City Gate in Palestine and its Foundations," *ZA* 74/2 (1984) 267-89.

[3] David Ussishkin, "The Borders and De Facto Size of Jerusalem in the Persian Period," in *Judah and the Judeans in the Persian Period*, 160.

[4] Concerning archaeological studies about the double gates at Tell en-Nasbeh, see Jeffrey R. Zorn, "An Inner and Outer Gate Complex at Tell en-Nasbeh," *BASOR* 307 (1997) 53-66; J. A. Emerton, " "The High Places of the Gates" in 2 Kings XXIII 8," *VT* 44 (1994) 455-67; and Amihai Mazar, *Archaeology of the Land of the Bible 10,000–586* BCE (New York: Doubleday, 1990) 467-69.

[5] Victor H. Matthews, "Entrance Ways and Threshing Floors: Legally Significant Sites in the Ancient Near East," *Fides et historia* 19/3 (1987) 25-40, here 26.

[6] Geoffrey Evans ("'Gates' and 'Streets': Urban Institutions in Old Testament Times," *The Journal of Religious History* 2 [1962] 2) points out that the citizens in antiquity were defined by their connection with the gate, such as "all those that went in by the gate of his city" in Gen 23:10.

[7] Tina Haettner Blomquist, *Gates and Gods: Cults in the City Gates of Iron Age Palestine An Investigation of the Archaeological and Biblical Sources* (ConBOT 46; Stockholm: Almqvist & Wiksell International, 1999) 16.

ties, such as a market place (2 Kgs 7:1, 18), a seat of juridical procedures and legal transactions (Gen 23:10; Ruth 4; Job 29:7; Prov 31:23), a place for public assemblies and proclamations (Gen 34:20; Jer 17:19; Ezra 10:9; Neh 8:3; 2 Chr 32:6; Prov 31:31), and the like.[8] The city square where the civic activities were carried out was usually situated inside the gate, so that the city square was often depicted as "the entrance of the gate (פתח שער)," or "the gateway of the city gate (פתח שער העיר)."[9]

Sufficient architectural points of contact between temple gates and city gates make it possible to apply findings about city gates to temple gates. The temple gates seem to have been built according to the basic pattern of the fortified, early Iron Age II monumental gates excavated at Gezer, Hazor, and Megiddo, with an initial threshold of the gate, three recessed chambers on both sides, and the inner vestibule of the gate, as Ezek 40:6-7 describes.[10]

In antiquity, temples were safeguarded by extraordinary measures since they symbolized a sacred precinct which had to be kept from profanation.[11] The temple enclosure was protected not only by the city walls but also by its own additional walls, and its gates were guarded by its own corps of gatekeepers.[12]

The duties of the temple guards were to safeguard the temple from profanation by controlling entry and to protect the temple property which was

[8] V. H. Matthews, "Entrance Ways and Threshing Floors," 26 and G. Evans, "'Gates' and 'Streets': Urban Institutions," 7.

[9] The phrase of "the entrance of the gate" or "the gateway of the city gate" appears at Num 4:26; Josh 8:29; 20:4; Judg 9:35, 40, 44; 18:16, 17; 2 Sam 10:8; 11:23; 1 Kgs 22:10; 2 Kgs 7:3; 10:8; 23:8; 1 Chr 9:21; 2 Chr 18:9; Jer 1:15; 19:2; 36:10; Ezek 8:3, 14; 10:19; 40:11, 13; and 46:3.

[10] Concerning early Bronze Age temples and their gate-ways, see Kempinski, "Chalcolithic and Early Bronze Age Temples," in *The Architecture of Ancient Israel*, 53-59; and for the temples of the Middle and Late Bronze Ages and the Iron Age, see, Amihai Mazar, "Temples and the Middle and Late Bronze Ages and the Iron Age," in *The Architecture of Ancient Israel*, 161-87. For an analysis of Ezek 40:6-7, see Walter Zimmerli, *Ezekiel 2: A Commentary on the Book of the Prophet Ezekiel Chapters 25-48* (Hermeneia; Philadelphia: Fortress Press, 1983) 352-53, 359-60.

[11] John W. Wright, "A Tale of Three Cities: Urban Gates, Squares and Power in Iron Age II, Neo-Babylonian and Achaemenid Judah," in *Studies in Politics, Class and Material Culture* (Vol. 3 of *Second Temple Studies*; ed. Philip R. Davies and John M. Halligan; JSOT-Sup 340; Sheffield: Sheffield Academic Press, 2002) 44-45.

[12] Othmar Keel, *The Symbolism of the Biblical World: Ancient Near Eastern Iconography and the Book of Psalms* (trans. Timothy J. Hallett; New York: The Seabury Books, 1978) 123.

kept in the Temple gate storehouses and treasuries.[13] In other words, the temple gates were a kind of checkpoint where people and their offerings were screened and the income collected before it was transferred to the store-chambers and treasuries. In this sense, having control over the temple gates implies that the gatekeepers exerted significant influence over the temple economy. The Chronicler's special attention to the *levitical* supervision of the temple gates *may* reflect his contemporary situation and the reality of expanded levitical roles. But if the Chronicler's depiction can be shown not to cohere with the preponderance of evidence from other sources, we must ask why the Chronicler took such pains to underline the connection of the Levites to the temple gates.

3.1.2. Locations of the Temple Gates

As I noted in the previous chapter, the Chronicler describes the locations of temple gates in 1 Chr 9:24 and 1 Chr 26:14-18. 1 Chr 9:24, which refers to situations of the Persian period, states that there were gate posts on each of the four sides of the Temple. Likewise, the other passage (1 Chr 26:14-18), which describes David's installation of temple gatekeepers for the future Temple, states that there would be gates at the four sides of the Temple. In this section, I shall question whether the Chronicler's brief portrait of temple gates presents an actual reconstruction of the temple gates in his own time. To answer this question, I compare the Chronicler's description with data that other sources provide. The comparison reveals, in fact, that the Chronicler's portrait of the gate complexes is consistent with realities of the late monarchic period, rather than those of the Persian period.

Since no excavation in Jerusalem has yet produced findings related to the temple gates of either the First Temple or the Second Temple of the post-exilic period, biblical texts, which provide some details on locations of temple gates, are crucial to my comparison.[14] In numerous references

[13] J. W. Wright ("Guarding the Gates," 79) argues that the gatekeepers described in 2 Chr 23:1-21 were "a paramilitary security force."

[14] Y. Shiloh, "Jerusalem," in *The New Encyclopedia of Archaeological Excavations in the Holy Land* (ed. Ephraim Stern; 5 vols.; New York: Simon & Schuster, 1993) 2:704; and Volkmar Fritz, "Temple Architecture: What can Archaeology Tell us About Solomon's Temple?" *BAR* 13 (1987) 38-49; and Eilat Mazar, "The Solomonic Wall in Jerusalem," in *"I Will Speak the Riddle of Ancient Things": Archaeological and Historical Studies in Honor of Amihai Mazar on the Occasion of his Sixtieth Birthday* (ed. Aren M. Maeir and Pierre de Miroschedji; Winona Lake: Eisenbrauns, 2006) 775-86.

to temple gates in the Bible, the temple gates are usually unnamed or not otherwise specifically designated (*e.g.*, in Jer 7:2; 1 Chr 16:42; and 2 Chr 31:2). But on several occasions various gates are identified with some precision.[15] These named gates are important for the present study because they provide information about their locations in the Temple. The narrative of Jehoiada's coup (2 Kgs 11: 4-20//2 Chr 23:1-21) offers the most valuable information about temple gates and provides ample material for a fruitful comparison with the Chronicler's descriptions of the gate complexes.

3.1.2.1. Guarding Posts in 2 Kgs 11:4-20//2 Chr 23:1-21

The narrative of Jehoiada's coup d'état against Athaliah in 2 Kgs 11: 4-20//2 Chr 23:1-21, provides interesting contrasts between the two versions' depictions of the guard posts associated with the Temple.[16] The Chronicler's version of the narrative (2 Chr 23:1-21) provides a very different picture than the Kings version (2 Kgs 11:4-20) in terms of the identifications of the guards and the gate names used by each. Additionally, the Chronicler places greater emphasis on guarding the Temple itself rather than the person of the future king, Joash. Since the two versions vary especially in the names of gates, I treat the Kings' version separately from the Chronicler's for the sake of clarity.

In Kings, Jehoiada commands the chiefs of the hundreds of the Carites and of the guards (הרצים) to watch the royal palace during the planned coup (2 Kgs 11:4-5).[17] These royal guards who were on duty at the hour

[15] In addition to the gates named in the narrative of Jehoiada's coup against Athaliah, two more named temple gates are found in the Hebrew Bible: "the Upper Gate of the Temple" (שׁער בית יהוה העליון, or שׁער העליון) (2 Kgs 15:35//2 Chr 27:3; cf. Jer 20:2) and "the New Gate" (שׁער־יהוה החדשׁ, or שׁער בית־יהוה החדשׁ) (Jer 26:10 and 36:10). However, none of these references to the Upper Gate or the New Gate provide explicit indications of their locations. Thus, without further archaeological or non-biblical data, they cannot be used to verify the existence of the gates at the four sides of the Temple, which the Chronicler describes in 1 Chr 9:24 and 1 Chr 26:14-16.

[16] Among various works on this narrative, specifically in terms of temple gate complexes, T. A. Busink's study is worth noting. See T. A. Busink, *Der Tempel von Jerusalem von Salomos bis Herodes: Eine archäologisch-historische Studie unter Berücksichtigung des westsemitischen Tempelbaus 1. Band: Der Tempel Salomos* (Leiden: E. J. Brill, 1970) 149-51.

[17] According to 2 Sam 15:18 and 20:23, the Carites, together with the Pelethites, were David's private army. Although their origin remains enigmatic, the Carites were apparently royal guards in the kingdom of Judah. See Mordecai Cogan and Hayim Tadmor, *II Kings: A New Translation with Introduction and Commentary* [AB 11; New York: Doubleday, 1988] 126. Another term for the guards in this passage, הרצים, should be understood as the royal guards. The occurrences of הרצים in the Old Testament are as follows: (1) as royal guards:

appointed for the coup were subdivided and positioned at three locations: "the royal palace" (בית המלך), "the Sur Gate" (שׁער סור), and "the gate behind the guards" (שׁער אחר הרצים) (2 Kgs 11:5-6). All those off-duty took up positions within the Temple to guard the king (2 Kgs 11:7). It appears that the manning of these three strategic positions in 2 Kgs 11:5-6 is intended to block the movement of Athaliah and her supporters from the palace to the Temple during the coronation of Joash. "The Sur Gate" and "the gate behind the guards," need further examination to identify their possible locations.

Concerning "the gate behind the guards": several commentators conjecture that it must have been located in the southern wall separating the Temple and palace compounds since 2 Kgs 11:19 states that Jehoiada and his supporters "went down" (ירד) from the Temple to the palace through "the way of the gate of guards" (דרך־שׁער הרצים).[18] 1 Kgs 14:27-28 also implies that the king regularly passed this gate to go into the Temple.[19]

---

1 Sam 22:17;1 Kgs 14:27- 28//2 Chr 12:10-11; 2 Kgs 11:4, 6, 11, 19; (2) as private body-guards: 2 Sam 15:1(Absalom's); 1 Kgs 1:5 (Adonijah's); 2 Kgs 10:25 (Jehu's); and (3) as royal messengers: 2 Chr 30:6, 10; Esth 3:13, 15; 8:10, 14. Considering the usage of the term הרצים, it is reasonable to interpret it as the royal guards in 2 Kings 11.

[18] Cogan and Tadmor, *II Kings*, 127; John Gray, *1 & II Kings: A Commentary* (OTL; Philadelphia: Westminster, 1963) 525; Volkmar Fritz, *1 & 2 Kings* (trans. Anselm Hagedorn; Continental Commentaries Old Testament; Minneapolis: Fortress, 2003) 300. Solomon's Temple was a royal sanctuary which located adjacent to the royal palace. This fact is verified by Ezek 43:8 where Ezekiel condemns the proximity of the royal palace to the Temple as the cause of contamination of the divine abode by the kings of Judah. A. Mazar's and M. Ottoson's separate studies about the temple-palace complexes in Palestine also support the close proximity of the Jerusalem Temple to the royal palace. See A. Mazar, "Temples and the Middle and Late Bronze Ages and the Iron Age," 184; and Magnus Ottosson, *Temples and Cult Places in Palestine* (Uppsala: Acta Universitatis Upsaliensis, 1980) 66, 76, and 112-13. Although no biblical texts indicate the location of the palace in relation to the Temple, the topographic features of the Temple Mount indicate that the Solomon's royal palace was connected to the Temple on the south side of the Temple. For the topographic features of the Temple Mount, see A. Mazar, *Archaeology of the Land of the Bible*, 417-20; D. Ussishkin, "King Solomon's Palaces," BA 36 (1973) 78-105; R. de Vaux, *Ancient Israel: Its Life and Institutions*, 312-17; and cf. D. Ussishkin, "Jerusalem as a Royal and Cultic Center in the 10th–8th Centuries BCE," in *Symbiosis, Symbolism, and the Power of the Past: Canaan, Ancient Israel, and Their Neighbors from the Last Bronze Age through Roman Palaestina* (ed. W. G. Dever and S. Gitin; Winona Lake: Eisenbrauns, 2003) 529-38. In this article, D. Ussishkin has suggested the possibility that the royal palace stood on the lower ground to the north of the temple.

[19] Cogan and Tadmor, *II Kings*, 131. For this reason, Busink calls this gate "Königstor" (Busink, *Der Tempel von Jerusalem von Salomos bis Herodes*, 149). However, Busink's naming seems not to be reconciled with other references to "the King's Gate" (1 Chr 9:18; Ezek

Regrettably, the Sur Gate appears only in 2 Kgs 11:6 and its location is unknown. Some scholars suggest emending סור as סוס, but there is no textual evidence for such emendation.[20] Moreover, the Horses' Gate (שׁער הסוסים) is always named with the plural form of סוס in its four occurrences in the Hebrew Bible (2 Kgs 11:16; Jer 31:40; Neh 3:28; and 2 Chr 23:15). K. Galling identifies the Sur Gate as the second gate in the southern wall of the Temple, which connects the palace to the Temple.[21] However, there is no scholarly consensus on the location of the Sur Gate. It is clear, however, that the two gates (the gate behind the guards and the Sur Gate) must be located where the palace is connected to the Temple, either in the south-west or south-east corner of the Temple or in the south of the Temple.[22]

We can gain additional ground by considering the practical logistics of Jehoida's coup. After the coup is accomplished, apparently, restrictions on Athaliah's movements are lifted and she passes freely from the palace to the Temple (2 Kgs 11:13//2 Chr 23:12). But by what route? According to 2 Kgs 11:14//2 Chr 23:13, Athaliah saw the king (Joash) standing by the pillar (על־העמוד) "as the custom" (כמשׁפט) when she entered the Temple. This pillar is one of the two pillars that Solomon set up at the vestibule of the Temple (לאלם ההיכל) (1 Kgs 7:21), which faced east. If Athaliah entered by the way of the eastern gate, as befitting her status as monarch, she would have immediately encountered the newly anointed Joash.

Additional evidence supports the picture of Athaliah's entrance from the eastern gate. The guards off-duty on the Sabbath who were commissioned to surround the king were also commanded to kill anyone who approached השׂדרות (2Kgs 11:8) S. Yeivin suggests that the term השׂדרות is an architectural term, which probably means the rows of semi-detached pillars adorning the inside of the gateway of the Temple (cf. 1 Kgs 6:9).[23]

44:3). 2 Kgs 11:5 implies the presence of a southern gate of the Temple, but the King's gate is identified with the eastern gate of the Temple in these two texts.

[20] Kurt Galling, "Die Halle des Schreibers: Ein Beitrag zur Topographie der Akropolis von Jerusalem," *Palästinajahrbuch des Deutschen evangelischen Instituts für Altertumswissenschaft* des *Heiligen Landes zu Jerusalem* 27 (1931) 51-57, here 51-52; and Curtis and Madsen, *The Books of Chronicles*, 427.

[21] Galling, "Die Halle des Schreibers," 51-52. T. A. Busink (*Der Tempel von Jerusalem von Salomos bis Herodes*, 149) also argues that the Sur Gate was the second gate in the southern wall of the altar court, which is connected to the courtyard of the palace. However, he does not provide any strong evidence for his argument. Lack of evidence makes any argument about the location of the Sur Gate inconclusive.

[22] Curtis and Madsen, *The Books of Chronicles*, 426.

[23] Yeivin, "Was There a High Portal in the First Temple?" 336. See also *HALOT*, 1310;

This highly ornamented gateway must have been the eastern gateway, that is, the main entrance to the inner court of the Temple, which fronted the façade of the Temple.[24] This was the place where Athaliah was arrested (2 Kgs 11:15).

Athaliah's final royal progress—toward her execution— may also shed some light on means of ingress and egress between the temple and the palace. 2 Kgs 11:16 states that Athaliah was killed at the Horses' entrance (דרך־מבוא הסוסים) located at the eastern end of the Ophel (the south-east corner of the Temple).[25] The Horses' Gate (שׁער הסוסים), leads into the Horses' entrance which in turn opens directly into the royal precinct.[26] S. Yeivin conjectures that the Horses' Gate would probably have been the main entrance to the palace from the outer court of the temple since it was wide enough to admit horse-drawn chariots.[27] If his conjecture is correct, Athaliah was pushed down from the eastern gate of the Temple to the Horses' Gate to be killed; that way must have been the shortest distance from the Temple to prevent any corpse-contamination in the temple precinct.

What can we conclude about Kings' depiction of temple gates in the story of Jehoida's coup? First, 2 Kgs 11:4-20 indicates the existence of the eastern gate of the Temple which led to the outer court of the Temple as well as the existence of at least two or three gates that joined the palace and the Temple complexes. Significantly, as we shall see below, this narrative does not contain any reference to the western gate.

The Chronicler's version of Jehoiada's coup (2 Chr 23:1-21) presents a different view on the temple gate complexes. In fact, the Chronicler alters the original narrative in Kings to convey his own concerns. First of all, in the Chronicler's version, neither the Carites nor the *royal* guards are mentioned (cf. 2 Kgs 11:4). According to 2 Chr 23:1-2, five captains of hundreds

---

and BDB 690. John M. Monson, *The Temple of Jerusalem: A Case Study in the Integration of Text and Artifact*, 125-26, also considers it as an architectural term, but argues that it means "wood beams," specifically, the paneling of the wall with rows of wooden planks (rather than "the ranks" which is found in the majority of modern translations).

[24] Yeivin, "Was There a High Portal in the First Temple?" 336.

[25] The reference to the place where Athaliah was executed (2 Kgs 11:16) seems to be intended to emphasize that incident happened outside of the temple precinct. See Robert L. Cohn, *2 Kings* (Berit Olam; Collegeville: Liturgical Press, 2000) 80. The repeated note of the execution of Athaliah "in the palace" in 2 Kgs 11:20 underlines such a religious concern about the profanation of the temple.

[26] Cogan and Tadmor, *II Kings*, 130; Gray, *I & II Kings*, 523.

[27] S. Yeivin, "Was There a High Portal in the First Temple?" 336.

(שׂרי המאות) came to Jehoiada to make a pact with him; then Jehoiada sent them to recruit the *Levites* for the upcoming coup against Athaliah. Thus, in the Chronicler's version, the main conspirators were not the royal guards, but the priests and the Levites (2 Chr 23:4). By this change, the Chronicler shows once again his preference for priestly class (priests and Levites) for work in the Temple, and at the same time successfully excludes foreigners (i.e., the Carites) from the Temple. The priests and Levites were commissioned to take up defensive positions in three locations: (1) "at the thresholds" (הספים); (2) "at the royal palace" (בית המלך); and (3) "at the Foundation Gate" (שׁער היסוד).

Except for the guard post at the royal palace, the other guard posts are described very differently from those in the Kings' version. For this reason, Raymond B. Dillard argues that this variation in the gate names may reflect updating or modernizing the gate names to those in use in the Chronicler's period.[28] This is possible, but the two versions do not seem to demonstrate the same concern about the guarding posts.

Clearly, the Chronicler is concerned to guard the Temple since the guards in 2 Chr 23:4-5 were the priests and Levites. 2 Chr 23:10 also emphasizes that the Temple was protected on three sides, south, north and east by the entire force.

The guard post at the royal palace (2 Chr 23:5) must be the southern gate(s) that linked the Temple with the palace. The guard post at the thresholds (2 Chr 23:4) must refer to a liminal area adjacent to the Temple structure itself on the eastern façade of the temple, as other references to the thresholds (הספים) indicate that they were part of the temple structure (2 Kgs 12:10; 22:4; 23:4; 25:18; 2 Chr 34:9; Jer 35:4 and 52:24). This proximity to the Holy place would explain why only priests and the Levites are assigned to guard this area. The ספים certainly cannot be identified with "the gate behind guards" (שׁער אחר הרצים) in 2 Kgs 11:6, *contra* T. A. Busink; there is no indication in Kings that that gate is part of the temple building.[29]

The location of the Foundation Gate is difficult to identify since there are no other references to it in the Hebrew Bible.[30] Nevertheless, we may be

[28] Dillard, *2 Chronicles*, 178. For instance, Dillard argues that the Chronicler did not mention "the gate behind the royal guards" (שׁער אחר הרצים) because the royal guards no longer frequented the entrance in his time.

[29] Busink, *Der Tempel von Jerusalem von Salomos bis Herodes*, 150.

[30] Japhet, *I & II Chronicles*, 831.

able to deduce its location. Jehoiada is said to have positioned the guards "from the south end to the north end of the Temple" to protect Joash "on every side (סביב)" (2 Chr 23:10).[31] The southern and eastern guard posts (the guard post at the royal palace and the guard post at the thresholds) are readily identified, but the northern post is not specified. Might the Foundation Gate have been at the north side of the Temple? If so, the Chronicler's picture of the gates here would cohere with his descriptions of the temple gates in 1 Chr 9:24 and 26:14-18, with one exception: as in 2 Kings 11, a western gate is not mentioned in 2 Chr 23:1-21. Is this because there was no western gate to be guarded during the era of the First Temple?

3.1.2.2. A Western Gate of the Temple

The only biblical reference to a western temple gate during the First Temple period occurs in 1 Chr 26:16. Does this reference reflect the historical reality of that era, or is it the Chronicler's creation? Despite the paucity of evidence, I suspect that it is highly probable that a western gate existed in the First Temple for several reasons.

First, the eastern gate of the Temple was used only for cultic purposes or by kings, and the southern gate was used primarily by court officials since it was located between the Temple and the palace. These gates' inaccessibility makes it likely that they were not used by the great majority of lay visitors to the temple precincts. Yet as the Temple of Jerusalem became the national sanctuary and the religious center of the nation, especially after Hezekiah's and Josiah's reforms, there would have been a need for a gate through which the people could easily enter the Temple grounds.

As it happens, archaeological findings reveal that Jerusalem expanded greatly to the west, almost completely covering the western hill of Jerusalem, in the later periods of the monarchy.[32] This urban development would have required a ramp to connect the Western Hill to the western enclosure of the Temple since there was a valley between the two. Thus, the Chronicler's description of the ascending gateway to the Temple and the gate of

[31] Raymond B. Dillard (2 *Chronicles*, 182) considers that the Sur (סור) Gate and the Foundation (יסוד) Gate are the same gate, the one a textual error to the other. See also Busink, *Der Tempel von Jerusalem von Salomos bis Herodes*, 160.

[32] A. Mazar, *Archaeology of the Land of the Bible*, 422-23; and Benjamin Mazar, *The Mountain of the Lord* (New York: Doubleday, 1975) 37-38. This new quarter (or the second quarters) of Jerusalem is mentioned in Zeph 1:10-11 and 2 Kgs 22:14. See A. Mazar, *Archaeology of the Land of the Bible* , 423-24).

chambers on the western wall of the Temple (1 Chr 26:16) may reflect, to a certain degree, situations of the later monarchic period.[33] S. Yeivin makes this point: "The description (of the First Temple) contained in the second book of Chronicles is based on the state of the building towards the last days of the kingdom of Judah, in the late VIIth (or early VIth) century B.C.E."[34]

Moreover, Benjamin Mazar's excavations in the Mishneh Quarter have shown that after the destruction of Jerusalem in 586 B.C.E. there was no new occupation of the Western Hill before the Hasmonean times (the second and first centuries B.C.E.).[35] Mazar's observation is corroborated by O. Lipschits and D. S. Vanderhooft's joint studies of Yehud Seal Impressions which report the total absence of Yehud stamps in the Western Quarter of Jerusalem until Hasmonean era.[36] Therefore, the gate of chambers on the west of the Temple mentioned in 1 Chr 26:16 is not likely to have been present in the Chronicler's own day. Rather, the Chronicler has probably preserved an accurate recollection of the existence, in the late monarchic period, of the gate of chambers and the ascending gateway associated with it.[37]

In conclusion, the Chronicler's descriptions of the temple gates in 1 Chr 9:24 and 26:14-16 are related to realities in the late monarchy rather than those of the Persian period. Thus, it will behoove us to reconsider the Chronicler's descriptions of other significant Temple loci, in particular, the temple treasuries and store-chambers.

[33] H. G. M. Williamson ("Nehemiah's Wall Revisited," 68, 71-72) also suggests a similar idea about the western wall in the late monarchic period. For the Chronicler's description of the ascending gateway to the Temple and the gate of chambers on the western wall, see section 2.1.2.2 of the present study.

[34] Yeivin, "Was There a High Portal in the First Temple?" 331

[35] B. Mazar, *The Mountain of the Lord*, 38.

[36] O. Lipschits and D. S. Vanderhooft, "Yehud Stamp Impressions in the Fourth Century BCE," in *Judah and Judeans in the Fourth Century BCE*, 80. The same understanding about the Western Hill of Jerusalem during the Persian period is also found in the following scholars' works: Finkelstein, "Jerusalem in the Persian (and Early Hellenistic) Period," 504-7; and Williamson, "Nehemiah's Wall Revisited," 66.

[37] At the present moment, the temple gate complexes of Zerubbabel's Temple remain completely unknown since the Persian stratum in Jerusalem is badly preserved because of later extensive construction in the Hasmonean and Herodian periods. Y. Shiloh, "Jerusalem," 709; and O. Lipschits, "Persian Period Finds From Jerusalem: Facts and Interpretations," *JHS* 9 (2009) Article 20:2-30.

3.1.3. The Temple Treasuries and Store-chambers

As we turn to the topics of temple treasuries and store-chambers, the lack of archaeological evidence again means that our discussion will depend largely on literary evidence from the pre-exilic period and from the exilic or post-exilic period. I first present here a summary of the Chronicler's description of store-chambers and treasuries in the Temple. Then, I treat each group of texts in separate sections.

3.1.3.1. The Chronicler's Description of the Store-chambers and Treasuries

In the Chronicler's narrative (1 Chr 28: 11-18), David's plan (תבנית) for the future temple includes store-chambers, the temple treasuries (אוצרות בית האלהים) and the treasuries of the dedicated things (אצרות הקדשים), which appear to be located between the priestly court and the court of the Israelites in the Chronicler's description (1 Chr 28:12).[38] David's plan for the temple treasuries is also elaborated in 1 Chr 26:20-28, where the two treasuries and their supervisors are introduced.

The Chronicler claims that Solomon completed all the work according to the plan that his father David passed down to him, and then stored the silver, the gold and all the vessels that David had dedicated in the temple treasuries (2 Chr 5:1). The Chronicler also asserts that Hezekiah built more store-chambers to store the gifts, the tithes, and the sacred things, which were to be allocated to the priests and Levites (2 Chr 31:11). The location of these chambers is not mentioned.

The Temple rebuilt in the post-exilic period, according to 1 Chr 9:26-29, also had both store-chambers (האצרות) and the temple treasuries (האצרות בית האלהים). While the treasuries of the dedicated things (האצרות הקדשים) are not mentioned, the Chronicler does report the existence of several additional chambers arranged by their contents: a chamber of the utensils of service (כלי העבודה); a chamber of the furniture and all the holy utensils (הכלים וכל־כלי הקדש); and a chamber(s) of the fine flour, wine, oil, incense, and spices (הסלת והיין והשמן והלבונה והבשׂמים).

When viewed against other literary descriptions of the Temple, The Chronicler's interest in the dual institutions of the temple treasuries and

[38] According to 2 Chr 4:9 Solomon made the court of the priests, and the great court, and also made doors between the two courts.

store-chambers is distinctive. The Chronicler uses his comments about these two institutions as a vehicle for praising David and highlighting other righteous kings (especially Hezekiah). In other words, as we shall see below, the Chronicler's descriptions of temple treasuries and store-chambers are by no means free of the tendentiousness and characteristic biases that we have noted previously.

3.1.3.2. Texts about the Pre-exilic Period

The store-chambers and treasuries of the Temple did not command the attention of the scribes of the pre-exilic era. Two texts, 2 Kgs 23:11 and Jer 35:4, contain brief mentions of the store-chambers of the Temple in the First Temple period, but they provide no concrete data that would help us construct an institutional portrait of the store-chambers.

On the other hand, the misfortunes of Judah at the hands of foreign sovereigns provided the author(s) of Kings with frequent opportunities to mention the temple treasuries: various Judean kings had no choice but to empty the temple treasuries in response to the depredations (threatened or actual) of imperial armies (1 Kgs 7:51; 14:26; 2 Kgs 12:18; 14:14; 16:8; 18:15; 24:13). However, these texts do not contain any organizational detail, such as interest in the ways in which the temple treasuries were administered. The lack of data about treasuries and store-chambers in pre-exilic texts brings into high relief the importance of these institutions in texts from the exilic and Persian eras.

3.1.3.3. Texts about the Exilic and Post-exilic Periods

Unlike the texts describing the temple treasuries and store-chambers of the pre-exilic period, the books of Ezekiel and Nehemiah display a growing interest in these features of the Second Temple. Ezekiel's plan for a future temple contains many cells in the outer and inner courts of the temple: he envisions thirty chambers in the outer court (Ezek 40:17), a chamber for washing burnt offerings (Ezek 40:38), chambers for the singers in the inner court (Ezek 40:44), chambers for the priests (Ezek 40:45-46; 42:13), chambers for the Levites (Ezek 45:5), the upper chambers (Ezek 42:5) and many other chambers. Ezekiel details the locations, dimensions and specific purposes of store-rooms especially in Ezekiel 40-42.

Nehemiah also provides some information about temple treasuries and store-chambers. First, the book specifies which items would be kept in the store-rooms: "the first part of dough, contributions, the fruit of every tree, wine and oil for the priests, and the tithes" (Neh 10:38; cf. Neh 13:12).[39] Nehemiah's concern about the store-chambers goes beyond specifying the items kept in them. Since the Temple's administration could be easily disrupted by an abusive administrator, we are told that Nehemiah appointed the four member treasurers' committee over the store-chambers (Neh 13:13).

Clearly, Ezekiel and Nehemiah treat the treasuries and store-chambers in ways which reflect their specific concerns. While Ezekiel is concerned primarily with laying out a structural plan for chambers in the Temple, Nehemiah' interest lies in describing how these institutions should be run. Similarly, as we have seen, the Chronicler's descriptions of the treasuries and store-chambers are distinctive in terms of his emphasis on who administers the institutions. Throughout his narrative the Chronicler associates Levites with the running of the treasuries and store-chambers; in lieu of supporting textual or archaeological evidence, there is no basis on which to conclude that the Chronicler's descriptions of temple treasuries and store-chambers either do or do not reflect the realities of his own time. All we can say with certainty is that the Chronicler's presentation of levitical involvement in these institutions' administrations is consistent with his overall picture of issues relating to the temple economy.

3.1.4. Summary

In section 3.1, I compared the Chronicler's description about *loci* of temple economy, specifically temple gates, store-chambers and treasuries with other sources. Based on this comparison, I draw the following conclusions:

First, the Chronicler's description of the four temple gates seems to reflect circumstances (or perhaps texts) of the late monarchic period rather than the Persian period. Second, the Chronicler's interest in the systematic organization and supervision of the store-chambers and treasuries reflects traditions that emerge in the Second Temple era rather than the First. However, one cannot demonstrate, due to the lack of evidence, that the Chronicler's portrayal of these institutions reflects the realities of his own day: how to account for the Chronicler's apparently consuming interest in the roles of the Levites in the Temple is a question that we will take up

[39] Mal 3:10 also implies that tithes were brought into the treasury of the temple.

following a discussion of the sources of funding for priests and Levites as envisioned by the Chronicler.

3.2. The Temple Revenue

In the previous chapter, my analysis of the selected texts showed that the Chronicler presents levitical temple personnel, both temple gatekeepers and treasurers, as in charge of at least certain aspects of matters relating to temple revenue. In this section, I shall examine the possible sources of temple revenue of the Second Temple in the Achaemenid Era, based on biblical or extra-biblical resources, and show how the Chronicler's depiction of these matters departs from what we find in other sources.

It is not clear what the major sources of revenue for the support of the Jerusalem Temple were in the post-exilic period. Did the Jerusalem Temple, like Babylonian temples under the Achaemenid Empire, own tracts of land, houses, or livestock that generated income through rent?[40] We simply do not know. What we can say is that in general, biblical texts mention three different sources of temple income: tithes, priestly gifts, and the temple tax. I pay special attention to the Chronicler's descriptions of who was in charge of collecting and storing funds and who benefitted from them.

As I demonstrate below, this study reveals the idiosyncrasy of the Chronicler's descriptions of matters related to temple revenue. For one thing, the Chronicler's description of the tithe is different from those of other biblical authors. Moreover, the Chronicler's treatment of the priestly gift is unique and notably different from Ezekiel's and Nehemiah's. Finally, the Chronicler does not mention the temple tax, but I suspect that his very silence merits our attention.

In the end of this section, I will examine the Chronicler's treatment of imperial taxes, although imperial taxes are not included in the category of temple revenue. Scholars have suggested that the temple administration was involved in collecting imperial taxes during the Persian period. However, there is no evidence that the Jerusalem Temple and the temple administration were directly involved in collecting and paying imperial taxes.

[40] Lynn Tatum, "Jerusalem in Conflict: The Evidence for the Seventh-Century B.C.E. Religious Struggle over Jerusalem," in *Jerusalem in Bible and Archaeology: The First Temple Period* (ed. A. G. Vaughn and A. E. Killebrew; SBLSS 18; Atlanta: Society of Biblical Literature, 2003) 315.

Indeed, Chronicles does not even betray knowledge of imperial taxes. Is this silence the result of ignorance, or should we understand it as indicating the Chronicler's general attitude toward the Achaemenid Empire and its relationship to the temple administration?

3.2.1. Tithes

Setting aside a portion of private income either for sacred or tax purposes was common throughout ancient Near East.[41] However, the exact nature of the tithe and the method of processing it in ancient Israel remain unclear. For instance, we do not know whether the tithe was understood to be exactly a tenth part or a certain kind of tax or gift; whether it was obligatory or voluntary; to which place(s) and in what season(s) of a year the collection of tithes was carried out; and the like.[42] In this section, I do not attempt to reconstruct the process of when and how the tithes were collected in ancient Israel. Rather, I seek to determine from biblical references where the tithe was stored, who was put in charge of these stores, and how, once having been collected, tithes were used. Attention to the changes in the institution of tithing over time reveals how the Chronicler interacted with his earlier traditions.[43]

[41] For the cases of rendering the tithes for sacred purposes in ancient Egypt, Mesopotamia, South Arabia and Ugarit, see, R. North, "עשׂר," *TDOT* 11:404-5; and Marc van de Mieroop, "Gifts and Tithes to the Temples in Ur," in *Dumu-E2-Dub-Ba-A: Studies in Honor of Ake W. Sjoberg* (ed. Hermann Behrens et al.; Philadelphia: University of Pennsylvania Museum Publication, 1989) 397-401; and Jacob Milgrom, *Leviticus 23-27: A New Translation with Introduction and Commentary* (AB 3B; New York: Doubleday, 2001) 2421-22.

[42] Not many books and articles on tithes have been published. The present study depends on the following sources: H. Jagersma, "The Tithes in the Old Testament," in *Remembering All the Way: A Collection of Old Testament Studies* (Leiden: Brill, 1981) 116-28; Martin S. Jaffee, *Talmud Yerushalmi. Ma'aserot* (Chicago: The University of Chicago Press, 1987); Menachem Herman, *Tithe as Gift: The Institution in the Pentateuch and in Light of Mauss's Prestation Theory* (San Francisco: Mellen Research University Press, 1991); Roger Brooks, *Talmud Yerushalmi. Ma'aser sheni* (Chicago: The University of Chicago Press, 1993); Jacob Milgrom, *Leviticus 23-27*, 2421-34; R. de Vaux, *Ancient Israel*, 140-41; R. North, "עשׂר," *TDOT* 11:404-9; and J. Christian Wilson, "Tithe," *ABD* 6:578-80.

[43] Tithes are mentioned in the Hebrew Bible with either a form of the verb עשׂר or of the noun מעשׂר. The word מעשׂר appears 32 times in the Bible, of which 30 occurrences are relevant to the present study (two cases in Ezekiel refer to "one-tenth" of a certain measuring unit). The references to מעשׂר: Gen 14:20 (once); Amos 4:4 (once); Deut 12:6, 11, 17; 14:23, 28; 26:12 (seven times in Deuteronomy); Lev 27:30, 31, 32 (thrice); Num 18:21, 24, 26 (thrice), 28 (six times in Numbers); Ezek 45:11, 14 (twice); Mal 3:8, 10 (twice); Neh 10:38, 39 (twice); 12:44; 13:5, 12 (six times in Nehemiah); and 2 Chr 31:5, 6 (twice), 12 (four times

References to the institution of the tithes before the exilic period are rare: Gen 14:20; Gen 28:22; 1 Sam 8:15, 17; and Amos 4:4. Gen 14:20 notes that Abraham gave a tenth of everything that he obtained in war to Melchizedek the king-priest of Salem. In Gen 28:22 Jacob vowed to pay a tithe at Bethel. M. Weinfeld interprets these two episodes as etiologies for the institution of the tithe in the royal sanctuary of Jerusalem and in one associated with northern Israel.[44] However, these two texts do not portray tithing as a systematic, continual practice but as an occasional, even exceptional, form of voluntary donation.[45] In both etiological narratives, it is likely that a single instance of tithing is highlighted to generalize the practice of tithing. Amos 4:4 also describes the tithe as a voluntary offering to the sanctuary.[46]

On the other hand, 1 Sam 8:15, 17 treats the tithe as a form of royal taxation, not as a sacred donation assigned to the Temple. Nowhere else in the Hebrew Bible are tithes explicitly mentioned as being owed to the king. However, ancient Mesopotamian and Egyptian documents show that the tithe could be a royal tax exacted by the king and granted as gifts or salaries to his officials.[47]

In contrast to the earlier texts, 2 Chronicles 31 gives more detailed information of the institution of the tithe. In 2 Chr 31:4, Hezekiah is said to make an ordinance for people to support the priests and Levites by giving tithes. This is one of a series of measures that Hezekiah takes in Chronicles to support the sacrificial worship in the Temple. 2 Chr 31:5-6 catalogues the property subject to tithing: the first fruits of grain, wine, oil, honey, and of all the produce of the field; the tithe of cattle and sheep; and the tithe of the dedicated things. The tithes were collected from the third month to the seventh month (2 Chr 31:7). Along with the contributions (התרומה) and the dedicated things (הקדשים), the tithes were stored in the chambers which

in Chronicles). The majority of references to the tithe occur in Pentateuchal regulations: the occurrences of the verb עשׂר which indicate the practice of tithing are found in Gen 28:22; Deut 14:22; 26:12; 1 Sam 8:15, 17 and Neh 10:38.

[44] Weinfeld, "Tithe," *EJ* 19:736. See also Milgrom, *Leviticus 23-27*, 2422, 2430.

[45] Andreas J. Köstenberger and David A. Croteau, "'Will a Man Rob God?' (Malachi 3:8): A Study of Tithing in the Old and New Testaments," *BBR* 16 (2006) 53-77.

[46] According to Francis I. Anderson (*Amos: A New Translation with Introduction and Commentary* [AB 24A; New York: Doubleday, 1989] 430), the tithes in Amos 4:4 are not "routine tithes, but special offerings promised on the eve of some hazardous enterprise or in a crisis."

[47] Milgrom, *Leviticus 23-27*, 2428; and Weinfeld, "Tithe," 736.

were newly built by the order of Hezekiah (2 Chr 31:7-8). These chambers in turn are put under the charge of Conaniah the Levite and eleven other chief officers of the Temple (2 Chr 31:12-13).

The Chronicler's description of Hezekiah's measure for the institution of the tithes has no parallel in Kings, nor does it reflect the Deuteronomic regulations concerning tithes.[48] However, Hezekiah's policy is quite similar to descriptions of the tithe in texts which portray or discuss post-exilic situations, such as Mal 3:10; Neh 10:38-39; 12:44; 13:5, 12-13. Thus, this passage in 2 Chronicles 31 will be treated along with the other texts which present the nature of the tithe and the way of processing and spending it in the post-exilic period. As we shall see, the description of Hezekiah's tithe policy is likely to have originated with the Chronicler himself and was probably intended to harmonize the contradictory tithing regulations contained in the Priestly traditions.

The Priestly laws concerning tithes are presented in Lev 27:30-33 and Num 18:21-32.[49] The former passage differentiates two kinds of tithes: the tithe of the land (מעשׂר הארץ) and the tithe of the herd and flock (מעשׂר בקר וצאן). The tithe of the land is taken from either "seed from the ground" or "fruit from the tree" (Lev 27:30). Monetary replacement of the tithe of the land is allowed with a twenty percent addition to it (Lev 27:31). On the

[48] Deuteronomy prescribes two different kinds of tithes: the annual tithe and the triennial tithe. For the annual tithe, all the Israelites are commanded to bring a tithe of their grain, new wine, and oil to the Temple and to consume these products on-site (Deut 12:6-7; 14:23). Thus, the annual tithe prescribed by Deuteronomy is not used for the maintenance of the Temple and its personnel. Similarly, the triennial tithe is not used for the upkeep of the central sanctuary. Rather, Deuteronomy requires that every third year all the landholding families should store the tithes of their increase in their village storehouse. This triennial tithe will be given to the Levites, the strangers, orphans and widows in their towns (Deut 14:28-29; 26:12 (cf. Deut 12:6-7; 14:23).

[49] Lev 27:30-33 is a part of "the Holiness Code" which A. Klostermann first named for the section of Leviticus 17-26 because of its linguistic and stylistic differences from the Priestly work. However, in the present work, we will not distinguish the Holiness Code from the other Priestly work since there is little scholarly consensus on the integrity of the Holiness Code, its composition, date or author, and its relationship to the Priestly work, and such differentiation is not necessary for our discussion. For an introduction to scholarly discussion about the relationship of the Holiness Code to the Priestly work, see I. Knohl, *The Sanctuary of Silence: The Priestly Torah and the Holiness School* (Winona Lake: Eisenbrauns, 2007) 1-7; Robert A. Kugler, "Holiness, Purity, the Body and Society: The Evidence for Theological Conflict in Leviticus," *JSOT* 76 (1997) 3-27; Gary A. Anderson, review of Baruch J. Schwartz, The Holiness Legislation Studies in the Priestly Code, *CBQ* 63 (2001) 128-29; and Michael D. Hildenbrand, *Structure and Theology in the Holiness Code* (North Richland Hills: Bibal Press, 2004).

contrary, the tithe of the herd and flock is not allowed to be redeemed.[50] M. Weinfeld suggests that the rationale behind this ordinance was the Temple's constant need of sacrificial animals.[51]

Both varieties of tithes are declared "holy to the Lord (קדש ליהוה)" (Lev 27:30, 32), and Lev 27:30 also states that the tithe of the land is assigned to Yahweh (ליהוה). The phrases "holy to the Lord" (קדש ליהוה) and "to Yahweh" (ליהוה), likely indicate that the tithes in Leviticus are rendered to the priests and their household.[52] The designation of the tithes as holy (קדש) means that they can be consumed only by the priests and their household since no Israelite can profane the holy things (קדשים) that belong to Yahweh (ליהוה) (Lev 22:15). Moreover, there are some cases in which the phrase "to the Lord (ליהוה)" is placed in apposition with the phrase of "to the priest (לכהן)": see Lev 23:30; Num 5:8; and cf. Num 18:28 (where תרומת יהוה is clearly allotted to the priests) and Neh 10:37 (where לבית אלהינו is supplemented with לכהנים).[53] Access to the tithe in Leviticus is thus strictly a priestly prerogative.[54] There are no cases in Leviticus where the Levites are specifically connected with either the word קדש or the phrase ליהוה.[55]

The laws of the tithe in Num 18:21-32 reflect a different view than that in Lev 27:30-33. Here the tithe *is* assigned to the Levites (Num 18:21, 24), and *not* to the priests. In turn, the Levites should set aside "a tithe of the tithe" (מעשׂר מן־המעשׂר) and give it to the priests (Num 18:26, 28).

[50] Lev 27:32 shows how tithing of animals could have been carried out. It is said that all the animals which pass under the shepherd's staff should be subject to tithing. Interestingly, tithing animals is mentioned only here and in 2 Chr 31:6. It is not so certain why the tithe of animals is not referred to elsewhere in the Bible. J. Wellhausen (*Prolegomena to the History of Israel*, 155) contends that the tithe of animals is a late invention which was never put into practice. M. Weinfeld ("Tithe," 738) disputes Wellhausen's contention based on the Mesopotamian texts in which the tithe of animals is often referred to. On the other hand, the Mishnah comments on this tithe as a second or festival tithe (*m. Bek.* 9:1-8). See Lester L. Grabbe, *Judaic Religion in the Second Temple Period: Belief and Practice from the Exile to Yavneh* (London/New York: Routledge, 2000) 138.

[51] Weinfeld, "Tithe," 737.

[52] J. Milgrom (*Leviticus 23-27*, 2425) also interprets Lev 27:30 as assigning tithes to the sanctuary priests.

[53] Weinfeld, "Tithe," 737.

[54] The followings scholars also suggest the same conclusion: Milgrom, *Leviticus 23-27*, 2386, 2397, 2425; Lester L. Grabbe, *Leviticus* (OTG; Sheffield: Sheffield Academic Press, 1993) 70; and Erhard S. Gerstenberger, *Leviticus: A Commentary* (OTL; Louisville: Westminster John Knox, 1996) 447.

[55] Jacob Milgrom (*Leviticus 23-27*, 2428) also comments: "The Priestly tradition consistently refrains from using קדש in regard to the Levites; this root is absent from even the Levites' ordination account, where the surrogate verb נתן is employed (Num 8:5-22)."

Thus, Lev 27:30-33 and Num 18:21-32 differ in terms of the beneficiaries of the tithes.[56] There is no scholarly consensus about which law is earlier or what caused a change in the ordinances, mainly because of the lack of evidence tracing the development of the laws concerning the tithe.[57] The differences between these two regulations are also reflected in later halakhic exegeses on the biblical laws of tithe which demonstrate the rabbis' efforts to make a consistent and systematic law code for the tithe by harmonizing the different ordinances.[58]

Several post-exilic texts (Mal 3:8, 10; Neh 10:38-39; 12:44; 13:5, 12) suggest that tithes were collected for the maintenance of the Temple from the beginning of the Second Temple era. Neh 12:47 asserts that even in the time of Zerubbabel, the daily portions of the singers and the gatekeepers were allocated from the people's contributions (מקדשים).[59] The Levites in turn are said to have paid a tenth of the tithes that they received to the priests (Neh 10:39; 12:47).[60] However, both Malachi and Nehemiah state that the institution of the tithe had not been well established either due to the people's laxity or due to the chief administrator's exploitation of it. For instance, Mal 3:8 denounces the people with "robbing God" by withholding tithes (המעשׂר) and offerings (התרומה) and exhorts them to "bring the full tithes into the storehouse (בית האוצר)" (Mal 3:10). A similar tithing crisis is noted in the time of Nehemiah when the chief officer Tobiah did not distribute the portions of the Levites (Neh 13:4-10).

[56] Milgrom, *Leviticus 23-27*, 2424.

[57] Milgrom, "Can the Tithe Laws be Harmonized," in *Leviticus 23-27*, 2431-34; and Tigay, *Deuteronomy*, 141.

[58] The harmonization of the Pentateuchal regulations concerning the tithe is witnessed from Tobit 1:6-8, *m. Ma'aś.* to *y. Ma'aś.* and *y. Ma'aś. Š.* Concerning the later development of the regulations of the tithe, refer to Martin S. Jaffee, *Talmud Yerushalmi. Ma'aserot* and Roger Brooks, *Talmud Yerushalmi. Ma'aser sheni.*

[59] The signers and gatekeepers are treated as independent orders from the Levites among the temple personnel in Ezra-Nehemiah. The gatekeepers are identified with Levites only exceptionally in Neh 13:15. In Ezra 2:41 and Neh 7:44, the singers are presented as the descendants of Asaph, which makes them Levites. Interestingly, these two texts do not include these singers in the same category of Levites which is introduced in a preceding verse (Ezra 2:40 and Neh 7:43). This fact implies that the Levites in Ezra-Nehemiah could designate a specific cultic function rather than a tribal name, although there exists a certain degree of obscurity in its differentiation of singers from the Levites in Nehemiah 12. However, for the Chronicler, the word "the Levites" means unambiguously "a tribal name" as which is used in Priestly texts.

[60] The regulation for the tithe of tithes that the Levites paid to the priests (Neh 10:39 and 12:47) is in conformity with the one of Num 18:26, 28. The Chronicler, however, does not mention this regulation.

In the post-exilic period, there seems to have been a distinction between the contribution (התרומה) as the share for priests and the tithe (המעשׂר) as for the Levites.[61] For example, Neh 10:36-38 differentiates between the priestly share and the share for the Levites, and provides a full list of the priestly share (תרומה): the first fruits of the soil and of every tree; the firstlings of the herds and flocks; and the first part of the dough, grain, fruit, wine and oil. In contrast, המעשׂר for the Levites is simply defined as "the tithe of the land."[62]

The practices described in Nehemiah reflect a combined and harmonized form of the regulations found in Leviticus 27 and Numbers 18. That is, the practices in Nehemiah seem to cover both the tithe of the herds and flocks (mentioned only in Leviticus 27) and the tithe assigned to the Levites (Numbers 18).[63]

According to Neh 10:38, 39, the Levites collected the tithe from all the towns, under the supervision of an Aaronide priest (Neh 10:39). Officials, according to Nehemiah, were appointed over the treasuries to oversee the contributions, first fruits and tithes, which they would also dispense to the priests and the Levites (Neh 12:44).[64]

In later texts, however, we can discern that the tithe designated for the Levites in Nehemiah has been diverted to the priests. According to Jdt 11:13, it seems that the levitical tithe was allowed to be given to the priests in the author's day.[65] Such diversion of the levitical tithes to the priests is also mentioned in Josephus, who refers to various situations concerning the processing of the tithe. First, in *Ant.* 4:68 and 205 the tithe is assigned to the priests as well as to the Levites. Second, in *Ant.* 20:181, 206; and *Life* 1:63, 80, Josephus takes it for granted that the tithe belonged exclusively to the priests.[66]

[61] Mal 3:8 gives two different categories that people should offer to God: the contributions and the tithe. However, Mal 3:8 does not specify which group would be the beneficiary of each category.

[62] Neh 12:44 presents a somewhat more complicated picture: there, three categories of offerings appear: the priests receive the contributions (תרומות) and the first fruits (ראשׁית), while the Levites continue to receive the tithes (מעשׂרות). In 2 Chr 31:12, the Chronicler also itemizes the donations of the people into three categories, but not exactly in the same way: contribution (התרומה), tithe (המעשׂר), and the sacred things (הקדשׁים).

[63] J. Blenkinsopp, *Ezra-Nehemiah* (OTL; Philadelphia: Westminster, 1988) 317-19.

[64] The text does not specify who appointed these officials or whether or not they were clerical officials.

[65] Baumgarten, "Critical Notes: On the Non-Literal Use of Ma'aser/Dekate," *JBL* 103 (1984) 245-61, here 247.

[66] Baumgarten, "Critical Notes: On the Non-Literal Use of Ma'aser/Dekate," 247; and

Yet the diversion of the levitical tithe to the priests is not reflected consistently across all sources: according to Tobit 1:6-7, the first fruits of the crops and the firstlings of the flock, the tithes of the cattle and the first shearing of the sheep are supposed to be given to the priests (τοῖς υἱοῖς Ααρων), but the tithe of the grain, wine, oil, pomegranates, figs, and the rest of the fruits is due to the Levites (τοῖς υἱοῖς Λευι).

The diversity of the depictions of tithing in post-exilic texts most probably indicates that there was no fixed system of submitting and consuming the tithe in the Second Temple period. (For a graphic presentation of the evidence, see Table 5 below.) The diversion of the levitical tithe to the priests appears to be a relatively late innovation, since it is not reflected in the sources from the early Second Temple period.[67]

The Chronicler's description of the institution of the tithe in 2 Chr 31:5-12 is unique in two key points. First, whereas the tithe is assigned to the Levites in Nehemiah and Malachi (as in Numbers 18), it is assigned to the *priests and the Levites* along with other kinds of donations in 2 Chr 31:4-6. Second, Nehemiah mentions the tithe of the tithes which the Levites should pay to the priests, as Numbers 18 does, but the Chronicler does not mention it in 2 Chronicles 31. (See Table 5, pp. 122-23.)

How can these differences be understood?[68]

Lester L. Grabbe, *Judaic Religion in the Second Temple Period*, 138. J. Milgrom (*Leviticus 23-27*, 2400) adds another text, 4QMMT B 62-64, to the list of later texts which indicate the diversion of the tithes to the priests. This text says: "Concerning the plantation of fruit trees planted in the land of Israel, it is like first-fruits, it is for the priests. And the tithe of the cattle and flocks is for the priests" (Martínez and Tigchelaar, eds., *The Dead Sea Scrolls Study Edition*, 795).

[67] J. Baumgarten ("Critical Notes: On the Non-Literal Use of Ma'aser/Dekate," 247) argues that the diversion of the levitical tithes to the priests must have been a Hasmonean innovation, specifically enacted by John Hyrcanus I. See also A. Oppenheimer, "Terumot and Ma'aserot," *EJ* 19:653. Oppenheimer argues that "the edict of Julius Caesar to Hyrcanus II," which Josephus cites, can also be evidence for the Hasmonean kings' appropriation of the tithe. A part of the edict says: "... they are to pay the same tithes to Hyrcanus and his sons, which they paid to their forefathers" (*Ant.* 14:203).

[68] For instance, Ziony Zevit ("Converging Lines of Evidence Bearing on the Date of P," *ZAW* 94 [1982] 492) holds a linear view about historical changes in practices of the levitical tithe when he argue as follows:

> The Biblical, Apocryphal and Rabbinic data attest to the continuous decline of levitical power and prestige from the last pre-exilic century on, and to the Levites' loss of control over their tithe from the beginning of the post-exilic period.

According to Zevit's contention, the Chronicler's description about the levitical tithes reflects an earlier practice than Nehemiah's. However, situations related to the levitical tithes as well as levitical status do not support such a linear view as I show below, and also in section 3.3.3.

In 2 Chr 31:4, the Chronicler asserts that Hezekiah commanded people to deliver the portion of the priests and the Levites (מנת הכהנים והלוים). Then, in 2 Chr 31:6, as I observed above, the Chronicler mentions "the tithe of the herds and flocks," which appears elsewhere only in Lev 27:32-33. This fact implies that the Chronicler knew the regulations of Leviticus 27. Hezekiah's policy could be a creative synthesis of different regulations in Leviticus 27, where the tithe is assigned to the priests, and Numbers 18, where the tithe is assigned to the Levites. Unlike Numbers 18, however, the Chronicler does not make any distinction between the priestly share and the levitical share.[69] According to the Chronicler, both groups will receive their due from the people's donations, which will include the first fruits of the grain, wine, oil, honey, and all kinds of agricultural produce, and tithes, which include tithes of cattle and sheep, and tithes of sacred things (מעשׂר קדשים), a term unique to the Chronicler (2 Chr 31:5-6).[70] In light of Lev 27:28 and 30,[71] the Chronicler's term "the tithe of sacred things"

[69] In 2 Chr 31:14-19 the Chronicler claims that Kore the gatekeeper, with six other assistants, was in charge of apportioning "the contribution and the most holy things" (תרומת יהוה וקדשי הקדשים) to the priests and Levites. The phrase "the contribution and the most holy things" is likely to include all the items that people brought to the Temple. With this phrase, the Chronicler seems to exclude any implication that the priestly share could be different from the levitical due.

[70] The term "the tithe of sacred things" (מעשׂר קדשים) appears only in 2 Chr 31:6. Thus, what it designates is not clear. In his article, Joseph Baumgarten ("Critical Notes: On the Non-Literal Use of Ma'aser/Dekate," 245) introduces Rashi's interpretation of this phrase: "it is the tithe that the Levites should give to the priests from their tithes." In other words, Rashi considered that "the tithe of sacred things" was the same with "the tithe of tithes," which the Levites should give to priests. Other scholars suggest either omitting the word מעשׂר from this phrase as a dittography, or adding a few words after the word מעשׂר to smooth the text, such as כל תבואת שׂדה to read "tithes of all produce of the field," based on 2 Chr 31:5. For the former view, see Curtis and Madsen, *The Books of Chronicles*, 479-80; and for the latter view, see Rudolph, *Chronikbücher*, 304. S. Japhet, H. G. M. Williamson, and S. L. McKenzie simply repeat both views without their own judgment in their commentaries on Chronicles. However, there is no textual evidence for any of these proposals. The manuscripts of LXX, Vulgate, Targum and Peshitta retain the phrase without any emendation of it.

[71] To clarify what this term (מעשׂר קדשים) designates, we need to examine first what קדשים might modify. Among numerous references to קדשים in the Biblical texts, the relevant cases are found in Lev 27:28, and 30. According to Lev 27:28, every dedicated thing (כל־חרם), whether man, or beast, or one's inherited land, is defined as most holy (קדשׁ־קדשים). According to N. Lohfink ("חרם." *TDOT* 5:180-99), חרם in Lev 27:28 is used "in the sense of something removed from the sphere of the profane and set apart for Yahweh." Lev 27:30 also defines "all tithes from the land" as holy to God (קדשׁ ליהוה).

Table 5. The Institution of Tithes

Text	The property subject to tithe	Beneficiary of the tithes	Administration	Storage	Others
Gen 14:20	A tenth of everything	Melchizedek the king-priest of Salem			
Gen 28:22	A tenth of all that God gives to Jacob	At the shrine of Bethel			
1 Sam 8:15, 17	The tenth of the grain and of the vineyards	The king's officers and servants			The tithe will be paid to the king
Deut 12:6-7; 14:23	The annual tithe (the tithes of grain, wine and oil)	It should be consumed by its offerer and his household in the central sanctuary during the festival			The tithe may be converted into silver for the people who dwell far from the central temple (Deut 14:23-24)
Deut 14:28-29; 26:12	The triennial tithe	It will be consumed by the Levite, the stranger, orphan and widow in each local village			
Lev 27:30-33	The tithe of the land (מעשׂר הארץ) and the tithe of the herd and flock (מעשׂר בקר וצא)	To the priests			Monetary replacement of the tithe of the land is allowed with 20% addition of it (Lev 27:31), but the tithe of the herd and flock may not be redeemed
Num 18:21-32	The tithe	To the Levites			The Levites should set aside the tithe of the tithes to give it to the priests

Text	The property subject to tithe	Beneficiary of the tithes	Administration	Storage	Others
2 Chr 31:5-6	The tithe of everything and the tithe of cattle and sheep	To the priests and the Levites	The supervision of collection of people's donations including tithes was in charge of Conaniah the Levite, and Shimei his brother as well as ten other overseers (2 Chr 31:12-13). For the allocation of these donations was in charge of Kore the Levite, the keeper of the East Gate and his six colleagues (2 Chr 31:14-19)	The chambers in the Temple (2 Chr 31:7-8)	The tithe of the tithes is not mentioned
Neh 10:38 (cf. Mal 3:8)	The tithe of the land	To the Levites	The collection of the tithe was in charge of the Levites under the supervision of an Aaronide priest (Neh 10:38-39). For the distribution of the tithe, the temple treasury committee was composed by Nehemiah (Neh 13:13)	The store-rooms of the Temple or the treasury	The Levites give the tithe of the tithes to the priests (Neh 10:39; 12:47)
Neh 13:5	the tithes of grain, wine, and oil	To the Levites, singers and gatekeepers			
Jud 11:13		To The priests			
Tobit 1:6-7	the tithe of the grain, wine, oil, pomegranates, figs, and the rest of the fruits	To the Levites			
Ant. 4:68 and 205	The tithe	To the priests and the Levites			
Ant. 20:181, 206; and *Life* 1:63, 80	The tithe	To Priests			

probably is equivalent to the tithe of every dedicated thing in Numbers 18, which is reserved as part of the priestly due.[72]

I argue, therefore, that 2 Chr 31:4-19 reflects the Chronicler's own exegesis of Leviticus 27 and Numbers 18 and his creative synthesis of the two contradictory laws. Whereas the author of Nehemiah 10 and 13 gave more weight to Numbers 18 in his application of the regulation for the tithe, the Chronicler produced a new regulation by combining two different regulations of Leviticus 27 and Numbers 18.

S. Japhet argues that the Chronicler's presentation of Hezekiah's measures in 2 Chr 31:11-13 "reflects a process of increasing centralization in the administration of the tithes, and probably reflects a specific development of the Second Temple period."[73] However, it is not certain that the Chronicler's description reflects the actual circumstances of the Temple in his time: 1 Chronicles 9, a text from the Persian period, where certain necessary items for the daily sacrifices are listed, does not mention explicitly the tithes. Thus, the Chronicler's own text does not verify that the Chronicler's view on the tithe in 2 Chronicles 31 has any relation to realities of his own time. Indeed, the temple staff that the Chronicler describes in 2 Chronicles 31 is not identical with the one that he portrays in 1 Chronicles 9. It is more likely that the Chronicler intends to provide a historical precedent for his own exegesis of the regulations for the tithe in Leviticus 27 and Numbers 18 by inserting an extended narrative into the Deuteronomistic History

[72] It should be noted that "every dedicated thing" (כל־חרם) is reserved as a part of the priestly due in Num 18:14. Num 18:8 also grants "all the sacred things of the Israelites" (כל־קדשי בני־ישׂראל) to the priests. Thus, the Chronicler's term, "the tithe of sacred things," can mean the tithe of the priestly share. It seems that the Chronicler alters the term "the tithe of the tithes" (מעשׂר מן־המעשׂר) of Num 18:26 to make it designate both the tithe of the priestly share and the tithe of the levitical share. Although the Chronicler's unique term מעשׂר קדשים has not been explained in this fashion by other commentators, this new interpretation makes better sense of it than other suggestions. My interpretation is corroborated by the fact that the subject who brought the tithe of the sacred things is not specified in 2 Chr 31:6. Those who brought the tithe of the sacred things were "the men of Israel and Judah living in the towns of Judah." By choosing a generic noun as the subject, the Chronicler seems to claim that everyone, *including the priests and the Levites themselves*, is obliged to bring the tithe. In his description of Hezekiah's measures for the maintenance of the Temple, the Chronicler clearly presents his egalitarian view about temple administration. The priests as well as the Levites would pay the tithe of their revenue as laymen did and would receive an equal share without any distinction in 2 Chr 31:4-19. To underpin his argument, the Chronicler asserts that whatever Hezekiah undertook in the service of the Temple was done "in accordance with the law and commandment" (בתורה ובמצוה).

[73] Japhet, *I & II Chronicles*, 966.

of King Hezekiah (2 Kings 18).[74] A brief one-verse statement concerning Hezekiah's reform in 2 Kgs 18:4 provides the opportunity for the Chronicler to elaborate it into three chapters (2 Chronicles 29–31). Whereas 2 Kgs 18:4 portrays Hezekiah's reform based on the Deuteronomistic ideology (the centralized worship at the chosen place and a thorough elimination of any idolatrous practices), 2 Chr 31:29-31 provides an alternative version of Hezekiah's reform, and embeds his own ideas about temple worship and administration, ideas which are also presented in 1 Chronicles 15-16, 23-28 and elsewhere.[75]

The Chronicler's innovative view concerning the tithe could not have been put into practice unless the highest authority over the temple administration strongly supported the Levites, as Hezekiah is portrayed as doing in 2 Chronicles 29–31. At any rate, it is likely that the Chronicler's innovation in the institution of the tithe must have been short-lived, if it was ever carried out, because the third-century B.C.E. texts report the diversion of the tithe to the priests, as we have noted.

3.2.2. Priestly Gifts (תרומות)

The second category of Temple revenue is a contribution or gift (תרומה). In general תרומה means "a part or portion which has been lifted and separated from a greater whole for another purpose."[76] In Priestly tradition, this portion is given to the priests (Lev 7:14; Num 5:9; and 18:8). Various items were offered as priestly gifts throughout the biblical era. Pentateuchal regulations command that all the Israelites should redeem the firstborn of their sons, and all their male livestock (Exod 13:2, 12-13, 22:28-29; 34:19-20; Num 18:15, 17; and cf. Deut 15:19-20) and the redemption money given to the priests (Num 18:15). Additionally, the priestly portion includes the choicest first fruits of their land (Exod 23:19; 34:26; Num 18:13); all the best of the oil, and all the best of the wine and of the grain (Num

[74] E. L. Curtis (*The Books of Chronicles*, 480) also gives a similar view on 2 Chronicles 31: "The Chronicler also gives an ideal picture of these contributions for the support of the priests and Levites as an object-lesson for his own times." His view that 2 Chronicles 31 reflects the Chronicler's concern about his own time is also found in the following works: Williamson, *1 and 2 Chronicles*, 374; and McKenzie, *1–2 Chronicles*, 347.

[75] Japhet, *I & II Chronicles*, 914.

[76] *HALOT*, 1789. Exod 35:5-24 provides a long list of items that could be offered as a contribution to God (תרומה ליהוה). In principle almost everything that is useful for the service in the Temple can be offered.

18:12: Deut 18:4); the first batch of dough (Num 15:20); all devoted things (כל־חרם) (Num 18:14); all the holy contributions (תרומת הקדשים) (Num 18:19); all the meat of sin offering and guilt offering (Leviticus 6-7); the breast or right thigh from well-being offerings (Leviticus 5; 7:32; cf. Deut 18:3: the shoulder, the two jowls, and the stomach of every animal to be sacrificed); the first of the fleece of the sheep (Deut 18:4); and the tithe of the tithes (Num 18:26, 28).[77]

The Chronicler's list of items (2 Chr 31:5-6) required to be offered as תרומה is extensive but less specific than Pentateuchal regulations, and includes the first fruits of grain, wine, oil, honey, and all the produce of the field; the tithe of everything; the tithe of cattle and sheep, and the tithe of the dedicated things. All of these contributions, not only the tithes, but also the other offerings, will be distributed to *both the priests and the Levites*, a claim of levitical standing that is unique to the Chronicler.[78]

How was this priestly share (תרומה) distributed? This question seems not to have been a major concern to biblical authors except for the Chronicler. The consumption of the priestly share is dealt with in Leviticus 10 and Numbers 18, but with an eye not to logistical matters but to the maintenance of ritual purity. There, the priestly gifts are divided into two categories: the most holy offerings (קדש הקדשים), and תרומות and תנופת.[79] The most holy offerings are anything reserved from the offerings by fire, such

[77] Ezekiel also explains the priestly share in detail. According to him, in the future temple, the following will be allocated to the priests: the meal offerings, sin offerings, guilt offerings, and every devoted thing (כל־חרם), all the choice first fruits of every kind, all the gifts of every kind (כל־תרומת כל) (Ezek 44:28-30). It is worth noting that Ezekiel's complete silence about the share of the Levites deviates from the regulations in Num 18:21, 24.

[78] Neh 10:36-38 lists the priestly share as part of the agreement (אמנה) that Nehemiah made with the returnees. The contributions that the returnees pledge to give to the priests are as follows: the first fruits of their soil, and of every fruit of every tree; the first-born of their sons and beasts; the firstlings of their cattle and flocks; the first part of their dough, and their gifts (תרומת) of grain, the fruit of every tree, wine and oil. As Neh 10:37 asserts that these items are required by the Torah (ככתוב בתורה), the list of required offerings is a good example of the harmonization of the regulations concerning the priestly share found in the Pentateuch. In a sense, Nehemiah's list is more conventional than the Chronicler's, in that it does not include the tithes (since they are considered by Nehemiah as the levitical share).

[79] These two terms, *tĕrûmôt* and *tĕnûpôt* are often translated as "the heave offerings" and "the wave offerings," respectively, partly based on *m. Menaḥ.* 5:6, but the exact meaning of these terms is still debated (Lev 7:29-36; 10:14-15; Num 6:20; 18:18). For this reason, I chose to put the transliteration of each term, instead of translating them. Concerning discussions about the precise meaning of these terms, refer to Grabbe, *Judaic Religion in the Second Temple Period*, 137.

as every meal offering, sin offering, and guilt offering (Num 18:9). This first category is designated exclusively for the priests and must therefore be consumed in a holy place (Num 18:10; and also Lev 10:12-13). The second category includes the priestly portions which are set aside from the well-being offerings, such as the breasts for the *tĕnûpôt*, and the right thighs for the *tĕrûmôt* (Lev 7:29-36; 10:14; Num 18:11), as well as all the best of the new oil, wine, and grain and the first fruits of everything in the land (Num 18:12-13). These are given to all the priestly families, and can be eaten in purity everywhere (Lev 10:14). These details notwithstanding, Leviticus 10 and Numbers 18 do not even hint at the existence of an administrative body to supervise the disbursement of the priestly share. In several places in Nehemiah and 2 Chr 31:12-19, however, bits of information about the process of apportioning the contributions can be found.

Neh 12:44 says that a certain group of people was appointed over the chambers where the contributions (תרומות), the first fruits, and the tithes were stored, at the time when Nehemiah made a firm agreement with the returnees. The numbers and affiliations of such people are not mentioned. Their main responsibility is to collect (כנס) the priestly and levitical portions in accordance with the law, and deposit them in the store-chambers. It is not stated explicitly whether they also had a responsibility to *distribute* the portions to the priests and the Levites. However, the later accusation against Tobiah for embezzlement of the levitical shares (Neh 13:10) implies that the officials of the chambers were likely responsible for allocating the portions to each group. According to Neh 13:13, Nehemiah, after dismissing Tobiah from his position, reorganized a treasury committee whose main duty was to distribute the portions to their associates. This committee was comprised of four members, who were perhaps two priests and two Levites.

The Chronicler appears to be relatively more concerned about the process of the storage and distribution of the portions to the priests and the Levites. 2 Chr 31:12-13 describes the establishment, during the reign of Hezekiah, of an administrative body whose duty was to supervise the process of the collection and storage of the people's contributions. Another administrative body is then introduced in 2 Chr 31:14-19, whose task is to apportion the contributions (תרומת יהוה) and the sacred things (קדשי הקדשים). Certainly, 2 Chr 31:12-19 shows a more elaborate bureaucratic tendency than Nehemiah. However, this does not necessarily imply that the Chronicler intended to retroject contemporary practices or institutions into the time of Hezekiah, *contra* S. Japhet.[80] The Chronicler's description of the administrative bodies is an unrealized ideal that the Chronicler projects but which does not exist in his own day. As I showed in section 2.2.3, the Chronicler's concern here seems to be to defend the Levites as eligible for the contributions in terms of equality. The Chronicler could have designed 2 Chr 31:12-19 as evidence of an historical precedent that he could rely on for a defense of his general stance regarding the temple administration and relatively elevated status of the Levites.

For this purpose, indeed, he again engages in creative—and harmonizing—exegesis of Pentateuchal regulations.[81] First, the Chronicler abolishes the distinction made in Leviticus 10 and Numbers 18 between the offerings required to be consumed in the sanctuary, and those that could be consumed by Priestly families away from the Temple. The Chronicler combines both types of offering into one category in 2 Chr 31:14, and designates both priests and Levites as their legitimate recipients: the gifts will be distributed to all the male priests from three years old and up (2 Chr 31:16) and all the Levites from twenty years old and up, including their dependents (2 Chr 31:17-18).[82]

In a second and related move, the Chronicler elevates the degree of the sanctity of the Levites by applying to them the terminology previously used exclusively for the priests.[83] Thus, in 2 Chr 31:18, the Chronicler asserts that the Levites are eligible for the portions (previously priestly portions) because they are faithfully keeping themselves holy (כי באמונתם יתקדשו־קדש).[84] In the Priestly source and in Ezekiel the Levites are never called "holy" (קדוש).[85] The Chronicler's two other references to the holiness of

[80] S. Japhet ("The Distribution of the Priestly Gifts according to a Document of the Second Temple Period," in *From the Rivers of Babylon to the Highlands of Judah: Collected Studies on the Restoration Period* [Winona Lake: Eisenbrauns, 2006] 292) argues: "The document in its present form (2 Chr 31:14-19) is undoubtedly from the Second Temple period, not only in terms of language and style but also in content, for the order of service described is based on the system of priestly courses, which certainly originated in the Second Temple Period."

[81] Japhet, *I & II Chronicles*, 969-72.

[82] A textual corruption found in this passage hinders its precise interpretation, but the basic idea is not changed regardless of different reconstructions of the text. Concerning the text-critical issues of this passage, see Japhet, *I & II Chronicles*, 970.

[83] Japhet, *I & II Chronicles*, 969-72.

[84] The phrase באמונתם is one of the Chronicler's favorite ones, which he uses to emphasize the virtue of the Levites in 1 Chr 9:22, 26, 31; 2 Chr 19:9 and 31:18.

[85] In the following places in the Pentateuch, it is the priests who are said to be holy (to God): Exod 28:36; 29:33; Lev 6:18, 27; 21:6, 7, 8; 23:20; Num 16:38. Num 16:3-40, where the

the Levites show a strong contrast to the Priestly traditions (2 Chr 23:6 and 35:3).

With these two changes, the Chronicler justifies the eligibility of the Levites for the priestly gifts.[86] But what is more surprising is his remarkable ability, which we have noted in several places, to adapt various scriptural traditions to his own purposes. It is not certain how successful the Chronicler's effort to promote the elevated status of the Levites was in his own time; but the fact that a similar effort to entitle the Levites to some of the priestly gift is found in a later text, the Temple Scroll (11QT) 60:6-8, implies that the Chronicler's perspective on this issue influenced later readers.[87] 11QT 60:6-8 reads:

> And it shall be for the Levites: a tenth of the grain, the new wine and the oil which they consecrate to me first; and the shoulder from those who slaughter the sacrifice; and a levy on the booty and spoil; and one percent of the catch of birds, animals and fish; and of the pigeons and of the tithe of the honey, one fiftieth. But to the priest belongs one percent of the pigeons ...[88]

In Deut 18:3, "The shoulder from the sacrificed animal" was assigned to the priests, along with the two cheeks and the stomach. Thus, here in the Temple Scroll the share of the Levites is much expanded in comparison with the former traditions of the Mosaic Law.

The above exploration concerning the priestly gifts suggests that issues surrounding the distribution of the priestly gifts remained unsettled not only in the immediate post-exilic period, but throughout the entire Second Temple era. This issue seems to have been ineluctably entangled with the question of who controlled the temple administration. The temple revenue, either the tithes or the priestly gifts, must have been vulnerable to

---

account of rebellion of Korah and his company is introduced, directly deals with the issue of who is holy to God. In this passage, to come near to God is defended as the exclusive priestly prerogative. However, the Chronicler's defense for the sanctity of the Levites could be supported by the following passages, which urge all the Israelites to be holy: Lev 11:44; 19:2; 20:7; 20:26; Deut 7:6; 14:2, 21; 26:19; 28:9. In addition, in Num 6:5, 8 the Nazirite is claimed to be holy to God.

[86] Japhet, "The Distribution of the Priestly Gifts," 293, 297, 301-3.

[87] Japhet, "The Distribution of the Priestly Gifts," 303-4.

[88] Translation from Martínez and Tigchelaar, eds., *The Dead Sea Scrolls Study Edition*, 795.

the influence of different groups which controlled the Temple at different times; hence the jockeying, in various sources, for various parties' access to the tithes or gifts.[89] One suspects, indeed, that to implement the Chronicler's pro-levitical policies would have been impossible without levitical control over the administration of the temple treasuries or store-chambers. Here, then, we begin to grasp more clearly why the Chronicler is so careful and even so relentless in presenting a wide variety of levitical powers as having originated with David and Hezekiah. If the Chronicler's claim that the Levites are legitimate partakers in the priestly gifts faced opposition in his own day, he must have intended their elevated status to be made to seem a matter of long-standing consensus, not a recent, and potentially illicit, innovation.

3.2.3. The Temple Tax

In analyses of issues relating to Temple revenue, the temple tax tends to loom large. Relying primarily on Exod 30:11-16; 38:25-26; 2 Chr 24:5-11; 34:8-13; and Neh 10:33, scholars have asserted that the payment of a temple tax was "a regular feature of temple administration" beginning in the Persian period and continuing down into the Roman period.[90] A close examination of these texts, however, reveals that none of them explicitly support that assumption. Contentions that 1 Chr 24:5-11 and 2 Chr 34:8-13 reflect practices of the temple administration during the Persian era are unwarranted.

In Exod 27:20-30:38, Moses explains the regular, daily activities to be performed in the Tent of Meeting. Exod 30:11-16, which belongs to this larger context, introduces a regulation to collect money from the populace

[89] Clearly, when compared with the view on the priestly gifts presented in Nehemiah, the Chronicler's perspective is quite pro-levitical. S. Japhet ("The Distribution of the Priestly Gifts," 303) compares the Chronicler's obvious pro-Levitical view in 2 Chr 31:14-19 with the Temple Scroll's emphasis of the status of the Levites, and concludes:

> It has become evident that the Chronicler's unique position of this work vis-à-vis Levites was not the personal inclination of one author, but a more widespread view, aspects of which are expressed in the writings of the Dead Sea sect.

[90] Blenkinsopp, *Ezra-Nehemiah*, 316; A. Lemaire, "Administration in Fourth-Century B.C.E. Judah," 59-60; Marthy E. Stevens, *Temples, Tithes, and Taxes: The Temple and the Economic Life of Ancient Israel* (Peabody, MA: Hendrickson, 2006) 108-13; and Charles E. Carter, "The Province of Yehud in the Post-Exilic Period: Soundings in Site Distribution and Demography," in *Temple Community in the Persian Period* (eds. T. C. Eskenazi and K. H. Richards; JSOTSup 175; Sheffield: JSOT Press, 1994) 140.

as a measure to maintain the service of the Tent of Meeting. According to this regulation, when a census is undertaken, every male from the age of twenty years and up is to pay a half shekel according to the sanctuary weight as the expiation money (כסף הכפרים) (Exod 30:12, 15, 16) to ransom their lives (כפר נפשו). The repetition of the word כפר four times in this short passage emphasizes the reason for the census tax collection. In addition, the phrase כפר נפשו implies that this money needs to be paid only once in one's lifetime.[91] That seems to be why this money is even defined as "a reminder (זכרון)" that one's life is ransomed before God (Exod 30:16b).

Exod 30:16a, where this money is assigned "to the service of the Tent of Meeting" (על־עבדת אהל מועד), does not exclude the possibility that the money can be collected at every census. However, after Exod 38:25-26, which indicates that the ransom money was collected in the wilderness period for the Tabernacle, a half-shekel tax never appears again in the biblical texts that describe the pre-monarchic or monarchic periods.

The Chronicler, we may recall, refers to this very regulation in his treatment of Joash's repair of the Temple (2 Chr 24:5-11). As I argued in section 2.3.1, the Chronicler uses the Mosaic regulation found in Exod 30:11-16 to justify collecting people's *voluntary* offerings for the upkeep of the Temple. The collection of the people's donation for the Temple is described again in 2 Chr 34:8-13, which proves to be similar to 2 Chr 24:5-11. In both texts, the Chronicler establishes legal precedents for the collection of the people's contribution for the management of the Temple and indicates who was eligible to handle the contributions.

However, neither of these "precedent-setting" passages provides any explicit evidence for the temple tax or for the presence of itinerant tax collectors; nor does the Chronicler evince any other sign of familiarity with an annual tax for the temple's upkeep. For one thing, the Chronicler gives no hint that he is familiar with Nehemiah's measure of an annual poll tax of one-third shekel of silver (Neh 10:33 asserts that the returnees agreed to give one-third of a shekel yearly for the service of the Temple).[92] The

[91] Several scholars have argued that Exod 30:11-16 is a regulation for a one-time donation, not a yearly tax. See Japhet, *I & II Chronicles*, 844; and McKenzie, *1–2 Chronicles*, 316.

[92] J. Blenkinsopp (*Ezra-Nehemiah*, 316) conjectures that the stipulation of Neh 10:33 would have been earlier than the one reflected in 2 Chr 24:4-14, mainly based on his assumption that taxation inexorably tends to increase. His suggestion relies on his unverified identification of the phrase משאת משה (2 Chr 24:9) with a half-shekel tax. This identification is untenable, as I argued before. Moreover, the amount of money to be paid for a tax is at most a precarious indicator determining the temporal sequence between two different stipula-

Chronicler's silence about the temple tax may imply that Nehemiah's stipulation for a poll tax for the Temple was a temporary measure, if indeed it had ever been put into practice.[93]

Apart from the texts noted above, there are no further references to a temple tax in the Hebrew Bible. Even in the Deutero-canonical texts, a half-shekel temple tax is not mentioned: Tob 1:6-8, where Tobit's offerings for the sanctuary are delineated in detail to emphasize his piety, does not allude to the temple tax. According to J. Liver, the earliest testimonies we have for an annual half-shekel tax for the temple service date to the period of Roman rule in Judea.[94]

There are some references to the regulation for the payment of a half-shekel as ransom for one's life in several texts in the Qumran corpus, such as 4Q159 2:6, 12; 11 QT 39:8, 10.[95] 4Q159, a fragmentary text of a part of a commentary on biblical laws, states clearly that a half-shekel payment is not an annual tax, but a single payment in one's life.[96] The regulation that 11QT 39:8 presents is similar to 4Q159. It states: "[...] for himself [a ransom] to YHWH (כופר] ...]) נפשו ליהוה) half a shekel, an eternal law."[97] However, these two texts seem not to confirm the practice of an actual annual collection of the temple tax. Rather, both texts appear to be an exegetical work on Exod 30:11-16, whose purpose is rather the establishment of communal ideals.

---

tions for taxes. There is no archaeological evidence for the collection of revenue in kind for the Temple during the Persian period; see H. G. M. Williamson, *Studies in Persian Period History and Historiography*, 52-53. On the contrary, C. E. Carter ("The Province of Yehud in the Post-Exilic Period," 140) argues that a temple tax imposed by Nehemiah supported temple operations, and that the income generated by the periodic influx of pilgrims also had wide effects on the economy of Jerusalem and Yehud. However, this seems to be overstated since the textual evidence as well as archaeological findings in the Persian period do not support Carter's argument.

93 Herbert Niehr ("Abgaben an den Tempel im Yehud der Achaimenidenzeit," in *Geschenke und Steuern, Zölle und Tribute: antike Abgabenformen in Anspruch und Wirklichkeit* [eds. H. Klinkott et al.; Leiden; Boston: Brill, 2007] 151) also asserts that the tax collection under Nehemiah soon came to a halt in that there are no references to the temple tax in the sources of the time after Nehemiah.

94 Jacob Liver, "The Half-Shekel Offering in Biblical and Post-Biblical Literature," *HTR* 56 (1963) 185-86.

95 4Q513 has one reference to a half-shekel, but the text itself is fragmentary, so that it is hard to know what the purpose of that half-shekel would be.

96 F. G. Martínez, *The Dead Sea Scrolls Translated: The Qumran Texts in English*, 86.

97 Translation is mine.

Josephus mentions the collection of a half-shekel tax from Babylonian Jewry in *Ant.* 18:312. This practice seems to have been understood to be in accordance with the custom of their ancestors (πάτριον). Moreover, in *Ant.* 16:160-172, Josephus provides almost a dozen imperial and local decrees, which grant Jews a privilege to send the sacred money (τὰ ἱερὰ χρήματα) to Jerusalem.[98] Philo refers explicitly to the annual temple tax in *Special Laws* 1:76-78: "It is ordained that everyone, beginning at his twentieth year, should make an annual contribution ... In fact, practically in every city there are banking places for the holy money where people regularly come and give their offerings." Matt 17:24 also provides textual evidence for the temple tax in its reference to "the collectors of the temple tax" (οἱ τὰ δίδραχμα λαμβάνοντες).[99]

With all these observations, it seems reasonable to conclude that the annual monetary payment of the temple tax did not become an established institution and was not fixed as an obligation imposed on every Jew until the end of the Hasmonean rule or somewhat later.[100] Therefore, the scholarly convention that the annual monetary payment of the temple tax became an established institution in the time in which Chronicles was written should be re-evaluated. Certainly, 2 Chr 24:5-11 and 2 Chr 34:8-13

[98] Lee I. Levine, *Jerusalem: Portrait of the City in the Second Temple Period (538 B.C.E.–70 C.E.)* (Philadelphia: The Jewish Publication Society, 2002) 247.

[99] In fact, what τὰ δίδραχμα indicates has been debated among the New Testament scholarship. Scholars relate it to the pre-70 C.E. tax paid to the Jerusalem Temple, or to the post-70 C.E. tax for the temple of Jupiter Capitolinus levied by Rome on Jews. Their views are dependent on the context in which they choose to read τὰ δίδραχμα. For the former view, that is, the pre-70 C.E. tax, see W. D. Davies and D. Allison, *A Critical and Exegetical Commentary on the Gospel According to Saint Matthew Vol. II: Commentary on Matthew VIII-XVIII* (ICC 26; Edinburgh: T&T Clark, 1988) 738-41. For the view of the post-70 C.E. tax, see Warren Carter, "Paying the Tax to Rome as Subversive Praxis: Matthew 17.24-27," *JSNT 16* (1999) 3-31; and R. J. Cassidy, "Matthew 17:24-27: A Word on Civil Taxes," *CBQ* 41 (1979) 571-80. Some scholars admit the polyvalence of the text (Matt 17:24-27) and accept both interpretations. See Edward J. Carter, "Toll and Tribute: A Political Reading of Matthew 17.24-27," *JSNT* 25/4 (2003) 414-16. Not only the identity of τὰ δίδραχμα, but also the method of paying it has been a subject of scholarly debate. Some scholars suggest that τὰ δίδραχμα should be regarded as a voluntary offering rather than as a tax in usual sense of the term. See Cassidy, "Matthew 17:24-27: A Word on Civil Taxes," 574; S. Mandell, "Who Paid the Temple Tax when the Jews were under Roman Rule?" *HTR 11* (1984) 223-32; and also D. Garland, "'Matthew's Understanding of the Temple Tax (Matt 17.24-27)," in *SBLSP 1987* (ed. K.H. Richards; Atlanta: Scholars Press, 1987) 197. These scholarly discussions indicate that the practices related to the temple tax even in the First Century C.E. were known only vaguely.

[100] Liver, "The Half-Shekel Offering in Biblical and Post-Biblical Literature," 190.

should not be considered as evidence for the temple tax. Rather, the two texts provide the Chronicler's rationale for the collection of people's voluntary contributions for the management of the Temple.

3.2.4 Imperial Taxes

The involvement of temples in the ancient Near East in collecting imperial taxes is widely attested in economic texts from the various temples during the Persian period.[101] If the Second Temple, as many scholars have argued, was the center of socio-economic activity in Achaemenid Yehud, it is natural to wonder how the temple administration was involved in collecting and paying imperial taxes.[102] Archaeological evidence suggests that imperial taxes were paid by Yehud during the Persian period; yet the Chronicler does not make any explicit comment on imperial taxes.[103] Why not? Can his silence be understood as a discreetly presented ideological stance? Does

[101] Such as the Eanna Temple at Uruk and the Ebabbar Temple at Sippar. The references to these temples will be introduced later when we discuss the administrative systems of these temples in section 3.3.

[102] The following scholars have contended that the Jerusalem Temple in the Achaemenid period functioned as a center of gathering imperial taxes, but they have not further examined how the temple administration was involved in gathering and paying the taxes to the central government, except for Joachim Schaper ("The Temple Treasury Committee in the Times of Nehemiah and Ezra," 200-206; and "The Jerusalem Temple as an Instrument of the Achaemenid Fiscal Administration," *VT* 45 [1995] 528-39). See Oded Lipschits, "Achaemenid Imperial Policy, Settlement Processes in Palestine, and the Status of Jerusalem in the Middle of the Fifth Century BCE," in *Judah and the Judeans in the Persian Period*, 38-40; Lester L. Grabbe, "The History of Israel: The Persian and Hellenistic Periods," in *Texts in Context: Essays by Members of the Society for Old Testament Study* (ed. A. D. H. Mayes; New York: Oxford University Press, 2000) 409; Rainer Albertz, "The Thwarted Restoration," in *Yahwism After the Exile* (ed. R. Albertz and Bob Becking; Assen: Royal Van Gorcum, 2003) 3; John Kessler, "Persia's Loyal Yahwists: Power Identity and Ethnicity in Achaemenid Yehud," in *Judah and the Judeans in the Persian Period*, 109-11; Jon L. Berquist, *Judaism in Persian's Shadow: A Social and Historical Approach* (Minneapolis: Fortress, 1995) 131-35; and Kenneth G. Hoglund, *Achaemenid Imperial Administration in Syria-Palestine and the Missions of Ezra and Nehemiah* (Atlanta: Scholars, 1992) 224-26.

[103] One may argue that it must have been intrinsically impossible for the Chronicler to mention anything about imperial taxes in his work since it mainly consists of narratives of the monarchic period of ancient Israel. However, if the Chronicler intended to rationalize practices of his own day through his re-writing of the former historical narratives, as scholars often argue, he could have made administrative staff in the Temple involved in collecting, keeping or paying tributes or taxes to an imperial power at a given time. In fact, there is no reference to such an activity by temple personnel in Chronicles. One may ask whether this silence would be intentional.

the Chronicler wish to underscore his view that the temple administration should be independent from non-cultic fiscal matters? Or might it indicate that the collection of imperial taxes was carried out by a different authority, such as the local governor, apart from the temple administration?[104]

A review of the available evidence reveals that in all likelihood, Yehud did pay imperial taxes to the Achaemenid Empire. But whether the temple administration at the time of the Chronicler was involved in collecting and paying imperial taxes is a much more difficult issue to settle. I will suggest below that the Chronicler's silence about imperial taxes was part of his idealistic presentation of temple administration, which he thought could and should be effectively managed in his own day without royal patronage.

3.2.4.1. Evidence for Imperial Taxes Paid by Yehud

Textual and archaeological evidence indicates that Yehud paid imperial taxes to the Achaemenid Empire. I shall present first the biblical and extra-biblical literary evidence, and then the archaeological evidence.

3.2.4.1.1. Textual Evidence

(1) Biblical Texts

There are several references to imperial taxes in Ezra-Nehemiah. The first appears in Ezra 4:13, which is ostensibly part of a letter (Ezra 4:11-16) that opponents of the returnees who were reconstructing Jerusalem sent to King Artaxerxes. In that letter, the opponents declare that if Jerusalem is rebuilt, the people of Jerusalem will not pay tribute (מדנה), poll-tax (בלו), or land-tax (הלך) (Ezr 4:13). Here, the payment of the imperial taxes is taken for granted, if we take the text at face value.

Artaxerxes' reply to that letter (Ezra 4:17-22) also confirms that the Judeans, under Achaemenid rule, paid tribute, poll-tax, and land-tax to the Persian kings (Ezra 4:20). Furthermore, in Darius' decree, which

[104] M. Heltzer ("The Provincial Taxation in the Achaemenid Empire and 'Forty Shekels of Silver' (Neh 5:15)," *Michmanim* 6 [1992] 15) argues that taxation inside the province could have been organized according to the decisions of the local governor (as in the case of Nehemiah). The central authorities of the Empire were interested in obtaining the tax in the amount due, but were concerned neither with how it was levied inside the province nor which group of the population paid it. See also M. Heltzer, "The Social and Fiscal Reforms of Nehemiah in Judah and the Attitude of the Achaemenid Kings to the Internal Affairs of the Autonomous Provinces," in *The Province Judah and Jews in Persian Times* (Tel Aviv: Archaeological Center Publications, 2008) 71-93.

allowed the returnees to resume rebuilding the Temple in Jerusalem (Ezra 6:8-12), Darius commands that the cost for rebuilding the Temple should be paid from "the tribute of the province Beyond the River" (מדת עבר נהרה) (Ezra 6:8). This text confirms that royal tribute was imposed on the satrapy "Beyond the River," to which the province of Yehud belonged. On the other hand, Artaxerxes' decree, addressed to all the treasurers (כל גזבריא) of the satrapy Abar-nahara (Ezra 7:21-24), grants an exemption from tribute, poll tax, or land tax for the cultic personnel of the Jerusalem Temple.[105] Regardless of the historical authenticity of this decree, the text shows that the author envisaged that the payment of imperial taxes was routine at that time.[106]

Other texts also indicate that the people of Yehud paid imperial tax levies. According to Neh 5:4, people in Yehud had to borrow money to pay the royal tax (מדת המלך). Neh 9:37 also describes people's regret over the fact that their riches flew to the kings. However, it is not known how these taxes were levied, nor does one find references in the biblical texts for how these taxes were remitted to the Persian Empire by Yehud.[107]

More information is available regarding the uses to which tax revenues of Yehud were ultimately put. The cost of the governor's salary and all the expenses for the maintenance of the province of Yehud were defrayed by the taxes of the people in the province, according to Neh 5:14-18. It is also reported that the governors before Nehemiah took food and wine from people, besides the forty shekels of silver, as their לחם הפחה. M. Heltzer argues that forty shekels of silver was the tax for a single peasant household to pay annually to their local governor.[108] The governor, then, was

[105] The historical authenticity of this text has been questioned among scholars. For instance, H. Niehr ("Abgaben an den Tempel im Yehud der Achaimenidenzeit," 146) argues that Ezra 7:12-26 originates in the Hellenistic period and it cannot be a portrayal of the Achaemenid period.

[106] Exemption of temple officials from taxation and tribute is attested to in several documents originating in the Persian period. For instance, Darius's letter to Gadatas mentions the exemption to the priests of Apollo from tribute and corvée labor. However, L. Fried (*The Priest and the Great King: Temple-Palace Relations in the Persian Empire* [Winona Lake: Eisenbrauns, 2004] 108-19) argues that the authenticity of this letter has been questioned from the beginning when the inscription was found. As for the authenticity of Ezra 7:21-24, Lester L. Grabbe ("The "Persian Documents in the Book of Ezra: Are They Authentic?" in *Judah and Judeans in the Persian Period*, 555) asserts: "Ezra 7:21-26 is not the decree of a Persian king, but the wishful thinking of a Jewish apologist."

[107] C. E. Carter, *The Emergence of Yehud in the Persian Period: A Social and Demographic Study* (JSOTSup 294; Sheffield: Sheffield Academic Press, 1999) 256.

[108] Heltzer, "The Provincial Taxation," 17-25.

amply provided for: Neh 5:17-18 suggests the scale of the daily expense for the governor's food was one ox and six choice sheep, fowl, and abundant wine for one hundred fifty people who sat at the governor's table.[109]

This picture corresponds with Dandamaev and Lukonin's and P. Briant's reconstructions of the administration of taxation in the Achaemenid Empire.[110] Provinces under the Empire had to pay imperial taxes and to provide for the satraps and governors, although in actual practice remarkable levels of diversity on the matter of taxation among the provinces existed within the Achaemenid Empire.[111]

(2) Extra-Biblical Texts

Although no extra-biblical economic documents are extant from Persian-era Yehud, a few texts that derive from Greece and Rome seem to confirm that the province of Yehud paid heavy tribute to the Achaemenid Empire just as other local provinces did.

Chapters 90–94 of Book III of Herodotus, for example, provide a list of the taxes and gifts that the satrapies paid to the Empire.[112] The fifth satrapy, that is, the whole of Phoenicia and Syria, is said to have paid a total of 350 talents.[113] The historical authenticity of Herodotus' report cannot be taken as a given, but Herodotus' description of the satrapial obligation to pay tribute to the Persian Empire is supported by archaeological findings.[114]

[109] P. Briant (*From Cyrus to Alexander: A History of the Persian Empire* [Winona Lake: Eisenbrauns, 2002] 402-3) points out how heavy the burden of hospitality would be for the province which had to host the king and his entourage or the satrap and his retinue when they visited. To prepare the royal dinner or "the Satrap's Table" was the most ponderous duty of all weighty obligations (Herodotus, VII.118-20; Xenophon, *Hellenica* III.1.12; Plutarch, *Alcibiades* 12; Athenaeus, *Deipnosophists* XII.534c-d).

[110] Dandamaev and Lukonin, *The Culture and Social Institutions of Ancient Iran*, 177-95; and Briant, *From Cyrus and Alexander*, 388-421.

[111] Dandamaev and Lukonin, *The Culture and Social Institutions of Ancient Iran*, 96-97, 192. P. Briant (*From Cyrus to Alexander*, 389) asserts that the tribute system did not undergo any revolutionary modifications throughout the Achaemenid Empire except the variations in extent and number of satrapies.

[112] Dandamaev and Lukonin, *The Culture and Social Institutions of Ancient Iran*, 184; Heltzer, "The Provincial Taxation," 15-16; and Briant, *From Cyrus to Alexander*, 388-98.

[113] M. Heltzer ("The Provincial Taxation," 15-16) conjectures that this amount of silver was paid only as the royal tribute, which did not include the local payments on the satrapial and provincial level of the regions.

[114] P. Briant (*From Cyrus to Alexander*, 388, 392) evaluates Herodotus' passage on tribute and taxes as follows:

> This text poses many difficult interpretive problems due to Herodotus' main focus on the immediate relationship between tribute levying and imperial dominion.

Josephus also states that Artaxerxes (II or III) imposed tribute on the Jews, so that they had to pay fifty shekels for every lamb which was offered for the daily sacrifices (*Ant.* 11.297).[115]

3.2.4.1.2. Archaeological Findings Concerning the Payment of Imperial Taxes

A variety of types of material provide evidence for the practices of taxation in a region during a certain period:[116] lists of taxable persons and property (which are necessary to assess the taxes and to collect them), records of assessment and collection of taxes[117] and any artifactual or documentary findings related to storage cities or granaries where the taxes were depos-

---

> However this text offers a wealth of information, even on the level of accounting practices, despite the fact that Herodotus himself is no expert in fiscal matters. ... Even though Herodotus made some arithmetic errors in converting to talents the amounts that had been furnished him in darics, it is apparent that the numerical information he gives must be considered reliable. The precision suggest quite strongly that he had access to official documents, such as, for example, quotations from the archive of Sardis and elsewhere.

On the other hand, Dandamaev and Lukonin (*The Culture and Social Institutions of Ancient Iran*, 179) cautions us that Herodotus' statement cannot be accepted without reservation. Both point out that Herodotus mentioned that the Persians were exempted from taxes since they were the ruling people (III, 97). However, the Persepolis Fortification tablets (henceforth PF) indicate apparently that the Persians were not exempt from taxes in kind (*e.g.*, PF 443, 451, 567, 2025, and 2070). For the cited texts, refer to Richard T. Hallock, *Persepolis Fortification Tablets* (Chicago: The University of Chicago Press, 1969).

[115] H. G. M. Williamson ("The Historical Value of Josephus' Jewish Antiquities xi. 297-301," in *Studies in Persian Period History and Historiography*, 74-89) suggests that the Artaxerxes mentioned in *Ant.*11.297 would be Artaxerxus III Ochus (358–338 B.C.E.). However, James C. VanderKam (*From Joshua to Caiaphas*, 60-63) argues that this incident happened during the reign of Artaxerxes II (404–358 B.C.E.), refuting Williamson's argument. Regardless of the debate on which Artaxerxes was intended in this story, it was cited here since it underscores the probability that the Jews in the province of Yehud paid imperial taxes.

[116] J. N. Postgate, *Taxation and Conscription in the Assyrian Empire* (Studia Pohl: Series Maior 3; Rome: Biblical Institute Press, 1974) 196-98.

[117] The following Aramaic documents found in Egypt belong to the second category. *TAD* C 3.11 dated to c. 416 BCE is a record of tax payments by various food processors. From *TAD* D 8.4 to *TAD* D 8.8, there are five accounts concerning silver. Especially, *TAD* D 8.7 is an account about silver "paid in(to) the treasury. *TAD* D 8.13 is a unique receipt for salt tax. For the text *TAD* C 3.11, see Bezalel Porten and Ada Yardeni, eds., *Literature, Accounts and Lists* (Vol. III of *Textbook of Aramaic Documents from Ancient Egypt*; Winona Lake: Eisenbrauns, 1993) 209-10. For the texts *TAD* D 8.4; D 8.5; D 8.6; D 8.7; D 8.8; and D 8.13, see B. Porten and A.Yardeni, eds., *Ostraca and Assorted Inscriptions* (Vol. IV of *Textbook of Aramaic Documents from Ancient Egypt*; Winona Lake: Eisenbrauns, 1999) 197-201.

ited, all provide valuable insight into procedures and policies relating to taxation.[118]

The first category, lists of taxable persons and property, encompasses items such as land registries or a census lists.[119] No such documents that date to the Persian period have been found from the province of Yehud. However, a copious amount of material that belonged to the second category (records of assessment and collection) is now available in the form of the Persian-period Aramaic ostraca excavated from several places in the province of Idumea, to the immediate south of the province of Yehud.[120] Although they are not from Yehud, those ostraca may shed some comparative light on practices of the taxation of Yehud during the Persian period.

At Tel Beer-sheva more than eighty Aramiac ostraca were found in the strata of the Persian period.[121] These ostraca are dockets that mention exact dates, specific amounts of wheat and barley and names of persons who presumably supplied these provisions. J. Naveh suggests that those ostraca were probably used as tags, attached to grain-sacks, which were brought as taxes to Beer-sheba.[122] Therefore, the excavators at Tel Beer-sheba conclude that Beer-sheba must have been an administrative center to which grain

[118] For example, *TAD* C 3.7, the Aramaic document from Elephantine, is a long list of monthly customs duty and tithe paid into the royal treasury dated to 475 BCE. For the text and its translation, see Porten and Yardeni, *Literature, Accounts and Lists*, 82-193.

[119] *TAD* D 8.3 is a land registry, which records a dozen Egyptian names and one Hebrew name with their properties. For the text and its translation, see Porten and Yardeni, *Ostraca and Assorted Inscriptions*, 196.

[120] Gerald A. Klingbeil ("A Semantic Analysis of Aramaic Ostraca of Syria-Palestine During the Persian Period," *AUSS* 35/1 [1997] 33-46) provides a semantic analysis of the Persian-period Aramaic ostraca for Syria-Palestine. Although he does not include Aramaic ostraca found in Maqqedah (Khirbet el-Kœm), his study gives a good introduction to Aramaic ostraca. According to Klingbeil, the genre of Persian-period Aramaic ostraca is classified as business administrative texts, which comprise lists of persons, receipts and order forms.

[121] Twenty-six Aramaic ostraca were found in the first and second seasons of excavation at Tel Beer-Sheba, all in refuse pits of the Persian period. All these ostraca were dated within the fourth century BCE, to the reigns of Artaxerxes II (404–359 B.C.E.) and Artaxerxes III (359–338 B.C.E.). An additional 54 Aramaic ostraca were discovered during the excavations held by Aharoni at Tell Beer-Sheba. These ostraca were found in silos. See J. Naveh, "The Aramaic Ostraca," in *Beer-Sheba I, Excavations at Tel Beer-Sheba 1969–1971* (ed. Y. Aharoni; Tel Aviv: Tel Aviv University-Institute of Archaeology, 1973) 79-82; idem, "The Aramaic Ostraca from Tell Beer Sheba (Seasons 1971–1976)," *Tel Aviv* 6 (1979) 182-98; and also Hanan Eshel, "Hellenism in the Land of Israel from the Fifth to the Second Centuries BCE in Light of Semitic Epigraphy," in *A Time of Change*, 116-24.

[122] Naveh, "The Aramaic Ostraca," 82.

was brought as taxes.[123] John W. Betlyon also argues that Tel Beer-sheba was a local collection point for the payment of agricultural taxes.[124]

Additionally, some 100 Aramaic ostraca from the fourth century B.C.E. were unearthed at Tel Arad on the eastern side of the Beer-sheba Valley, where the existence of a Persian-era fortress is also proved by archaeological finds.[125] Most of these ostraca are notes instructing the recipient to provide supplies, including various types of food, for men and animals (horses, donkeys and camels) to the bearer. The bearers of these "requisition forms" were horsemen and donkey-drivers serving in the Persian army or administration. We also have evidence that a commander of ten, the *ganzabar* (treasurer) ʿAqabiah, who was in charge of ten donkey drivers, and ʿAnani, who seems to have been in charge of a granary, were also in possession of such ostraca.[126] Most of the names of the bearers were Jewish, but most taxpayers were Arabs and Idumeans.[127] The Jewish involvement in taxation in the province of Iduamea underscores the probability that the Judean taxes were similar to the Idumean taxes.[128] The Arad

[123] Naveh, "The Aramaic Ostraca," 82; and also E. Stern, *Archaeology of the Land of the Bible Vol. II: The Assyrian, Babylonian, and Persian Period (732–332 BCE)* (New York: Doubleday, 2001) 446.

[124] John W. Betlyon, "A People Transformed: Palestine in the Persian Period," *NEA* 68 (2005) 4-60.

[125] J. Naveh, "The Aramaic Ostraca from Tel Arad," in *Arad Inscriptions* (ed. Y. Aharoni; Jerusalem: Israel Exploration Society, 1981) 153-76; Hanan Eshel and Boaz Zissu, "Two Notes on the History and Archaeology of Judea in the Persian Period," in *"I Will Speak the Riddle of Ancient Things": Archaeological and Historical Studies in Honor of Amihai Mazar on the Occasion of his Sixtieth Birthday* (ed. A. M. Maeir and P. de Miroschedji; Winona Lake: Eisenbrauns, 2006) 830; and Stern, *Archaeology of the Land of the Bible*, 372.

[126] E. Stern, *Archaeology of the Land of the Bible*, 446, 452.

[127] According to Esther Eshel ("The Onomasticon of Mareshah in the Persian and Hellenistic Periods," in *Judah and Judeans in the Fourth Century B.C.E.*, 150), the majority of names recorded on the Arad Aramaic ostraca are Jewish names with the –YH theophoric element. For this reason, she asserts that in Arad most of the soldiers were Jews. On the other hand, A. Kloner and I. Stern examined the ethnic backgrounds of about 1,300 names recorded on the Aramaic ostraca from late-Persian-period Idumea, and provided the following result: "The enthnic breakdown reflected by the ostraca reveals a very mixed population: approximately 32% Arab names, 27% Idumean names, 25% West Semitic names, 10% Judean names, 5% Phoenician names and 1% other minor ethnicities." The divergence of ethnicity in Arad Aramaic ostraca, however, reveals an interesting feature: 61.22% the Judahites, 14.29% Idumeans, 12.25% the West Semites, and 12.24% Arabs. See, A. Kloner and I. Stern, "Idumea in the Late Persian Period (Fourth Century B.C.E.)," in *Judah and the Judeans in the Fourth Century B.C.E.* (ed. Oded Lipschits, Gary N. Knoppers, and Rainer Albertz; Winona Lake: Eisenbrauns, 2007) 139-44, here 141-43.

[128] André Lemaire, "New Aramaic Ostraca from Idumea and Their Historical Interpretation," in *Judah and the Judeans in the Persian Period*, 415.

ostraca indicate that Tel Arad probably functioned as a way station where barley was supplied to horsemen and their beasts.[129] These ostraca support the possibility that most of the imperial taxes were consumed in the local provinces or satrapies, rather than delivered to the central government. At any rate, there is no material evidence for the payment of imperial taxes by the province of Yehud to the Achaemenid Empire in the areas where the imperial centers were located.

Makkedah ostraca provide direct evidence of tax-collection in the province of Idumea between 362 and 312 B.C.E.[130] These ostraca were used as tags attached to sacks or jars with agricultural produce that were submitted to the Persian authority as taxes.[131] According to A. Lemaire, most of the ostraca are connected with a land-tax paid in kind and collected in the Makkedah storerooms (מסכנת מנקדה). Evidence for a poll-tax paid in silver is also found in a few ostraca.[132]

All these Aramaic ostraca are not direct evidence for the payment of imperial taxes by the province of Yehud, they do indicate that imperial taxes were probably paid by the province of Yehud.[133]

Additional textual evidence contained in a fourth-century B.C.E. papyrus document from Ketef Yeriḥo may fill in the picture of imperial taxation in Yehud a bit more. The document consists of a list of 23 names (mostly

[129] Stern, *Archaeology of the Land of the Bible*, 446.

[130] A. Lemaire, "Taxes et impôts dans le sud de la Palestine (IVᵉs. av. J.-C.)," *Transpeuphratène* 28 (2004) 133-42; H. Lozchmeur and A. Lemaire, "Nouveaux ostraca araméens d'Idumée," 123-42; S. Ahituv and A. Yardeni, "Seventeen Aramaic Texts on Ostraca from Idumea: The Late Persian to the Early Hellenistic Periods," *Maarav* 11/1 (2004) 7-23; and B. Porten and A. Yardeni, "Social, Economic, and Onomastic Issues in the Aramaic Ostraca of the Fourth Century B.C.E.," in *Judah and the Judeans in the Persian Period*, 457-88.

[131] Eshel, "Hellenism in the Land of Israel," 121-22.

[132] A. Lemaire, "Administration in Fourth-Century B.C.E. Judah in Light of Epigraphy and Numismatics," in *Judah and the Judeans in the Fourth Century B.C.E.*, 58. Some Makkedah ostraca apprear to be drafts of a land registry, such as the ostracon published by Shmuel Aḥituv ("An Edomite Ostracon," 33-34).

[133] In my brief survey on imperial taxation in Egypt, Idumea, and Yehud during the Perisan period, I noticed the fact that the various terms for taxation are used in the documents originated from these three regions. For instance, in the Hebrew Bible, מנדה, בלו, or הלך are used to designate imperial taxes, while אשכר is used in Aramaic ostraca. In Aramaic texts from ancient Egypt, מנדה and מכס are used. We do not know how these terms were used or why different terms were used in different regions. An extensive study of the terminology of taxation in the Achaemenid period is in great need, although it is beyond the scope of the present study. The following article is related to this topic, but it does not include the Achaemenid period: Maria deJ. Ellis, "Taxation in Ancient Mesopotamia: the History of the Term *miksu*," *JCS* 26 (1974) 211-50 (the Persian period is not included).

Yahwistic), with a sum of money in shekels (ש), *rib'în* (ר) or *ma'at* (מ) noted next to each name.[134] Most of the sums listed are of either 1 or 2 shekels, or a half shekel. The purpose of this document is not clear. H. Eshel and H. Misgav conjecture that the *recto* is a record of money lent to various people, amounting to twenty-one shekels, while the *verso* lists the amount of money received as repayment of these loans.[135] Interestingly, though, a few ostraca from Makkedah also preserve a list of personal names followed by a half shekel or a multiple of a half shekel. Thus, following M. Heltzer, I suspect that the papyrus from Ketef Yeriḥo may be connected with the taxes of the province of Yehud.[136]

The third category of evidence for imperial taxes paid by the province of Yehud includes findings related to the storage cities or granaries, where the levies of grain, wine, and the like deposited. In Palestine during the Persian period, there were many granary cities, such as Meggido, Tell Jemmeh, Makkedah, and Beer-sheva.[137] Meggido, a major city, served as an important urban center furnished with several storehouses down to the end of the Persian period.[138] Tell Jemmeh also had a storehouse consisting of five rectangular-shaped rooms with mud-brick walls, as well as some ten round granaries (silos) in its latest stratum to the Persian period dated to as early as 460 B.C.E.[139] Four ostraca were found in this city. Two of them are notes instructing the recipient to provide supplies to the bearer, similar to the Arad ostraca, but the other two are wine dockets.[140]

The inscribed seal impressions belonging to the officials of the local Persian provincial administration are a valuable indicator of such storage cities. Recent studies by O. Lipschits and D. Vanderhooft of Yehud seal impressions (abbreviated as YSI hereafter) have shown that among the 570 stamp impressions of different types, 80 percent of the YSIs were found in Ramat Raḥel and Jerusalem. About 95 percent of the entire corpus was found in a

[134] Hanan Eshel and Hagai Misgav, "A Fourth Century B.C.E. Document from Ketef Yeriµo," *IEJ* 38/3 (1988) 165; and idem, "Jericho papList of Loans ar," in *Miscellaneous Texts from the Judaean Desert* (ed. J. Charlesworth et al; DJD 38; Oxford: Clarendon, 2000) 21. Here, the shekel was equal to four רבעין, and a רבע was equal to six מעה.

[135] Eshel and Misgav, "Jericho papList of Loans ar," 22.

[136] Heltzer, "The Provincial Taxation," 171.

[137] Morris Silver, *Prophets and Markets: The Political Economy of Ancient Israel* (Boston: Kluwer-Nijhoff, 1983) 35-38.

[138] Stern, *Archaeology of the Land of the Bible*, 373.

[139] Stern, *Archaeology of the Land of the Bible*, 412.

[140] J. Naveh, "Aramaic Ostraca and Jar Inscriptions from Tell Jemmeh," *Atiqot* 21 (1992) 49-53.

small circle between Tell en-Naṣbeh in the region of Benjamin and Ramat Raḥel.[141] According to Lipschits and Vanderhooft, YSIs found at Ramat Raḥel constitute the largest and most varied group of impressions found in one place from the Persian period.[142] On the basis of this fact, excavators suggest that in the Persian period the seat of the governor of the province was located in Ramat Raḥel.[143] However, the fact that the highest percentage of the jars were found in Ramat Raḥel can be explained in a different way: Ramat Raḥel could have been a major storage center, where goods were collected and stored.[144] The official nature of YSIs strongly suggests that the goods stored in Ramat Raḥel were related to a process of collecting goods (as taxes) within the province of Yehud.[145] These taxes could have been consumed by the province of Yehud or delivered to another collection point in its proximity. This conclusion contradicts J. Schaper's argument that the Jerusalem Temple was the only tax-collection point in the Yehud province.[146]

While none of the evidence that I examined above proves definitively that the province of Yehud paid imperial taxes, my study strongly of data from biblical and extra-biblical sources suggests that the province of Yehud paid them, just as neighboring provinces did. This suggestion, in turn,

[141] Lipschits and Vanderhooft, "Yehud Stamp Impressions," 75-94.

[142] O. Lipschits, D. Vanderhooft, Y. Gadot, and M. Oeming, "Twenty-Four New *Yehud* Stamp Impressions from the 2007 Excavation Season at Ramat-Raḥel," *Maarav* 15/1 (2008) 8. See also Stern, *Archaeology of the Land of the Bible*, 436-37.

[143] Y. Aharoni et al., *Excavations at Ramat Rahel: Seasons 1959 and 1960* (Rome: Centro di studi semitici, 1962); idem, *Excavations at Ramat Rahel: Seasons 1961and 1962* (Rome: Centro di studi semitici, 1964); Stern, *Archaeology of the Land of the Bible*, 437; and also O. Lipschits et als, "Palace and Village, Paradise and Oblivion: Unraveling the Riddles of Ramat Raḥel," *NEA* 74 (2011) 2-49.

[144] D. Vanderhooft (O. Lipschits et al., "Twenty-Four New *Yehud* Stamp Impressions," 12) comments on the fact that Ramat Raḥel is the only site where stamp impressions of all three *pḥwʿ* types have appeared as such:

> It would be hazardous to conclude that Ramat Raḥel, and not Jerusalem, was the seat of the governor of Yehud during the period when these seals were used. Nevertheless, it is clear that the site played a key role in the distribution of the commodities associated with the jars.

Melody D. Knowles (*Centrality Practiced*, 118-119) agrees with D. Vanderhooft by suggesting that Ramat Raḥel was probably the economic center for the Persian era Yehud, which was related to the collection of taxes in kind. C. E. Carter (*The Emergence of Yehud in the Persian Period*, 267) also considers that both Ramat Raḥel and Tell en-Naṣbeh functioned as administrative centers, perhaps for collecting of goods in-kind or other taxable items.

[145] O. Lipschits et als, "Palace and Village, Paradise and Oblivion," 34.

[146] Schaper, "The Temple Treasury Committee," 205.

leads to the conclusion that the Chronicler's silence about imperial taxes should not be understood as indicating either the lack of such taxation or the Chronicler's lack of knowledge of such taxation. The question most relevant to the Chronicler's presentation is whether the temple administration was directly involved in collecting and paying the imperial taxes.

3.2.4.2. The Temple Administration's Involvement in Collecting Imperial Taxes

Scholars who agree that the province of Yehud paid imperial taxes to the Persian Empire typically assert that the Jerusalem Temple played the central role in collecting and remitting those taxes. For instance, K. G. Hoglund argues that Jerusalem was established by the Persian Empire as a location to collect and store imperial revenue during the time of Darius' administrative restructuring.[147] Similarly, Jon L. Berquist asserts that the imperial government supervised the collection of taxes through the Temple since the Temple functioned as the civic and political center of Yehud.[148] These scholars effectively challenged the view that the province of Yehud enjoyed socio-political autonomy during the Achaemenid period, as in J. Weinberg's hypothesis of the Citizen-Temple Community.[149] However, theories that assert the Jerusalem Temple's crucial role in collecting imperial taxes require scrutiny. Since J. Schaper's work has served as the foundation of others who followed, I want to examine his claims about the temple administration staff's role with regard to imperial taxes.

J. Schaper argues that "the Jerusalem temple administration acted as the interface between the tax-paying population of Judah and the Persian government."[150] Elsewhere, he says that "no other institution except the temple treasury committee could have fulfilled the task of collecting and administering the tithes or any other taxes, and indeed no other institution would have received permission from the Persians to do so."[151] The basis for his argument is rooted in two observations: (1) the roles of the Babylonian temples in collecting taxes on behalf of the king during the Achaemenid era; and (2) the presence of a foundry in the Jerusalem Temple.

[147] Hoglund, *Achaemenid Imperial Administration*, 224.

[148] Berquist, *Judaism in Persian's Shadow*, 135.

[149] Joel P. Weinberg, *The Citizen-Temple Community*.

[150] Schaper, "The Jerusalem Temple as an Instrument of the Achaemenid Fiscal Administration," 537.

[151] Schaper, "The Temple Treasury Committee," 205-6.

However, Schaper's argument that temples were the sole agencies for taxation and the only viable collection points in the Achaemenid Empire is not tenable. Even in Babylon during the Achaemenid period, temples were in fact neither the sole collection point for imperial taxes nor the only imperial taxation agency.[152] Rather, the Achaemenid rulers recruited local entrepreneurs, such as the Egibi,[153] Iddin-Marduk,[154] and the Murašû,[155] into the upper ranks of their political administration, and these commercial houses became efficient agents for collecting imperial taxes as well as an effective means to suppress the power of influential Babylonian aristocrats.[156] Further, many storehouses or local treasuries of the Persian period which are not attached to the temples are known to us, apart from the granary cities that I mentioned above.[157]

With regard to his second point, the presence of the foundry in the Temple, Schaper argues:

> Throughout the Achaemenid Empire state taxes could be paid in kind or in precious metals. All over the empire, temples served as collection and storage centers for these metals, and their foundries conveniently melted down and recast them where necessary. In the

[152] Concerning the techniques of the Persian Empire for collecting state taxes, refer to Dandamaev and Lukonin, *The Culture and Social Institutions of Ancient Iran*, 188-95.

[153] Kathleen Abraham (*Business and Politics Under the Persian Empire* [Bethesda: CDL, 2004]) collected more than 300 tablets from the Egibi archive pertaining to *Marduk-nāṣir-apli*, a Babylonian entrepreneur, who led his family business from 521 B.C.E. to 490 B.C.E. In her work on the Egibi archive from Babylon, she shows how the Achaemenid Empire collected their taxes through the collaboration of the local power which was not connected to temple administrations.

[154] Cornelia Wunsch, *Die Urkunden des babylonischen Geschäftsmannes Iddin-Marduk: Zum Handel mit Naturalien im 6. Jahrhundert v. Chr* (Groningen: STYX, 1993).

[155] M. Stolper, *Entrepreneurs and Empire: The Murashu Archive, the Murashu Firm, and Persian Rule in Babylonia* (Leiden: Nederlands Historische-Archaeologisch Instituut te Istanbul, 1985).

[156] M. Stolper, "Mesopotamia, 482–330 B.C.," in *The Cambridge Ancient History* Vol. VI*: The Fourth Century* B.C. (ed. D. M. Lewis et al; 2nd ed.; Cambridge: Cambridge University Press, 1994) 249.

[157] According to Peter R. Bedford ("The Economic Role of the Jerusalem Temple in Achaemenid Judah: Comparative Perspectives," in *Shai le-Sarah Japhet: Studies in the Bible, its Exegesis and its Languages* [ed. Mosheh Bar-Asher et al.; Jerusalem: Bialik Institute, 2007] 17), the Elamite administrative texts from Persepolis also identify about nineteen local treasuries/storehouses, which are not temples. See also Dandamaev and Lukonin, *The Culture and Social Institutions of Ancient Iran*, 208-9; and Briant, *From Cyrus to Alexander*, 428-29. According to Briant, these local treasuries included warehouses and a sizable staff, and their primary functions were to collect, warehouse, and process agricultural and animal products.

Yehud province, the Jerusalem Temple was the only institution which provided the infrastructure needed for such an enterprise.[158]

As I observed above, the Aramaic ostraca found in Idumea indicate that imperial taxes were paid by agricultural products as well as silver in kind. If Yehud paid imperial taxes by agricultural products, and these taxes were sent to the granary cities where Persian authorities were in charge, then the Jerusalem Temple need not have been involved in collecting imperial taxes. Moreover, Schaper's supposition that the Jerusalem Temple had the only foundry in the province of Yehud and that it was used to recast silver collected as taxes in order to mint it into a standard denomination, needs to be re-evaluated.[159] His argument includes two assumptions which have not been proved: first, that the foundry of the temple in Jerusalem was used as a part of a minting facility, and second, that the existence of the foundry of the Temple proves the Temple's involvement in collecting and paying imperial taxes.

If imperial taxes were paid in silver by people in Yehud, the standardization of the metal for further transactions or for the payment of tribute to the Persian Empire would likely have been necessary, since the metal was usually circulated in irregular shape and purity. The process of refining and recasting requires a facility, such as a foundry. This fact seems to support Schaper's claim. The existence of the foundry in the Jerusalem Temple during the Persian period can *perhaps* be inferred: J. Schaper heavily relies on the term יוצר in Zech 11:13 in order to support his argument that the Temple was the sole institution to recast silver. יוצר can be rendered as "potter" (Ps 2:9; Jer 18:2, 4, 6), "maker," or "caster" who melts down metal vessels and tools into ingots.[160] The context of Zech 11:13 requires this term to be rendered as "caster" or "foundry," because the prophet was told to throw his wages (thirty shekels of silver) into the יוצר in the temple. In addition to Zech 11:13, 2 Kgs 12:11 may also imply that a foundry was a crucial part of the temple administration during the monarchic period.[161]

[158] Schaper, "The Temple Treasury Committee," 204; and idem, "The Jerusalem Temple," 531.

[159] Schaper, "The Jerusalem Temple," 536.

[160] *HALOT*, 429. The interpretation of יוצר as "caster," or "founder" was first suggested by Charles C. Torrey ("The Foundry of the Second Temple at Jerusalem," *JBL* 55 [1936] 247-60). See also C. C. Torrey, "The Evolution of a Financier in the Ancient Near East," *JNES* 2 (1943) 295-31, esp. 298-99.

[161] See section 2.3.

Nevertheless, contrary to Schaper, the possible existence of a foundry in the Jerusalem temple does not prove the Temple's involvement in collecting and sending imperial taxes to the central treasuries in Persepolis and Susa.[162] J. Schaper argues: "The treasury committee instituted by Nehemiah oversaw the collection and administration of both "holy" and "secular" taxes. This means that its members acted both as temple officials and as Achaemenid tax collectors."[163] However, Neh 13:13 does not support Schaper's contention. The treasury committee was organized mainly to distribute the proper share of priestly gifts and tithes to the temple personnel. Even if the foundry had been used for the secular tax, the whole process of collecting and sending the imperial taxes could have been supervised by the local governor, and not by the temple administrative staff.[164] There is no direct evidence, at present, that the Jerusalem Temple and the temple administration were directly involved in collecting and paying imperial taxes.[165]

[162] J. Schaper's argument is followed by H. Niehr ("Abgaben an den Tempel im Yehud der Achaimenidenzeit," 141-57).

[163] Schaper, "The Temple Treasury Committee," 205. J. Schaper ("The Jerusalem Temple," 539) also argues that the priests and Levites seem to have been given a regular stipend from the imperial government since the central government wanted a fiscal system to be operated efficiently. However, there is no evidence for his argument.

[164] Evidence from the Yadua coins demonstrates the existence of minting facilities in Yehud. The Yehud coinage consists of a series of tiny silver coins, one of the earliest of the Yehud coin series, which seems to be dated to c. 360 B.C.E. Thus, one may argue that it is highly possible that some types of foundries existed in the Jerusalem Temple, and minting facilities in Yehud. However, there is no archaeological evidence for the existence of foundries in the province of Yehud. Indeed, even in Ramat Raḥel, no vestiges of foundries have been found in the strata of the Persian period. Moreover, it is questionable whether the existence of Yadua coins in the late Persian period implies that the foundry of the Jerusalem Temple was used for minting coins. Without further evidence, it is not possible to prove that the foundry in the Temple of Jerusalem, even if we assume that it existed, was used as a part of a minting facility. See, L. Mildenberg, "On Fractional Silver Issues in Palestine (Pls VIII-XI)," *Transeuphratene* 20 (2000) 89-100; idem, "Numismatic Evidence," *Harvard Studies in Classical Philology* 91 (1987) 381-95, esp. 388-89; Yigal Ronen, "Some observations on the Coinage of Yehud," *Israel Numismatic Journal* 15 (2003) 28-31; and Ya'akov Meshorer, *Ancient Jewish Coinage* (2 vols.; Dix Hills: Amphora Books, 1982).

[165] Melody D. Knowles (*Centrality Practiced*, 120) also argues:

> Evidence for the temple as a depot for taxes is less clear. Although some of the tithe money would ultimately be sent to the imperium, it is hard to say whether all of Yehud had to pay their taxes at the temple. Besides Zech 11:13 there is no clear evidence for the existence of a "king's chest" at the Jerusalem temple. The יהד coins may point to the relation of the temple with a foundry late in the Persian period, but there is no necessary connection.

3.2.4.3. Summary

A brief survey on the evidence for imperial taxes in Persian-era Yehud led us to conclude that the province of Yehud was not freed from the duties of imperial taxes that the Achaemenid Empire imposed. In this sense, one can say that the Chronicler's silence about imperial taxes does not reflect realities of his own day.

On the other hand, no evidence is found that the temple administrative staff was involved in collecting and paying taxes to the central government of the Empire. In the Chronicler's description of the temple administration, no cultic personnel were involved in collecting or sending imperial taxes to any imperial government at a given time. The Chronicler's silence about imperial taxes should be considered together with his failure to indicate Achaemenid political control of Yehud in his book: the Persians make only a brief onstage appearance in the Chronicler's work, and then only at the end of the work (2 Chr 36:20, 22-23). Thus, while *historically*, the Persian presence may have been inescapable, in the Chronicler's fictive world, the profile of Persia is considerably diminished. The Chronicler's silence about imperial taxes, in fact, reveals that his account has been idealized considerably. By not mentioning any circumstances related to the Empire, the Chronicler envisions an ideal world in which the Temple is administered wholly from within and free from geopolitical entanglements with imperial overlords. Clearly, then, the Chronicler's silence about imperial taxes was not a reflection of his own time, but a deliberate attempt to promote his ideal world where temple administration could be operated independently from any possible political interventions.

3.3. Temple Staff

Information about the bureaucratic systems of temple administration is plenteous in Persian era literary sources.[166] Typically, in temple adminis-

[166] Bezalel Porten (*Archives from Elephantine: The Life of an Ancient Jewish Military Colony* [Berkeley: University of California Press, 1968] 46-47) points out that in the Persian period the officials always appear in groups in biblical and extra-biblical material. He also asserts that the system was created to place checks upon the absolute exercise of authority by any single individual and to guard against unlawful usurpation. Several documents from ancient Near East give witnesses to such usurpation or a monopoly of power in a temple. In the Neo-Assyrian period, for example, Letter No. 134, among the letters from priests to the kings Esarhaddon and Assurbanipal, mentions that Pulu, the lamentation priest, ran

trations from this period, cultic staff were divided into two corps of personnel, often comprised of an upper echelon and a lower echelon. Additionally, the upper echelon was frequently headed by two chief officials. To some degree, the Chronicler's presentation of issues pertaining to the administration of the Jerusalem Temple corresponds with trends toward increasing bureaucratization of temple staffs in the Persian Empire as a whole. As we have seen at various points in this study, the Chronicler envisions the existence of a body or bodies of temple administrators with specialized duties throughout the book, such as in 1 Chr 9:26-29; 26:20-28; 2 Chr 31:11-13 and 34:12-13. The bureaucratic system that the Chronicler describes has been treated by several scholars as a reflection of the practices of his own day.[167] Yet it has become apparent, I hope, that the Chronicler's interest in providing levitical genealogies for the non-priestly temple officials of his own day, his consistent concern to situate the origins of offices held by Levites to the era of David, and his adept reinterpretation of Pentateuchal regulations indicate that he is not simply concerned with recording the realities of his day, but with shaping them or with arguing for his view of how the temple *should* operate. There is no question that the Chronicler consistently—and, one suspects, ahistorically— describes non-priestly members of the Jerusalem temple's administration, including gatekeepers, musicians, and treasurers, as Levites. We established over the course of Chapter 2 that each of these interpretive moves is intended to establish the legitimacy of the offices and those who hold them. The question that remains is, "why?"[168] That is, why was such an effort on the Chronicler's part necessary? Or what effect was he trying to produce in the circle of readers to whom he directed his work?

In order to discern more clearly the ideological interests that contributed to the Chronicler's presentation of the administrative structures in the

---

the temple of Nabû arbitrarily by appointing officials of his own and by controlling all the treasuries under his supervision. Another letter, No. 138, shows that the priest of Ea committed a theft in the Temple. For the texts of these letters, refer to Steven W. Cole and Peter Machinist, *Letters from Priests to the Kings Esarhaddon and Assurbanipal* (Helsinki: Helsinki University Press, 1998) 102-4, 110. These letters indicate a possible background for the development of the bureaucratic system in the temple administration. M. Jursa (*Neo-Babylonian Legal and Administrative Documents: Typology, Contents and Archives* [Münster: Ugarit-Verlag, 2005] 49-54) also provides a succinct introduction to the structure of temple administrations of Neo-Babylonian temples.

[167] Japhet, *I & II Chronicles*, 454, 966; Williamson, *1 and 2 Chronicles*, 400-401; and McKenzie, *1–2 Chronicles*, 198, 341.

[168] See section 2.2.3 above.

Jerusalem Temple, it is worth undertaking a brief examination of literary sources that describe the administrations of the Ebbabar temple of Babylon, the Eanna temple of Uruk and the Judean Temple in Elephantine, as well as the portraits of temple administration embedded in other biblical sources. I will then ask if these comparative sources give us a glimpse into the Chronicler's ideological goals: is he an anti-priestly partisan? Does his pro-levitical stance jibe with other portraits of the Levites in the Persian era and thereafter? Or might his shaping of his narrative be intended to achieve a practical, rather than political, end?

3.3.1. Bureaucratic Systems of Temple Administration in the Persian Period

Our first task is to examine several key examples which illustrate the bureaucratic system of temple administration. They show that the diarchic model of governance in Yehud (governor and priest) fits the general pattern of the "two chief" system seen at Ebbabar and elsewhere.

Documents from the archive of the Ebabbar temple show that in the Neo-Babylonian period,[169] the upper echelon of the temple personnel operated under the "two chief" system: this level of management consisted of the "resident" (*qīpu*) of Ebabbar and the "temple administrator" (*šangû*) of Sippar, who were assisted by the "scribes of Ebabbar" (*ṭupšarrū ša*

[169] This archive contains more than 35,000 tablets and fragments from the Neo-Babylonian period to the early Achaemenid period. The documents from the archive reflect the everyday practice of the temple administration. According to John MacGinnis (*Letter Orders from Sippar and the Administration of the Ebabbar in the Late-Babylonian Period* [Poznan: Bonami, 1995] 8), the staff in the Ebabbar temple can be divided into five categories: administrators, ritualists, food offering preparers, craftsman and temple oblates. The terms *qīpu*, *šangû*, and *ṭupšarrū ša Ebabbar* have been translated in various ways by different scholars. Here I follow Bongenaar's translation of these terms except for *ṭupšarrū ša Ebabbar* for which Bongenaar prefers to translate "College scribes" instead of "scribes of Ebabbar." I prefer to use the latter since it is a more literal translation of *ṭupšarrū ša Ebabbar*. See A. C. V. M. Bongenaar, *The Neo-Babylonian Ebabbar Temple at Sippar: Its Administration and its Prospography* (Leiden: Nederlands Historisch-Archaelogisch Instituut te Istanbul, 1997) 6-7. See also M. A. Dandamayev, "Neo-Babylonian and Achaemenid State Administration in Mesopotamia," in *Judah and Judeans in the Persian Period*, 388-95. In the cited article, Dandamayev gives various usages of these titles of officials.

Ebabbar).[170] The lower echelon of the temple administration consisted of overseers (*šāpirū*) and chiefs (*rabûtu*).[171]

The administration of the Ebabbar temple in the Achaemenid period followed a similar pattern to that of Neo-Babylonian period, with some minor modifications.[172] The Achaemenid kings respected the basic structure of the Ebabbar temple administration, but they attempted to co-opt the power of the temple administration by appointing members of the local elite to administrative positions in which they would work for the king's benefit.

A second example of temple administration is found in the archives of the Eanna temple in Uruk, the sanctuary of the goddess Ishtar, which contains over 8,000 tablets. The majority of these tablets date to the Neo-Babylonian and early Achaemenid periods (626–520 B.C.E.).[173] In the Eanna temple, the *qīpu ša Eanna* and the *šatammu ša Eanna* formed the top echelon of the temple administration. Their management was executed in close

[170] It is not always clear whether there was an explicit distinction between the role of *šangû* of Sippar and that of *qīpu* of Ebabbar as the top administrators in the Ebabbar temple. A. C. V. M. Bongenaar (*The Neo-Babylonian Ebabbar Temple at Sippar*, 23) divides the administrative tasks of the *šangû* of Sippar into three categories: (1) management of the property of the temple of Ebabbar consisting of farm land, cattle outside the city and houses in the city; (2) supervision of temple personnel; (3) control over the movements of goods, i.e. the issue and receipt of commodities. It appears that the *qīpu* of Ebabbar was considered superior to the *šangû* of Sippar during the Neo-Babylonian period. From the beginning of the reign of Cambyses, however, this ranking is reversed. See MacGinnis, *Letter Orders from Sippar*, 117 and and Bongenaar, *The Neo-Babylonian Ebabbar Temple at Sippar*, 6-7.

[171] Bongenaar, *The Neo-Babylonian Ebabbar Temple at Sippar*, 142. From the third millennium onwards certain groups of institutional personnel acquired status and income by performing a specific role in the cult. Their ultimate successors were the prebendal elites of the Neo-Babylonian towns of the First Millennium. Some high-ranking temple officials and the groups of brewers, bakers, butchers, fishermen and herdsmen owned the prebendal right which was principally heritable, but could be leased, sold, or transmitted through adoption. Royal officials and the temple scribes were not regarded as prebendaries through their roles in the temple administration unless they acquired a prebendal right by other means. For the prebendal right, see G. van Driel, *Elusive Silver: In Search of a Role for a Market in an Agrarian Environment Aspects of Mesopotamia's Society* (Leiden: Nederlands Instituut Voor Het Nebije Oosten, 2002) 64-86. According to Bongenaar, such a prebendal system continued to exist until the end of Hellenistic period. The main source of the prebendal income was the remnants of the sacrifices offered to the deities.

[172] The upper echelon of the temple administration consisted of the *šangû* of Sippar, the *qīpu* of Ebabbar, and the five scribes of Ebabbar plus an Aramaic scribe (*sepīru*). See Briant, *From Cyrus to Alexander*, 71-72.

[173] Paul-Alain Beaulieu, *Late Babylonian Texts in the Nies Babylonian Collection* (Bethesda: CDL Press, 1994), 6; and M. Jursa, *Neo-Babylonian Legal and Administrative Documents*, 138-39.

collaboration with the *ṭupšarrū bīti* (temple scribes) and the *sepīru* (the Aramaic scribe).[174]

A third set of texts, which has more direct bearing on our study and which illustrates a bureaucratic system of temple administration in the Achaemenid period, can be found in the Elephantine archive. This archive, dating from the fifth century B.C.E., was discovered in the first decade of the twentieth century C.E. in the location of a former Jewish military colony on the island of Elephantine at the southern border of Egypt.[175] The Elephantine texts shed some light on the administrative structure of the Yahweh Temple in Elephantine: a collection of ten documents, known as the archive of Jedaniah ben Gemariah, is of particular interest.[176] These documents consistently indicate that this Jedaniah, who is described as "the priest" (הכהן) in several letters, was a chief official in the temple of Elephantine. He was assisted by five or six subordinates, whose identities vary.[177] In several letters, Jedaniah the priest (הכהן) and his colleagues

[174] L. S. Fried (*The Priest and the Great King*, 9-13) includes *zazakku* and *šākin ṭēmi Uruk* in the list of the Eanna temple personnel, but the *zazakku* (DUB.SAR.ZAG.GA) was a high royal official in charge of the national tax system and the *šākin ṭēmi Uruk* belonged to the city bureaucracy as the governor. M. A. Dandamayev ("State and Temple in Babylonia in the First Millennium B.C." in *State and Temple Economy in the Ancient Near East* [ed. Edward Lipinski; Leuven: Department Oriëntalistiek, 1979] 590) also points out that in the case of the Eanna temple, the involvement of the *šākin ṭēmi Uruk* (the governor of Uruk) and the *rēš šarri bēl piqitti ša muḫḫi quppi* [*makkūr*] *Eanna* (the royal courtier in charge of the cash box of Eanna) in the temple administration was much more visible than in the case of the Ebabbar temple. Nevertheless, they were not regular members of temple administration. Thus, I do not include them in the category of the temple staff.

[175] Porten, *Archives from Elephantine*, vii-viii.

[176] The ten documents in the archive of Jedaniah mostly deal with communal affairs. Most of them concerned the relations between Jews and Egyptians and the destruction of the Jewish Temple. Porten, *Archives from Elephantine*, 278.

[177] It is not clear how many colleagues assisted Jedaniah at any one time. In *TAD* A4.2 or C 37, "Jedaniah, Mauziah, Uriah and the garrison" appear as recipients of the letter sent by someone who introduced himself as their servant. *TAD* A4.3 or C 38 is a letter that Mauziah son of Nathan sent to his lords Jedaniah, Uriah and "the priests of YHW the god" (כהני יהו האל), Mattan and Berechiah (Porten and Yardeni, eds., *Letters*, 56-57). *TAD* A4.10 or C 33 contains an offer of payment for reconstruction of the temple, which was written by five representatives: Jedaniah, Mauzi, Shemaiah, Hosea son of Jathom, and Hosea son of Nattun (Porten and Yardeni, eds., *Letters*, 58-59). *TAD* A4.3 or C 38 is a letter that Mauziah son of Nathan sent to his lords Jedaniah, Uriah and "the priests of YHW the god" (כהני יהו האל), Mattan and Berechiah.Porten and Yardeni, eds., *Letters*, 56-57. *TAD* A4.10 or C 33 contains an offer of payment for reconstruction of the temple, which was written by five representatives: Jedaniah, Mauzi, Shemaiah, Hosea son of Jathom, and Hosea son of Nattun (Porten and Yardeni, eds., *Letters*, 58-59).

the priests (הכהנים) appear as either senders or recipients, with Jedaniah's name appearing prominently in the first position.[178]

Of particular interest to the present study, *TAD* A4.7:18-19 or C 30:18-19 mentions a letter that Jedaniah and his colleagues in Elephantine sent to Bagohi the governor of Judah, to Jehohanan the high priest and his colleagues the priests in Jerusalem, and to Ostanes brother of Anani and the nobles of the Jews.[179] This document implies that Jehohanan the high priest and his colleagues (priests) administered the Jerusalem Temple at that time, a datum that might seem initially to be of limited importance. Yet when we line up biblical texts about the temple administration in the fifth century B.C.E. for comparison with this document, an interesting contrast emerges: whereas *TAD* A4.7:18-19 seems to envision a temple administration comprised of a chief executive assisted by several subordinates, other biblical and post-biblical sources tend to envision a more complex bureaucracy, wherein specific committees oversaw various aspects of the temple's economic management. (See Table 6, p. 154.)

Clearly, the biblical sources take for granted that an administrative body (or bodies) managed day-to-day economic operations in the Temple; it is possible that the *TAD* letter addressed to Jehohanan was intended to bypass layers of bureaucracy. In Ezra-Nehemiah, temple staffs are composed of four members, although the composition of each staff shows slight differences.[180] The Chronicler, unlike the author of Ezra-Nehemiah, insists that non-priestly temple staff (in this case, gatekeepers) were all Levites, and

[178] For example, the so-called "Passover Letter" (*TAD* A4.1 or C 21) was sent to "Jedaniah and his colleagues (ידניה וחבריו)" (*TAD* A4.1:1, 10 or C 21:1, 10) by Hananiah. See Porten and Yardini, eds., *Letters* (Vol. I of *TAD*; Winona Lake: Eisenbrauns, 1986) 54-55. Similarly, (Porten and Yardini, eds., *Letters*, 68-71 and 72-75) it was "Jedaniah and his colleagues the priests (ידניה וחבריו הכהנים)" who wrote letters to Bagohi governor of Judah (*TAD* A4.7 or C 30; *TAD* A4.8 or C 31), and to Delaiah and Shelemiah sons of Sanballat, governor of Samaria (*TAD* A4.7: 29).

[179] Porten and Yardini, eds., *Letters*, 68-71. The purpose of this letter from Jedaniah in Elephantine is to request the Jewish center in Jerusalem to write a recommendation letter to the satrap of Egypt on behalf of the community in Elephantine to permit them to rebuild the Temple of YHW.

[180] A possible relationship between the temple treasuries in Ezra 8:33 and in Neh 13:13 is still debated among scholars. H. G. M. Williamson (*Ezra, Nehemiah* [WBC 16; Waco: Word Books] 388-89) argues that they are two different ones, but J. Schaper ("The Temple Treasury Committee," 200-206) contends, against Williamson, that Nehemiah set up the treasury committee as a permanent one, and the committee mentioned in Ezra 8:33 was the same one that Nehemiah installed. Both arguments are closely related to each scholar's opinion on whether Ezra preceded Nehemiah or not.

Table 6. Temple Staff, Post-exilic Period to the Post-biblical Period

Texts	The composition of the temple staff	The function of the temple staff
Ezra 8:33-34	Two priests and two Levites	To weigh out the gold and silver and the vessels that Ezra brought from Babylon and to record them
Neh 13:13[182]	A priest, a scribe, a Levite and one officer	To distribute the tithes to their kinsmen
1 Chr 9:26-29	The four chief gatekeepers (the four Levites)	To guard the utensils of service and the furniture and all the holy utensils; and to supply flour, wine, oil, incense, and spices for daily sacrificial services
TAD A4.7:18-19	Jehohanan the high priest and his colleagues the priests	
m. Šeqal. 5:2[183]	The three treasurers, together with the seven administrators	To manage the finances and property of the Temple; to keep the holy vessels and priestly vestments; to distribute funds, flour for meal offerings and wine for libations; to handle any donations; and to supply wood, animals, flour and oil to make offerings. Many of these tasks were divided among fifteen officers, whose names are listed in *m. Šeqal.* 5:1

[181] J. Schaper ("The Temple Treasury Committee," 201-2) argues that the scribe in Neh 13:13 belongs to the Zadokites since his name is Zadok, and another layman to the Levites because of his genealogy. Thus, according to J. Schaper, the treasurers' committee is composed of two priests and two Levites.

[182] Levine, *Jerusalem*, 243. Although Mishnah was written in c. 200 C.E. when the Temple no longer existed, *m. Šeqal.* 5:2 is included in Table 10 since it provides detailed information about the temple administration (though it is not certain which period the information refers to) and at the same time, it indicates that the temple administration gradually developed into a sophisticated bureaucratic system.

presents them as being charged with the care of cultic items. The Mishnah's description of the temple staff and their duties seems to reflect a more sophisticated bureaucratic system than those found in Ezra-Nehemiah and Chronicles. The Mishnah's description may have been related to practices of a much later period than the Chronicler's time (perhaps the practices of the Herodian temple), if indeed it is meant to reflect the realities of a certain time. The fact that *m. Šeqal* 5:1 provides names of the fifteen officers who performed specific tasks in the Temple implies that the descriptions derive from recent memory, rather than from the fourth century B.C.E.

When viewed against contemporary works, Chronicles' incorporation of non-priestly temple staff (i.e. gatekeepers) into the corps of Levites by genealogical means and its emphasis on their access to the most valuable cultic items remains distinctive enough to demand further investigation. If we are to gain ground on the Chronicler's intentions *vis-à-vis* his depictions of Levites we must first determine first whether the Chronicler's pro-Levitical tendency pairs with a negative treatment of the priesthood. How does the Chronicler's depiction of for example, the high priest, compare with depictions of this figure in Ezra-Nehemiah, *et al.*? Second, we must inquire whether the Chronicler's favoritism to the Levites has any proponents in the later period, such as the Hellenistic or Hasmonean period.[183] If it does, the Chronicler's partiality to the Levites should be understood within a larger context where various interpretations about participants in the cult were produced.

3.3.2. The Chronicler's Treatment of the High Priesthood

The majority of the references to the title "high priest" (הכהן הגדל) or "chief priest" (הכהן הראש) appear in texts written after the Persian period.[184]

[183] This question will be dealt with in the next chapter, which concludes the present work, where I propose why the Chronicler incorporated all the non-priestly temple personnel into the Levites. See section 4.2. I shall argue that extra-biblical sources of Hellenistic or Hasmonean period reflect conflicts among the various parties who defended their own right to serve in the Temple and that the Chronicler's description of the temple staff could indeed have been a product of his engagement in a dynamic conversation with them.

[184] The references to the title הכהן הגדל: Num 35:25, 28 ; Josh 20:6; 2 Kgs 22:4, 8; 23:4; 2 Chr 34:9; Neh 3:1, 20; 13:28; Hag 1:1, 12, 14; 2:2, 4; Zech 3:1, 8; 6:11. The title הכהן הגדל is translated into ὁ ἱερεὺς ὁ μέγας in the LXX of all the cited passages except for Josh 20:6 (the title does not appear in the LXX). On the other hand, the title הכהן הראש appears in 2 Kgs 25:18; Jer 52:24; Ezra 7:5; 1 Chr 27:5; 2 Chr 19:11; 24:11; 26:20; 31:10. Unlike the title הכהן הגדל, the title הכהן הראש is translated in various ways in the LXX. For instance, הכהן

Indeed, Persian era texts in general do not tend to focus on the office of high priest. The references to Joshua in Ezra, for example, do not even use the term "high priest," even though we know, from Hag 1:1, 12, 14; 2:2, 4; Zech 3:1, 8, that that office is meant. Joshua's priestly status is known in Ezra only from his patronym and from his association with other priests.[185] The title "high priest" is used only once in Chronicles (2 Chr 34:9) for Hilkiah during the reign of Josiah.[186] Similarly, we might note Neh 12:10-11, 22-23, 26, which is believed, based on Josephus' list of the high priests (*Ant.* 11.121, 297, and 302), to contain the names of high priests in the Persian era.[187] Yet the names on the list in Nehemiah 12 are not identified explicitly as high priests.[188] In contrast, there is *TAD* A4.7 = C 30, according to which, Jehohanan was the high priest (כהנא רבא) of the Jerusalem Temple in the year 401 B.C.E. This Johohanan seems to be the same figure who appears in the list of Neh 12:22 and was one of the recipients of the letter that the Jews of Elephantine wrote asking for support in their efforts to rebuild their temple.[189] This fact implies that the office of the high priest in Jerusalem was highly regarded by the Jews in Elephantine.

הראש is translated into ὁ ἱερεὺς ὁ πρῶτος (in LXX 2 Kgs 25:18; Jer 52:24; Ezra 7:5; 2 Chr 26:20); ὁ ἱερεὺς ὁ ἄρχων (in LXX 1 Chr 27:5; 2 Chr 31:10); ὁ ἱερεὺς ἡγούμενος (in LXX 2 Chr 19:11); or ὁ ἱερεὺς ὁ μέγας (in LXX 2 Chr 24:11). However, the most frequently used title for the high priest in the Greek texts is ὁ ἀρχιερεύς: see 1 Macc 10:20, 32, 38, 69; 12:3, 6, 7; 13:36, 42; 14:17, 23, 27, 30, 35, 41, 47; 15:17, 21, 24; 16:12, 24; 2 Macc 3:1, 4, 9, 10, 16, 21, 32, 33; 4:13; 14:3, 13; 15:12; 1 Esd 5:40; 9:39, 40, 49; 3 Macc 1:11; 2:1; 4 Macc 4:13, 16, 18. The title ὁ ἱερεὺς ὁ μέγας also appears in the following Greek texts: Jdt 4:6, 8, 14; 15:8; Sir 50:1; 1 Macc 12:20; 14:20; 15:2. These data indicate that more than 66% of the occurrences of the title "high priest" or "chief priest" appear in the texts which originated from the Hellenistic period. The frequent appearance of the high priest in literature could imply the significance of his role in the community.

[185] VanderKam, *From Joshua to Caiaphas*, 19-20.

[186] It is likely to be a simple repetition of its source 2 Kgs 22:4. Interestingly, the Chronicler omits Hilkiah's title in the other two cases where his source refers to Hilkiah with his title (see 2 Kgs 22:8//2 Chr 34:15 and 2 Kgs 23:4 which is omitted in Chronicles). Moreover, the Chronicler gives Hilkiah a lesser role in the account of Josiah's reforms than that found in Kings as I observed in section 2.3.2.

[187] Levine, *Jerusalem*, 35.

[188] The only one called high priest in the book of Nehemiah is Eliashib (Neh 3:1). Eliashib and his fellow priests participated in Nehemiah's task to rebuild the wall of Jerusalem. This Eliashib was the high priest when Nehemiah came to Jerusalem in the twentieth year of Artaxerxes I (=445 B.C.E.; Neh 1:1; 2:1). When Tobiah's exploitation of the temple revenue is reported in Neh 13:4-9, he is the one who appointed Tobiah over the storerooms of the Temple. But he is named there as "the priest Eliashib" (Neh 13:4), not the high priest Eliashib. See VanderKam, *From Joshua to Caiaphas*, 50-51.

[189] Bezalel Porten with J. J. Farber et al, *The Elephantine Papyri in English: Three Millennia of Cross-Cultural Continuity and Change* (Leiden: Brill, 1996) 142, n. 59.

The Chronicler seems to prefer another title for the high priest, הכהן הראש, which appears five times in Chronicles.[190] In another case, the Chronicler uses a different title for the chief priest, נגיד בית־האלהים, for Azariah during the reign of Hezekiah (1 Chr 9:11 and 2 Chr 31:12).[191] In all of these cases, the Chronicler's treatment of the high priesthood is similar to the portraits of the high priesthood that we find in Ezra-Nehemiah or in Josephus' *Antiquities*.

According to the Chronicler, the chief priest had the highest authority in cultic matters, but no power in civic matters. For instance, in 2 Chr 19:11 Jehoshaphat appoints Amariah, the chief priest, to oversee religious matters (לכל דבר־יהוה), but sets Zebadiah over the king's matters (לכל דבר־המלך). Such a distinction between spheres of sacerdotal and political responsibility is also found in 1 Chr 26:30 and 32, where matters pertaining to royal administration (דבר המלך) are distinguished from religious matters (דבר האלהים). For this reason, several commentators consider the Chronicler's narrative of Jehoshaphat's judiciary reform as the Chronicler's own work, in which he retrojected the circumstances of his own day into the time of Jehoshaphat.[192]

The Chronicler's perspective on the division of civil and religious jurisdictions appears again in his treatment of Azariah during the reign of King Uzziah (2 Chr 26:20). When King Uzziah violates the priestly privilege of offering incense, Azariah, as a representative of the priests, defends their prerogative against the king (2 Chr 26:16-17).

In section 2.3.1, I discussed the Chronicler's specific treatment of his source, 2 Kgs 12:5-11, which deals with Joash's temple renovations. The Chronicler's version (2 Chr 24:5-11) prohibits Jehoiada, the chief priest, from securing or handling funds for the temple renovation, most likely in order to emphasize the Levites' responsibility to guard and handle the funds. Nevertheless, Jehoiada is portrayed as the chief executive of the cultic staff since he is reprimanded for the Levites's failure to implement the king's command.

[190] There are four priests termed "chief priest" (הכהן הראש) in Chronicles: Amariah under Jehoshaphat (2 Chr 19:11); Jehoiada under King Joash (1 Chr 27:5; 2 Chr 24:6, 11); Azariah under Uzziah (2 Chr 26:20); and Azariah of the house of Zadok under Hezekiah (2 Chr 31:10). See Steven James Schweitzer, "The High Priest in Chronicles," 393.

[191] This title is used once by Jeremiah in a slightly different formula, הכהן והוא־פקיד נגיד בבית יהוה (Jer 20:1).

[192] Paul K. Hooker, *First and Second Chronicles* (Louisville: Westminster John Knox, 2001) 200; and Gary N. Knoppers, "Jehoshaphat's Judiciary," 80.

The fourth chief priest mentioned in Chronicles appears in the narrative of Hezekiah's provisioning of the priests and Levites (2 Chr 31:2-21; and see section 2.2.3). Azariah the chief priest is portrayed by the Chronicler as in charge of the priests and the Levites. Azariah exercises his administrative authority over the cultic domain by participating in the appointment of officials of the storerooms along with King Hezekiah.

All of these observations indicate that in Chronicles, the high priest or the chief priest is presented as the highest authority within the cultic arena, responsible for adjudicating cultic matters, defending priestly privilege, or for being accountable for the actions of all the temple personnel, including the Levites. However, the chief priest is never portrayed as being independent of the king, or as having any authority over civic affairs.[193]

The Chronicler's distinction between cultic and civic matters also appears in other biblical sources that date to the Persian period.[194] The differentiation between the office of the governor and the office of high priest is found in Haggai and Zechariah as well as Ezra-Nehemiah. For instance, the diarchic leadership of the governor and the high priest is expressed with the phrase "Zerubbabel the governor of Judah (פחה יהודה) and Joshua the high priest (הכהן הגדול)" in Hag 1:1, 12, 14; 2:2, 4; Ezra 3:8; and 5:2.[195] Such leadership is also portrayed in the book of Zechariah, using metaphorical or indirect expressions, such as "two olive trees" (Zech 4:11); "two branches of the olive trees," (Zech 4:12) and "the two anointed ones" (שני בני־היצהר) (Zech 4:14). In Ezekiel's program for the future Temple, the careful distinction between the offices of princes and priests is also found (Ezek 37:24-28; 44:1-3; 45:4-5, 7-25; 46:1-10, 12, 16-18; 48:21-22).[196]

According to Ezra 4:1, it was "Zerubbabel and the heads of families" that the adversaries of Judah and Benjamin approached to ask to participate in rebuilding the Temple. Joshua, the high priest, is not mentioned here, even though he was in charge of the construction work itself (Ezra 3:9). This omission indicates that the ability to authorize temple construc-

[193] Schweitzer, "The High Priest in Chronicles," 402; Deborah W. Rooke, *Zadok's Heirs: The Role and Development of the High Priesthood in Ancient Israel* (New York: Oxford University Press, 2000) 238-39; and also Klein, *1 Chronicles*, 212-13.

[194] Knoppers, "Jehoshaphat's Judiciary," 80.

[195] It is worth noting that Joshua is always mentioned second after Zerubbabel in these references. VanderKam, *From Joshua to Caiaphas*, 21.

[196] G. N. Knoppers, "An Achaemenid Imperial Authorization of Torah in Yehud?" in *Persia and Torah: The Theory of Imperial Authorization of the Pentateuch* (ed. James W. Watts; Atlanta: Society of Biblical Literature, 2001) 128.

tion falls under the jurisdiction of the civil authority, even though the execution of the work itself falls to the chief priest. Interestingly, the answer to this request was given by "Zerubbabel, Joshua, and the rest of the heads of fathers' houses in Israel" (Ezra 4:3).

Evidently there was a boundary between the responsibilities that the two leaders assumed, but this boundary, always porous, seems to shift over the course of time, as we see in the edict of Artaxerxes (Ezra 5:12-26), which clearly indicates that the tasks of Ezra were cultic in nature. Yet Ezra's involvement in excommunicating assimilationists due to their exogamic status (Ezra 10) cannot have been solely a cultic matter. More startlingly, according to Neh 7:1, it was Nehemiah, the governor, not Eliashib the high priest, who appointed the cultic personnel, such as gatekeepers, singers and the Levites, even though, clearly, the appointment of cultic personnel is related to cultic matters.[197] All these facts indicate that while during the Persian period there was a differentiation between the cultic sphere and the civic sphere, the boundary between the two spheres fluctuated depending on the balance of power at various times. Compared to Ezra-Nehemiah, the Chronicler's depiction of the division of authority is on the whole much more sharply and consistently drawn.[198]

It is only at the close of the Persian period that the high priest seems to have achieved the exalted status that scholars often associate with it. For example, Josephus' story about Alexander's meeting with Jaddua the high priest (*Ant.* 11.329-39) suggests that Jaddua was a leader not only in cultic affairs, but also in political, and even military ones.[199] However,

[197] J. W. Cataldo (*A Theocratic Yehud?* 103) interprets Nehemiah's reformation as a political move, by which Nehemiah solidified his power over the religious administration. According to Cataldo, Nehemiah's measures to secure the positions and income of the Levites were intended to counterbalance the priestly pursuit of power.

[198] Josephus also presents a story of a high priest named Johanan. According to *Ant.* 11.297-301, Johanan killed his brother Jesus in the Temple. While it is not clear whether this Johanan the high priest was the same as Johanan the high priest in *TAD* A4.7, Josephus' story implies that the office of high priest was subject to intervention by Persian officials, such as Bagoses, the general of Artaxerxes' army (*Ant.* 11.298-301). H. G. M. Williamson ("The Historical Value of Josephus' Jewish Antiquities xi. 297-301," 80-88) argues that they are not the same individuals by suggesting Josephus' Johanan as a later priest paired with Bagoses, a Persian general of Artaxerxes III (358–338 B.C.E.). In contrast, L. S. Fried (*The Priest and the Great King*, 229-30) proposes that the high priest in *Ant.* 11.297 and Johanan in *TAD* A4.7 are the same individual as another Johanan who minted his coins between 378–368B.C.E. In this case, this Johanan had been in office of high priesthood for 40 years. The identity of Johanan is hard to reach a scholarly consensus without any further evidence.

[199] VanderKam, *From Joshua to Caiapas*, 67.

this is an exceptional case. In general, during the Persian period, the high priest never gained any autonomous authority in the province of Yehud, as studies of bullae, seals, and coins from the Persian period corroborate.[200] The records of the governors' names from these sources indicate that a governor was present in the province of Yehud as a civic ruler in almost all the years of Persian control.[201] Recently, O. Lipschits et al. have argued that "the wide distribution of the several YSI types that include the term *pḥwʾ* (פחוא)" and "the existence of a stamp type with the reading *yhwd pḥwʾ*, but no personal name, strongly suggests that there was one, lone governor of Yehud [at a given time] and the office was widely recognized."[202] All of these facts indicate that civil authority during this era rested in the hands of civil imperial appointees, not in the hands of the high priest.[203]

Readers might object that the coins minted in the name of יוחנן הכוהן, i.e., "Yoḥanan the priest," seem to challenge this conclusion. The fact that the priest could mint the coins in the mid-fourth century B.C.E. has been interpreted in several ways:[204] either as evidence for the involvement of Yehud in the Tennes rebellion of the 340s B.C.E.,[205] or as a concrete example for the high priest's control over the secular government.[206] However, these hypothetical interpretations are open to question. There is no evidence to support such hypothetical argument.[207] Moreover, the existence of the coins

[200] Nahman Avigad, *Bullae and Seals from a Post-Exilic Judean Archive* (Jerusalem: The Institute of Archaeology, The Hebrew University of Jerusalem, 1976); E. Stern, *Material Culture of the Land of the Bible in the Persian Period 538–332 B.C.E.* (Jerusalem: Israel Exploration Society, 1982); D. Barag, "Some Notes on a Silver Coin of Johanan the High Priest," *BA* 48 (1985) 166-68.

[201] J. W. Cataldo (*A Theocratic Yehud?*, 90-93, 103, 117) argues that governors continued to function in the province of Yehud after Nehemiah through almost the entirety of the Persian period based on the testimony of the extra-biblical evidence, such as bullae and seals which have either or both *yhd* and *pḥh* signs. See also Fried, *The Priest and the Great King*, 184-87.

[202] Lipschits et al, "Twenty-Four New *Yehud* Stamp Impressions," 11.

[203] VanderKam, *From Joshua to Caiaphas*, 111.

[204] Barag, "Some Notes on a Silver Coin of Johanan the High Priest," 166-68.

[205] D. Barag, "The Effects of the Tennes Rebellion on Palestine," *BASOR* 183 (1966) 6-12; M. Smith, *Palestinian Parties and Politics that Shaped the Old Testament* (New York: Columbia University Press, 1971) 60; and also, John Wilson Betlyon, "The Provincial Government of Persian Period Judea and the Yehud Coins," *JBL* 105 (1986) 637.

[206] Betlyon, "The Provincial Government," 641; and H. G. M. Williamson, "Judah and the Jews," in *Studies in Persian Period History and Historiography*, 44-45.

[207] Archaeological evidence also does not support the involvement of Yehud in these revolts. Moreover, the coins of Yoḥanan were minted on the Persian shekel standard, not on the Attic standard, which most provinces adopted, and the coins are two *gerah* (1/20th of

of Yeḥezqiyah the governor, which can hardly antedate the mid-fourth century B.C.E., attenuates the merit of the argument that the high priest assumed power over the civic matters as well as the cultic matters in the later part of the Persian period.[208]

For the purposes of the present study, what can we now conclude? First, that the Chronicler's treatment of the high priesthood does not deviate from the general thrust of textual and archaeological evidence from the Persian period. In other words, while the Chronicler does not exalt the high priest, neither does he exhibit any strong anti-priestly sentiment in his presentation of temple staff. Thus, it is unlikely that the Chronicler's emphasis on the Levites' status, which runs like a red thread through the work, is based on hostility toward priests.

Having evaluated the Chronicler's portrayal of cultic administrative offices and practices against the evidence of contemporary sources, we may now proceed to the final task of this work, namely, the question of why the Chronicler shaped his material on gatekeepers, treasurers and tax-collectors in the ways that he did.

---

the Persian shekel) pieces. B. W. Root ("Coinage, War, and Peace in Fourth-Century Yehud," *Near Eastern Archaeology* 68/3 [2005]: 134) suggests that this fact may indicate that the one who minted the coins of Yoḥanan was on friendly terms with the Persian king. L. S. Fried (*The Priest and the Great King*, 227-31) also argues that Yoḥanan could mint some coins with his name on them only with Persian permission. Thus, the hypothesis that the coins of Yoḥanan would have been related to the involvement of Judah in the Tennes revolt is far from conclusive.

[208] For the date of these coins, see Barag, "Some Notes on a Silver Coin of Johanan the High Priest," 168; and H. Gitler and C. Lorber, "A New Chronology for the Ptolemaic Coins of Judah," *AJN* 18 (2006) 1-41.

CHAPTER FOUR

The Chronicler's Agenda and Influence

In the previous chapters, I demonstrated how the Chronicler incorporated all the non-priestly temple personnel into one category, that is, the Levites; how he singled out the Korahites to claim the continuity of the office of the gatekeepers throughout the history of Israel; and how he expanded the levitical involvement in certain cultic duties, even though he certainly knew that such expansion deviated from Priestly traditions which he considered authoritative. In the final chapter of the present work we will consider two questions: first, why was the Chronicler so invested in matters pertaining to the Levites? What was he trying to achieve? Second, did his work succeed in accomplishing its aim? These two questions are indispensably related to the historical descriptions of the Levites. I shall try to answer the first question in the context of the depictions of the Levites in the Hebrew Bible by comparing various scholarly interpretations (in Section 4.1). I shall deal with the second question by comparing the Chronicler's view on the Levites with descriptions of the Levites in later works, such as texts that originated in the Hellenistic and Hasmonean periods, including Deutero-canonical and pseudepigraphic works as well as the Dead Sea Scrolls (in Section 4.2).

4.1. The Levites in Chronicles and the History of the Levites in the Hebrew Bible

Throughout the Hebrew Bible, the Levites are presented in various ways which reflect different views on cultic personnel and its roles in the temple administration. All the occurrences of the Levite (הלוי) or Levites (הלוים) in the Hebrew Bible present very interesting patterns.[1]

[1] There are 26 occurrences of the singular noun "the Levite," and 263 occurrences of the plural noun, "the Levites" in the Hebrew Bible: 4 times in Exodus, 2 in Leviticus, 31 in

First, the references of the Levite(s) in the books of Exodus, Leviticus, and Numbers, i.e. so-called Pentateuchal Priestly traditions, hold an almost consistent description of the Levites as a cultic assistant of the priests. In Priestly traditions, the genealogies of Levi (in Exod 6:16-25; Num 3:14-39) were divided into two units: the sons of Aaron (the Aaronide priesthood) and the remaining families of Levi (including Moses and his descendants).[2] The descendants of Aaron are clearly separated as priests from the remaining families of Levi whose roles are mainly to carry the tabernacles and all its equipment (Num 1:50), to substitute for all the firstborn (Num 3:12) and to serve at the Tabernacle (Num 8:15). All these roles of the Levites are overseen by the priests (see Exod 38:21; Num 3:9, 32; 8:11). Thus the Priestly tradition only allows the Levites to be hierodules for the priests. The references of the book of Ezekiel follow this pattern. According to the view of Ezekiel, the levitical priests, who are defined as descendants of Zadok, are solely eligible to perform all the priestly duties in his future temple. The Levites, who are distinguished from the priests, shall be "ministers in the sanctuary" as cultic assistants to the priests and as "gatekeepers" of the temple (Ezek 44:11; 45:5). The secondary status of the Levites is explicit in Ezekiel, where the Levites are accused of having led the house of Israel astray (probably by doing wrong cultic practices) (44:12-13).[3]

Secondly, Deuteronomy and Joshua represent a very different picture of the Levites from the Priestly tradition. Deuteronomy presents two classes of the Levites: the poor Levites in the local sanctuaries and the levitical priests. The first class of the Levites is an object of a charitable concern: people are recommended to take care of the Levites along with the foreigners, widows and orphans because they did not have any portion in the inheritance of the land (Deut 12:12, 18; 14:27, 29; 18:6; 26:13). The second class of the Levites is presented in apposition to the priests, i.e., הכהנים

Numbers, 17 in Deuteronomy, 11 in Joshua, 6 in Judges, 2 in 1/2 Samuel, 1 in 1 Kings, 92 in Chronicles, 18 in Ezra, 33 times in Nehemiah, 1 in Isaiah, 2 in Jeremiah, and 6 in Ezekiel.

2 In Exod 6:15-26, as G. Galil ("The Sons of Judah and the Sons of Aaron in Biblical Historiography," *VT* 35.4 [1985] 488-95) observes, the sons of Aaron and the remaining Levites are introduced by two different formulas: for the sons of Aaron by the formula of "X (male name) married Y (female name) + (her pedigree) and she bore him A,B,C ..." and for the sons of Levi by the formula of "the sons of X: A, B, C...."

3 G. Knoppers (*1 Chronicles 10-29*, 809) interprets Ezekiel's peculiar accusation of the Levites as an implication of the fact that some Levites were involved in the priestly functions in former times.

הלוים (Deut 17:9, 18; 18:1; 24:8; 27:9).[4] By this distinctive expression, the author of Deuteronomy seems to regard all the Levites having basically the same status of the priests. Such a Deuteronomic stance is also found in the book of Joshua. It does not distinguish the Levites from the priests. The term "levitical priests" occurs two times (Josh 3:3; 8:33). Their functions are presented to carry the Ark of the Covenant (Josh 3:3; 8:33) and to bless the people (Josh 8:33). Josh 18:7 explicitly states that the priesthood is the Levites' heritage, and because of that, they have no portion in the land (18:7). The levitical towns are given to them from each tribe instead of the land (Josh 14:3-4; 21). The genealogical information of the descendants of Aaron the priest (Joshua 21) is not separated from the other Levites. "The children of Aaron the priest" are clearly defined as "the Levites" (21:4).

Interestingly, the term Levite very rarely appears in the last books of the Deuteronomistic History. The Levites are mentioned only three times in the books of Samuel and Kings (1 Sam 6:15; 2 Sam 15:24 and 1 Kgs 8:4). In these references, the role of the Levites is consistently defined as the carriers of the Ark, and the Levites are distinguished from the priests.

The social status of the Levites seems to have changed through the history of the monarchic Israel, and may have been affected by historical incidents, such as the building of the central temple in Jerusalem by Solomon and his appointment of Zadok as the chief priest (1 Kgs 2:26-27), Jeroboam's appointment of non-Levite priests (1Kgs 12:31) for the northern cultic centers and several kings' cultic reforms.

Lastly, the depiction of the Levites in the post-exilic texts, such as the books of the Ezra-Nehemiah and Chronicles, is very different from the other biblical sources, specifically with their remarkably high occurrences of the Levites.

In the book of Ezra-Nehemiah, the organization of the temple personnel is much more elaborated than the Priestly tradition. Not only the priests and the Levites, but also the singers, the gatekeepers, the temple servants, and the descendants of Solomon's servants are included among the temple personnel (Ezra 2:40-55; Neh 7:43-60; 7:73; 10:28). However, the singers and gatekeepers are not included into the Levites, unlike in Chronicles.

[4] The term "levitical priests" also appears in the book of Jeremiah (33:18, 21). Here Jeremiah foresees a time when the levitical priests will flourish again. On the other hand, in the book of Ezekiel, the term "the levitical priests" always appears in apposition to the descendants of Zadok (43:19; 44:15). By defining the levitical priests as the descendants of Zadok, Ezekiel intends to exclude all non-Zadokite Levites from the priestly prerogatives.

In Ezra-Nehemiah the Levites are distinguished from the priests and their cultic role is to assist priests (Neh 12:47). In that sense, Ezra-Nehemiah follows the traditional stance on the Levites observed in the Priestly tradition. However, the functions of the Levites are expanded; Levites are members of the assembly which is composed of priests, the Levites and the heads of the families (Ezra 1:5; 2:70; 3:12 *et als.*), and are described as teachers (Neh 8:7, 9), treasurers (Neh 13:13), tithe collectors (Neh 10:37-39) and officers (Ezra 3:9) as well as cultic personnel.

In Chronicles, as we have observed in the previous chapters, non-priestly cultic personnel are all incorporated among the Levites.

The Chronicler's incorporation of the non-priestly temple personnel into the Levites has been the subject of much scholarly speculation. Many scholars who have devoted themselves to reconstructing the development of the cultic hierarchy in the Jerusalem Temple agree (although the details of their theories differ) that the Chronicler's assimilation of the other ranks of lower clergy into the Levites is an accurate reflection of the final stage of the historical development of the cultic hierarchy. For example, A. H. J. Gunneweg concludes his study of the history of cultic personnel in Israel with this comment:[5]

> Although the incorporation into the Levites (*Levitisierung*) is theoretical, it was not a theory invented by the Chronicler - the process had already begun in the pre-exilic period- but it would have complied with the actual self-understanding of these groups.

R. Numela, who studied the historical process of emergence of the Levites as a second-class priesthood in the post-exilic period, identifies the Levites with "former royal priests of the Northern Kingdom, living under impoverished circumstances in the South," and differentiates them from the priests of the high places.[6] According to Numela, these two groups were assimilated into one category as the Levites in Chronicles: "The Chronicler reflects the latest stage of this development, as he includes them

[5] A. H. J. Gunneweg, *Leviten und Priester: Hauptlinien der Traditionsbildung und Geschichte des israelitisch-jüdischen Kultpersonals* (Göttingen: Vandenhoeck & Ruprecht, 1965).

[6] R. Numela, *The Levites: Their Emergence as a Second-Class Priesthood* (Atlanta, Scholars, 1998).

(the singers and gatekeepers who might have originated from the priests of the high places) into the Levites."[7]

Unlike Numela, J. Schaper identifies the Levites as a small group of priests of the high places, who were enfranchised as minor clergy in the Jerusalem Temple during the reforms of Josiah.[8] Schaper conjectures that Nehemiah promoted Levites in order to create a balance with the strong priestly families, and this promotion of the Levites continued to be strengthened by Ezra, who came to Jerusalem after Nehemiah. Thus, J. Schaper considers the Chronicler's assimilation of the non-priestly temple personnel to the Levites a natural result of this promotion of the Levites by Nehemiah and Ezra.[9]

Thus, these scholars do not consider the incorporation of the entire minor clergy (gatekeepers, musicians, etc.) into the Levites as the Chronicler's formulation and therefore do not question the Chronicler's intention behind that formulation.

In contrast, Gabriele Boccaccini interprets the Chronicler's assimilation of non-priestly cultic personnel into the Levites not as a reflection of historical reality, but as a rhetorical case, that is, the priestly aristocracy's response to the shortage of Levites in the post-exilic period. According to Boccaccini, the priests of the Jerusalem Temple during the post-exilic period introduced a series of measures to respond to the shortage of the Levites, such as lowering the age of admission to the levitical rank, broadening the definition of the Levites to include all temple personnel, and securing separate financial support for the Levites.[10]

[7] Numela, *The Levites*, 175.

[8] Joachim Schaper, *Priester und Leviten im achämenidischen Juda: Studien zur Kult- und Sozialgeschichte Israels in persischer Zeit* (Tübingen: Mohr Siebeck, 2000).

[9] J. Schaper (*Priester und Leviten*, 300) states:

> The association between the Levites, singers and gatekeepers might have emerged after 398 BCE. The Levites had been strengthened by Ezra and Nehemiah and been provided with additional tasks. .... That Ezra entrusted the Levites with the task of religious teaching led this development to its culmination. The Levites, in addition to the priesthood, were the second pillar of the religious life of Judah. Their teaching was the germ cell, from which later grew the Pharisaic movement. With the acquisition of the duties of religious teaching, the Levites became an increasingly important counterweight to the priesthood. However, these new tasks added to the workload which rested on the shoulders of the Levites. The very reason for the association with singers and gatekeepers likely lay right here. The three groups joined together not out of power-political motivations, but from practical-organizational considerations.

[10] G. Boccaccini, *Roots of Rabbinic Judaism: An Intellectual History, from Ezekiel to Daniel* (Grand Rapids: Eerdmans, 2002) 69-70.

Even scholars who have interpreted the Chronicler's incorporation of the non-priestly cultic personnel into the Levites primarily as a rhetorical move still tend to see it as reflection of his contemporary circumstances, and read the material relating to the Levites as an attempt to legitimize contemporary realities,[11] as an *apologia pro* Levites,[12] or as a part of the Chronicler's plan to establish a more legitimate YHWH cult according to Pentateuchal traditions.[13]

It is this last possibility that I suspect drives the Chronicler's treatment of the Levites. Certainly, aside from questions pertaining to the Levites, prevailing *scholarly consensus* holds that the Chronicler's principal agenda is to emphasize the value of the Jerusalem Temple as the cultic center for all Israel.[14] Scholars' interpretations of the Chronicler's motivations are various: some assert that his goal was to encourage the inhabitants of the prov-

[11] See Timothy D. Goltz, "The Chronicler as Elite: Establishing an Atmosphere of Perpetuity in Jerusalem Yehud," in *The Function of Ancient Historiography in Biblical and Cognate Studies* (ed. Patricia G. Kirkpatrick and Timothy Goltz; LHBOTS 489; New York: T & T Clark, 2008) 97; Mark J. Boda, "Identity and Empire, Reality and Hope in the Chronicler's Perspective," in *Community Identity in Judean Historiography: Biblical and Comparative Perspectives* (ed. G. N. Knoppers and Kenneth A. Ristau; Winona Lake: Eisenbrauns, 2009) 251, 256; and Antti Laato, "The Levitical Genealogies in 1 Chronicles 5-6 and the Formation of Levitical Ideology in Post-exilic Judah," *JSOT* 62 (1994) 77-99.

[12] Some scholars argue that the Chronicler, as one of the Levites in the Persian period, tried to defend rights of the Levites to participate in the Temple cult through his work. See Von Rad, *Das Geschichtsbild des chronistischen Werkes*, 81-119; P. R. Ackroyd, "The Theology of the Chronicler," *LTQ* 8 (1973) 111-12; Williamson, *1 and 2 Chronicles*, 16-17; Paul D. Hanson, "1 Chronicles 15-16 and the Chronicler's View on the Levites," in *"Sha'arei Talmon" Studies in the Bible*, 69-77; I. Kalimi, "Placing the Chronicler in his own Historical Context: A Closer Examination," *JNES* 68 (2009) 179-92, here 190; De Vries, "Moses and David as Cult Founders in Chronicles," 636; and McKenzie, *1–2 Chronicles*, 28-29.

[13] See among others: Kalimi, "Placing the Chronicler in his own Historical Context," 185-89; Fishbane, Biblical Interpretation, 385-87, 394, 401; Kenneth A. Ristau, "Reading and Rereading Josiah: The Chronicler's Representation of Josiah for the Postexilic Community," in *Community Identity in Judean Historiography*, 219-47; Antti Laato, "The Levitical Genealogies in 1 Chronicles 5-6," 88; and Thomas Willi, "Leviten, Priester und Kult in vorhellenistischer Zeit: Die Chronistische Optik in ihrem geschichtlichen Kontext," in *Gemeinde ohne Tempel = Community without Temple: Zur Substituierung und Transformation des Jerusalemer Tempels und seines Kults im Alten Testament, antiken Judentum und frühen Christentum* (ed. Beate Ego, Armin Lange, und Peter Pilhofer; WUNT 118; Tübingen: Mohr Siebeck, 1999) 75-98.

[14] See Kalimi, "Placing the Chronicler in his own Historical Context," 189-91; idem, "Jerusalem—The Divine City: The Representation of Jerusalem in Chronicles Compared with Earlier and Later Jewish Compositions," in *The Chronicler as Theologian*, 189-205; Kenneth A. Ristau, "Reading and Rereading Josiah," 241; Jonathan E. Dyck, *The Theocratic Ideology of the Chronicler*, 166; Gary N. Knoppers, " 'The City Yhwh Has Chosen'," 307, 313-16.

ince of Yehud as well as Jews from the Diaspora to move to Jerusalem and live in the city;[15] others claim that he wished to highlight the holiness as well as the significance of his own contemporary, small, poorly built and furnished Temple;[16] still others maintain that he wanted to ensure the authoritative centrality of the Jerusalem Temple among several Jewish sanctuaries in neighboring regions in the fifth or fourth century B.C.E.,[17] such as the Samaritan temple,[18] a Jewish sanctuary at Elephantine,[19] a Persian-period Judean sanctuary at Lachish,[20] and a sanctuary of "Yaho" in Idumea.[21]

Undoubtedly, the Chronicler's emphasis on the legitimacy of the Jerusalem Temple is related to a variety of internal and external challenges that the Jerusalem Temple encountered in the Chronicler's time. His descriptions of the temple administration, including the passages about the roles of the Levites, emerge in this larger context: indeed, the Chronicler's (apparently ahistorical) incorporation of all the temple functionaries into the Levites is of a piece with his larger literary program, namely, to ensure

[15] See, Kalimi, "Placing the Chronicler in his own Historical Context," 189-90; Knowles, *Centrality Practiced*, 91.

[16] Kalimi, "Placing the Chronicler in his own Historical Context," 189.

[17] Kalimi, "Placing the Chronicler in his own Historical Context," 189-91; Knoppers, " 'The City Yhwh Has Chosen'," 319-20; idem, "Mt. Gerizim and Mt. Zion: A Study in the Early History of the Samaritans and Jews," *SR* 34/3-4 (2005) 320, 322, 325-26; idem, "Revisiting the Samarian Question in the Persian Period," in *Judah and Judeans in the Persian Period*, 279; and Knowles, *Centrality Practiced*, 127; Jörg Frey, "Temple and Rival Temple—The Case of Elephantine, Mt. Gerizim, and Leontopolis," in *Gemeinde ohne Tempel = Community without Temple*, 171-203.

[18] For the Samaritan Temple at Mt. Gerizim in the Persian period, refer to: Yizhak Magen, Haggai Misgav and Levana Tsfania, *Mount Gerizim Excavations* Vol. I: *The Aramaic, Hebrew and Samaritan Inscriptions* (Jerusalem: Israel Antiquities Authority, 2004) 1-3; Ingrid Hjelm, *Jerusalem's Rise to Sovereignty: Zion and Gerizim in Competition* (London: T& T Clark, 2004) 215; Bob Becking, "Do the Earliest Samaritan Inscriptions Already Indicate a Parting of the Ways?" in *Judah and Judeans in the Fourth Century* B.C.E., 220; Knoppers, "Revisiting the Samarian Question in the Persian Period," in *Judah and Judeans in the Persian Period*, 265-89.

[19] Concerning the Jewish Temple at Elephantine and its religious practices, see Stephen G. Rosenberg, "The Jewish Temple at Elephantine," *NEA* 67 (2004): 4-13; Paul-Eugène Dion, "La religion des papyrus d'Éléphantine: un reflet du Juda d'avant l'exil," in *Kein Land für sich allein* (ed. Ulrich Hübner und Ernst Axel Knauf; Göttingen: Vandenhoeck & Ruprecht, 2002) 243-54; and Thomas M. Bolin, "The Temple of יהו at Elephantine and Persian Religious Policy," in *The Triumph of Elohim: From Yahwism to Judaisms* (ed. Diana Vikander Edelman; Grand Rapids: Eerdmans, 1996) 127-42.

[20] Ephraim Stern, "The Religious Revolution in Persian-Period Judah," in *Judah and Judeans in the Persian Period*, 200.

[21] A. Lemaire, "New Aramaic Ostraca from Idumea and Their Historical Interpretation," 416-17.

that cultic practices and traditions should be grounded in Pentateuchal regulations, as John Van Seters states:

> The nature of Chronicler's historiography is revisionist, reading into the past all the necessary structures and institutions, and ideological legitimation to support the later religious community. The Priestly Code had already laid down the foundation for this religious constitution. What was lacking was the specific continuity from this Mosaic law through the political and religious authority of Jerusalem. The Samaritan community or their predecessors could and did claim that continuity through the sanctuary of Gerizim. The Chronicler's history is the Jerusalem community's attempt to establish the continuity of the Pentateuchal law in final form through Jerusalem.[22]

However, in the process of his rewriting the history of Israel in light of the Pentateuchal traditions, the Chronicler does not simply follow the traditions. He freely harmonizes different legal traditions about the same matter; presents creative interpretations of certain traditions from his own perspective; and sometimes deviates from the Priestly tradition to make his own points concerning a specific matter. I see the Chronicler's presentation of the non-priestly cultic personnel as Levites as one product of such dialectic approaches to the traditions. By emphasizing the eligibility of the Levites to perform various cultic duties, and by providing the non-priestly cultic personnel with levitical lineage, the Chronicler formulates the legal basis for the payment of the cultic personnel of the Jerusalem Temple, which was, in the Persian period, without royal sponsorship. Lacking funding from a royal patron, the main source of income for the Jerusalem Temple was the people's donations and contributions, including the tithes, which had to cover all the expenses necessary to run the Temple. But as we saw in the previous chapter, according to the Priestly tradition, *only* the priests and Levites can be paid with people's donations and contributions for the Temple, which are categorized into "the priestly gifts" and "the tithes." Thus, the Chronicler's legal interpretations and historical revisionism with regard to the Levites have a practical purpose, namely, to make the non-priestly cultic personnel eligible to be paid out of the Temple's coffers. For this purpose, the Chronicler emphasized the eligibility of the Levites for various cultic

[22] John Van Seters, "The Chronicler's Account of Solomon's Temple-Building: A Continuity Theme," in *The Chronicler as Historian*, 300.

duties, and, in a kind of reciprocal arrangement, provided the non-priestly cultic personnel with levitical lineage. The Chronicler's new formulation was a product of his creative interpretation of Priestly traditions, which rested on the particular methods I discussed in section 2.5.

Why, if we accept that the Chronicler's goal was to provide legal cover for these personnel in the form of levitical genealogies and putative historical precedents for their appointments, did the Chronicler choose the Korahites to establish the continuity of the office of gatekeepers throughout the history of Israel? The Chronicler could have chosen a different, and a less controversial, branch of the Levites, such as the Gershonites or the Merarites. The Chronicler's special interest in the Korahites may be polemical; perhaps a priestly opponent group used the tradition of Korah's rebellion (Numbers 16) as an argument against any attempt to expand the corps of Levites to include cultic personnel previously identified as members of the laity.[23] The Chronicler's deviations from the Priestly tradition in his descriptions of specific cultic duties could thus be understood in the context of conflicts among the various groups that argued for different interpretations of cultic practices. By projecting his own ideals for cultic practices and levitical roles onto David's institution of the temple's administrative structures, the Chronicler attempts not only to justify his own perspective, but also to instruct his own generation to follow his ideal.[24]

[23] R. Numela also interprets the story of Korah's rebellion in Numbers 16 in a similar way. He (*The Levites*, 132) suggests:

> The story might also have been in harmony with the priestly writer's intention to portray the Levites' opposition against the Aaronites as a revolt against Moses, as Moses is the mediator in P of the divine regulations concerning the division of the priesthood into different ranks. If we so suppose an older P-story about a revolt of the people against the priests, we should also ask which historical situation such an account might reflect. This interpretation would imply that the distinction between priests and laymen as such had been challenged by some group in the post-exilic period. It is not historically feasible to assume that the prerogative of the priests concerning the cultic duties could be contested in the post-exilic period, when the division into different ranks within the priesthood was given its final legitimation, though there were conflicts as regards it.

On the other hand, J. Schaper (*Priester und Leviten*, 218) suggests that the Korahites were the most important group among the class of the minor clergy of the Jerusalem Temple in the late Achaemenid era.

[24] Mark J. Boda ("Identity and Empire, Reality and Hope in the Chronicler's Perspective," 251) also comments that the book of Chronicles not only justifies present reality but also project future hope. However, some scholars assert that the Chronicler's work is an attempt to justify the power of the priestly elite in Yehud. See Timothy D. Goltz, "The Chronicler as Elite: Establishing an Atmosphere of Perpetuity in Jerusalem Yehud," 97.

Did the Chronicler succeed? Did the corps of Levites expand as the Persian era progressed, and did the Levites, as a consequence, gain increased influence in the cultic arena? Again, only literary sources can shed light on this question, and again, the verdict is mixed.

4.2. The Levites in the Writings of the Second Temple Period

In this section, I examine references to the Levites in texts that originated in the Hellenistic and Hasmonean period, including Deutero-canonical and pseudepigraphic works as well as the Dead Sea Scrolls.

4.2.1. The Levites in Deuterocanonical Works

The only two mentions of the Levites in deuterocanonical works are found in Tob 1:7 (which I mentioned above) and in LXX Esther 10:3 where a certain Dositheus is introduced as a priest and a Levite.[25] The absence of references to the Levites in these texts can be explained in several ways: (1) as an indication of the disappearance of the Levites as a distinct body; (2) as evidence that the Levites had been integrated into the priestly group, or that the author understood the category "priests" to include all temple personnel; or (3) as evidence of intentional downplaying of the Levites as a reflection of conflicts between the Levites and other priestly groups.

Arguments from silence are not always convincing, but the silence of the books of Ben Sira and 1 and 2 Maccabees may speak volumes, given these works' passionate interest in issues relating to the priesthood of the Temple in Jerusalem. The author of Ben Sira shows an intense concern about the priesthood. Sir 7:29-31 equates fearing God with treating his priesthood as holy, and loving God with not forgetting one's relationship with the priesthood.[26] When Sir 46:6-25 describes the priestly covenant with Aaron and his descendants, it emphasizes that Aaron's priesthood is eternal (vv. 7, 15, and 24) and exclusive (vv. 18-19). It also introduces the priestly duties, such as to offer sacrifices, to make atonement for Israel, to guard and teach the Torah (vv. 16-17); but it does not mention the Levites' teaching role, which 2 Chr 17:7-8; 35:3; Neh 8:7, 9 explicitly highlight.[27] Furthermore,

[25] Levine, *Jerusalem*, 244; and Cana Werman, "Levi and Levites in the Second Temple Period," *DSD* 4/2 (1997) 211-25, here 214.

[26] Saul M. Olyan, "Ben Sira's Relationship to the Priesthood," *HTR* 80 (1987) 263.

[27] In 2 Chr 35:3, the Chronicler uses a specific word מבנים (instructors) to designate the

Sir 45:18-19, by alluding to the rebellion of Korah, Dathan and Abiram of Numbers 16, underscores the exclusivity of Aaron's priesthood, defines other priestly groups as illegitimate, and provides a hint of Korah's literary afterlife as a figure used polemically by competing parties.

Ben Sira's silence about the Levites thus likely reflects his concern to defend the Aaronide priesthood: the author's silence does not necessarily indicate the absence of the Levites in the second century B.C.E., *contra* C. Werman.[28] In fact, Ben Sira ignores not only the Levites, but also Moses' role as a priest (Exod 6:16-25), as well as Zadok and his descendants, and the Zadokite scribe Ezra.[29] Thus, S. M. Olyan is right to conclude that Ben Sira's silence about the Levites reflects his own tactic of attacking rival group(s) by ignoring them as completely as if they did not exist.[30] In other words, the Levites could have existed as a rival group, which competed with Ben Sira's pan-Aaronide ideology.

The books of 1 and 2 Maccabees clearly portray the high priests and priests as occupying prominent roles in the second century B.C.E., but they do not contain any references to the Levites.[31] Since the two books take different perspectives on the history of the Maccabean revolt, I will treat each book separately.[32]

Levites' teaching role (see also Neh 8:7 and 9). Based on this term, Aelred Cody (*A History of Old Testament Priesthood* [Rome: Pontifical Biblical Institute, 1969] 187-90) argues that the Levites' teaching role is distinguished from the priests' one, which is often designated by a *Hiphil* participle of verb ירה, such as in 2 Chr 15:3 (a teaching priest, כהן מורה). However, in 2 Chr 26:5, Zechariah the priest during the time of Uzziah is described as the king's "instructor" (המבין). Furthermore, Ezr 8:16 also mentions a certain group of people as מבנים. These are not definitely Levites since they are the people whom Ezra sent to fetch some Levites from Casiphia. Thus, the word מבנים cannot be limited to designate the Levites' specific role, and at the same time, this term cannot be used as a supporting evidence for the argument that the Levites' teaching role is distinguished from the priests' one.

[28] C. Werman ("Levi and Levites in the Second Temple Period," 214-15) argues that there were no Levites in the Second Temple period, and Ben Sira's silence about the Levites serves for her as supporting evidence.

[29] Olyan, "Ben Sira's Relationship to the Priesthood," 275.

[30] Olyan, "Ben Sira's Relationship to the Priesthood," 275.

[31] The book of 1 Maccabees is dated to sometime between the rule of John Hyrcanus I (134–104 B.C.E.) and Pompey's conquest of Jerusalem in 63 B.C.E. The book of 2 Maccabees was written in Greek sometime between 124 and 63 B.C.E. See John R. Bartlett, *1 Maccabees* (Sheffield: Sheffield Academic Press, 1998) 33-34; Robert Doran, *Temple Propaganda: The Purpose and Character of 2 Maccabees* (Washington: The Catholic Biblical Association of America, 1981) 1; Daniel J. Harrington, *The Maccabean Revolt: Anatomy of a Biblical Revolution* (Wilmington: Michael Glazier, 1988) 36-39, 57-59; and Daniel R. Schwartz, *2 Maccabees* (Berlin: Walter de Gruyter, 2008) 10-15.

[32] Concerning the differences between 1 Maccabees and 2 Maccabees, refer to J. R. Bartlett, *1 Maccabees*, 45-49, 66-67, 73-74. Due to these differences, J. R. Bartlett (*1 Mac-*

In 1 Maccabees, there are several references to priests which can be categorized into two groups.[33] The first category includes references to priestly activities in the Temple.[34] The second category comprises references that present priests as one of the representative parties of the Jews.[35] Levites are not mentioned in either category.[36]

Clearly, the author of 1 Maccabees is pro-Hasmonean, since his main focus is on asserting the legitimacy of the Hasmoneans' assumption of the office of the high priesthood.[37] The priesthood itself or temple administra-

---

cabees, 102) suggests reading the two books as a separate work: "It is unlikely that the historian of 1 Maccabees knew the work of the Epitomist (the author of 2 Maccabees) or of his source, Jason of Cyrene, and it is important to try to understand the picture given by 1 Maccabees without confusion from 2 Maccabees."

[33] 1 Macc 4:42-43, 57; 7:33; 11:23-24; 12:6; 14:20, 41, 44, and 47.

[34] The author states that Judas Maccabeus chose "blameless priests" and made them purify the sanctuary for the rededication of the Temple (1 Macc 4:42-43). He also mentions "the chambers of the priests" (1 Macc 4:57). However, the activities of the Levites in the Temple are not mentioned.

[35] When Nicanor, the general of Demetrius I, came to kill Judas Maccabeus, the ones who welcomed him to prevent a worse situation were "some priests and the elders" (1 Macc 7:33). When Jonathan visited Demetrius II to win his favor, he chose "some elders of Israel and some priests" to accompany him (1 Macc 11:23-24). Here, the representatives of people fall into only two groups: the elders of Israel and the priests. This categorization is also found in a letter of Jonathan to the Spartans (1 Macc 12:6) and a letter that the Spartans sent to Simon (1 Macc 14:20). In both letters, the elders (οἱ πρεσβύτεροι) or the senate of the nation (ἡ γεροουσία τοῦ ἔθνους) and the priests appear with the high priest as a representative of the people. The same categorization appears in 1 Macc 14:41, 44, and 47 where the hereditary high priesthood in Simon's family was confirmed by the Jews and their priests. There is one case in which the priests are not mentioned as a representative of people. In 1 Macc 13:36, Demetrius II sent a letter to the high priest (Simon) and to the elders, but the priests are not included as addressees.

> The categorization of 1 Maccabees certainly contrasts with the Chronicler's categorization, such as that of 1 Chr 9:2 (Israelites, priests, Levites, and temple servants); that of 1 Chr 23:2 (all the officers of Israel and the priests and the Levites); that of 2 Chr 30:25 (All the congregation of Judah and the priests and the Levites and all the congregation that came from Israel); that of 2 Chr 35:18 (by the priests and the Levites, by all Judah and Israel). See also Ezra 3:12; 8:29 which categorize the representatives of people as the priests, Levites and heads of fathers' *households*; Ezra 6:16 which catalogues the people of Israel, the priests, the Levites, and the rest of the returned exiles; Ezra 10:5 which groups the leading priests, the Levites, and all Israel; and Neh 10:34 categorizes the priests, the Levites, and the people. All of these categorizations include the Levites in contrast with 1 Maccabees. Such a difference makes one wonder about the destiny of the Levites in post-Chronistic period.

[36] Joan Annandale-Potgieter, "The High Priests in 1 Maccabees and in the Writings of Josephus," in *VII Congress of the International Organization for Septuagint and Cognate Studies* (ed. Clause E. Cox; Atlanta: Scholars, 1989) 393-429.

[37] The author of 1 Maccabees simply ignores Onias, Jason and Menelaus. See Schwartz,

tion is not the author's concern.[38] Thus, silence about the Levites cannot prove the absence of Levites, just as the author's silence about Onias, Jason and Menelaus does not indicate their non-existence. Might the Levites have been absorbed by the author's time into the category of the priests? Or were they ignored intentionally? It is certainly possible that the Levites could have been opponents of the Hasmoneans because of the latter party's unlawful possession of both the high priesthood and the secular authority, and their untraditional religious practices.[39]

---

2 *Maccabees*, 469. There is no reference to Onias III although the book begins with the accession of Antiochus Epiphanes (175 BCE). Interestingly, Onias III is highly praised in 2 Maccabees (see 2 Macc 3:1-3; 15:12). There is no explicit reference to Jason, but some allusions to Jason and his followers, the so-called pro-Hellenists. For instance, the term "lawless men" (υἱοὶ παράνομοι) in 1 Macc 1:11 alludes to Jason and his followers. The term is used throughout 1 Maccabees to describe the Hellenizers. See John R. Bartlett, *The First and Second Books of the Maccabees* (Cambridge: Cambridge University Press, 1973) 22.

On the other hand, the high priest Alcimus was vehemently criticized: see 1 Macc 7:5, 9, 14, 23; 9:53-56. This is contradictory to 2 Macc 14:3, where Alcimus was introduced as a former high priest. D. R. Schwartz (2 *Maccabees*, 469) explains 1 Macc 7:5 as "a pro-Hasmonean author's way of undermining Alcimus' legitimacy."

To the contrary, the high priesthood of Jonathan is legitimized with triple confirmation by the Seleucid kings: by Alexander Balas in 152 B.C.E. (1 Macc 10:20-21), Demetrius II (1 Macc 11:27) and Antiochus VI Epiphanes (145–142 B.C.E.) (1 Macc 11:57). The author's intentional emphasis on the foreign kings' confirmation on the high priesthood of Jonathan does not seem to be harmonized with his anti-Hellenizing sentiment. Perhaps, it is being employed to underline the fact that Jonathan did not take the high priesthood of his own will. The high priesthood of Simon is also legitimized by multiple confirmations from various authorities, such as Demetrius II (1 Macc 13:36; 14:38-39), the Spartans (14:20), the Jews (14:35, 41-43) and Antiochus VII (138–129 BCE), who gave Simon permission to mint his own coinage (15:6). The Jews and their priests decided to make the high priesthood of Simon hereditary (14:41-43) and publicized this decision by a decree (14:44-49). In addition, Simon's membership in a priestly family is underlined with genealogical information (14:29). Simon's father Mattathias is claimed to have been a priest of the sons of Joarib. If Mattathias was a priest of the sons of Joarib, the Hasmoneans belonged to the first division among 24 priestly courses as 1 Chr 24:7 shows. Thus, they were of the line of Aaron. See Rooke, *Zadok's Heirs*, 280. However, this claim is doubtful in two points as S. Schwartz (*Imperialism and Jewish Society 200* B.C.E. *to 640* C.E. [Princeton: Princeton University Press, 2001] 33-36) argues. First, their ties to Jerusalem seem not to have been strong since they were influential mainly in Modein. The additional information about Mattathias' family's relocation from Jerusalem to Modein in 1 Macc 2:1 seems to be rather tendentious. Second, the Hasmoneans behaved in very untraditional ways to the extent that the traditionalists could not imagine. For instance, they did not bother much with the fact that their constant exposure to corpse impurity was not compatible with the purity requirement for the high priest. Moreover, their integration of the gentiles in their conquered territory into Jews by means of forcible circumcision produced a wide range of skepticism about the Hasmoneans among many Judean traditionalists.

[38] Bartlett, *1 Maccabees*, 33.

[39] There is evidence for strong opposition to the Hasmoneans and their claims to the

2 Maccabees is mainly a history of Jerusalem from the beginning of Hellenization under the high priest Jason around 175 B.C.E. up to Judas Maccabeus' victory over the Seleucid general Nicanor in 161 B.C.E.[40] In 2 Maccabees, the priesthood itself is not of much concern.[41] For instance, according to 2 Macc 10:1-9, those who purified the Temple were not the priests, but "Maccabeus and his followers." Moreover, the priests are not a separate category in the phrases which designate the whole nation, such as in 2 Macc 1:10 ("the people of Jerusalem and of Judea and the senate and Judas"), in 11:6 ("Maccabeus and his men and all the people"), and in 11:27 ("to the senate of the Jews and to the other Jews").

On the other hand, in 2 Macc 1:23; 3:15; 14:31, 34, those who prayed before the altar or offered sacrifices are always designated as "the priests" (οἱ ἱερεῖς); no Levites are mentioned. Even the hymn singers are "the priests," (not the Levites) in 2 Macc 1:30, unlike Chronicles and Josephus (*Ant.* 20.216-218). Does this omission confirm the absence of the Levites at that time? D. R. Schwartz suggests another possibility to explain the absence of the Levites in 2 Maccabees. Schwartz states: "Note that it is difficult to render "Levites" in Greek; indeed, in *Antiquities* 20.216 Josephus felt the need to gloss "the Levites" and explain to his readers that they are "a tribe."[42] Accordingly, it would be understandable if some references to Levites were rendered by the word "priests" in Greek texts, such as 2 Maccabees.

Consequently 1 and 2 Maccabees do not resolve the question of whether the silence of the authors about the Levites was deliberately intended or

---

high priesthood. The Qumran Habbakkuk Commentary (1QpHab) implies that the Teacher of Righteousness was the legitimate claimant to the high priesthood after Alcimus' death and before the accession of Jonathan to that office. D. Harrington (*The Maccabean Revolt*, 120-21) suggests that the Wicked Priest's illegitimate claim to the high priesthood had been a deciding factor for the Teacher of Righteousness to split himself from the existing religious institutions and to find the Qumran community. On the other hand, Aloson Schofield and James C. Vanderkam ("Were the Hasmoneans Zadokites?" *JBL* 124 [2005] 73-87) have recently argued that the Hasmoneans were a Zadokite family, based on the phrases "a priest of the family of Joarib" in 1 Macc 2:1 and "Phinehas our ancestor" in 1 Macc 2:54, which have been regarded as a pro-Hasmonean propaganda justifying their assumption of the high priesthood. The argument that Schofield and Vanderkam suggest does not nullify successfully the traditional view. If the Hasmoneans were Zadokites as they argue, it seems to be very strange not to have revealed their Zadokite descent explicitly since such disclosure could have eliminated all the potential oppositions to their claim to the high priesthood.

[40] D. R. Schwartz, *2 Maccabees*, 3.

[41] 2 Macc 1:10, 23, 30; 3:15; 4:14; 14:31 and 34.

[42] D. R. Schwartz, *2 Maccabees*, 157.

whether the category of "the priests" was meant to be inclusive of all the temple personnel.

Unlike 1 and 2 Maccabees and Ben Sira, Josephus refers to the Levites in *Antiquities*. The following is a brief sketch of Josephus' treatment of the Levites, especially in the post-biblical period.[43]

4.2.2. The Levites in *Antiquities*

Christopher T. Begg's studies of the terms "Levi," "Levite(s)," and "levitical" in *Antiquities* provide a comprehensive view of Josephus' portrayal of the Levites.[44] According to Begg, the Levites in *Antiquities* are clearly distinguished from the priests and subordinate to them. Josephus consistently avoids the term "levitical priests," transfers certain levitical roles to the priests, and ignores the Levites' prophetic role.[45]

Since my concern is with the Levites in the post-biblical period, two pericopae from *Antiquities* are relevant: *Ant.* 13.62-73 and *Ant.* 20.216-218. The first text is Josephus' account of the construction of a Jewish temple at Leontopolis in Egypt sometime in the second century B.C.E.[46] According to *Ant.* 13.63, Onias (probably Onias IV, the son of Onias III) asked permission from King Ptolemy and Queen Cleopatra to build a temple in Egypt in order to "ordain Levites and priests out of their own family." Then Onias found the priests and Levites who would perform divine service at the temple (*Ant.* 13.73).[47]

[43] Josephus covers the post-biblical period in Antiquities 11.297-20.268. See Christopher T. Begg, "The Levites in Josephus," *HUCA* 75 (2004) 19.

[44] According to C. T. Begg ("The Levites in Josephus," 1-22), the terms "Levi," "Levite(s)," and "Levitical" occurs some 93 times in *Antiquities* with the following distribution: Ληουίς, Λευίς (the proper name of Jacob's son Levi, 5/6 times), Ληουίτης, -αι, Λευιτῆς, -αι (the collective noun, "Levite(s)," 82/83 times); λευουτικός (the adjective "levitical," once), and ληουῖτις, λευῖτις (another adjectival form, "levitical," 5/6 times).

[45] Begg, "The Levites in Josephus," 20-21.

[46] Concerning a Jewish temple at Leontopolis, refer to M. Delcor, "Le temple d'Onias en Égypte," *RB* 75 (1968) 88-203; Robert Hayward, "The Jewish Temple at Leontopolis: A Reconsideration," *JJS* 33 (1982) 429-43; Boulos Ayad, "The Temple of the God Yahweh in Leontopolis (Tell el-Yahudiya) East of the Nile Delta," *Coptic Church Review* 14 (1993) 99-108; and David Noy, "The Jewish Communities of Leontopolis and Venosa," in *Studies in Early Jewish Epigraphy* (ed. Jan Willem van Henten and Pieter Willem van der Horst; Leiden: Brill, 1994) 162-82.

[47] Josephus' information about the matter of Leontopolis is not consistent. His information given in *Ant.* 13.62-73 and in *War* 7.422-32 is somewhat contradictory with regard to the identity of Onias as well as his descriptions about the temple. Furthermore, his refer-

The other pericope (*Ant.* 20.216-218) is about levitical singers and indicates that questions regarding the relative status of priests and Levites continued to be controversial up through the first century C. E. Here, Josephus explains that the Levites are a tribe (*Ant.* 20.216). In *Ant.* 20.218, this tribe is presented as "the one who performs a religious service in the Temple." Josephus states that many of the levitical singers of hymns persuaded King Agrippa to seek permission from the Sanhedrin for them to wear linen robes "on equal terms with the priests" (ἐπίσης τοῖς ἱερεῦσιν) (*Ant.* 20.217).[48] Josephus goes on to note that Agrippa granted this request and that "all this was contrary to the laws of the country" (*Ant.* 20.218).

4.2.3. The Levites in Dead Sea Scroll Texts

In contrast to their low profile in deuterocanonical and historical sources, in the Dead Sea Scrolls, the Levites experience something of a literary renaissance.[49] References to the Levites are found in the Damascus Document (CD), the Community Rule (1QS), the Rule for the Congregation (1QSa) the War Scroll (1QM), and the Temple Scroll (11QT).[50] These references

ences to the Levites are not consistent in the two books. In *War* 7.422-32 Josephus does not mention the Levites, but only the priests (esp. *War* 7.430). See Hayward, "The Jewish Temple at Leontopolis: A Reconsideration," 430 and Begg, "The Levites in Josephus," 20.

[48] Begg, "The Levites in Josephus," 1.

[49] Several scholars have published studies about the Levites in the Qumran corpus. Among them, Robert C. Stallman's studies ("Levi and the Levites in the Dead Sea Scrolls," *JSP* 10 [1992] 163-89) are most extensive. He has examined all the references to Levi and the Levites throughout the Dead Sea Scrolls corpus. The references to the Levites that I examined in this section are mostly taken from his lists. The following works were also consulted: Jacob Milgrom, "Studies in the Temple Scroll," *JBL* 97 (1978) 501-23; idem, "The Qumran Cult: Its Exegetical Principles," in *Temple Scroll Studies*, 165-80; C. G. Kruse, "Community Functionaries in the Rule of the Community and the Damascus Document: A Test of Chronological Relationship," *RevQ* 10 (1981) 543-51; Barbara E. Thiering, "*Mebaqqer* and *Episkopos* in the Light of the Temple Scroll," *JBL* 100 (1981) 59-74; Terry L. Donaldson, "Levitical Messianology in Late Judaism: Origins, Development and Decline," *JETS* 24 (1981) 193-207; and George J. Brooke, "Levi and the Levites in the Dead Sea Scrolls and the New Testament," in *Mogilany 1989: Papers on the Dead Sea Scrolls offered in Memory of Jean Carmignac Part I: General Research on the Dead Sea Scrolls Qumran and the New Testament the Present State of Qumranology* (ed. Zdzislaw J. Kapera; Krakow: Enigma, 1993) 105-29.

[50] The following references to the Levites are taken from Stallman, "Levi and the Levites in the Dead Sea Scrolls," 172-88. CD 3:1-4:4; 10:4-10; 12:23-13:7; 14:3-4; ; 1QS 1:19; 1:21-2:1; 2:5; 2:19-20; 1QSa 1:22-24; 1QM 1:3; 2:2-5; 3:13-4:17; 5:1; 7:13-14; 8:9-10; 13:1-2; 15:4; 16:3-9; 17:12-13; 18:5; and 11QT 21:2-6; 44:4-45:2; 60:6-9.

prove that the Chronicler was not the sole promoter of the elevated status of the Levites in the Second Temple period. It is worth noting, however, that the authors of the DSS had their own unique ideological concerns, and that, while some of their texts treat actual life within the Qumran sect, others portray a restored, idealized, eschatological Israel and its temple. References to Levites tend to occur more frequently in eschatological passages and therefore may not reflect historical practices.[51] Nevertheless, the Scrolls provide a consistent portrait of the Levites as occupying a middle status, higher than the great majority of Israelites, but lower than the priestly corps.

The first text whose references to Levites we shall examine, the Damascus Document (CD), includes congregational and disciplinary rules which regulated the life of the sect. Scholars suggest that this document may have been produced around 100 B.C.E.[52] CD has four different sections in which Levites are mentioned: CD 3:21-4:4; 10:4-10; 12:23-13:7; 14:3-4.

For the purposes of this study, the role of the Levites in the Rule for the Camps should be noted (CD 12:22b-13:7a). In these statutes, an educated priest is required to preside over gatherings of ten or more men. If a learned priest is not available, a learned Levite can take his place. Thus, the Rule for the Camps presupposes the presence of Levites in the Camps and indicates their position as leaders.[53]

[51] Since 4QMMT is considered a key text about the sectarian community's history and identity, the absence of references to the Levites in 4QMMT needs to be addressed. 4QMMT presents twenty two laws regarding sacrificial law, priestly gifts, ritual purity, and other matters over which the writers disagree with the Jerusalem authorities. Considering the fragmentary nature of the text and the fact that the main focus of the text is not on who performs sacrifices, the lack of references to the Levites in 4QMMT does not negate my argument that the references of the Levites in the corpus of Dead Sea Scrolls indicate that the Levites were considered significant in the late Second Temple period. As for scholarly discussion about 4QMMT, see James C. VanderKam, *The Dead Sea Scrolls Today* (2nd ed.; Grand Rapids: Eedermans, 2010) 83; Albert L. A. Hogeterp, "4QMMT and Paradigms of Second Temple Jewish Nomism,"*DSD* 15 (2008) 359–379; Azzan Yadin, "4QMMT, Rabbi Ishmael, and the Origins of Legal Midrash," *DSD* 10 (2003) 130-49; and Lawrence H. Schiffman, "The New Halakhic Letter (4QMMT) and the Origins of the Dead Sea Sect," *BA* 53 (1990) 64-73, here 64.

[52] Joseph M. Baumgarten, Ada Yardeni and Stephen J. Pfann, eds., *Qumran Cave 4. V. XIII: The Damascus Document (4Q266-273)* (DJD 18; Oxford: Clarendon, 1996) 1-2, 26-30; Hartmut Stegemann, *The Library of Qumran: On the Essenes, Qumran, John the Baptist and Jesus* (Grand Rapids: Eerdmans, 1998) 117; and Charlotte Hempel, *The Damascus Texts* (Sheffield: Sheffield Academic Press, 2000) 21-24.

[53] Nevertheless, the issue of Levites' presence and role is not clear when the immediately following rule (CD 13:4-7) is considered. CD 13:4-7 governs a case of a skin disease: If

A similar indication of the Levites' status appears in the Rule for mustering the assembly of the Camps (CD 14), which states that the Levites are enrolled after the priests and followed by the Israelites and the proselytes at the annual assembly at which a priest presides (CD 14:4-6). This three-tiered hierarchy of priests-Levites-Israelites is also found in 1QS 2:21-22, which states rules for idealized assemblies.[54]

The Levites appear again in CD 3.21-4.4, an allegorical interpretation of Ezek 44:15, where הכהנים הלוים בני צדוק (the levitical priests descended from Zadok) are singled out to be ministers in the future temple. In CD 3:21-4.4, the phrase, הכהנים הלוים בני צדוק, is interpreted as three different groups: "the priests" who founded the sect, "the Levites" who joined them, and "the sons of Zadok" who were the members of the sect. Once again, then, the Levites are designated as an important corps.

Lastly, CD 10:4-10 presents the Levites as members of the judicial committee of the congregation, which consists of four members from the tribe of Levi and Aaron and six from all Israel. The phrase "למטה לוי ואהרן" of CD 10:5 indicates that the sect did not always differentiate the tribe of Levi (or the Levites) from the sons of Aaron.[55]

These references to the Levites in CD seem to indicate that the Levites held leadership and judicial positions in the Camps and that their overall status was just below the priesthood.[56] Nevertheless, it remains difficult to determine to what extent these references should be interpreted as a historical indication of the status of the Levites in the sect because the references to the Levites in CD tend to appear in sections of that document which present rules for the idealized assemblies. While it is not possible to know exactly what role Levites played in actual sectarian life, it is clear that the Covenanters shared the Chronicler's ideal view that while Levites were distinct from and subordinated to Aaronide priests, they should nevertheless play crucial roles in cultic activity.

---

a member of a Camp has a skin disease, a priest must come into the Camp to inspect it. If the priest does not know the law of skin disease, the Examiner, not a learned Levite, must explain the law and its application to the case. Since the Examiner's levitical lineage is never addressed throughout CD, the role of Levites in the Camp remains obscure.

[54] The idealized nature of 1QS 2:21-22 will be dealt with below.

[55] In the Testimonia (4Q175) the distinction between Levites and priests is also obscured. The text states that an eschatological priests will come from Levi (4Q175 2:14-20) based on Deut 33:8-11.

[56] Stallman, "Levi and the Levites in the Dead Sea Scrolls," 180.

Like CD, the Community Rule (1QS) contains clearly idealized components that anticipate the restoration of Israel at the End of Days. For instance, according to 1QS 2:21-22, the great assembly is to be organized by groups of thousands, hundreds, fifties and tens at the covenant renewal rite. However, these numbers are likely symbolic and/or hyperbolic. By the same token, CD 12:22–13:2, which mentions rules for meetings of individual camps in a similar way, cannot be a reflection of the realities of the community.

All five references to Levites in the Community Rule occur within the section that deals with entrance into the covenant community (1:16–3:12).[57] At the initiation ceremony, the Levites take a leading role along with the priests. They bless God together with the priests (1QS 1:19), and recount the iniquities of Israel during the reign of Belial (1QS 1:21–2:1a). Then, the priests bless the men of the lot of God, and the Levites will curse the men of the lot of Belial (1QS 2:5) as prescribed for the covenant ceremony at Mt. Gerizim in Deuteronomy 27 and 28. This annual initiation rite will be repeated until the dominion of Belial ends (1QS 2:19). In this ceremony, the priests will always be ranked first, then the Levites, and then all the people (1QS 2:19-20). Thus, the liturgical section of the Community Rule (1QS 1:1–3:12) implies the existence of the Levites as an identifiable and prominent class in the community.[58]

[57] All the references to the Levites in the Community Rule occur in its liturgical section (1QS 1:1-3:12). This causes a problem in determining the status of the Levites in the Qumran community. Twelve copies of the Rule of the Community have been found from the Qumran caves. Apart from 1QS, there are ten significant fragmentary manuscripts from Cave 4, one or possibly two from Cave 5, and one additional text combining QS and the Damascus Document (4Q265). 4QS[b] and 4QS[d] are the practically identical manuscripts and paleographically several decades later than 1QS, but 4QS[d] does not have any parallel to columns 1QS 1-4. This fact leads to the serious question of which manuscript of the Rule of the Community, among several manuscripts, would reflect the community's ideology most accurately, as J. C. VanderKam (*The Dead Sea Scrolls Today*, 77-80) points out. See also Sarianna Metso, "The Textual Traditions of the Qumran Community Rule," in *Legal Texts and Legal Issues: Proceedings of the Second Meeting of the International Organization for Qumran Studies, Cambridge, 1995: Published in Honour of Joseph M. Baumgarten* (ed. Moshe J. Bernstein, Florentino García Martínez and John Kampen; STDJ 23. Leiden: Brill, 1997) 141-47. This question is indeed an obstacle for my study of the status of the Levites in the Qumran community. However, the following point still makes it doable: The references to the Levites occur not only in 1 QS 1:1-3:12, but also in other sectarian texts, such as CD, 1QSa, 1QM, and the like, and all these references produce a relatively consistent portrayal of the Levites, as C. G. Kruse ("Community Functionaries," 544-45) states.

[58] The Levites' role in reciting blessings and curses in 1QS is also mentioned in 1QM 13:1-2, 4; 18:5. Stallman, "Levi and the Levites in the Dead Sea Scrolls," 182.

In two other texts which focus more exclusively on a restored, eschatological Israel and its temple, the presence of Levites is again assumed. I first deal with the references to the Levites in the Rule for the Congregation or the Messianic Rule (1QSa) since it was copied by the same scribe and sewn to the same scroll as 1QS.[59] This rule pertains to restored Israel at the End of Days (1QSa 1:1), and therefore must be read as an ideal portrait of Israelite society, not as a description of the sect's own time. In this future, eschatological Israel, the Levites shall hold office as the leaders, judges, and officers, "under the authority of the sons of Aaron" (1QSa 1:22). Whenever the assembly of the congregation is mustered either for a legal verdict, a council of the community, or for war, the Levites will usher in and out all who attend certain assemblies (1QSa 1:22-23). The Levites are also included in the list of officials (1QSa 1:27–2:3) who attend meetings that the Council of Yahad convenes.

Another highly eschatological text, the War Scroll (1QM), contains the ordinances for the future final battle to be waged between the forces of light and darkness and presents a highly idealized view of the community.[60] In the War Scroll, the Levites play leadership roles in both cult and combat. They, together with the sons of Judah, Benjamin, and the exiles in the desert, will participate in the future battle against the sons of darkness (1QM 1:3). The name of Levi is to be inscribed on the shield of the prince of the congregation in the order of "Israel and Levi and Aaron," (1QM 5:1); the names of the other twelve tribes will follow. According to 1QM 7:9–9:9, during the battle itself, the priests and Levites will serve as commanders who carry no weapons. The priests' trumpets sound the advance, and the Levites' horns will follow (7:13-14). Here, the priests' trumpet blasts function differently from the Levites' horns (8:9-10; 16:3-9; 17:12-13), thus emphasizing the superiority of the priests. In the cultic arena, the Levites, ranked after the priests, are to officiate as the gatekeepers of the sanctuary and cultic functionaries (1QM 2:2-5), to pronounce blessings and curses (1QM 13:1-2; 18:5) and to offer prayers (1QM 15:4) together with the priests. The covenanters' depiction of the Levites here may be an instance where, at least on a literary level, the Chronicler's view of the Levites as vital, legitimate, high-status cultic functionaries has gained adherents.

[59] Geza Vermes, *The Complete Dead Sea Scrolls in English* (Rev. ed.; London: Penguin Books, 2004) 159.

[60] Stallman, "Levi and the Levites in the Dead Sea Scrolls," 176.

Lastly, the Temple Scroll (11QT), which presents a plan for an ideal sanctuary for the restored twelve tribes, insists on the significance of the Levites in the temple cult.[61] The Temple Scroll describes cultic worship and the Temple, based on an effort to synthesize and reinterpret the biblical laws about sacrifices on Sabbaths and annual feasts, the temple building and furniture, purity regulations, the judicial system, specific regulations for the preparation for the sacrificial animals, regulations about vows, stipulations for the tithes and the like.[62] In this systematization, the Levites receive attention along with the priests, and in several places, the tribe of Levi is prominent. Of particular interest, for our purposes, is that fact that the tribe of Levi is assigned to the central gate on the eastern side in the naming of the gates of the middle and outer courts (11QT 39:12 and 40:14).[63] This could be another indication that the Chronicler's focus on Levites as gatekeepers has gained adherents among the covenanters. Furthermore, the sacrifices of the tribe of Levi will be offered before those of any of the other tribes. According to 11QT 23:9-10, 12, when the high priest offers the sacrifices for the twelve tribes for six consecutive days, he will offer the sacrifices of Levi and Judah on the first day.[64]

[61] The Qumran sectarian origin of the Temple Scroll has been debated. Y. Yadin (*The Temple Scroll* [3 vols.; Jerusalem: Israel Exploration Society, 1977–1983] 1:393-99) argues that it was composed as a "sectarian Torah in the Qumran community." For similar opinions, see Barbara Thiering, "The Date of Composition of the Temple Scroll," in *Temple Scroll Studies*, 101-6. However, several scholars point out that there is no specific connection between the Qumran community and the composition of the Temple Scroll. See Hartmut Stegemann, "The Literary Composition of the Temple Scroll and its Status at Qumran," in *Temple Scroll Studies*, 123-48; Lawrence H. Schiffman, "The Enigma of the Temple Scroll," in *Reclaiming the Dead Sea Scrolls: The History of Judaism, the Background of Christianity, the Lost Library of Qumran* (ABRL; New York: Doubleday, 1995) 257-71; and Baruch A. Levine, "The Temple Scroll: Aspects of its Historical Provenance and Literary Character," *BASOR* 232 (1978) 5-23, here 12. The origin of the Temple Scroll in term of its connection to the Qumran community does not affect much my discussion here since the concern is to investigate how the Levites are portrayed in the texts from the Second Temple period.

[62] Johann Maier, "The Architectural History of the Temple," 23.

[63] Stallman, "Levi and the Levites in the Dead Sea Scrolls," 166.

[64] R. C. Stallman ("Levi and the Levites in the Dead Sea Scrolls," 166) mentions 11QT 44:4-45:2 as another example for the special treatment of the Levites in the Temple Scroll. This section deals with the assignment of chambers in the Temple. Stallman interprets that the Levites were given more sections than the priests, but his interpretation is not correct. In fact, the priests, "the sons of Aaron," were allotted 108 chambers with their rooms in the sections to the north and south of Levi's gate (11QT 44:3-7). To the Levites, especially to the sons of Kohath, however, one section from the gate of Joseph to the gate of Benjamin is assigned (11QT 44:14).

Nevertheless, the Levites are still inferior to the priests: the shares that the Levites receive from the offerings are less than the priests' portions. Still, the Levites' shares are more expanded in the Temple Scrolls (11QT 21:2-6; 60:6-9) than in any biblical source, including Chronicles (see above, section 3.2.2).[65] During the feast of the new wine, the Levites will drink the new wine after the priests (11QT 21:4). Similarly, the cultic function of the Levites in the Temple is distinguished from that of the priests. According to 11QT 22:4, the Levites perform the slaughtering (שחט) of the animal for the well-being offerings, while the priests sprinkle the blood on the altar, burn the fat, and the like.[66] The Levites are also mentioned, along with the priests and judges, as court members (11QT 61:8-9; see also Deut 21:5 and 2 Chr 19:8), and, with the twelve priests and twelve leaders, as members of the royal cabinet (11QT 57:11-13).

Thus, even though the Levites occupy prominent roles, they themselves are consistently distinguished from and subordinate to the priests in the Temple Scroll.[67] R. C. Stallman views the Temple Scroll's treatment of the Levites as elevating their status above that assigned to them in the Pentateuchal materials or even in the pro-levitical Chronicler's work.[68] However, except for the allotment of shoulder from the sacrificed animal to the Levites, the treatment of the Levites in the Temple Scroll seems largely to cohere with the Chronicler's descriptions of the Levites as an elite group

[65] According to 11QT 21:2-5, the Levites will receive the shoulder from the well-being offerings. Deut 18:13 defines the shoulder of the offered animals as the priestly share. For this reason, J. Milgrom ("Studies in the Temple Scroll," *JBL* 97 [1978]:502-3) comments on 11QT 21:2-5 as "the most radical innovation" in the Temple Scroll. On the other hand, 11QT 58:13 deals with the allotment of booty. The Levitical portion will be a hundredth of the booty, but the priestly portion will be a thousandth of booty. This stipulation follows exactly the one of Num 31:28, 30, and 47, as R. C. Stallman ("Levi and the Levites in the Dead Sea Scrolls," 167) points out.

[66] In biblical texts, Levitical involvement in the slaughtering is also mentioned, as in Ezek 44:11; 2 Chr 30:17; 35:6, 10-11. See Stallman, "Levi and the Levites in the Dead Sea Scrolls," 170 and Milgrom, "Studies in the Temple Scroll," 503.

[67] Barbara E. Thiering ("*Mebaqqer* and *Episkopos* in the Light of the Temple Scroll," 61) argues that in the Temple Scroll, there are two kinds of members of the levitical class: levitical priests (sons of Levi, sons of the Levites) and Levites. However, Thiering's argument is not tenable. First, the priests are identified with sons of Aaron in 11QT 22:5; 34:13. Second, in the Temple Scroll, the expression, "the priests, the sons of Levi" which is the main basis for her argument, appears only one time in 11QT 63:3. This expression is more likely influenced by its source Deut 21:5, rather than the author's intentional addition. For a critical view on Thiering's argument, refer to S. M. Oylan, "Ben Sira's Relationship to the Priesthood," 277.

[68] Stallman, "Levi and the Levites in the Dead Sea Scrolls," 171.

which nevertheless is subordinate to the priests. It is possible, moreover, that the allotment of the shoulder piece to the Levites in 11QT may reflect the author's exegetical efforts to harmonize[69] or homogenize[70] the various biblical laws in order to present a hopeful portrait of an ideal system that will be implemented when God restores Israel.[71]

At any rate, the prominent presence of the Levites in the three texts (1QSa, 1QM, and 11QT) indicates that the Levites were considered as a significant group in the Covenanters' eschatological views of Israel. This picture of the Levites is consistent with the first group of texts (CD and 1 QS) which regulate the actual life of the Covenanters.

Scholarly evaluations of the references to the Levites in the Qumran sectarian texts are quite diverse, as is the construction of the sect's eschatology in general. Very broadly, the issue comes down to whether the Levites were fictitiously inserted into these texts for a variety of authorial purposes or whether people identified as "Levites" were actually members of the sect. For a sense of just how broadly divergent perspectives on these matters are, we may first consider C. Werman's position:

> The assumption that the Levites' absence was the subject of controversy can be strengthened by the observation that other documents from the Second Temple period that represent the priestly view, namely the Qumran Scrolls also struggle to explain the lack of Levites. The scrolls, however, give another solution. The writers of the Qumran literature create a fictive existence for the Levites, a literary creation designed to camouflage their scarcity. For example, in Column 2 of the Rule of the Community, the Levites appear in the ceremony of the covenant but not in the description of the ordering of the Yahad.[72]

[69] Y. Yadin (*The Temple Scroll*, 1:74-77) suggests that harmonization, that is, the fusion of the various laws on a single subject into one law, is one of the main organizing features of the Scroll.

[70] According to J. Milgrom ("The Qumran Cult: Its Exegetical Principles," 165-80), another exegetical principle that the author of the Temple Scroll uses is the technique of homogenization, which means that a law which applies to specific objects, animals, or persons is extended to other members of the same species. It is the forerunner of rabbinic *binyan 'ab*.

[71] J. Milgrom ("The Qumran Cult," 177-78) reaches the same conclusion even though he does not deny the possible existence of tensions between priests and the Levites in the Second Temple, and R. C. Stallman ("Levi and the Levites in the Dead Sea Scrolls," 172) also follows Milgrom's view.

[72] Werman, "Levi and Levites in the Second Temple Period," 212.

On the contrary, R. C. Stallman reaches the opposite conclusion:

> The very fact that the Levites surface so often in the literature and that they are afforded such esteem is evidence that this tribe was both highly respected and the subject of extensive theological reflection. This observation fortifies the conclusion that such prominence in eschatological or otherwise future-oriented material paralleled the exalted stature of Levites who were involved at the center of the life of the Qumran community.[73]

Clearly, scholars' interpretations are varied, but we can say that the Dead Sea Scrolls' presentation of the Levites is similar to the Chronicler's, in terms of the positive light in which Levites are presented, the positions of authority which are ascribed to them, and in the emblems of status (such as the shoulder portion) with which they are endowed.

4.2.4. The Levites in the Apocryphal Levi-Priestly Tradition

The status of the Levites in the late Second Temple period is also illuminated in the apocryphal Levi-Priestly Tradition, attested in *Aramaic Levi*, *Jubilees* 30:1-32:9 and *Testament of Levi*.[74] In this tradition, Levi, the third son of Jacob, is portrayed as having been chosen by God for the priestly office because of his zeal for Israel's purity.[75] R. Kugler traces this tradition back to a synoptic reading of four passages in the Pentateuch, Gen 34; Exod 32:25-29; Num 25:6-13; and Deut 33:8-11.[76] A

[73] Stallman, "Levi and the Levites in the Dead Sea Scrolls," 189.

[74] Concerning the Levi-Priestly Tradition, refer to Robert A. Kugler, *From Patriarch to Priest: The Levi-Priestly Tradition from Aramaic Levi to Testament of Levi* (Atlanta: Scholars Press, 1996); James Kugel, "Levi's Elevation to the Priesthood in Second Temple Writings," *HTR* 86 (1993) 1-64; C. Werman, "Levi and Levites in the Second Temple Period," 211-25; and also H. C. Kee, "Testaments of the Twelve Patriarchs (Second Century B.C.E.): A New Translation and Introduction," in *The Old Testament Pseudepigrapha Vol. I: Apocalyptic Literature & Testaments* (ed. James H. Charlesworth; ABRL; New York: Doubleday, 1983) 777.

[75] Kugler, *From Patriarch to Priest*, 2-3.

[76] R. A. Kugler (*From Patriarch to Priest*, 9-16) argues that each of the four passages cannot work alone as a cornerstone for the Levi-Priestly Tradition, but later exegetes could have built such tradition based on a common denominator of these four scriptural passages: Levi's zeal revealed through his ferocious attack on Shechem in Gen 34, the Levites' involvement in punishing the participants in the act of apostasy and Moses' instruction for them to fill their hands (מלאו ידכם) in Exod 32:25-29, Phinehas' zeal for God, and God's granting him "the covenant of peace" and "the covenant of eternal priesthood" in Num 25:6-13 and

comparable synoptic reading is first witnessed in Mal 2:4-7, where these passages, most noticeably Num 25:6-13 and Deut 33:8-11, are integrated into Malachi's portrait of the ideal priest.[77] Julia M. O'Brien points out that Malachi uses several terms in his description of the priesthood, such as "the priests" (הכהנים), "the sons of Levi" (בני־לוי), and "the covenant of Levi" (ברית הלוי), but never uses the terms: "sons of Aaron," "sons of Zadok," or "the Levitical priests."[78] In Malachi, the Levites are not treated as subordinate to the priests, because there is no distinction of functions between the priests and the Levites.[79] Malachi's reference to "the covenant with Levi" is intended to suggest an alternative to the incumbent priests, who failed to adhere to the Pentateuchal norms for sacrifice and teaching. Since the observance of the Mosaic law is considered a prerequisite for the priesthood in Malachi, a strong emphasis is given to the teaching role of the priests (Mal 2:5-7).

The author of *Aramaic Levi* furthers Malachi's covenant with Levi to the extent of promoting Levi as a proper model of the priesthood.[80] Levi's priesthood is confirmed in three ways: through his own vision (vv. 3a-7); by Jacob's ordination of Levi to the priesthood (vv. 9-10); and with Isaac's instructions for the priesthood, which he gives to Levi (vv. 14-61). This triple confirmation affirms an ideal for the priesthood in *Aramaic Levi*, which appears to have been a polemic against another form of the priesthood. An ideal priesthood should have the following qualities: (1) Levi's passion for the purity of cult and community; (2) strict observance of priestly regula-

---

Moses' blessing for Levi to give him the prerogatives of the priesthood (to keep Thummim and Urim, to teach the Torah, and to officiate at the altar) in Deut 33:8-11 (cf. Deut 10:8, where God chose the Levites for their future priestly role). Deut 33:8-11 is also quoted in 4QTestimonia (4Q175), which is a collection of messianic proof-texts. This quotation indicates the community's anticipation of the Priest-Messiah. For 4QTestimonia (4Q175), see G. Vermes, *The Complete Dead Sea Scrolls in English*, 527-28.

[77] Kugel, "Levi's Elevation to the Priesthood in Second Temple Writings," 60; and also Kugler, *From Patriarch to Priest*, 17-18.

[78] Julia M. O'Brien, *Priest and Levite in Malachi* (SBLDS 121; Atlanta: Scholars, 1990) xiv.

[79] O'Brien, *Priest and Levite in Malachi*, 47.

[80] Kugler, *From Patriarch to Priest*, 224. The fragments of *Aramaic Levi* were discovered in the Cairo Geniza, as well as in the Qumran caves. All these fragments evidence kinship with *Testament of Levi* and with *Jubilees*. For the reconstruction of the text of *Aramaic Levi* and its date and relationship with *Jubilees* and *Testament of Levi*, we follow R. A. Kugler. Some scholars suggest different opinions about its date and its literary dependence from Kugler's, but they do not affect my discussion.

tions; and (3) instructional functions (to teach the Torah); the priest as sage and scribe.[81]

C. Werman argues that *Aramaic Levi* 48-49 denies the existence of the non-priestly descendants of Levi[82] when it states: "And now, my child, listen to my words and pay heed to my commandments, and let not these my words leave your heart all your days, for you are a holy priest of the Lord, and your seed will be priests."[83] However, Werman's interpretation of this verse appears to be contradicted in Levi's testament to his children:

> [And you will] be leaders, judges, and magis[trates] and workers (works?) [ ] Also priests and kings you will te[ach] (*Aramaic Levi* 99-100).[84]

This reference to the Levites' instructional role does not assume that those who engage in teaching are necessarily priestly. The existence of priestly and non-priestly Levites appears also in *Jubilees* 30:1-32:9, where Levi is presented as the model priest:[85]

> And the seed of Levi was chosen for the priesthood and levitical (orders) to minister before the Lord always just as we [the host of angels] do. And Levi and his sons will be blessed forever because he was zealous to do righteousness and judgment and vengeance against all who rose up against Israel (*Jubilees* 30:18).[86]

In this quotation, non-priestly Levites ("levitical orders" in the text) are mentioned as a separate group from those with priestly status, and Levi is the father of both Levites and priests.[87] The following quotations also reflect this tradition:

[81] Kugler, *From Patriarch to Priest*, 223; and Werman, "Levi and Levites in the Second Temple Period," 218.

[82] Werman, "Levi and Levites in the Second Temple Period," 211.

[83] Kugler, *From Patriarch to Priest*, 98.

[84] Kugler, *From Patriarch to Priest*, 121.

[85] Kugler, *From Patriarch to Priest*, 169; and Kugel, "Levi's Elevation to the Priesthood," 5-7.

[86] The quotation is taken from O. S. Wintermute, "Jubilees (Second Century B.C.E.): A New Translation and Introduction," in *The Old Testament Pseudepigrapha* (ed. James H. Charlesworth; 2 vols.; New York: Doubleday, 1985) 2:113.

[87] Werman, "Levi and Levites in the Second Temple Period," 221-22.

> And a spirit of prophecy came down his [Isaac's] mouth. And he took Levi in his right hand and Judah in his left hand. ... "May the Lord give you and your seed very great honor. May he draw you and your seed near to him from all flesh to serve in his sanctuary as the angels of the presence and the holy ones. May your sons' seed be like them with respect to honor and greatness and sanctification. And may he make them great in every age. And they will become judges and rulers and leaders for all of the seed of the sons of Jacob (*Jubilees* 31:12, 14-15).[88]

> And he stayed that night in Bethel. And Levi dreamed that he had been appointed and ordained priest of the Most High God, he and his sons forever (*Jubilees* 32:1).[89]

The Levi-Priestly Tradition also shows up in *Testament of Levi*. R. Kugler argues that one concern of this text was to legitimate the joint assumption by the Hasmoneans of military and sacerdotal power.[90] However, there is no explicit reference to any of the Maccabean priest-kings in *Testament of Levi*. *Testament of Levi* 18 is a hymn anticipating the glorious epoch of the eschatological priest. Nothing there connects "a new priest" that God will raise in the future (*Testament of Levi* 18:1) to any of the Hasmonean rulers. What is certain is that *Testament of Levi* defends Levi's priesthood and his offspring's possession of the priestly office. The following quotation proves this point, and notes the existence of the non-priestly descendants of Levi:

> And I saw seven men in white clothing, who were saying to me, "Arise, put on the vestments of the priesthood.... From now on be a priest, you and all your posterity. ... From among them will be priests, judges, and scribes, and by their word the sanctuary will be controlled" (*Testament of Levi* 8:2, 3, 17).[91]

The Levi-Priestly Tradition in *Aramaic Levi*, *Jubilees* and *Testament of Levi*, then, holds that Levi himself was ordained as a priest in his lifetime, and his descendants were also blessed, through Levi, to serve before God

[88] Wintermute, "Jubilees (Second Century B.C.E.)," 115.

[89] Wintermute, "Jubilees (Second Century B.C.E.)," 116-17.

[90] Kugler, *From Patriarch to Priest*, 224.

[91] The quotation is taken from H. C. Kee, "Testaments of the Twelve Patriarchs," 791.

as priests, judges, scribes and leaders. Thus, Levi's offspring includes the priests as well as non-priestly Levites. The origins of these interesting texts are mysterious, but four main lines of inquiry merit our attention.

First, C. Werman asserts that the Levi-Priestly Tradition grew out of "a priestly need to explain, in the course of a dispute with their opponents, the dearth of Levites."[92] She argues that the potential opponents of the priestly trend were the sages, who could employ the dearth of Levites to their advantage. In other words, the sages could have quoted Jacob's curse of Levi in Genesis 49 to give a reason for the disappearance of the Levites and at the same time, to reject the priests' claim to power.[93] However, this reasoning is principally based on an incorrect observation that the tradition denies the existence of non-priestly descendants of Levi.

Second, R. Kugler states that the Levi-Priestly Tradition could have been produced by "a wide range of opponents of the incumbent priesthood," or by "some of the occupants of the office."[94] The latter case is closely related to Kugler's interpretation of *Testament of Levi* as a text designed to defend the double assumption of military and priestly roles.

Third, J. Kugel suggests two different candidates for the authorship of *Testament of Levi*: (1) Levites in the Second Temple period who felt themselves disenfranchised by the current Aaronide priests' monopoly; or (2) A priest who wished to trace his own priesthood to his ancestor Levi. J. Kugel seems to be more inclined toward the second hypothesis, but he does not clarify what would have been this priest's reason to create such a tradition.[95]

Lastly, S. M. Olyan argues that the Levi-Priestly Tradition was produced by non-Aaronide levitical circles to oppose to the Zadokite and Aaronide ideologues who sought to exclude the rest of Levi from the priesthood. His argument is based on his interpretation of the Tradition's polemics against the chief priests (*Testament of Levi* 14:2) and the corrupt priesthood (*Testament of Levi* 14:4-8).[96] However, it is not clear whether the polemics were against the Zadokite priests or the Aaronide priests. H. C. Kee suggests that *Testament Levi* 14 could reflect disillusionment with the increasingly secularized Maccabean priests.[97]

92 Werman, "Levi and Levites in the Second Temple Period," 212.
93 Werman, "Levi and Levites in the Second Temple Period," 213.
94 Kugler, *From Patriarch to Priest*, 225.
95 Kugel, "Levi's Elevation to the Priesthood," 43-44.
96 Oylan, "Ben Sira's Relationship to the Preisthood," 279-80.
97 Kee, "Testaments of the Twelve Patriarchs," 793.

All of these opinions about the producers of the Levi-Priestly Tradition, in spite of their differences, point to the fact that conflicts over the Levites' roles, whether as priests or as cultic functionaries, known from the exilic and post-exilic periods, continued into the late Second Temple period. Moreover, such a variety of interpretations of the levitical role implies a possibility that the Levites themselves participated in these controversies.

This overview of Second Temple texts reveals that the Chronicler's description of the temple staff could indeed have been a product of his engagement in a dynamic conversation with the various parties who defended their own right to serve in the Temple. The Chronicler's positions vis-à-vis the Levites may have found allies among those who defended the Levi-Priestly Tradition. At any rate, matters relating to the identity of priests and the status of Levites clearly remained controversial throughout the Second Temple era; certainly Levites could be used symbolically as figures opposed to prevailing cultic powerholders.

4.3. Conclusion

In this study I have aimed to get a better understanding of the Chronicler's portrayal of the roles of Levites within the administration of the Jerusalem Temple. In particular, I have focused on two related points. First, I have attempted to elucidate the variety of interpretive methods that the Chronicler used to underscore the Levites' legitimate access to important cultic offices and prerogatives.[98] Secondly, in the hope of gaining insight into the Chronicler's distinctive concerns, I have asked how his depiction of the Levites compares with those found in a wide range of other contemporary biblical and extra-biblical literary sources, and in sources that predate and postdate the probable composition of Chronicles. I now want to propose an explanation for why the Chronicler took such pains to describe all the non-priestly temple personnel as Levites.

As I showed in section 4.1, scholars have offered various hypotheses about the Chronicler's incorporation of non-priestly temple personnel among the Levites. The first such interpretation holds that the incorporation of non-levitical personnel into the Levites reflects the final stage of the development of the cultic hierarchy.[99] The second maintains that the

[98] See section 2.5 (pp. 141-49).

[99] The view held by Gunneweg, Numela, and Schaper. For more detailed information, see section 3.4.

incorporation constituted the priestly aristocracy's response to a shortage of Levites in the post-exilic period.[100] And the third line of interpretation argues that legitimization of contemporary realities lies at the heart of the Chronicler's agenda.[101] While I agree with scholars who argue that the Chronicler's careful creation of links between non-priestly personnel and the Levites was a part of his plan to establish a legitimate YHWH cult,[102] I think that a better interpretation of the evidence is available. I have made every effort to demonstrate that the Chronicler's incorporation of all the non-priestly personnel into the Levites largely does not cohere with the realities of the temple administration of his day. Rather, it seems most probable that the Chronicler's interpretive moves, particularly those that concern Pentateuchal regulations, contain the author's arguments for policies and practices he wished to see adopted.[103] Essentially, the Chronicler formulated the legal grounds for the payment of the cultic personnel of the Jerusalem Temple, which was left without any royal sponsorship during the Persian period.

My analyses of the Chronicler's descriptions of the temple administration also illuminate situations of conflict among various groups that upheld different interpretations about cultic practices during the post-exilic period.[104] For example, the Chronicler's choice of the Korahites to establish the continuity of the office of gatekeepers throughout the history of Israel can be understood as an argument against a priestly opponent group that used the tradition of Korah's rebellion (Numbers 16) as a polemic against the Levites. Likewise, the Chronicler's deviations from, or in some

[100] Boccaccini, *Roots of Rabbinic Judaism*, 69-70.

[101] E.g., Goltz, Boda, Laato and the like. For more detailed information, see section 3.4.

[102] Such as, Kalimi, Fishbane, Ristau, and Willi.

[103] Throughout the present work, I demonstrated the Chronicler proposal for policies and practices for ideal administration of the Temple. In summary, they can be enumerated as follows: (1) The Chronicler's cultic organization consisted of four groups: gatekeepers, priests, non-priestly cultic assistants, and singers. All of these cultic personnel belong to the tribe of Levi (see section 1.1.5); (2) In the Chronicler's administrative system, the priests possess the exclusive right to certain cultic activities, such as atonement and burning incense, and the levitical personnel has a subordinate role to the priests. Nevertheless, the extent of levitical engagement in cultic activities is greatly expanded in Chronicles, when compared with the Priestly tradition (see sections 1.1.2 and 1.1.3); (3) The Chronicler emphasizes the levitical supervision of the temple gates (see section 2.1.1.3), and also associates Levites with the running of the treasuries and store-chambers which were vital to the running of the temple economy (see section 2.2.4); and (4) The Chronicler does not make any distinction between the priestly share and the levitical share. Both groups will receive their due from the people's donations (see section 3.2.1).

[104] See section 3.3.2.

cases, reworking of, Priestly traditions in his descriptions of specific cultic duties should be understood in the context of conflicts between the various groups that presented different interpretations about cultic practices, which continued to appear in later works than Chronicles.

Thus, the Chronicler's descriptions of the temple administration are a product of his dialectic approach, not only to Pentateuchal traditions but also to his contemporary circumstances in which various interpretations about cultic practices were put forward. In other words, the Chronicler's descriptions of the temple administration were formulated in the context of the post-exilic period, but they were not intended to present "what really happened" with regard to the temple administration of his own time. Rather, the Chronicler attempted to present his views on who should run the Temple, and how the Temple is supposed to be administered. To legitimize his own views on the temple administration, the Chronicler provided the legal bases for it from Pentateuchal traditions and also gave historical precedents for it in his own version of the historical narratives of the exemplary kings, especially David, Hezekiah and Josiah. By presenting his idealistic temple administration as deeply rooted in ancient cultic traditions, the Chronicler proposed that his own generation should implement his plans.[105] In this sense, following I. Kalimi, I can say that the Chronicler presented his view on the temple administration "to make it applicable to his time and generation, rather than [as] an accurate representation" of the temple administration of his own day.[106]

The book of Chronicles presents myriad challenges, but its study affords ample rewards to those who will approach it with patience and perseverance. It challenges our notions of literary genre; it prevents and indeed, upends, scholarly complacency about the history of Yehud in the Persian era; and it requires us to bring to use every scholarly tool at our disposal to address adequately the textual, exegetical, and compositional puzzles that it poses. Further, in its treatment of issues relating to

[105] Kenneth A. Ristau's study of the Chronicler's reinterpretation of Josiah reaches a similar view on the Chronicler's intention. Ristau ("Reading and Rereading Josiah," 240) comments: "Historical impulses of the text constitute an ideological re-presentation of the community's historical traditions with the purpose of making them (intellectually and/or pragmatically) relevant to the community's present. A text such as this, then, aims to inscribe its ideological re-presentation on its audience in order to persuade them to a certain world view and to actions that reflect that world view."

[106] Kalimi, "Placing the Chronicler in his own Historical Context," 189.

temple administration, the book of Chronicles gives us an unparalleled glimpse into some of the logistical and practical problems that the people of Yehud faced as they sought a way forward in a time of uncertainty, and as they worshipped their God in a temple whose foundations, they hoped, would prove firm.

Bibliography

Abraham, Kathleen. *Business and Politics under the Persian Empire.* Bethesda: CDL Press, 2004.

Ackroyd, Peter R. "The Theology of the Chronicler." *Lexington Theological Quarterly* 8/4 (1973) 101-16.

Aharoni, Y. "Megiddo: The Neolithic Period to the End of the Bronze Age." in *The New Encyclopedia of Archaeological Excavations in the Holy Land.* Edited by Ephraim Stern. 5 vols. New York: Simon & Schuster, 1993. Pp. 3:1003-12.

—— et al., *Excavations at Ramat Rahel: Seasons 1959 and 1960.* Rome: Centro di studi semitici, 1962.

——. *Excavations at Ramat Rahel: Seasons 1961 and 1962.* Rome: Centro di studi semitici, 1964.

Ahituve, Shmuel. "An Edomite Ostracon." in *Michael: Historical, Epigraphical and Biblical Studies in Honor of Prof. Michael Heltzer.* Edited by Yitzhak Avishur and Robert Deutsch. Tel Aviv-Jaffa: Archaeological Center Publication, 1999. Pp. 33-37.

—— and A. Yardeni. "Seventeen Aramaic Texts on Ostraca from Idumea: The Late Persian to the Early Hellenistic Periods." *Maarav* 11 (2004) 7-23.

Albertz, Rainer. *Israel in Exile: The History and Literature of the Sixth Century* B.C.E. Translated by D. Green. Atlanta: Society of Biblical Literature, 2003.

——. "The Thwarted Restoration." In *Yahwism After the Exile.* Edited by Rainer Albertz and Bob Becking. Assen: Royal Van Gorcum, 2003. Pp. 1-17.

Albright, William F. "The Judicial Reform of Jehoshaphat." Pages 61-82 in *Alexander Marx Jubilee Volume* on the Occasion of his Seventieth Birthday. New York: The Jewish Theological Seminary of America, 1950.

Aletti, Jean-Noël. "Proverbs 8:22-31: étude de structure." *Biblica* 57 (1976) 25-37.

Allen, Leslie C. "Kerygmatic Units in 1 and 2 Chronicles." *Journal for the Study of the Old Testament* 41 (1988) 21-36.

——. *The Translator's Craft*. Vol. 1 of *The Greek Chronicles: The Relation of the Septuagint of I and II Chronicles to the Massoretic Text*. Supplements to Vetus Testamentum 25. Leiden: E.J. Brill, 1974.

——. *Textual Criticism*. Vol. 2 of *The Greek Chronicles: The Relation of the Septuagint of I and II Chronicles to the Massoretic Text*. Supplements to Vetus Testamentum 27. Leiden: E.J. Brill, 1974.

Ambar-Armon, Einat and Amos Kloner, "Archaeological Evidence of Links Between the Aegean World and the Land of Israel in the Persian Period." In *A Time of Change: Judah and Its Neighbors in the Persian and Early Hellenistic Periods*. Edited by Yigal Levin. Library of Second Temple Studies 65. New York: T & T Clark, 2007. Pp. 1-22.

Anderson, Francis I. and David Noel Freedman, *Amos: A New Translation with Introduction and Commentary*. Anchor Bible 24A. New York: Doubleday, 1989.

Anderson, Gary A. Review of Baruch J. Schwartz, *The Holiness Legislation Studies in the Priestly Code*. *Catholic Biblical Quarterly* 63 (2001) 128-29.

Annandale-Potgieter, Joan. "The High Priests in 1 Maccabees and in the Writings of Josephus." In *VII Congress of the International Organization for Septuagint and Cognate Studies*. Edited by Clause E. Cox. Atlanta: Scholars Press, 1989. Pp. 393-429.

Avigad, Nahman. *Bullae and Seals from a Post-Exilic Judean Archive*. Translated by R. Grafman. Qedem 4. Jerusalem: Institute of Archaeology, The Hebrew University of Jerusalem, 1976.

Barag, D. "A Silver Coin of Yohanan the High Priest and the Coinage of Judaea in the Fourth Century BC." *Israel Numismatic Journal* 9 (1986–1987) 4-21.

——. "The Effects of the Tennes Rebellion on Palestine." *Bulletin of the American Schools of Oriental Research* 183 (1966) 6-12.

Bartlett, John R. *1 Maccabees*. Guides to Apocrypha and Pseudepigrapha. Sheffield: Sheffield Academic Press, 1998.

——. *The first and Second Books of the Maccabees*. The Cambridge Bible Commentary. Cambridge: University Press, 1973.

Baumgarten, Joseph M. "Critical Notes: On the Non-Literal Use of Maʿaser/Dekate." *Journal of Biblical Literature* 103 (1984) 245-61.

——, Ada Yardeni and Stephen J. Pfann, eds. *Qumran Cave 4. V. XIII: The Damascus document (4Q266-273).* Discoveries in the Judean Desert 18. Oxford: Clarendon Press, 1996.

Beaulieu, Paul-Alain. *Late Babylonian Texts in the Nies Babylonian Collection*. Bethesda: CDL Press, 1994.

Becking, Bob. "Do the Earliest Samaritan Inscriptions Already Indicate a Parting of the Ways?" in *Judah and Judeans in the Fourth Century* B.C.E. Edited by Oded Lipschits, Gary N. Knoppers, and Rainer Albertz. Winona Lake: Eisenbrauns, 2007. Pp. 213-22.

—— and Marjo C.A. Korpel. eds. *The Crisis of Israelite Religion: Transformation of Religious Traditions in Exilic and Post-Exilic Times*. Oudtestamentische Studiën 42. Leiden: Brill, 1999.

Bedford, Peter Ross. "The Economic Role of the Jerusalem Temple in Achaemenid Judah: Comparative Perspectives" In *Shai le-Sarah Japhet: Studies in the Bible, its Exegesis and its Languages*. Edited by Mosheh Bar-Asher et al; Jerusalem: Bialik Institute, 2007. Pp. 3-20.

Beentjes, Pancratius C. *Tradition and Transformation in the Book of Chronicles* Studia Semitica Neerlandica 52. Leiden; Boston: Brill, 2008.

——. "Psalms and Prayers in the Book of Chronicles." In *Psalms and Prayers:* Papers *Read at the Joint Meeting of the Society of Old Testament Study and the Oudtestamentische Werkgezelschap in Nederland en Belgie, Apeldoorn August 2006*. Edited by Bob Becking and Eric Peels. Oudtestamentische Studiën 55. Leiden; Boston: Brill, 2007. Pp. 9-44

——. "Prophets in the Book of Chronicles." In *The Elusive Prophet: The Prophet as a Historical Person, Literary Character and Anonymous Artist*. Edited by Johannes C. de Moor. Oudtestamentische Studiën 45. Leiden: Brill, 2001. Pp. 45-53

——. "Tradition and Transformation: Aspects of Innerbiblical Interpretation in 2 Chronicles 20." *Biblica* 74 (1993) 258-68.

Begg, Christopher T. "The Levites in Josephus." *Hebrew Union College Annual* 75 (2004) 1-22.

Ben Zvi, Ehud. "Revisiting 'Boiling in Fire' in 2 Chronicles 35:13 and Related Passover Questions: Text, Exegetical Needs and Concerns, and General Implications." In *Biblical Interpretation in Judaism and Christianity*. Edited by Isaac Kalimi and Peter J. Haas. Library of Hebrew Bible/Old Testament Studies 439. New York; London: T & T Clark, 2006. Pp. 238-50

Bennett, Harold V. "Triennial Tithes and the Underdog: A Revisionist Reading off Deuteronomy 14:22-25 and 26:12-15." In *Yet with a steady beat:* Contemporary U.S. Afrocentric Biblical Interpretation. Edited by Randall C. Bailey. Society of Biblical Literature Semeia Studies 42. Atlanta: Society of Biblical Literature, 2003. Pp. 7-18.

Berger, Yitzhak. *The Commentary of Rabbi David Kimhi to Chronicles: A Translation with Introduction and Supercommentary*. Providence, RI: Brown Judaic Studies, 2007.

Betlyon, John Wilson. "A People Transformed: Palestine in the Persian Period." *Near Eastern Archaeology* 68 (2005) 4-60.

——. "The Provincial Government of Persian Period Judea and the Yehud Coins." *Journal of Biblical Literature* 105 (1986) 633-42.

Berquist, Jon L. *Judaism in Persian's Shadow: A Social and Historical Approach*. Minneapolis: Fortress Press, 1995.

Blenkinsopp, Joseph. *Ezra-Nehemiah: A Commentary*. Old Testament Library. Philadelphia: Westminster Press, 1988.

Blomquist, Tina Haettner. *Gates and Gods: Cults in the City Gates of Iron Age Palestine An Investigation of the Archaeological and Biblical Sources*. Coniectanea Biblica Old Testament Series 46. Stockholm: Almqvist & Wiksell International, 1999.

Boccaccini, Gabriele, *Roots of Rabbinic Judaism: An Intellectual History, from Ezekiel to Daniel*. Grand Rapids: Eerdmans, 2002.

Boda, Mark J. "Identity and Empire, Reality and Hope in the Chronicler's Perspective." In *Community Identity in Judean Historiography: Biblical and Comparative Perspectives*. Edited by G. N. Knoppers and Kenneth A. Ristau. Winona Lake: Eisenbrauns, 2009. Pp. 249-72.

Bolin, Thomas M. "The Temple of יהו at Elephantine and Persian Religious Policy." In *The Triumph of Elohim: from Yahwism to Judaisms*. Edited by Diana Vikander Edelman. Contributions to Biblical Exegesis and Theology 13. Grand Rapids: Eerdmans, 1996. Pp. 127-42.

Bongenaar, A. C. V. M. *The Neo-Babylonian Ebabbar Temple at Sippar: Its Administration and its Prospography*. Uitgaven van het Nederlands Historisch-Archeologisch Institut te Istanbul 80. Leiden: Nederlands Historisch-Archaelogisch Instituut te Istanbul, 1997.

Braun, Roddy. *1 Chronicles*. Word Biblical Commentary 14. Waco: Word Books, 1986.

——. "Chronicles, Ezra and Nehemiah: Theology and Literary History." In *Studies in the Historical Books of the Old Testament*. Edited by J.A. Emerton. Supplements to Vetus Testamentum 30. Leiden: Brill, 1979. Pp. 52-64.

Briant, Pierre. *From Cyrus to Alexander: A History of the Persian Empire.* Winona Lake: Eisenbrauns, 2002.

Brooke, A. E., N. McLean, and H. St. John Thackeray, eds. *The Old Testament in Greek.* 3 vols. London: Cambridge University Press, 1906–1940.

Brooke, George J. "Levi and the Levites in the Dead Sea Scrolls and the New Testament." In *Mogilany 1989: Papers on the Dead Sea Scrolls offered in Memory of Jean Carmignac Part I: General Research on the Dead Sea Scrolls Qumran and the New Testament the Present State of Qumranology*. Edited by Zdzislaw J. Kapera. Qumranica Mogilanensia 2. Krakow: The Enigma Press, 1993. Pp. 105-29.

Brooks, Roger. *Talmud Yerushalmi. Ma'aser sheni.* Chicago: The University of Chicago Press, 1993.

Burrell, Barbara. *Neokoroi: Greek Cities and Roman Emperors.* Leiden: Brill, 2004.

Busink, Th. A., *Der Tempel Solomos.* Vol. 1 of *Der Tempel von Jerusalem,* von *Salomo bis Herodes; eine archäologisch-historische Studie unter Berücksichtigung des westsemitischen Tempelbaus.* Studia Francisci Scholten memoriae dicata 3. Leiden: Brill, 1970.

——. *Von Ezechiel bis Middot.* Vol. 2 of *Der Tempel von Jerusalem,* von *Salomo bis Herodes; eine archäologisch-historische Studie unter Berücksichtigung des westsemitischen Tempelbaus.* Studia Francisci Scholten memoriae dicata 3. Leiden: Brill, 1980.

Carter, Charles E. *The Emergence of Yehud in the Persian Period: A Social and Demographic Study.* Jouranl for the Study of the Old Testament: Supplement 294. Sheffield: Sheffield Academic Press, 1999.

——."The Province of Yehud in the Post-Exilic Period: Soundings in Site Distribution and Demography." In *Temple Community in the Persian Period.* Vol. 2 of *Second Temple Studies.* Edited by Tamara C. Eskenazi and Kent H. Richards. Journal for the Study of the Old Testament: Supplement Series 175. Sheffield: JSOT Press, 1994. Pp. 106-45.

Carter, Edward J. "Toll and Tribute: A Political Reading of Matthew 17.24-27." *Journal for the Study of the New Testament* 25 (2003) 413-31.

Carter, Warren. "Paying the Tax to Rome as Subversive Praxis: Matthew 17.24-27." *Journal for the Study of the New Testament* 16 (1999) 3-31.

Cassidy, Richard J. "Matthew 17:24-27: A Word on Civil Taxes." *Catholic Biblical Quarterly* 41 (1979) 571-80.

Cataldo, Jeremiah W. *A Theocratic Yehud? Issues of Government in a Persian Province*. Library of Hebrew Bible/Old Testament studies 498. New York: T & T Clark, 2009.

Charlesworth, James H., ed. *The Old Testament Pseudepigrapha*. 2 vols. New York: Doubleday, 1985.

Clines, David J. A. *Ezra, Nehemiah, Esther*. New Century Bible Commentary. Grand Rapids: Eerdmans, 1984.

Cody, Aelerd. *A History of Old Testament Priesthood*. Analecta Biblica 35. Rome: Pontifical Biblical Institute, 1969.

Cogan, Mordechai and Hayim Tadmor, *II Kings: A New Translation with Introduction and Commentary*. Anchor Bible 11. New York: Doubleday, 1988.

Coggins, R. J. *The Books of Ezra and Nehemiah*. Cambridge Bible Commentary. New York: Cambridge University Press, 1976.

Cohn, Robert L. *2 Kings*. Berit Olam. Collegeville: Liturgical Press, 2000.

Cole, Steven W. and Peter Machinist. eds. *Letters from Priests to the Kings Esarhaddon and Assurbanipal*. With Contributions by Simo Parpola. Illustrations Edited by Julian Reade. State Archives of Assyria 13. Helsinki: Helsinki University Press, 1998.

Crüsemann, Frank. *The Torah: Theology and Social History of Old Testament Law*. Translated by Allan W. Mahnke. Minneapolis: Fortress Press, 1996.

Curtis, Edward Lewis and Albert Alonzo Madsen. *A Critical and Exegetical Commentary on the Books of Chronicles*. The International Critical Commentary 11. New York: Scribner's, 1910.

Dandamayev, Muhammed A. and Vladimir G. Lukonin. *The Culture and Social Institutions of Ancient Iran*. English Edition by Philip L. Kohl with the Assistance of D. J. Dadson. Cambridge; New York: Cambridge University Press, 1989.

Davies, William David and Dale C. Allison, *Commentary on Matthew VIII–XVIII*. Vol. 2 of *A Critical and Exegetical Commentary on the Gospel According to Saint Matthew*. The International Critical Commentary 26. 3 vols. Edinburgh: T & T Clark, 1988.

De Vaux, Roland. *Ancient Israel: Its Life and Institutions*. Translated by John McHugh. Grand Rapids: Eerdmans, 1997.

De Vries, Simon J. *1 and 2 Chronicles*. The Forms of the Old Testament Literature 9. Grand Rapids: Eerdmans, 1989.

——. "Moses and David as Cult Founders in Chronicles." *Journal Biblical Literature* 107 (1988) 619-39.

De Wette, William Martin Leberecht. *A Critical and Historical Introduction to the Canonical Scriptures of the Old Testament.* Translated and Enlarged by Theodore Parker; 2 vols. 3rd ed. Boston: Rufus Leighton, 1859.

Delcor, M. "Le temple d'Onias en Égypte." *Revue Biblique* 75 (1968) 88-203.

Demsky, Aaron. "The Genealogy of Gibeon (1 Chronicles 9:35-44): Biblical and Epigraphic Considerations." *Bulletin of the American Schools of Oriental Research* 202 (1971) 16-23.

Dillard, Raymond B. 2 *Chronicles.* Word Biblical Commentary 15. Waco: Word Books, 1987.

Dion, Paul-Eugène. "La religion des papyrus d'Éléphantine: un reflet du Juda d'avant l'exil." In *Kein Land für sich allein: Studien zum Kulturkontakt in Kanaan, Israel/Palästina und Ebirnari* für *Manfred Weippert zum 65 Geburtstag.* herausgegeben von Ulrich Hübner und Ernst Axel Knauf. Orbis Biblicus et Orientalis 186. Göttingen: Vandenhoeck & Ruprecht, 2002. Pp. 243-54.

Dirksen, Peter B. *1 Chronicles.* Historical Commentary on the Old Testament. Leuven; Dudley, MA: Peeters, 2005.

——. "1 Chronicles 9:26-33: Its Position in Chapter 9." *Biblica* 79 (1998) 91-96.

——. "The Composition of 1 Chronicles 26:20-32." *JNSL* 24 (1988) 144-55.

Donaldson,Terry L. "Levitical Messianology in Late Judaism: Origins, Development and Decline." *Journal of the Evangelical Theological Society* 24 (1981) 193-207.

Doran, Robert. *Temple Propaganda: The Purpose and Character of 2 Maccabees.* Catholic Biblical Quarterly: Monograph Series 12. Washington: The Catholic Biblical Association of America, 1981.

Dörfuss, Ernst Michael. *Mose in den Chronikbüchern: Garant theokratischer Zukunftserwartung.* Beiheft zur Zeitschrift für die alttestamentliche Wissenschaft 219. Berlin: W. de Gruyter, 1994.

Dorsey, David A. "Another Peculiar Term in the Book of Chronicles: מְסִלָּה, 'Highway'?" *Jewish Quarterly Review* 75 (1985) 385-91.

Driver, Samuel Rolles, *A Critical and Exegetical Commentary on Deuteronomy.* The International Critical Commentary 5. Edinburgh: T & T Clark, 1951.

Duggan, Michael W. *The Covenant Renewal in Ezra-Nehemiah (Neh 7:72B-10:40): An Exegetical, Literary, and Theological Study*. Society of Biblical Literature Dissertation Series 164. Atlanta: Society of Biblical Literature, 2001.

Duke, Rodney K. *The Persuasive Appeal of the Chronicler: A Rhetorical Analysis*. Journal for the study of the Old Testament: Supplement Series 88. Sheffield: Almond Press, 1990.

——. "A Rhetorical Approach to Appreciating the Books of Chronicles." In *The Chronicler as Author: Studies in Text and Texture*. Edited by M. P. Graham and S. L. McKenzie. Journal for the Study of the Old Testament: Supplement Series 263. Sheffield: Sheffield Academic Press, 1999. Pp. 100-135.

Dyck, Jonathan E. *The Theocratic Ideology of the Chronicler*. Biblical Interpretation Series 33. Leiden; Boston; Köln: Brill, 1998.

Eerdmans, Bernardus Dirk, *The Hebrew Book of Psalms*. Oudtestamentische Studiën 4. Leiden: Brill, 1947.

Eissfeldt, Otto. "Eine Einschmelzstelle am Tempel zu Jerusalem." *Forschungen und Fortschritte* 13 (1937) 163-64.

Ellis, Maria deJ. "Taxation in Ancient Mesopotamia: the History of the Term *miksu*." *Journal of Cuneiform Studies* 26 (1974) 211-50.

Emerton, J. A. " 'The High Places of the Gates' in 2 Kings XXIII 8." *Vetus Testamentum* 44 (1994) 455-67.

Endres, John C., William R. Millar and John Barclay Burns. eds. *Chronicles and its Synoptic Parallels in Samuel, Kings, and Related Biblical Texts*. Collegeville: Liturgical Press, 1998.

Ephʿal, Isreal. "The Western Minorities in Babylonia in the 6th-5th Centuries B.C.E.: Maintenance and Cohesion." *Orientalia* 47 (1978) 74-90.

——. "Syria-Palestine under Achaemenid Rule." In *Persia, Greece and the Western Mediterranean c. 525 to 479 BCE*. Vol. 4 of *The Cambridge Ancient History*. Edited by John Boardman , N. G. L. Hammond, D. M. Lewis, M. Ostwald. 2nd ed. New York: Cambridge University Press, 1988. Pp. 139-64.

Eshel, Hanan and Boaz Zissu. "Two Notes on the History and Archaeology of Judea in the Persian Period." In *"I Will Speak the Riddle of Ancient Things": Archaeological and Historical Studies in Honor of Amihai Mazar on the Occasion of his Sixtieth Birthday*. Edited by A.M. Maeir and P. de Miroschedji. Winona Lake: Eisenbrauns, 2006. Pp. 823-831.

—— and Hagai Misgav. "A fourth-century BCE document from Ketef Yeriho." *Israel Exploration Journal* 38 (1988) 158-76.

—— and Hagai Misgav. "Jericho papList of Loans ar." In *Miscellaneous Texts from the Judaean Desert*. Edidted by J. Charlesworth et als. Discoveries in Judean Desert 38. Oxford: Clarendon Press, 2000. Pp. 21-30.

Evans, Geoffrey. " 'Gates' and 'Streets': Urban Institutions in Old Testament Times." *The Journal of Religious History* 2 (1962) 1-12.

Even-Shoshan, A. ed. *A New Concordance of the Bible: Thesaurus of the Language of the Bible Hebrew and Aramaic Roots, Words, Proper Names, Phrases and Synonyms*. Yerushalayim: Kiryat-Sefer, 2000.

Ferguson, Everett. *Backgrounds of Early Christianity*. 3rd ed. Grand Rapids: Eerdmans, 2003.

Finkelstein, Israel. "The Historical Reality behind the Genealogical Lists in 1 Chronicles." *Journal of Biblical Literature* 131 (2012) 65-83.

Fishbane, Michael. *Biblical Interpretation in Ancient Israel*. Oxford: Oxford University Press, 1985.

Fox, Nili Sacher. *In the Service of the King: Officialdom in Ancient Israel and Judah*. Monographs of Hebrew Union College 23. Cincinnati: Hebrew Union College Press, 2000.

Frey, Jörg. "Temple and Rival Temple—The Case of Elephantine, Mt. Gerizim, and Leontopolis." In *Gemeinde ohne Temepl = Community without Temple: Zur Substituierung und Transformation des Jerusalemer Tempels und seines Kults im Alten Testament, antiken Judentum und frühen Christentum*. Edited by Beate Ego, Armin Lange and Peter Pilhofer. Wisenschaftliche Untersuchungen zum Neuen Testament 118. Tübingen: J.C. B. Mohr (Paul Siebeck), 1999. Pp. 171-203.

Fried, Lisbeth S. *The Priest and the Great King: Temple-Palace Relations in the Persian Empire*. Biblical and Judaic Studies from the University of California, San Diego 10. Winona Lake: Eisenbrauns, 2004.

——. "A Silver Coin of Yoµanan Hakkôhēn (Pls II-V)." *Transeuphratene* 26 (2003) 65-85.

Fritz, Volkmar, *1 & 2 Kings: A Continental Commentary*, Translated by Anselm Hagedorn. Continental Commentaries. Minneapolis: Fortress Press, 2003.

——. "Temple Architecture: What can Archaeology Tell us About Solomon's Temple?" *BAR* 13 (1987) 38-49.

Galling, Kurt. *Die Bücher der Chronik, Esra, Nehemiah*. Das Alte Testament deutsch 12. Göttingen: Vanderhoeck & Ruprecht, 1954.

———. "Die Halle des Schreibers: Ein Beitrag zur Topographie der Akropolis von Jerusalem." *Palästinajahrbuch des Deutschen evangelischen Instituts für Altertumswissenschaft* des *Heiligen Landes zu Jerusalem* 27 (1931) 51-57.

Gerson, Stephen N. "Fractional Coins of Judea and Samaria in the Fourth Century B.C.E." *Near Eastern Archaeology* 64/3 (2001) 106-21.

Gerstenberger, Erhard S. *Leviticus: A Commentary* (Old Testament Library; Louisville: Westminster John Knox Press, 1996.

Gitin, Seymour and Amir Golani. "A Silver-Based Monetary Economy in the Seventh Century BCE: a Response to Raz Kletter." *Levant* 36 (2004) 203–205.

Gitler, Haim and Oren Tal, *The Coinage of Philistia of the Fifth and Fourth Centuries B.C.: A Study of the Earliest Coins of Palestine*. Milan/New York: Edizioni Ennerre, 2006.

———, Oren Tal and Peter Van Alfen. "Silver Dome-shaped Coins from Persian-period Southern Palestine." *Israel Numismatic Research* 2 (2007) 47-62.

——— and C. Lorber, "A New Chronology for the Ptolemaic Coins of Judah." *American Journal of Numistmatics* 18 (2006) 1-41.

Gitlin, Emmanuel. "The Tithe in Deuteronomy." *Religion in Life* 32 (1963) 574-85.

Goltz, Timothy D. "The Chronicler as Elite: Establishing an Atmosphere of Perpetuity in Jerusalem Yehud." In *The Function of Ancient Historiography in Biblical and Cognate Studies*. Edited by Patricia G. Kirkpatrick and Timothy Goltz. Library of Hebrew Bible/Old Testament Studies 489. New York: T & T Clark, 2008. Pp. 91-110

Grabbe, Lester L. "The "Persian Documents in the Book of Ezra: Are They Authentic?" in *Judah and Judeans in the Persian Period*. Edited by Oded Lipschit and Manfred Oeming; Winona Lake: Eisenbrauns, 2006. Pp. 531-70.

———. "The History of Israel: The Persian and Hellenistic Periods." In *Texts in Context: Essays by Members of the Society for Old Testament Study*. Edited by A. D. H. Mayes. New York: Oxford University Press, 2000. Pp. 403-27.

———. *Judaic Religion in the Second Temple Period: Belief and Practice from the Exile to Yavneh*. London; New York: Routledge, 2000.

———. *Leviticus*. Old Testament Guides. Sheffield: Sheffield Academic Press, 1993.

Gray, John. *I & II Kings*. Old Testament Library. 2nd, fully revised, ed. Philadelphia: The Westminster Press, 1970.

Gregori, B. "Three-Entrance' City-Gates of the Middle Bronze Age in Syria and Palestine.." *Levant* 18 (1986) 83-102.

Gunneweg, A. H. J. *Leviten und Priester: Hauptlinen der Traditionsbildung und Geschichte des israelitisch-jüdischen Kultpersonals*. Forschungen zur Religion und Literatur des Alten und Neuen Testaments 89. Göttingen: Vanderhoeck & Ruprecht, 1965.

Hallock, Richard T. *Persepolis Fortification Tablets*. University of Chicago Oriental Institute Publications 92. Chicago: The University of Chicago Press, 1969.

Hanson, Paul D. "1 Chronicles 15-16 and the Chronicler's View on the Levites" in *"Sha'arei Talmon" Studies in the Bible, Qumran, and the Ancient Near East Presented to Shemaryahu Talmon*. Edited by Michael Fishbane and Emmanuel Tov with the assistance of Weston W. Fields. Winona Lake: Eisenbrauns, 1992. Pp. 69-77.

——. *Dawn of Apocalyptic: The Historical and Sociological Roots of Jewish Apocalyptic Eschatology*. Philadelphia, Fortress Press, 1975.

Harrington, Daniel J. *The Maccabean Revolt: Anatomy of a Biblical Revolution*. Old Testament Studies 1. Wilmington: Michael Glazier, 1988.

Hayward, Robert, "The Jewish Temple at Leontopolis: A Reconsideration." *Journal of Jewish Studies* 33 (1982) 429-43.

Heltzer, Michael. *The Province Judah and Jews in Persian Times*. Tel Aviv: Archaeological Center Publication, 2008.

——. "The Provincial Taxation in the Achaemenid Empire and 'Forty Shekels of Silver' (Neh 5:15)." *Michmanim* 6 (1992) 15-25.

Hempel, Charlotte. *The Damascus Texts*. Sheffield: Sheffield Academic Press, 2000.

Herman, Menachem. *Tithe as gift: The Institution in the Pentateuch and in Light of Mauss's Prestation Theory*. San Francisco: Mellen Research University Press, 1991.

Herzog, Zeev. "Settlement and Fortification Planning in the Iron Age." In *The Architecture of Ancient Israel: From the Prehistoric to the Persian Periods*. Edited by A. Kempinski and Ronny Reich. Jerusalem: Israel Exploration Society, 1992. Pp. 231-74.

Hildenbrand, Michael D. *Structure and Theology in the Holiness Code*. North Richland Hills: Bibal Press, 2004.

Hjelm, Ingrid, *Jerusalem's Rise to Sovereignty: Zion and Gerizim in Competition*. Journal for the Study of the Old Testament: Supplement Series 404. London; New York: T& T Clark International, 2004.

Hoglund, Kenneth. "The Chronicler as Historian: A Comparativist Perspective." In *The Chronicler as Historian*. Edited by M. Patrick Graham, Kenneth G. Hoglund and Steven L. McKenzie. Journal for the Study of the Old Testament 238. Sheffield: Sheffield Academic Press, 1997. Pp. 19-29.

——. *Achaemenid Imperial Administration in Syria-Palestine and the Missions of Ezra and Nehemiah*. Society of Biblical Literature Dissertation Series 125. Atlanta: Scholars Press, 1992.

Hogeterp, Albert L. A. "4QMMT and Paradigms of Second Temple Jewish Nomism." *Dead Sea Discoveries* 15 (2008) 359–379.

Hognesius, Kjell. *The Text of 2 Chronicles 1-16: A Critical Edition with Textual Commentary*. Coniectanea Biblica 51. Stockholm: Almqvist & Wiksell International, 2003.

Hooker, Paul K., *First and Second Chronicles*. Westminster Bible Companion. Louisville: Westminster John Knox Press, 2001.

Hurvitz, Avi. "Terms and Epithets Relating to the Jerusalem Temple Compound in the Book of Chronicles: The Linguistic Aspect." In *Pomegranates and Golden Bells: Studies in Biblical, Jewish, and Near Eastern Ritual, Law, and Literature in Honor of Jacob Milgrom*. Edited by David P. Wright, D. N. Freedman, and Avi Hurvitz. Winona Lake: Eisenbrauns, 1995. Pp. 165-83.

Jackson, Bernard S. "Law in the Ninth Century: Jehoshaphat's 'Judicial Reform'." Pages 369-97 in *Understanding the History of Ancient Israel*. Edited by H. G. M Williamson. Proceedings of the British Academy 143. Oxford; New York: Oxford University Press, 2007.

Jaffee, Martin S. *Talmud Yerushalmi. Ma'aserot*. Chicago: The University of Chicago Press, 1987.

Jagersma, H. "The Tithes in the Old Testament." In *Remembering All the Way: A Collection of Old Testament Studies*. Edited by Adam S van der Woude. Leiden: Brill, 1981. Pp. 116-28.

Japhet, Sara. "The Relationship between Chronicles and Ezra-Nehemiah." Pages 169-82 in *From the Rivers of Babylon to the Highlands of Judah*. Winona Lake: Eisenbrauns, 2006.

——. *I & II Chronicles: A Commentary*. Old Testament Library. London: SCM Press, 1993.

——. *The Ideology of the Book of Chronicles and Its Place in Biblical Thought*. Beiträge zur Erforschung des Alten Testaments und des Antiken Judentums 9. Frankfurt: Peter Lang, 1989.

——. "The Supposed Common Authorship of Chronicles and Ezra-Nehemiah Investigated Anew." *Vetus Testamentum* 18 (1968): 330-71.

——. "The Distribution of the Priestly Gifts according to a Document of the Second Temple Period." In *From Rivers of Babylon to the Highlands of Judah: Collected Studies on the Restoration Period*. Winona Lake: Eisenbrauns, 2006. Pp. 289-306.

Johnson, Marshall D. *The Purpose of the Biblical Genealogies: With Special Reference to the Setting of the Genealogies of Jesus*. Society for New Testament Studies Monograph Series 8. 2nd ed. Cambridge: Cambridge University Press, 1988.

Johnstone, William. *1 Chronicles 1–2 Chronicles 9: Israel's Place among the Nations*. Vol. 1 of *1 and 2 Chronicles*. 2 Volumes. Journal for the Study of the Old Testament: Supplement Series 253. Sheffield: Sheffield Academy Press, 1997.

——. *2 Chronicles 10-36 Guilt and Atonement*. Vol. 2 of *1 and 2 Chronicles*. 2 Volumes. Journal for the Old Testament: Supplement Series 254. Sheffield: Sheffield Academy Press, 1997.

Jones, Gwilym H. *1 &2 Chronicles*. Old Testament Guides. Sheffield: JSOT Press, 1993.

Jonker, Louis C., *Reflections of King Josiah in Chronicles: Late Stages of the Josiah Reception in 2 Chr 34f.* Textpragmatische Studien zur Literatur- und Kulturgeschichte der Hebräischen Bibel 2. Gütersloh: Gütersloher Verlagshaus, 2003.

——. "The Chronicler and the Prophets: Who were his Authoritative Sources?" *Scandinavian Journal of the Old Testament* 22 (2008) 275-95.

Jursa, M. *Neo-Babylonian Legal and Administrative Documents: Typology, Contents, and Archives: Guides to the Mesopotamian Textual Record*. Guides to the Mesopotamian Textual Record 1. Münster: Ugarit-Verlag, 2005.

Kalimi, Isaac. "Placing the Chronicler in his own Historical Context: A Closer Examination." *Journal of Near Eastern Studies* 68 (2009) 179-92.

——. *An Ancient Israelite Historian: Studies in the Chronicler, his Time, Place and Writing*. Studia Semitica Neerlandica 46. Assen: Van Gorcum, 2005.

——. *The Reshaping of Ancient Israelite History in Chronicles*. Winona Lake: Eisenbrauns, 2005.

——. "Jerusalem—The Divine City: The Representation of Jerusalem in Chronicles Compared with Earlier and Later Jewish Compositions." In *The Chronicler as Theologian: Essays in Honor of Ralph W. Klein*. Edited by M. Patrick Graham, Steven L. McKenzie and Gary N. Knoppers. Journal for the Study of the Old Testament: Supplement Series 371. London: T & T Clark, 2003. Pp. 189-205.

——. "The View of Jerusalem in the Ethnographical Introduction of Chronicles (1 Chr 1-9)." *Biblica* 83 (2002) 556-62.

Kaufman, Stephen. *The Akkadian Influences on Aramaic*. Assyriological Studies 19. Chicago: University of Chicago, 1974.

Kee, H. C. "Testaments of the Twelve Patriarchs (Second Century B.C.E.): A New Translation and Introduction." In *The Old Testament Pseudepigrapha Vol. I: Apocalyptic Literature & Testaments*. Edited by James H. Charlesworth; New York: Doubleday, 1983. Pp. 777-828.

Keel, Othmar, *The Symbolism of the Biblical World: Ancient Near Eastern Iconography and the Book of Psalms*. Translated by Timothy J. Hallett. New York: The Seabury Books, 1978.

Kempinski, Aharon., "Middle and Late Bronze Age Fortifications." In *The Architecture of Ancient Israel: From the Prehistoric to the Persian Periods*. Edited by A. Kempinski and Ronny Reich. Jerusalem: Israel Exploration Society, 1992. Pp. 127-42.

Kessler, John. "Diaspora and Homeland in the Early Achaemenid Period: Community, Geography and Demography in Zechariah 1–8." In *Approaching Yehud: New Approaches to the Study of the Persian Period*. Edited by Jon L. Berquist. Society of Biblical Literature Semeia Studies 50. Atlanta: Society of Biblical Literature, 2007. Pp. 137-66.

Kitz, Anne Marie, "The Hebrew Terminology of Lot Casting and Its Ancient Near Eastern Context." *Catholic Biblical Quarterly* 62 (2000) 207-14.

——. "Undivided Inheritance and Lot Casting in the Book of Joshua." *Journal of Biblical Literature* 119 (2000) 601-18.

Klein, Ralph W. *1 Chronicles*. Hermeneia. Minneapolis: Fortress Press, 2006.

Kleinig, John W. *The Lord's Song: The Basis, Function and Significance of Choral Music in Chronicles*. Journal for the Study of the Old Testament: Supplement Series 156. Sheffield: Sheffield Academic Press, 1993.

Kletter, R. "Iron Age Hoards of Precious Metals in Palestine - an 'Underground Economy'?" *Levant* 35 (2003) 139-52.

——. "Coinage before Coins? A Response." *Levant* 36 (2004) 207–210.

Klingbeil, Gerald A. "A Semantic Analysis of Aramaic Ostraca of Syria-Palestine During the Persian Period" *Andrew University Seminary Studies* 35/1 (1997) 33-46.

Knohl, Israel. *The Sanctuary of Silence: The Priestly Torah and the Holiness School*. Winona Lake: Eisenbrauns, 2007.

——. "Between Voice and Silence: The Relationship between Prayer and Temple Cult." *Journal of Biblical Literature* 115 (1996) 17-30.

Knoppers, Gary N. "Mt. Gerizim and Mt. Zion: A Study in the Early History of the Samaritans and Jews." *Studies in Religion* 34 (2005) 309-38.

——. "Classical Historiography and the Chronicler's History: A Re-examination." *Journal of Biblical Literature* 122 (2004) 627-50.

——. " 'The City Yhwh Has Chosen': The Chronicler's Promotion of Jerusalem in Light of Recent Archaeology." In *Jerusalem in Bible and Archaeology: The First Temple Period*. Edited by Andrew G. Vaughn and Ann E. Killebrew. Society of Biblical Literature Symposium Series 18. Atlanta: Society of Biblical Literature, 2003. Pp. 307-26.

——. *1 Chronicles 1-9: A New Translation with Introduction and Commentary*. Anchor Bible 12. New York: Doubleday, 2003.

——. *1 Chronicles 10-29: A New Translation with Introduction and Commentary*. Anchor Bible 12A. New York: Doubleday, 2003.

——. "An Achaemenid Imperial Authorization of Torah in Yehud?" in *Persia and Torah: The Theory of Imperial Authorization of the Pentateuch*. Edited by James W. Watts. Atlanta: Society of Biblical Literature, 2001. Pp. 115-34.

——. "Sources, Revisions and Editions: The Lists of Jerusalem's Residents in MT and LXX Nehemiah 11 and 1 Chronicles 9." *Textus* 20 (2000) 141-68.

——. "Hierodules, Priests, or Janitors? The Levites in Chroniclers and the History of the Israelite Priesthood." *Journal of Biblical Literature* 118 (1999) 49-72.

——. "Jehoshaphat's Judiciary and 'The Scroll of YHWH's Torah'." *Journal of Biblical Literature* 113 (1994) 59-80.

——. "Reform and Regression: The Chronicler's Presentation of Jehoshaphat." *Biblica* 72 (1991) 500-524.

Knowles, Melody D. *Centrality Practiced: Jerusalem in the Religious Practice of Yehud and the Diaspora in the Persian Period*. Society of Biblical Literature: Archaeology and Biblical Studies 16. Atlanta: Society of Biblical Literature, 2006.

Köstenberger, Andreas J. and David A. Croteau. " 'Will a Man Rob God?' (Malachi 3:8): A Study of Tithing in the Old and New Testaments." *Bulletin for Biblical Research* 16 (2006) 53-77.

Kruse, Colin G. "Community Functionaries in the Rule of the Community and the Damascus Document: A Test of Chronological Relationships." *Revue de Qumrân* 10 (1981) 543-51.

Kugel, James. "Levi's Elevation to the Priesthood in Second Temple Writings." *Harvard Theological Review* 86 (1993) 1-64.

———. *In Potiphar's House*. San Francisco: Harper, 1990.

Kugler, Robert A. "Holiness, Purity, the Body and Society: The Evidence for Theological Conflict in Leviticus." *Journal for the Study of the Old Testament* 76 (1997) 3-27.

———. *From Patriarch to Priest: The Levi-Priestly Tradition from Aramaic Levi to Testament of Levi*. Early Judaism and its Literature 9. Atlanta: Scholars Press, 1996.

Laato, Antti. "The Levitical Genealogies in 1 Chronicles 5-6 and the Formation of Levitical Ideology in Post-exilic Judah." *Journal for the Study of the Old Testament* 62 (1994) 77-99.

Labahn, Antje. "Antitheocratic Tendencies in Chronicles." Pages 115-35 in *Yahwism After the Exile: Perspectives on Israelite Religion in the Persian era*. Edited by Rainer Albertz and Bob Becking. Assen: Royal Van Gorcum, 2003.

Lemaire, André. "Administration in Fourth-Century B.C.E. Judah in Light of Epigraphy and Numismatics." In *Judah and Judeans in the Fourth Century B.C.E.* Edited by Oded Lipschits, Gary N. Knoppers, and Rainer Albertz. Winona Lake: Eisenbrauns, 2007. Pp. 53-74.

———. "New Aramaic Ostraca from Idumea and Their Historical Interpretation." In *Judah and the Judeans in the Persian Period*. Edited by Oded Lipschits and Manfred Oeming. Winona Lake: Eisenbrauns, 2006. Pp. 413-56.

———. "Another Temple to the Israelite God: Aramaic Hoard Documents Life in Fourth Century BCE." *Biblical Archaeology Review* 30 (2004) 38-44, 60.

———. "Taxes et impôts dans le sud de la Palestine (IV[e]s.av. J.-C.)." *Transpeuphratène* 28 (2004) 133-42.

Levine, Baruch A. "The Temple Scroll: Aspects of its Historical Provenance and Literary Character." *Bulletin of the American Schools of Oriental Research* 232 (1978) 5-23.

Levine, Lee I. *Jerusalem: Portrait of the City in the Second Temple Period (538 B.C.E.-70 C.E.)*. Philadelphia: The Jewish Publication Society, 2002.

Levin, Yigal. "Who Was the Chronicler's Audience? A Hint from His Genealogies." *Journal of Biblical Literature* 122 (2003) 229-45.

Lewis, D. M. "The King's Dinner (Polyaenus IV 3,32)." Pages 79-87 in *Achaemenid History* II. *The Greek Sources: Proceedings of the Groningen* 1984 *Achaemenid History Workshop*. Edited by Helen Sancisi-Weerdenburg and Amélie Kuhrt. Leiden: Nederlands Instituut Voor Het Nabije Oosten, 1987.

Lindblom, Johannes. "Lot-casting in the Old Testament." *Vetus Testamentum* 12 (1962) 164-78.

Lipschits, Oded. "Persian Period Finds From Jerusalem: Facts and Interpretations" *Journal of Hebrew Scriptures* 9 (2009) Article 20:2-30.

——. "Achaemenid Imperial Policy, Settlement Processes in Palestine, and the Status of Jerusalem in the Middle of the Fifth Century B.C.E." In *Judah and the Judeans in the Persian Period* Edited by Oded Lipschits and Manfred Oeming. Winona Lake: Eisenbrauns, 2006. Pp. 19-52.

——. "Literary and Ideological Aspects of Nehemiah 11." *Journal of Biblical Literature* 121 (2002) 423-40.

—— and D. Vanderhooft. "Yehud Stamp Impressions in the Fourth Century BCE: A Time of Administrative Consolidation?" in *Judah and the Judeans in the Fourth Century BCE*. Edited by Oded Lipschits, Gary N. Knoppers, and Rainer Albertz. Winona Lake: Eisenbrauns, 2007. Pp. 75-94.

——, David Vanderhooft, Y. Gadot and Manfred Oeming. "Twenty-Four New *Yehud* Stamp Impressions from the 2007 Excavation Season at Ramat-Raḥel." *Maarav* 15 (2008) 7-25.

——, Yuval Gadot, Benjamin Arubas, and Manfred Oeming. "Palace and Village, Paradise and Oblivion: Unraveling the Riddles of Ramat Raḥel." *Near Eastern Aarchaeology* 74 (2011) 2-49.

Liver, Jacob. *Chapters in the History of the Priests and Levites: Studies in the Lists of Chronicles and Ezra and Nehemiah*. Jerusalem: The Magness Press, 1968.

——. "The Half-Shekel Offering in Biblical and Post-Biblical Literature." *Harvard Theological Review* 56 (1963) 173-98.

Lozachmeur, H. and André Lemaire. "Nouveaux ostraca araméens d'Idumée (Collection Sh. Moussaïeff)." *Semitica* 46 (1996) 123-42.

Luckenbill, Daniel D. *Ancient Records of Assyria and Babylonia Vol. II: Historical Records of Assyria*. New York: Greenwood Press, 1968.

MacGinnis, John. *Letter Orders from Sippar and the Administration of the Ebabbar in the Late-Babylonian Period*. Poznan: Bonami, 1995.

Magen, Yizhak, Haggai Misgave and Levana Tsfania. *The Aramaic, Hebrew and Samaritan Inscriptions*. Vol. 1 of *Mount Gerizim Excavations*. Judea and Samaria Publications 2. Jerusalem: Israel Antiquities Authority, 2004.

Maier, Johann. "The Architectural History of the Temple in Jerusalem in the Light of the Temple Scroll." In *Temple Scroll Studies: Papers Presented at the International Symposium on the Temple Scroll, Manchester, December 1987*. Edited by George J. Brooke. Journal for the Study of the Pseudepigrapha Supplement Series 7. Sheffield: Sheffield Academic Press, 1989. Pp. 23-62.

Mandell, S. "Who Paid the Temple Tax when the Jews were under Roman Rule?" *Harvard Theological Review 11* (1984) 223-32.

Mankowski, P. V., S.J. *Akkadian Loanwords in Biblical Hebrew*. Harvard Semitic Studies 47. Winona Lake: Eisenbrauns, 2000.

Martínez, Florentino García. *The Dead Sea Scrolls Translated: The Qumran Texts in English*. Translated by Wilfred G. E. Watson. 2nd ed. Leiden; New York: Brill; Grand Rapids: Eerdmans, 1996.

———, and Eibert J. C. Tigchelaar, eds. *The Dead Sea Scrolls Study Edition*. 2 vols. Leiden; Boston; Köln: Brill, 1997–1998.

Matthews, Victor H. "Entrance Ways and Threshing Floors: Legally Significant Sites in the Ancient Near East." *Fides et historia* 19 (1987) 25-40.

Mattingly, Gerald L. "Gateways and Doors." In *Dictionary of the Ancient Near East*. Edited by Piotr Bienkowski and Alan Ralph Millard. Philadelphia: University of Pennsylvania Press, 2000. P. 125.

Mayes, Andrew David Hastings, *Deuteronomy*. New Century Bible Commentary. London: Oliphants; Grand Rapids: Eerdmans, 1979.

Mazar, Amihai. *Archaeology of the Land of the Bible 10,000–586* BCE. Anchor Bible Reference Library. New York: Doubleday, 1990.

Mazar, Benjamin. *The Mountain of the Lord*. New York: Doubleday, 1975.

Mazar, Eilat. "The Solomonic Wall in Jerusalem." In *"I Will Speak the Riddle of Ancient Things": Archaeological and Historical Studies in Honor of Amihai Mazar on the Occasion of his Sixtieth Birthday*.

Edited by Aren M. Maeir and Pierre de Miroschedji. Winona Lake: Eisenbrauns, 2006. Pp. 775-86.

McEntire, Mark Harold. *The Function of Sacrifice in Chronicles, Ezra, and Nehemiah*. Lewiston, NY: Mellen Biblical Press, 1993.

McKenzie, Steven L. *1–2 Chronicles*. Abingdon Old Testament Commentaries. Nashville: Abingdon Press, 2004.

——. "The Chronicler as Redactor." In *The Chronicler as Author: Studies in Text and Texture*. Edited by M. P. Graham and S. L. McKenzie. Journal for the Study of the Old Testament: Supplement Series 263. Sheffield: Sheffield Academic Press, 1999. Pp. 70-90.

Meshorer, Ya'akov. *Ancient Jewish Coinage*. 2 vols. Dix Hills: Amphora Books, 1982.

—— and Shraga Qedar. *Samarian Coinage*. Jerusalem: The Israel Numismatic Society, 1999.

Metso, Sarianna. "The Textual Traditions of the Qumran Community Rule." In *Legal Texts and Legal Issues: Proceedings of the Second Meeting of the International Organization for Qumran Studies, Cambridge, 1995: Published in Honour of Joseph M. Baumgarten*. Edited by Moshe J. Bernstein, Florentino García Martínez and John Kampen. Studies on the Texts of the Desert of Judah 23. Leiden: Brill, 1997. Pp. 141-47.

Mildenberg, Leo. "On Fractional Silver Issues in Palestine: (Pls VIII-XI) (A propos des problems d'argent en Palestine [Pls VIII-XI])." *Transeuphratène* 20 (2000) 89-100.

——. "Numismatic Evidence." *Harvard Studies in Classical Philology* 91 (1987) 381-95.

Milgrom, Jacob. *Leviticus 23-27: A New Translation with Introduction and Commentary*. Anchor Bible 3B. New York: Doubleday, 2000.

——. "The Qumran Cult: Its Exegetical Principles." In *Temple Scroll Studies: Papers Presented at the International Symposium on the Temple Scroll, Manchester, December 1987*. Edited by George J. Brooke. Journal for the Study of the Pseudepigrapha: Supplement Series 7. Sheffield: Sheffield Academic Press, 1989. Pp. 165-80.

——. "Studies in the Temple Scroll." *Journal of Biblical Literature* 97 (1978) 501-23.

Monson, John Michael. *The Temple of Jerusalem: A Case Study in the Integration of Text and Artifact*. Ph.D. diss., Harvard University, 1998.

Montgomery, James A. *A Critical and Exegetical Commentary on the Books of Kings*. The International Critical Commentary. Edinburgh: T & T Clark, 1951.

Mosis, Rudolph. *Untersuchungen zur Theologie des chronistischen Geschichtswerkes*. Freiburger theologische Studien 92. Freiburg: Herder, 1972.

Myers, Jacob M. *II Chronicles*. Anchor Bible 13. Garden City, N.Y.: Doubleday, 1965.

Naveh, Joseph. "Aramaic Ostraca and Jar Inscriptions from Tell Jemmeh." *Atiqot* 21 (1992) 49-53.

——. "The Aramaic Ostraca from Tel Arad." In *Arad Inscriptions*. Edited by Yohanan Aharoni, in cooperation with Joseph Naveh. Judean Desert Studies. Jerusalem: Israel Exploration Society, 1981. Pp. 153-76.

——. "The Aramaic Ostraca." In *Excavations at Tel Beer-Sheba 1969–1971 Seasons*. Vol. 1 of *Beer*-Sheba. Edited by Yohanan Aharoni. Publications of the Institute of Archaeology 2. Tel Aviv: Tel Aviv University-Institute of Archaeology, 1973. Pp. 79-82.

——. "The Aramaic Ostraca from Tel Beer Sheba (Seasons 1971–1976)." *Tel Aviv* 6 (1979) 182-98.

Niehr, Herbert. "Abgaben an den Tempel im Yehud der Achaimenidenzeit." In *Geschenke und Steuern, Zölle und Tribute: antike Abgabenformen in Anspruch und Wirklichkeit*. herausgegeben von H. Klinkott, S. Kubisch, and R. Müller-Wollermann. Culture and History of the Ancient Near East 29. Leiden; Boston: Brill, 2007. Pp. 141-57.

North, Robert, S.J. "The Chronicler: 1–2 Chronicles, Ezra, Nehemiah." Pages 362-98 in *The New Jerome Biblical Commentary*. Edited by Raymond E. Brown et al. 2nd ed. New Jersey: Englewood Cliffs, 1990.

Noth, Martin. *The Chronicler's History*. Translated by H. G. M. Williamson, with an Introduction. Journal for the Study of the Old Testament: Supplement Series 50. Sheffield: JSOT, 1987.

Noy, David. "The Jewish Communities of Leontopolis and Venosa." In *Studies in Early Jewish Epigraphy*. Edited by Jan Willem van Henten and Pieter Willem van der Horst. Arbeiten zur Geschichte des antiken Judentums und des Urchristentums 21. Leiden; New York; Köln: Brill, 1994. Pp. 162-82.

Numela, Risto. *The Levites: Their Emergence as a Second-Class Priesthood*. South Florida Studies in the History of Judaism 193. Atlanta, Scholars, 1998.

O'Brien, Julia M. *Priest and Levite in Malachi*. Society of Biblical Literature. Dissertation Series 121. Atlanta: Scholars Press, 1990.

Oeming, Manfred. *Das wahre Israel: Die 'genealogische Vorhalle' 1 Chronik 1-9*. Beiträge zur Wissenschaft vom Alten und Neuen Testament 7. Stuttgart: W. Kohlhammer, 1990.

Olson, Dan. "What Got the Gatekeepers into Trouble?" *Journal for the Study of the Old Testament* 30 (2005) 223-42.

Olyan, Saul M. "Ben Sira's Relationship to the Priesthood." *Harvard Theological Review* 80 (1987) 261-86

Oppenheim, A. Leo. "Babylonian and Assyrian Historical Texts." In *Ancient Near Eastern Texts Relating to the Old Testament*. Edited by James B. Pritchard. 3rd edition, Princeton: Princeton University Press, 1969. pp. 265-317.

Oppenheimer, A'hron. "Terumot and Ma'aserot." In *Encyclopedia Judaica*. Edited by Fred Skolnik et als. 22 vols. 2nd ed. Detroit: Macmillan Reference USA in association with the Keter Publishing House Ltd., 2007. Pp. 19:652-54.

Ottosson, Magnus. *Temples and Cult Places in Palestine*. Acta Universitatis Upsaliensis: Boreas 12. Uppsala: Acta Universitatis Upsaliensis, 1980.

Peltonen, Kai. "A Jigsaw without a Model? The Date of Chronicles." In *Did Moses Speak Attic? Jewish Historiography and Scripture in the Hellenistic Period*. Edited by Lester L. Grabbe. Journal for the Study of the Old Testament: Supplement Series 317. Sheffield: Sheffield Academic Press, 2001. Pp. 225-71

Porten, Bezalel. *Archives from Elephantine: The Life of an Ancient Jewish Military Colony*. Berkeley: University of California Press, 1968.

—— with J. J. Farber et al, *The Elephantine Papyri in English: Three Millennia of Cross-Cultural Continuity and Change*. Leiden: Brill, 1996.

—— and Ada Yardeni. "Makkedah and the Storehouse in the Idumean Ostraca." In *A Time of Change: Judah and its Neighbors in the Persian and Early Hellenistic Periods*. Edited by Yigal Levin. Library of Second Temple Studies 65. New York: T & T Clark, 2007. Pp. 125-70.

—— and Ada Yardeni. "Social, Economic, and Onomastic Issues in the Aramaic Ostraca of the Fourth Century B.C.E." In *Judah and Judeans in the Persian Period*. Edited by Oded Lipschit and Manfred Oeming; Winona Lake: Eisenbrauns, 2006. Pp. 457-88.

—— and Ada Yardeni. *Textbook of Aramaic Documents from Ancient Egypt*. 4 vols. Winona Lake: Eisenbrauns, 1986–1999.

Postgate, J. N. *Taxation and Conscription in the Assyrian Empire*. Studia Pohl: Series Maior 3. Rome: Biblical Institute Press, 1974.

——. "The Role of the Temple in the Mesopotamian Secular Community." In *Man, Settlement and Urbanism: Proceedings of a Meeting of the*

Research Seminar in Archaeology and Related Subjects Held at the Institute of Archaeology, London University. Edited by Peter J Ucko, Ruth Tringham and G. W. Dimbleby. Cambridge: Schenkman, 1972. Pp. 811-825.

Rawlinson, H. C. *The Cuneiform Inscriptions of Western Asia Vol V: A Selection from the Miscellaneous Inscriptions of Assyria and Babylonia*. London: Trustees of the British Museum, 1884. Plates 1-10.

Reade, Julian. *Assyrian Sculpture*. 2nd ed. Cambridge: Harvard University Press, 1998.

Rendtorff, Rolf. "Chronicles and the Priestly Torah." In *Texts, Temples and Traditions: A Tribute to Menahem Haran*. Edited by Michael V. Fox, Victor Avigdor Hurowitz, Avi Hurvitz, Michael L. Klein, Baruch J. Schwartz, and Nili Shupak. Winona Lake: Eisenbrauns, 1996. Pp. 259-66.

Reviv, Hanoch. "The Traditions Concerning the Inception of the Legal System in Israel: Significance and Dating." *Zeitschrift für die alttestamentliche Wissenschaft* 94 (1982) 566-75.

Riley, William. *King and Cultus in Chronicles: Worship and the Reinterpretation of History*. Journal for the Study of the Old Testament: Supplement Series 160. Sheffield: JSOT Press, 1993.

Ristau, Kenneth A. "Reading and Rereading Josiah: The Chronicler's Representation of Josiah for the Postexilic Community." In *Community Identity in Judean Historiography: Biblical and Comparative Perspectives*. Edited by Gary N. Knoppers and Kenneth A. Ristau. Winona Lake: Eisenbrauns, 2009. Pp. 219-47

Robertson, J. F. "The Social and Economic Organization of Ancient Mesopotamia Temples." In *Civilizations of the Ancient Near East*. Edited by Jack M. Sasson. New York: Simon & Schuster Macmillan, 1995. Pp. I: 443-54.

Ronen, Yigal. "Twenty Unrecorded Samarian Coins." *Israel Numismatic Research* 2 (2007) 29-33.

———. "Some observations on the Coinage of Yehud." *Israel Numismatic Journal* 15 (2003) 28-31.

Rooke, Deborah W. *Zadok's Heirs: The Role and Development of the High Priesthood in Ancient Israel*. Oxford Theological Monographs. Oxford; New York: Oxford University Press, 2000.

Root, Bradley W. "Coinage, War, and Peace in Fourth-Century Yehud" *Near Eastern Archaeology* 68 (2005) 131-34.

Rosenberg, Stephen G. "The Jewish Temple at Elephantine." *Near Eastern Archaeology* 67 (2004) 4-13.

Rothstein, Johann Wilhelm, and Johannes Hänel. *Kommentar zum ersten Buch der Chronik*. Vol. 2 of *Das erste* Buch der Chronik. Kommentar zum Alten Testament 18/2. Leipzig: A. Deichert, 1927.

Rudolph, Wilhelm. *Chronikbücher*. Handbuch zum Alten Testament 21. Tübingen: J.C.B. Mohr, 1955.

Runnalls, Donna. "The Parwār: A Place of Ritual Separation?" *Vetus Testamentum* 41 (1991) 324-31.

Russell, John Malcolm. *Sennacherib's Palace Without Rival at Nineveh*. Chicago: The University of Chicago Press, 1991.

Schaper, Joachim. *Priester und Leviten im achämenidischen Juda: Studien zur Kult- und Sozialgeschichte Israels in persischer Zeit*. Forschungen zum Alten Testament 31. Tübingen: Mohr Siebeck, 2000.

——. "The Temple Treasury committee in the Times of Nehemiah and Ezra." *Vetus Testamentum* 47 (1997) 200-206.

——. "The Jerusalem Temple as an Instrument of the Achaemenid Fiscal Administration." *Vetus Testamentum* 45 (1995) 528-39.

Schiffman, Lawrence H. "The New Halakhic Letter (4QMMT) and the Origins of the Dead Sea Sect." *Biblical Arachaeologist* 53 (1990) 64-73.

——. "The Enigma of the Temple Scroll." In *Reclaiming the Dead Sea Scrolls: The History of Judaism, the Background of Christianity, the Lost Library of Qumran*. Anchor Bible Reference Library. New York: Doubleday, 1995. Pp. 257-71.

Schmidt, Frances. "Gôrâl versus Payîs: Lots at Qumran and in the Rabbinic Tradition." In *Defining Identities: We, You, and the Other in the Dead Sea Scrolls: Proceedings of the Fifth Meeting of the IOQS in Groningen*. Edited by Florentino García Martínez and Mladen Popović. Studies on the Texts of the Desert of Judah 70. Leiden; Boston: Brill, 2008. Pp. 175-85.

Schniedewind, William M. "The Chronicler as an Interpreter of Scripture." Pages 158-80 in *The Chronicler as Author: Studies in Text and Texture*. Edited by M. P. Graham and S. L. McKenzie. Journal for the Study of the Old Testament: Supplement Series 263. Sheffield: Sheffield Academic Press, 1999.

——. *The Word of God in Transition: From Prophet to Exegete in the Second Temple Period*. Journal for the Study of the Old Testament: Supplement Series 197. Sheffield: Sheffield Academic Press, 1995.

Schofield, Aloson and James C. Vanderkam. "Were the Hasmoneans Zadokites?" *Journal of Biblical Literature* 124 (2005) 73-87.

Schwartz, Daniel R. *2 Maccabees*. Commentaries on Early Jewish literature. Berlin; New York: Walter de Gruyter, 2008.

Schwartz, Seth. *Imperialism and Jewish Society 200 B.C.E. to 640 C.E.* Princeton: Princeton University Press, 2001.

Schweitzer, Steven James. "The High Priest in Chronicles: An Anomaly in a Detailed Description of the Temple Cult." *Biblica* 84 (2003) 388-402.

Shaver, Judson Rayford. *Torah and the Chronicler's History Work: An Inquiry into the Chronicler's References to Laws, Festivals, and Cultic Institutions in Relationship to Pentateuchal Legislation*. Brown Judaic Studies 196. Atlanta: Scholars Press, 1989.

Shiloh, Y. "Jerusalem." In *The New Encyclopedia of Archaeological Excavations in the Holy Land*. Edited by Ephraim Stern. 5 vols. New York: Simon & Schuster, 1993. Pp. 2:698-712

Silver, Morris. *Prophets and Markets: The Political Economy of Ancient Israel*. Boston: Kluwer-Nijhoff Publishing, 1983.

Sparks, James T. *The Chronicler's Genealogies: Towards an Understanding of 1 Chronicles 1-9*. Academia Biblica 28. Atlanta: Society of Biblical Literature, 2008.

Spencer, John R. "The Tasks of the Levites: šmr and ṣbʾ." *Zeitschrift für die alttestamentliche Wissenschaft* 96 (1984) 267-71.

——. *The Levitical Cities: A Study of the Role and Function of the Levites in the History of Israel*. Ph.D. diss., The University of Chicago, 1980.

Stallman, Robert C. "Levi and the Levites in the Dead Sea Scrolls." *Journal for the Study of the Pseudepigrapha* 10 (1992) 163-89.

Stegemann, Hartmut. *The Library of Qumran: On the Essenes, Qumran, John the Baptist and Jesus*. Grand Rapids: Eerdmans, 1998.

——. "The Literary Composition of the Temple Scroll and its Status at Qumran" in *Temple Scroll Studies: Papers Presented at the International Symposium on the Temple Scroll, Manchester, December 1987*. Edited by George J. Brooke. Journal for the Study of the Pseudepigrapha Supplement Series 7. Sheffield: Sheffield Academic Press, 1989. Pp. 123-48.

Steins, Georg. *Die Chronik als kanonisches Abschulussphänomen: Studien zur Entstehung und Theologie von 1/2 Chronik*. Bonner biblische Beiträge 93. Weinheim: Beltz Athenäum, 1995.

Stern, Ephraim. "The Religious Revolution in Persian-Period Judah." In

Judah and Judeans in the Persian Period. Edited by Oded Lipschit and Manfred Oeming; Winona Lake: Eisenbrauns, 2006. Pp. 199-205.

——. *Archaeology of the Land of the Bible, Vol. II: The Assyrian, Babylonian and Persian Periods*. New York: Doubleday, 2001.

——. *Material Culture of the Land of the Bible in the Persian Period 538–332 B.C.E.* Warminster: Aris & Phillips; Jerusalem: Israel Exploration Society, 1982.

Stevens, Marthy E. *Temples, Tithes, and Taxes: The Temple and the Economic Life of Ancient Israel*. Peabody, MA: Hendrickson, 2006.

Stolper, Matthew W. "The Governor of Babylon and Across-the-River in 486 B.C.E." *Journal of Near Eastern Studies* 48 (1989) 283-305.

——. *Entrepreneurs and Empire: The Murašû Archive, the Murašû Firm, and Persian rule in Babylonia*. Uitgaven van het Nederlands Historisch-Archaeologisch Instituut te Istanbul 54. Leiden: Nederlands Historische-Archaeologisch Instituut te Istanbul, 1985.

Streck, M. *Assurbanipal und die letzten assyrischen Könige bis zum Untergang* II: Teil: Texte. Leipzig: Hinrichs, 1916.

Sweeney, Marvin A. *I & II Kings: A Commentary*. Old Testament Library. Louisville: Westminster John Knox Press, 2007.

Tal, Oren. "Coin Denominations and Weight Standards in Fourth-Century BCE Palestine" *Israel Numismatic Research* 2 (2007) 17-28.

Talmon, Shemaryahu and Israel Knohl. "A Calendrical Scroll From A Qumran Cave: Mišmarot B[a], 4Q321." In *Pomegranates and Golden Bells: Studies in Biblical, Jewish, and Near Eastern Ritual, Law, and Literature in Honor of Jacob Milgrom*. Edited by David P. Wright, Daivd Noel Freedman, and Avi Hurvitz. Winona Lake: Eisenbrauns, 1995. Pp. 267-301

Tan, Nancy. "The Chronicler's 'Obed-dom': A Foreigner and/or a Levite?" *Journal for the Study of the Old Testament* 32 (2007) 217-30.

Tatum, Lynn. "Jerusalem in Conflict: The Evidence for the Seventh-Century B.C.E. Religious Struggle over Jerusalem." In *Jerusalem in Bible and Archaeology: The First Temple Period*. Edited by A. G. Vaughn and A. E. Killebrew. Society of Biblical Literature Symposium Series 18; Atlanta: Society of Biblical Literature, 2003. Pp. 291-306.

Thiering Barbara E. "*Mebaqqer* and *Episkopos* in the Light of the Temple Scroll." *Journal of Biblicla Literature* 100 (1981) 59-74.

——. "The Date of Composition of the Temple Scroll." In *Temple Scroll Studies: Papers Presented at the International Symposium on the*

Temple Scroll, Manchester, December 1987. Edited by George J. Brooke. Journal for the Study of the Pseudepigrapha Supplement Series 7. Sheffield: Sheffield Academic Press, 1989. Pp. 99-120.

Throntveit, Mark A. *When Kings Speak: Royal Speech and Royal Prayer in Chronicles*. Society of Biblical Literature Dissertation Series 93. Atlanta: Scholars Press, 1987.

Tidwell, N. L. "No Highway! The Outline of a Semantic Description of *Mesillâ*." *Vetus Testamentum* 45 (1995) 251-69.

Tigay, Jeffrey H. *Deuteronomy*. JPS Torah Commentary. Philadelphia: The Jewish Publication Society, 1996.

Torrey, Charles Cutler. "The Evolution of a Financier in the Ancient Near East." *Journal of Near Eastern Studies* 2 (1943) 295-301.

———. "The Foundry of the Second Temple at Jerusalem." *Journal of Biblical Literature* 55 (1936) 247-60.

Tov, Emanuel. *Textual Criticism of the Hebrew Bible*. 2nd ed. Minneapolis: Fortress Press, 2001.

Tuell, Steven S. *First and Second Chronicles*. Interpretation, a Bible Commentary for Teaching and Preaching. Louisville: John Knox Press, 2001.

Tuplin, C. "The Administration of the Achaemenid Empire." In *Coinage and Administration in the Athenian and Persian Empires: The Ninth Oxford Symposium on Coinage and Monetary History*. Edited by Ian Carradice. Oxford: B.A.R., 1987. Pp. 109-66.

Ussishkin, David. "Big City, Few People: Jerusalem in the Persian Period." *Biblical Archaeology Review* 31/4 (2005) 27-35.

———. "The Borders and De Facto Size of Jerusalem in the Persian Period." In *Judah and the Judeans in the Persian Period*. Edited by Oded Lipschits and Manfred Oeming. Winona Lake: Eisenbrauns, 2006. Pp. 147-66.

———. "Jerusalem as a Royal and Cultic Center in the 10th–8th Centuries BCE." Pages 529-38 in *Symbiosis, Symbolism, and the Power of the Past: Canaan, Ancient Israel, and Their Neighbors from the Last Bronze Age through Roman Palaestina*. Edited by William G. Dever and Seymour Gitin. Winona Lake: Eisenbrauns, 2003.

Van de Mieroop, Marc. "Gifts and Tithes to the Temples in Ur." In *Dumu-E2-Dub-Ba-A: Studies in Honor of Ake W. Sjoberg*. Edited by Hermann Behrens, Darlene Loding, Martha T. Roth. Occasional Publications of the Samuel Noah Kramer Fund 11. Philadelphia: University of Pennsylvania Museum Publication, 1989. Pp. 347-401.

Van Driel, G. *Elusive Silver: In Search of a Role for a Market in an Agrarian Environment Aspects of Mesopotamia's Society*. Leiden: Nederlands Instituut Voor Het Nebije Oosten, 2002.

Van Seters, John. "The Chronicler's Account of Solomon's Temple-Building: A Continuity Theme." In *The Chronicler as Historian*. Edited by M. Patrick Graham, Kenneth G. Hoglund and Steven L. McKenzie. Journal for the Study of the Old Testament 238. Sheffield: Sheffield Academic Press, 1997. Pp. 283-300.

Van Wijk-Bos, Johanna W. H., *Ezra, Nehemiah, and Esther*. Westminster Bible Companion. Louisville: Westminster John Knox Press, 1998.

VanderKam, James C. *The Dead Sea Scrolls Today*. 2nd ed. Grand Rapids: Eerdmans, 2010.

——. *From Joshua to Caiaphas: High Priests after the Exile*. Minneapolis: Fortress Press, 2004.

Vaughn, Andrew G. *Theology, History, and Archaeology in the Chronicler's Account of Hezekiah*. Archaeology and Biblical Studies 4. Atlanta: Scholars Press, 1999.

Vermes, Geza. *The Complete Dead Sea Scrolls in English*. Revised edition. London: Penguin Books, 2004.

Von Rad, Gerhard. *From Genesis to Chronicles: Exploration in Old Testament Theology*. Translated by E. W. Trueman Dicken. Edinburgh; London: Oliver & Boyd, 1966. Translation of *Gesammelte Studien zum Alten Testament*. Theologische Bücherei 8; Munich: Kaiser Verlag, 1958. Repr., Minneapolis: Fortress Press, 2005.

——. *Das Geschichtsbild das chronistischen Werkes*. Beiträge zur Wissenschaft vom Alten und Neuen Testament 4. Stuttgart: W. Kohlhammer, 1930.

Weinberg, Joel P. *The Citizen-Temple Community*. Trans. by Daniel L. Smith-Christopher. Journal for the Study of the Old Testament: Supplement Series 151. Sheffield: Sheffield Academic Press, 1992.

Weinfeld, Moshe. "Tithe." In vol. 19 of *Encyclopaedia Judaica*. Edited by Fred Skolnik and Michael Berenbaum. 22 vols. 2nd ed. Detroit: Macmillan Reference USA in association with the Keter Pub. House, 2007. Pp. 736-39.

Welch, Adam C. *The Work of the Chronicler, its Purpose and its Date*. The Schweich Lectures of the British Academy 1938. London: Oxford University Press, 1939.

Wellhausen, Julius. *Prolegomena to the History of Ancient Israel*. Translated by J. Sutherland Black and Allan Enzies, with preface by W. Robertson Smith. Edinburgh: Adam & Charles Black, 1885. Tranlsation of *Prolegomena zur Geschichte Israels*. 2nd ed. Berlin: G. Reimer, 1883. Repr., Atlanta: Scholars Press, 1994.

Welten, Peter. *Geschichte und Geschichtsdarstellung in den Chronikbüchern*. Wissenschaftliche Monographien zum Alten und Neuen Testament 42. Neukirchen-Vluyn: Neukirchener Verlag, 1973.

Werman, Cana. "Levi and Levites in the Second Temple Period" *Dead Sea Discoveries* 4 (1997) 211-25.

Willi, Thomas. "Leviten, Priester und Kult in vorhellenistischer Zeit. Die chronistische Optik in ihrem geschichtlichen Kontext." In *Gemeinde ohne Temepl = Community without Temple: Zur Substituierung und Transformation des Jerusalemer Tempels und seines Kults im Alten Testament, antiken Judentum und frühen Christentum*. Edited by Beate Ego, Armin Lange and Peter Pilhofer. Wisenschaftliche Untersuchungen zum Neuen Testament 118. Tübingen: J.C. B. Mohr (Paul Siebeck), 1999. Pp. 75-98.

———. *Die Chronik als Auslegung: Untersuchungen zur literarischen Gestaltung der historischen Überlieferung Israels*. Forschungen zur Religion und Literatur des Alten und Neuen Testaments 106. Göttingen: Vandenhoeck & Ruprecht, 1972.

Williamson, Hugh Godfrey Maturin. "The Temple in the Books of Chronicles." In *Templum Amicitae: Essays on the Second Temple Presented to Ernst Bammel*. Edited by Wiliam Horbury. Journal for the Study of the New Testament: Supplement Series 48. Sheffield: JSOT Press, 1991. Pp. 15-31.

———. *Ezra, Nehemiah*. Word Biblical Commentary 16. Waco, Texas: Word Books, 1985.

———. *1 and 2 Chronicles*. New Century Bible Commentary. Grand Rapids: Eerdmans; London: Marshall, Morgan & Scott Pub. Ltd., 1982.

———. "The Origins of the Twenty-four Priestly Courses: A Study of 1 Chronicles 23-27." In *Studies in the Historical Books of the Old Testament*. Edited by J. A. Emerton. Supplements to Vetus Testamentum 30. Leiden: Brill, 1979. Pp. 251-68

———. *Israel in the Books of Chronicles*. Cambridge; New York: Cambridge University Press, 1977.

Wilson, Robert R. "Israel's Judicial System in the Preexilic Period." *The Jewish Quarterly Review, New Series* 74 (1983) 229-48.

Wright, G. R. H. "The Monumental City Gate in Palestine and its Foundations." *Zeitschrift für Assyriologie und vorderasiatische Archäologie* 74 (1984) 267-89.

Wright, John W. "A Tale of Three Cities: Urban Gates, Squares and Power in Iron Age II, Neo-Babylonian and Achaemenid Judah." In *Studies in Politics, Class and Material Culture*. Vol. 3 of *Second Temple Studies*. Edited by Philip R. Davies and John M. Halligan. 3 vols. Journal for the Study of the Old Testament: Supplement Series 340. New York: Sheffield Academic Press, 2002. Pp. 19-50.

——. "Guarding the Gates: 1 Chronicles 26:1-19 and the Roles of Gatekeepers in Chronicles." *Journal for the Study of the Old Testament* 48 (1990) 69-81.

Wunsch, Cornelia. "Neo-Babylonian Entrepreneurs." In *The Invention of Enterprise: Entrepreneurship from Ancient Mesopotamia to Modern Times*. Edited by David S. Landes, Joel Mokyr and William J. Baumol. Kauffman Foundation Series on Innovation and Entrepreneurship New Jersey: Princeton University Press, 2010. Pp. 40-61.

——. *Die Urkunden des babylonischen Geschäftsmannes Iddin-Marduk: Zum Handel mit Naturalien im 6. Jahrhundert v. Chr*. Groningen: STYX, 1993.

Yadin, Azzan. "4QMMT, Rabbi Ishmael, and the Origins of Legal Midrash." *Dead Sea Discoveries* 10 (2003) 130-49.

Yadin, Yigael, ed. *The Temple Scroll*. 3 vols. Jerusalem: Israel Exploration Society, 1977–1983.

Yardeni, Ada. "Maritime Trade and Royal Accountancy in an Erased Customs Account from 475 B.C.E. on the Aḥiqar Scroll from Elephantine." *Bulletin of the American Schools of Oriental Research* 293 (1994) 67-78.

Yee, Gale A. "An Analysis of Prov 8:22-31 According to Style and Structure." *Zeitschrift für die alttestamentliche Wissenschaft* 94 (1982) 58-66.

Yeivin, S. "Was There a High Portal in the First Temple?" *Vetus Testamentum* 14 (1964) 331-43.

Zadok, Ran. "Remarks on Ezra and Nehemiah." *Zeitschrift für die alttestamentliche Wissenschaft* 94 (1982) 296-98.

Zevit, Ziony. "Converging Lines of Evidence Bearing on the Date of P." *Zeitschrift für die alttestamentliche Wissenschaft* 94 (1982) 481-511.

Zimmerli, Walther. *Ezekiel* 2. Hermeneia. Philadelphia: Fortress Press, 1983.

Zorn, Jeffrey R. "An Inner and Outer Gate Complex at Tell en-Nasbeh." *Bulletin of American Schools of Oriental Research* 307 (1997) 53-66.

Index of Biblical Passages and Extrabiblical Sources